CHRISTIANITY, ISLAM
AND THE
NEGRO RACE

EDWARD W. BLYDEN, LL.D.

CONTENTS.

PREFACE TO THE SECOND EDITION ... ...

PREFACE TO THE FIRST EDITION ... ...

INTRODUCTORY BIOGRAPHICAL NOTE ... ...

MOHAMMEDANISM AND THE NEGRO RACE ... ...
  Fraser's Magazine, November, 1875.

CHRISTIANITY AND THE NEGRO RACE ... ...
  Fraser's Magazine, May, 1876.

CHRISTIAN MISSIONS IN WEST AFRICA ... ...
  Fraser's Magazine, October, 1876.

THE AIMS AND METHODS OF A LIBERAL EDUCATION FOR AFRICANS ...
  Inaugural Address as President of Liberia College, January 5, 1881.

ORIGIN AND PURPOSE OF AFRICAN COLONISATION ... ...
  Discourse at the Anniversary of the American Colonisation Society, January, 1883.

ETHIOPIA STRETCHING OUT HER HANDS UNTO GOD (AFRICA'S SERVICE TO THE WORLD) ... ...
  Discourse delivered in the United States in 1880.

ECHOES FROM AFRICA ... ...
  The American Missionary, Dec., 1878, Jan. and Feb. 1879; and *The Three Despised Races in the United States*, an Address by Joseph Cook, New York, 1878.

PHILIP AND THE EUNUCH ... ...
  Discourse delivered in the United States in 1882.

MOHAMMEDANISM IN WESTERN AFRICA ... ...
  Methodist Quarterly Review, January, 1871.

SIERRA LEONE AND LIBERIA ... ...
  Lecture at Sierra Leone, April, 1884.

ISLAM AND RACE DISTINCTIONS ... ...
  Fraser's Magazine, November, 1876; *Islam under the Arabs*, 1876; *Mohammed and Mohammedanism*, 1874.

AFRICA AND THE AFRICANS ... ...
  Fraser's Magazine, August, 1878.

LIFE OF LORD LAWRENCE AND ITS LESSONS ... ...

THE MOHAMMEDANS OF NIGRITIA... ... ...

AFRICAN COLONISATION ... ...

APPENDIX ... ...

PREFACE TO SECOND EDITION.

THE generosity which has made a second edition of this volume necessary is no less surprising than gratifying. It was originally written chiefly with a view of instructing Negro youth in Christian lands eager to study the history, character and destiny of their race. In my early years I sorely felt the need of some such work to assist my own studies and direct my aspirations. Wherever I turned for light and guidance, I found only what the dominant white man had said in his own way and for his own purposes; or discovered, now and then, some crude literary effort of the Negro in exile and bondage, giving in broken utterances and *in forma pauperis* the conceptions of a blurred past and the hopes of an indistinct and troubled future. As I advanced in my studies and researches, difficult and hampered as they were, I determined to do, as soon as I felt able, whatever in me lay to supply the desideratum. The reception which my first effort in this direction has met has far exceeded my expectations. The volume appears to have been read with interest and profit, not only by my own people, but by foreigners in the highest literary walks, both in Europe and America.

One very interesting and important effect of the generous reception accorded to the work will be to convince the intelligent Negro youth, first, that in the Republic of Letters, as Mr. Herbert Spencer once said to me, there is no such thing as caste; and, secondly, that if any man, whatever his race, has anything to say worth listening to, men of all races who think will give him more than a respectful hearing.

The Christian Negro has, hitherto, as I have tried to show throughout this volume, rarely been trained to trust his own judgment, or to think that he can have anything to say which foreigners will care to hear. His subordinate position everywhere in Christian countries has made him believe that what his foreign teachers think is the only proper thing to think and that what they say is the only right thing to say. He is, therefore, untrue to the natural direction of his powers, and attempts to soar into an atmosphere not native to his wing. This is what often brings that shadow of disappointment over the brows of his best friends, as his profound disqualifications for the work for which they suppose they had trained him, become apparent. The faulty estimate which he himself entertains of the true field for his energies is not corrected by his guides, who, familiar with and strong on their own ground, can conceive of no other, and do not suspect the vicious estimate of himself and of his destiny in the mind of their *protégé*. It is difficult for the European to put himself in the place of the Christian Negro. But it is evident that there can be hope for the future improvement of the African only as he finds out his work and destiny and, as a consequence, learns to trust his own judgment; and it is hoped that this volume and the reception it has met, while stimulating effort in that direction on the part of the rising generation of Africans, will encourage their European guides and patrons to allow greater scope and freedom, not only for their mental and moral, but for their social and political evolution.

Of the numerous reviews of the work which I have had the opportunity of seeing, I have studied none with greater attention and respect than those which have appeared in the *Church Missionary Intelligencer*, as expressing the views of that large and influential body of Christians who, of all Missionary organisations labouring in Africa, must take precedence for the magnificence of their liberality and the breadth of their conception in planning for the erection of a Christian Church in Africa, and to whose patient and untiring efforts it is owing, notwithstanding existing perplexities, that so many difficulties have been overcome and so many drawbacks removed from the normal development of a genuine African Church.

But I have noticed with regret that the reviewer in the *Intelligencer* for November, 1887, proceeding upon the assumption that Mohammedanism is eulogised in this volume to the disparagement of Christianity, devotes a large portion of his article to bringing charges against Islam. The *tu quoque* argument is never satisfactory, dignified or edifying; and in this case it is especially and sadly irrelevant, when the necessity is so pressing for a careful consideration of the elements in the methods of foreign Christian workers in Africa which prevent wider and more permanent results—a subject to the discussion of which the work is chiefly devoted, but which the reviewer seems either to ignore or to deliberately put aside. Most reviewers, however, have discovered no attack upon Christianity itself, but only a serious arraignment of the methods of the Christian teachers of the Negro.

The earlier Missionaries laboured for the people to the extent of the possibilities of that time, and they did noble and exemplary work. The later Missionaries seem not to recognise the altered circumstances and the tendencies created by previous training to growth on racial lines, but wish to walk in the footsteps of their predecessors, as if they still had to deal with a *tabula rasa*. The result is, that all real life is strangled in a body whose form, notwithstanding advancing years, they strive to retain. They increase their expenditure in certain directions, and wonder that the reproductive power of their work does not fulfil its earlier promise or is not commensurate with the pecuniary outlay. "So long as you treat us like children," said a wealthy African merchant to the

Rev. Henry Venn, late Honorary Secretary of the Church Missionary Society, more than thirty years ago, "we shall behave like children. Treat us like men and we shall behave like men."[1]

The foreign teachers of the African are able to deal with accidental and external peculiarities—like the names and dress of the people. They secure by large expenditures of money outward conformity, but they have no means of shaping a healthful evolution; indeed, the word "evolution" implies spontaneity. It demands, for its effective operation, the *carrière ouverte aux talents* in Church and State. Nature suppressed, if vigorous, will make an outlet for itself, and there is no telling the shape it will take when once it has found or made that outlet. But it certainly will not conform to the regulations of those who would keep it down. It is by due attention to these things that Mohammedanism, with its more elastic social and political system, threatens the whole of Africa. What our religious and political teachers should pray for is the gift to recognise the necessity of increasing measures of freedom on the part of their *protégés* as the condition of social as well as spiritual advancement, so as to afford full scope for the expansion of the inherent energies of the mind. But, as long as they believe that there are no inherent energies to be expanded, they will aim at making the Negro what they think he ought to be, by the plastic hand of European religious organisations and the moulding force of European laws; and these will have no influence beyond European settlements, and, even there, they will stifle all true life in the people. The intelligent Negro of the interior, whether Pagan or Mohammedan, looks upon many of these regulations and laws as not only despotic but absurd, and will reject them as calculated to put him and his people in an awkward and helpless position.

---

[1] Memoir of Rev. Henry Venn, B.D., p. 546.

The reviewer in the *Church Missionary Intelligencer* for November, says, "Another topic is abundantly dwelt upon in Dr. Blyden's volume. It is largely devoted to hymning the praises of Liberia."

Perhaps explanation is necessary. That Republic represents two principles for which, in common with all intelligent Christian Negroes, I should contend: First, the return of the exiled African from the house of bondage; and, secondly, Christian Negro autonomy in Church and State on African soil. Liberia is the only country which redeems Christianity, or rather Christians, from the charge of appropriating the country of another people as a reward for giving them the highest religion. There is no other country in the world belonging to any dark race which, evangelised by Christians, has been left to the control of the natives. All Christian countries, excepting Liberia and Haïti, are under the government of Europeans or white people. But we have Mohammedan countries under the rule of men of all the races—Caucasian, Mongolian and Negro—from North-western China to West Africa. Mohammedan conquests mean subjugation to the Koran, and not to Arab or Turk. If I have "hymned the praises of Liberia," it is because, whatever its present difficulties or failures, it represents an important principle, and may be made the instrument of a great work.[2]

Did Sir William Hunter realise the full effect upon the minds of thinking people among unevangelised races of the eloquent utterances at the close of his able lecture on "The Religions of India," delivered a few weeks ago before the Society of Arts? He said, "Speaking as an Englishman, I declare my conviction that English missionary enterprise is the highest modern expression of the world-wide national life of our race. I regard it as the spiritual complement of England's instinct for *colonial expansion and Imperial rule*."

---

[2] See Appendix.

Does he know that Chinese, Japanese and African critics of "English missionary enterprise" attribute the energy and zeal displayed to the restless desire for foreign possessions— "for colonial expansion and Imperial rule?"

I am convinced that it is utterly impossible for Christianity to penetrate this continent by the methods now in general favour. I venture to think that if the desire is to convert Mohammedans, Christians should give up their bitter hostility and study Islam—not at second hand, but as far as possible in its original records—with greater sympathy and liberality. The agency of the press diffuses rapidly to the remotest parts of the earth everything said and done in Christian countries. Mohammedan newspapers are reporting foreign intelligence to their people. When Missionary Societies, in their official publications, denounce Mohammed as a "false prophet," still reproducing the unchastened conceptions of the Middle Ages, they cannot expect that their agents will be received without, to say the least, suspicion in Mohammedan countries.

In view of the past and present position of Islam, Christians have no ground for special exultation. Ishmael holds his own before Isaac. The Cross has surrendered to the Crescent the very locality which it first consecrated. The voice of the Muezzin is heard in the plain of Sharon and in the hill country of Judea; on the banks of the Jordan, and by the waters of Abana and Pharpar; at Bethlehem, Hebron, Nazareth. Over one of the gates of the "Holy City," the Muslim formula is displayed, "There is no God but God and Mohammed is the Apostle of God." If in those countries Islam has lost its productive and conquering energy as a dominant force, Christianity has not regained its ancient influence. Intelligence furnished by Christian missionaries in the Turkish Empire does not show that Mohammedanism is growing any weaker at its centre. As a rejoinder to the attacks made upon Islam in the recent or pending controversy in England and America, the highest Turkish authorities propose the enactment of a law restricting or abolishing the privileges formerly enjoyed by Christian missionaries in the establishment and conduct of schools. Dr. Washburn, the President of Robert College, at Constantinople, has just furnished in the New York *Independent* (Feb. 9) the translation of an important letter written by the Sheikh-ul-Islam, giving an official statement of Mohammedan doctrine for the instruction of recent and expected converts to Islam.[3]

As to India, Sir William Hunter has recently told us of the new vitality awakened among the Mohammedans of that country. "The sternly religious character," he says, " of their early teaching gives a vigorous coherence to Islam in India which may yet be productive of great political results."[4]

In Central Africa, the religion of Arabia shows its pristine vitality and expansive power, carrying on its operations by indigenous agents and simple methods ; while Christianity attempts to confront it by an expensive missionary system and exotic agencies—by various sects and a complicated ecclesiasticism. The experience of each day, especially when we contrast the results of the two systems, convinces the careful and earnest student of the question that an effective missionary among the Natives of interior Africa, whether Pagan or Mohammedan, must begin with "Silver and gold have I none" and continue with, "Stand up; I myself also am a man." And it is becoming more and more apparent that an enterprise which requires so much and such continuous foreign aid and oversight—such an apparatus of alien training and directing agencies—is ill-adapted to compete with that energetic and cosmopolitan system from Arabia, whose agents are indigenous and stand on their own legs, pursuing methods, which, if under the inspiration of the Koran, are "racy of the soil."

WEST AFRICA, *March 20th*, 1888.

---

[3] See Appendix.   [4] *Religions of India.*

PREFACE TO FIRST EDITION.

THE Colonial and Indian Exhibition of 1886, which has brought together in London men of all races and climes, and of almost every degree of civilisation, has been the immediate occasion—not the cause—of the publication of this volume, and it is hoped that the interest in West Africa which may have been awakened by the "Exhibits" from this part of the world may lead many, who might not otherwise have been attracted by the subject, to a perusal of its pages.

The chapters which it contains have, many of them, appeared, at various times, in the shape of articles in English periodicals, or in those of the United States. They are an attempt to deal with the grave questions which affect Africa and the Negro race—to set forth to Africans and to their foreign helpers, secular and religious, some of the conditions of the problem before them, as they have presented themselves to an African who has enjoyed exceptional opportunities of travel and observation in the Eastern and Western hemispheres—in Central Africa, in Egypt and Syria, in Europe, in North and South America, and in the West Indies.

Much has been written about Africa and the African. The character, position and destiny of the Negro race have been discussed by Europeans of every nationality. Travellers from all parts of the civilised world have visited the country, and have furnished facts—or what seemed to be facts—for brilliant essayists and incisive critics. But very little has been written by the African himself of his country and people—very little, that is, which has attracted the attention of the higher class of readers in Europe and

America. Africans at home have no problems to solve except those which pertain to their local or domestic affairs. They are not forced, either by intellectual, or by social, or by material exigencies, to take interest in the outside world. Were it not for foreign interference, they would never, in any numbers, have left their ancestral homes for residences in other lands.

It is different with the outside, especially the European, world. Europe and America, for the multifarious purposes of their complex life and wonderful growth, have, during the last three hundred years, needed the aid of Africa and the African. And in return for the services which, though forced from them, have been effectually rendered, many and noble have been the efforts put forward towards the opening and improvement of the continent, by those who have been benefited by the labours of her children. Religious convictions and philanthropic impulses have induced active and self-denying exertions for the amelioration of the people; but the drawbacks have been, and are still, numerous and diversified.

Two great religious systems are exerting their influence in Africa —Christianity and Mohammedanism. These systems have many things in common. Christians speak of Abraham as "the Father of the Faithful," and "the pattern of believers," and Mohammedanism professes to be a revival of the Abrahamic faith and worship. The Koran admits the Divine authority of the Scriptures of the Old and New Testaments. It is with these two great systems in their effect upon the African, through the methods of their respective propagators, that many of the following pages deal.

Another subject dealt with in this book is the important part in the development of Africa that may be played by the settlement therein of civilised and Christian Negroes, drawn from the Western hemisphere. It is now universally admitted that the acclimatisation of Europeans in Tropical Africa is impossible. No Europeans will ever be able to live in the Soudan or Congo and work as farmers, mechanics or labourers. But, without the example of communities engaging steadily in such employments, the task of civilising the natives, in any large numbers, is hopeless. The Republic of Liberia presents an example of the, at least, comparative, success which

B

attends the efforts of civilised Africans living and working in organised communities, with their farms, workshops, stores, school-houses and churches.

The other method, of a few Europeans settled as missionaries, Government officials, or traders, has, so far, made very little impression on the Continent. We have no example in tropical Africa of hundreds of Europeans living together, and engaged in the arts and practices of civilised life. But, even if this were possible, a few hundreds of Europeans could exert no influence capable of spreading civilisation among the millions in Africa, and of developing the industrial and commercial resources of so vast a continent

It is the African converts to Mohammedanism and the Negro colonists from Christian countries, who have, thus far, done most for the permanent advance of civilisation in equatorial Africa; and it is these who seem to me to be the only capable and efficient agencies for the work of African regeneration. Mohammedanism— by its simple, rigid forms of worship, by its literature, its politics, its organised society, its industrial and commercial activities—is rapidly superseding a hoary and pernicious Paganism. The exiled Negro in the Western hemisphere, on the other hand, in spite of slavery, in spite of the bitter prejudices, the dark passions of which he has been the victim, has come under influences which have given him the elements of a nobler civilisation. The seed of a spiritual, intellectual, industrial life has been planted in his bosom, which, when he is transferred to the land of his fathers, will grow up into beauty, expand into flower, and develop into fruit which the world will be glad to welcome.

It is gratifying to know that there are thousands in America looking to Africa as their future home, who have been kept so much apart from the alien race in whose country they live, that their race-strength has not been undermined nor their race-vitality absorbed, by surrounding influences. They will return to their ancestral home bearing, it is true, the marks of slavery to a foreign race, but it will be only a superficial mark. Within they will have the noble and manly traits of those who, while outwardly slaves to foreigners, have been free servants to truth, to Africa, and to the race. They have never been crushed under the pressure, or forced into the mould, of foreign prejudices. Christians and Mohammedans will meet face to face, as they have never confronted each other before, and in a field where there are no other disputants; the professors of each being of the same race, and both believing in their duty to convert the Pagans. And it is an advantage that the Negro Christian who is thus brought into a religious rivalry should be of that class which brings nothing to the conflict but an unwavering belief in the truth of Christianity; for he will confront Mohammedans whose unreasoning adherence to their faith has not been influenced by the disease of European casuistry. The new comer from the West will infuse spiritual life into the formalism of the Muslims, a vital and spontaneous activity into the mechanical regularity of their worship; while the Muslims by their disciplined intellect and respect for order, will confront the pretentions of ignorant and unlettered religious guides, and rebuke the wild impulses of religious fervour, the indifference to learning, the license (mistaken for liberty) imported from the house of bondage.

It is chiefly to point out these things that the following pages have been written, with the conviction that, if Christianity cannot conquer the whole of Africa—a task which it can never accomplish through European agency alone—it may, by the efforts and influence of its African converts, at least divide the empire of the Continent with Islam; Paganism, with all its horrors and abominations, having been forever abolished.

LIBERIA, WEST AFRICA,
    May, 1887.

INTRODUCTORY BIOGRAPHICAL NOTE,

BY THE

HON. SAMUEL LEWIS.

THE opportunity which has been unexpectedly offered to me of writing a brief biographical introduction to Dr. Blyden's work on "Christianity, Islam and the Negro Race," will not, I trust, be misemployed if, at the outset, I venture to express a hope that its bearings on the great question of Negro progress may secure for it an extensive circulation, as well as the sympathetic study of all who are interested in the condition of Africa. Nor can I doubt that a careful consideration of its contents will ultimately lead, if not to the adoption of methods altogether new, at least to an extensive modification of those older methods which have been, hitherto, regarded as most conducive to the civilisation of the Dark Continent.

A Negro myself, of unadulterated African blood, I believe that, in the ideas which underlie and interpenetrate this volume, and which lead up, by different but converging paths, to the general conclusion that the aim of philanthropists should be, not to distort or to destroy any of the characteristics which are most distinctive of the Negro race, but to ensure to them, as far as possible, their normal and natural development, Dr. Blyden is only giving eloquent expression and emphasis to the sentiments and aspirations of every enlightened member of his race. Foreign influence may—indeed it must—for some time to come do much for Africa, but not least, by recognising the fundamental fact that when all has been said and done by Europeans and Americans that they can either say or do, the African himself is, and must always remain, the fittest instrument for the development of his country. He it is who can best be trained to utilise the vast resources of Africa, not only for her own good, but for the benefit of the human race.

What may be the precise means which are best adapted for that end, I need not here enquire; nor whether it is Mohammedanism or Christianity which, under the present condition of Africa is likely to be the most important factor in its development. Many enlightened Africans are inclined to think, on grounds which are sufficiently explained in this volume, that Islam is, at the present moment, able to do more for the Pagan Negro than its great rival. But those who, like myself, believe in the ultimate triumph, throughout Negroland, of the Christian faith, will, none the less, be glad to learn that Dr. Blyden does not, in any degree, attribute the spread of Mohammedanism in Africa to its sensualism. Such an explanation is, at once, unworthy of a great religion and insulting to the Negro race, although it is one to which some European travellers of recent date—more qualified to traduce an unfortunate people than to engage in the philosophical investigation of their character and history—have not been ashamed to attribute its rapid spread and its wide influence. The facts and arguments accumulated in Dr. Blyden's Essays on this important subject will, I am convinced, repay the study of the Christian Evangelist no less than of the Christian Statesman.

Edward Wilmot Blyden was born in the Danish Island of St. Thomas, West Indies, and is of the purest Negro parentage. Inspired, in early youth, with a love for the Fatherland, and a desire to labour for its amelioration, he went to the United States in his seventeenth year, with a view of pursuing certain studies to fit himself to work in Africa. Influential friends endeavoured to secure for him admission to some institution of learning there, but so strong was the prejudice against his race at that time that the effort proved unavailing. He was advised to proceed at once to Liberia, where the Board of Foreign Missions of the Presbyterian Church in the United States was about to establish a High School, under the care of Rev. David A. Wilson, M.A., a graduate of Princeton College, now Dr. Wilson of Missouri. After a few months' residence in Liberia, young Blyden entered the new institution among its first pupils. By diligence and perseverance he soon rose to the headship of the school, and, after filling that office for three years, to the satisfaction of all concerned, was, in 1862, elected to a Professorship in the newly-founded College of Liberia. In 1864, he was appointed Secretary of State by the President of Liberia, and managed, for two years, to combine the duties of that office with his educational work. In 1869, he made a journey to the East, visiting Egypt and Syria, chiefly with the view of studying the Arabic language, in order to its introduction into the curriculum of the College.

In 1871, he resigned his Professorship, and, after a brief visit to Europe, spent two years in Sierra Leone, during which time he was sent by the Governor of the Colony—which was then under the administrations, successively, of Sir Arthur Kennedy and Sir John Pope Hennessy—on two diplomatic missions to the powerful chiefs of the interior. His Report on one of these Expeditions was published at length in the Proceedings of the Royal Geographical Society.

In 1877, he was appointed Minister Plenipotentiary of the Republic of Liberia at the Court of St. James', and was received by Her Majesty at Osborne, July 30, 1878, being introduced by the Marquess of Salisbury, then Secretary of State for Foreign Affairs. He was soon after elected an Honorary Member of the Athenæum Club. In 1880, he was elected a Fellow of the American Philological Association. In 1882, he was made a Corresponding and Honorary Member of the Society of Science and Letters of Bengal. In 1884, he was elected Vice-President of the American Colonisation Society. The honorary degrees of Master of Arts, Doctor of Divinity and Doctor of Laws have been conferred upon him by different American Colleges. In 1885, he was nominated by the Republican Party of Liberia a candidate for the Presidency of the Republic.

Dr. Blyden has, in the course of his labours, been brought into contact—epistolary or personal—with some of the most remarkable literary men of his day. Among them may be mentioned Lord Brougham, Mr. Gladstone, Dean Stanley, Charles Dickens, Charles Sumner.

He seems from his earliest years to have had a central idea, a dominant conviction, about the Negro and his country, which has, all along, guided and sustained him in his efforts. He believes his views to be true, and he is only gradually elaborating the exact method by which they may be brought home to others.

The following articles, though written at different times, will appear, when read carefully, to be linked together. They are not only the sentiments of a careful observer and diligent student, but they are the exponent of a purpose—the patriotic purpose of a lover of his race.

Many of the thoughts are new, but they are such as will be read with profit by all who are interested in the solution of the great problems which beset the work of the civilisation of Africa, and the genuine progress of humanity.

SAMUEL LEWIS.

FREETOWN, SIERRA LEONE,
October 14th, 1886.

Mohammedanism and the Negro Race.

TO students of general literature in Europe and the United States, until within the last few years, the Orientals most celebrated in religion or politics, in literature or learning, were known only by name. The Oriental world, to the student aiming at practical achievements, presented a field of so little promise that he scarcely ever ventured beyond a distant survey of what seemed to him a boundless and impracticable area. But, thanks to the exigencies of commerce, to philanthropic zeal, and to the scientific impulse, the East is daily getting to be " nearer seen and better known," not only in its outward life, but in those special aspects which, in religion and government, in war and policy, differentiate Eastern from Western races. It has been recently stated by a distinguished authority that " the intimate acquaintance with the languages, thoughts, history and monuments of Eastern nations is no longer a luxury, but a necessity." And the visits, within the last ten years, of Oriental rulers to Europe—the Sultan of Turkey, the Khedive of Egypt, the Shah of Persia, and the Seyyid of Zanzibar—have stimulated in the popular mind a livelier curiosity as to the character, condition, and influence of Mohammedan countries.

Drawn away from the beaten track of Roman and Greek antiquity by considerations, for the most part, of a material nature, and wandering into paths which, heretofore, were trodden only by such enthusiastic pioneers as Sir William Jones, the Western student finds rewards far rarer and richer than he had anticipated. And even those who have not the opportunity of familiarising themselves with Oriental languages find enough in translations—inadequate and unsatisfactory as they often are—to inspire them with a desire not only to increase their acquaintance with Eastern subjects, but to impart the knowledge they glean to others.

To the latter class belongs Mr. R. Bosworth Smith, the author of the work before us.[1] He informs us at the outset that "the only qualification he would venture to claim for himself," as a writer on Islam, "is that of a sympathetice interest in his subject," his work having been "derived in the main from the study of books in the European languages."

Mr. Bosworth Smith, who is a graduate of one of the English Universities, of only twelve years' standing, and therefore, we gather, a comparatively young man, may be regarded as one of the earliest collateral results of that increased activity in Oriental research which Dr. Birch has told us "marks the advance of civilization." And if he does stand upon the shoulders of Caussin de Perceval, Sprenger, Muir, and Deutsch, he may, without immodesty, claim to be taller than they; for we are very much mistaken if his book does not form an important starting-point on the road to a more tolerant—if not sympathetic—view among popular readers of the chief religion of the Oriental world. The works of the writers just mentioned were designedly not popular, but written by scholars for scholars, maintaining or opposing theories for the most part of merely literary or historical significance. Mr. Bosworth Smith has brought to his work not only a thorough appreciation of the literary and historical questions involved, but an earnest respect "for the deeper problems of the human soul," cherishing the sound and fruitful conviction, which he strives to impart to his readers, "that Mohammedans may learn much from Christians, and yet remain Mohammedans; that Christians have something at least to learn from Mohammedans,.

---

[1] *Mohammed and Mohammedanism.*—Lectures delivered at the Royal Institution of Great Britain, in February and March, 1874, by R. Bosworth Smith, M.A., Assistant-Master in Harrow School, late Fellow of Trinity College, Oxford.—London: Smith, Elder and Co.

which will make them not less but more Christian than they were before."

Mr. Bosworth Smith pursues the discussion of this important subject, which, as a labour of love, he entered upon, with a degree of earnestness, perspicuity, catholicity, and force of reasoning that renders his work not only most instructive, but highly interesting as an indication of the tendency and direction of cultivated thought in England. He has entered into the spirit of Islam in a manner which, but for the antecedent labours of Lane, Sprenger, Deutsch, and Weil, would be astounding in a Western scholar and an Englishman.

Dean Stanley's lecture on the same subject, though marked by the breadth of view, generous impartiality, and geniality of spirit which so honourably distinguish all the writings of that scholarly and Christian divine, is fragmentary—necessarily limited in its range by the nature and scope of the work. To Mr. Bosworth Smith, then, must be awarded the credit not only of having fully, fairly, and freely investigated the practical features of Islam, but of having rendered a clear, unbiassed, and unambiguous verdict, the influence of which, whether acknowledged or not, must be felt throughout the literary world. Such works as those of Maracci, Prideaux, and White are hereafter impossible in polemico-religious literature. No cultivated man, however inquisitorial his temperament, will ever, in the future, be tempted—or at least yield to the temptation—to subject any religious system to the Procrustean ordeal.

And, so far as Islam is concerned, scholars are arising within its ranks imbued with Western learning, and taking the part not only of defenders of their faith, but of interpreters between the Eastern and Western world. It has recently occasioned some surprise and comment that a Mohammedan writer should have written an able work in the English tongue, "challenging European and Christian thinkers on their own ground."[3] Since the

---

[3] *British Quarterly Review* for January, 1872, in a Review of 'A Series of Essays on the Life of Mohammed,' &c.; by Syed Ahmed Khan Bahador, C.S.I., Vol. I.—London, Trübner and Co., 1870.

appearance of Syed Ahmed's essays, another work has appeared in the English language, written by a young Mohammedan, in which he has briefly, temperately, and ably discussed the various subjects in relation to which Islam is usually assailed.[8]

But it is not only in recent days, as the writer in the *British Quarterly Review* would seem to imply, that Mohammedans have availed themselves of the power of the pen, in defence of their faith. There have always been, and there are now, able controversialists among them altogether unknown to Western fame. The celebrated work of Dr. Pfander, the Mizan-al-Hakk, attacking the Mohammedan system, has been reviewed in the Arabic language by a Mohammedan scholar, Rahmat Allah, in a learned and incisive reply, in which he reveals a marvellous acquaintance with European literature. We have heard of no attempt at a rejoinder to the work of Rahmat Allah. We saw a copy of this book in the hands of a West African Mohammedan at Sierra Leone, who was reading and commenting upon it to a number of his co-religionists.

We are glad to notice that Mr. Bosworth Smith's book has been republished in the United States, and that the able article of Deutsch on Islam has been reproduced in the same volume as an appendix. They are fit companions—*par nobile fratrum*. The traveller, contemplating a visit to Mohammedan countries, or the theologian wishing to get a clear view of a religious system which is shaping the destiny of millions of the race, may now carry in his pocket a complete compendium of Mohammedan literature. If we except the very remarkable article on the 'Historical Statements in the Koran,' written in 1832, by the then stripling reviewer, Mr. J. Addison Alexander, of Princeton, and the able 'Review of the Koran,' by Professor Draper, of the New York University, in his *History of the Intellectual Development of Europe*, American scholarship has as yet, as far as we are aware, produced nothing of importance in this branch of literature.

---

[8] *A Critical Examination of the Life and Teachings of Mohammed;* by Syed Ameer Ali Moulvi, M.A., LL.B., of the Inner Temple, Barrister-at-Law, &c.—London: Williams and Norgate, 1873.

Mohammedanism and the Negro Race.

The portion of the interesting work now before us, which we propose more particulary to notice, is that part of the first lecture which refers to the character and influence of Islam in Western and Central Africa. Dean Stanley says:—

> It cannot be forgotten that Mohammedanism is the only higher religion which has hitherto made progress in the vast continent of Africa. Whatever may be the future fortunes of African Christianity, there can be no doubt that they will be long affected by its relations with the most fanatical and the most proselytising portion of the Mussulman world in its Negro converts.[4]

If this view is correct, then the Christian world cannot be indifferent to the discussion of a subject so full of importance affecting one branch of the philanthropic interests into which the Christian Church, more than ever before, is now pouring its most eager life.[5]

Three streams of influence have always penetrated into Negroland: one, from Egypt, through Nubia, to Bornou and Hausa; another, from Abyssinia to Yoruba and Ashantee; the third, from the Barbary States across the desert to Timbuktu. By the first two, Egypt and Arabia exchanged their productions for the raw materials of the Soudan. By the third, the ports of the Mediterranean, through the Great Desert, having Timbuktu as a centre, became outlets for the wealth of Nigritia. Even in the days of Herodotus there appears to have been intercourse between the region of the Tsad and the Mediterranean, and the valuable products collected at various centres by the itinerant traffic, which still flourishes in the interior, shared by numerous caravans, found their way by means of Phœnician ships to different countries of Europe and the Levant.

Central Africa has never been cut off commercially from European and Asiatic intercourse. But it was not until the ninth

---

[4] *Eastern Church*, p. 259.

[5] Mr. Monier Williams, the Boden Professor of Sanscrit at Oxford, has recently expressed the opinion, in a paper read at the Conference on Foreign Missions, held at the Cannon Street Hotel in London (June 22, 1875), that, unless a fresh and powerful impulse is given to Christian missionary effort, Mohammedanism will speedily overrun the whole African continent.

century of the Christian era that any knowledge of the true God began to penetrate into Negroland. To Akbah, a distinguished Muslim general, belongs the credit or discredit of having subdued North Africa to Islam. He marched from Damascus at the head of ten thousand enthusiastic followers, and in a short time spread his conquests along the shores of North Africa, advancing to the very verge of the Atlantic, whose billows alone checked his westward career.[6] But the energy which could not proceed westward turned northward and southward. In its southern progress it crossed the formidable wastes of the Sahara, penetrated into the Soudan, and established the centre of its influence at Timbuktu. In less than a century from that time several large Nigritian tribes had yielded to the influence of Islam; and it shaped so rapidly the ideas, the manners, and the history of those tribes, that when in the Middle Ages Ibn Batoutah, an Arab traveller, visited those regions, he found that Islam had taken firm root among several powerful peoples, had mastered their life and habits, and dominated their whole social and religious policy. Among the praiseworthy qualities which attracted his attention as a result of their conversion, he mentions their devotion to the study of the Koran, and relates the following illustrative incidents, which we give in the French version now before us:—

> Ils ont un grand zèle pour apprendre par cœur le sublime Coran. Dans le cas où leurs enfants font preuve de négligence à cet égard, ils leur mettent des entraves aux pieds et ne les leur ôtent pas qu'ils ne le sachent réciter de mémoire. Le jour de la fête, étant entré chez le juge, et ayant vu ses enfants enchaînés, je lui dis: "Est-ce que tu ne les mettras pas en liberté?" Il repondit: "Je ne le ferai que lorsqu'ils sauront par cœur le Coran." Une autre jour, je passai devant un jeune nègre, beau de figure, revêtu d'habits superbes, et portant aux pieds une lourde chaîne. Je dis à la personne qui m'accompagnait: "Qu'a fait ce garçon? Est-ce qu'il a assassiné quelqu'un?" Le jeune nègre entendit mon propos et se mit à rire. On me dit: "Il a été enchaîné uniquement pour le forcer à apprendre le Coran de mémoire."[7]

Mohammedanism in Africa counts in its ranks the most energetic and enterprising tribes. It claims as adherents the only people

---

[6] Gibbon's *Decline and Fall*, &c., chap. li.

[7] *Voyages d'Ibn Batoutah*, texte et traduction; par Defremery et Sanguinetti.—Paris, 1858; vol. iv, pp. 422, 423.

Mohammedanism and the Negro Race.

who have any form of civil polity or bond of social organisation. It has built and occupies the largest cities in the heart of the continent. Its laws regulate the most powerful kingdoms—Futah, Masina, Hausa, Bornou, Waday, Darfur, Kordofan, Senaar, &c. It produces and controls the most valuable commerce between Africa and Foreign countries; it is daily gaining converts from the ranks of Paganism; and it commands respect among all Africans wherever it is known, even where the people have not submitted to the sway of the Koran.

No one can travel any distance in the interior of West Africa without being struck with the different aspects of society in different localities, according as the population is Pagan or Mohammedan. Not only is there a difference in the methods of government, but in the general regulations of society, and even in the amusements of the people. The love of noisy terpsichorean performances, so noticeable in Pagan communities, disappears as the people come under the influence of Mohammedanism. It is not a fact that "when the sun goes down, all Africa dances;" but it might be a fact if it were not for the influence of Islam. Those who would once have sought pleasure in the excitement of the tom-tom, now repair five times a-day to the mosque, where they spend a quarter of an hour on each occasion in devotional exercises. After the labours of the day they assemble in groups near the mosque to hear the Koran recited, or the Traditions or some other book read. In traversing the region of country between Sierra Leone and Futah Jallo in 1873, we passed through populous Pagan towns; and the transition from these to Mohammedan districts was striking. When we left a Pagan and entered a Mohammedan community, we at once noticed that we had entered a moral atmosphere widely separated from, and loftier far than, the one we had left. We discovered that the character, feelings, and conditions of the people were profoundly altered and improved.

It is evident that, whatever may be said of the Koran, as long as it is in advance of the Shamanism or Fetichism of the African tribes who accept it—and no one will doubt that Islam as a creed is an enormous advance not only on all idolatries, but on all

Christianity, Islam and the Negro Race.

systems of purely human origin—those tribes must advance beyond their primitive condition.

The Koran is, in its measure, an important educator. It exerts among a primitive people a wonderful influence. It has furnished to the adherents of its teachings in Africa a ground of union which has contributed vastly to their progress. Hausas, Foulahs, Mandingoes, Soosoos, Akus, can all read the same books and mingle in worship together, and there is to all one common authority and one ultimate umpirage. They are united by a common religious sentiment, by a common antagonism to Paganism. Not only the sentiments, but the language, the words of the sacred book are held in the greatest reverence and esteem. And even where the ideas are not fully understood, the words seem to possess for them a nameless beauty and music, a subtle and indefinable charm, incomprehensible to those acquainted only with European languages. It is easy for those not acquainted with the language in which the Koran was written, and therefore, judging altogether as outsiders, to indulge in depreciation of its merits.[8] Such critics lose sight of the fact that the Koran is a poetical composition, and a poetical composition of the earliest and most primitive kind, and that therefore its ideas and the language in which they are conveyed cannot well be separated. The genuine poet not only creates the conception, but the word which is its vehicle. The word becomes the inseparable drapery of the idea. Hence the highest poetry cannot be translated. We see this in the numerous versions by which it has been sought in every age to reach the sense of the poetical portions of the Bible. No words yet furnished by Greek, Roman, or Teutonic literature have been fully adequate to bring out the subtle beauties of the Semitic original. Among Mohammedans, written or printed translations of the Koran are discouraged. The Chinese, Hindoos, Persians, Turks, Mandingoes

---

[8] The case cited by Dr. Mühleisen Arnold, in his work on Islam, of an Arab philosopher and unbeliever in Mohammed, who lived in the eighth century, depreciating the literary merits of the Koran, is no more in point as an argument against the book, it appears to us, than if a Mohammedan controversialist were to quote from Voltaire or Tom Paine against the Bible.

Mohammedanism and the Negro Race.

Foulahs, &c., who have embraced Islam, speak in their "own tongues wherein they were born," but read the Koran in Arabic.

Mr. Bosworth Smith was right to begin his preparations for the valuable work he has written by a careful study of the Koran. But it is to be regretted that he had not access to the force and beauty of the original, which neither Sale, Kasimirsky, Lane, nor Rodwell have been able—though they laboured hard to do so—to retain in their excellent translations. A distinguished Oriental scholar and critic says:—

> There can be no doubt that, to understand thoroughly this wonderful book the aid of those learned men, Arabs and others, who have devoted themselves to the careful study of it, is not only desirable, but necessary. . . . The subject is of sufficient importance to men of research to render it advisable that it should be examined from all points of view, for by no other means can we hope to obtain as clear an insight into the origin of Islam, as by a careful study of the book which contains its fundamental principles.[9]

To the outside world, easily swayed by superficial impressions, and carried away by matters of mere dramatic interest, there may be nothing attractive in the progress of Islam in Africa, because, as far as known to Western readers, the history of African Mohammedanism is deficient in great characters and in remarkable episodes. There has been, it is supposed, no controlling mind developed, which has moved great masses of men. But the words of Horace are applicable here:—

> Omnes illacrimabiles
> Urgentur, ignotique longa
> Nocte, carent quia vate sacro.

It is not, however, that no bard has written, but they have had very few readers in Christian countries. To those acquainted with the interior of Africa—to the Mohammedan world of North Africa and Arabia—it is well known that numerous characters have arisen in Africa—Negro Muslims—who have exerted no little influence in the military, political, and ecclesiastical affairs of Islam, not only in Africa, but in the lands of their teachers. In the biographies of

---

[9] W. Nassau Lees, in the preface to his edition of the *Commentary of Zamakhshari*.

Ibn Khallikan are frequent notices of distinguished Negro Mohammedans. Koelle, in his *Polyglotta Africana*, gives a graphic account of the proceedings of the great Fodie, whose zeal, enthusiasm, and bravery spread Islam over a large portion of Nigritia.

One of the most remarkable characters who have influenced the history of the region of country between Timbuktu and the West Coast was a native of Futah Toro, known as the Sheikh Omaru Al-Hajj. He is said to have been a Waleeu,[10] a man of extraordinary endowments, of commanding presence, and great personal influence. He was educated by the Sheikh Tijani, a Muslim missionary from Arabia. Having spent several years under the instruction of this distinguished teacher, visiting Mecca in the meanwhile, he became profoundly learned in the Arabic language. After the death of his master, he went twice to Mecca on pilgrimage. On his return to his country the second time, he undertook a series of proselytising expeditions against the powerful Pagan tribes on the east and south-east of Futah Toro. He conquered several powerful chiefs and reduced their people to the faith of Islam. He banished Paganism from Sego, and purified the practices of several Mohammedan districts which had become imbued with heathenish notions. He thus restored Jenne, and Hamd-Allahi, and was on his way to Timbuktu, about ten years ago, when, through the treachery of the Arabs of that region, he was circumvented and killed at a town in Masina. One of his sons, Ahmadu, is now King of Sego, another rules over Hamd-Allahi, two of the largest cities in Central Africa.

Al-Hajj Omaru wrote many Arabic works in prose and poetry. His poems are recited and sung in every Mohammedan town and village, from Futlah-town, in Sierra Leone, to Kano. His memory is held in the greatest respect by all native students, and they

---

[10] This word is used by the Mohammedans of Negroland in a peculiar sense. It means one called of God, and endowed with special gifts to exercise authority in ecclesiastical and sometimes political matters, inferior in official rank—according to their estimation—only to a prophet. Such men have, from time to time, arisen among African Mohammedans, and have carried out important reforms in Church and State.

Mohammedanism and the Negro Race.

attribute to him many extraordinary deeds, and see in his successful enterprises, literary and military, proofs of divine guidance."[11]

We have heard of numerous instances of these "half-military, half-religious geniuses," as Mr. Bosworth Smith calls them, "which Islam always seems capable of producing."

To the Mohammedans of Negroland, far away from the complex civilisation of European life, with its multifarious interests, the struggle for the ascendancy of Islam is the one great object which should engage the attention of a rational being. It is a struggle between light and darkness, between knowledge and ignorance, between good and evil. The traditional enthusiasm of their faith makes them utterly indifferent to the sufferings of any who stand in the way of the dissemination of the truth, and patient of any evils they may have to endure in order to ensure the triumph of their cause. "Paradise is under the shadow of swords," is one of their stimulating proverbs.

There is one passage in Mr. Bosworth Smith's book, of which we do not think that the author, who, as it seems, has not himself been in Africa, perceived the full import, but which the Christian world, it appears to us, would do well to ponder. It is as follows:—

Christian travellers, with every wish to think otherwise, have remarked that the Negro[12] who accepts Mohammedanism acquires at once a sense of the dignity of human nature not commonly found even among those who have been brought to accept Christianity.[18]

Having enjoyed exceptional advantages for observation and comparison in the United States, the West Indies, South America,

---

[11] Report on the Expedition to Timbo made to the Governor of Sierra Leone, 1873. See also the *African Sketch Book*, by Winwood Reade, vol. i, p. 317.

[12] Mr. Bosworth Smith writes this word with a small "n," but we do not see why, if it is used to designate one of the great families of man, it should not be entitled to the same distinction as such words as Indian, Hindoo, Chinaman, &c. Why give more dignity to the specific than to the general? Why write Ashantee, Congo, Mandingo, with capitals, and Negro, the generic appellation, with a small "n"? Is not this in deference to the sort of prejudice against which Mr. B. Smith himself protests?

[18] Lecture I, p. 32.

Christianity, Islam and the Negro Race.

Egypt, Syria, West and Central Africa, we are compelled, however reluctantly, to endorse the statement made by Mr. B. Smith. And we are not surprised at his seizing hold, in his researches, of this most important fact and giving it such prominence—a prominence it richly deserves—in the discussion. Wherever the Negro is found in Christian lands, his leading trait is not docility, as has been often alleged, but servility. He is slow and unprogressive. Individuals here and there may be found of extraordinary intelligence, enterprise, and energy, but there is no Christian community of Negroes anywhere which is self-reliant and independent. Haïti and Liberia, so-called Negro Republics, are merely struggling for existence, and hold their own by the tolerance of the civilised powers.[14] On the other hand, there are numerous Negro Mohammedan communities and states in Africa which are self-reliant, productive, independent, and dominant, supporting, without the countenance or patronage of the parent country, Arabia, whence they derived them, their political, literary, and ecclesiastical institutions. In Sierra Leone, the Mohammedans, without any aid from Government—Imperial or local—or any contributions from Mecca or Constantinople, erect their mosques, keep up their religious services, conduct their schools, and contribute to the support of missionaries from Arabia, Morocco, or Futah when they visit them. The same compliment cannot be paid to the Negro Christians of that settlement. The most enlightened native Christians there look forward with serious apprehension—and, perhaps, not without good grounds—to the time when, if ever, the instructions and influence from London will be withheld. An able paper on the 'Condition and Wants of Liberia,' by an intelligent and candid Liberian, has the following:

> We want, as a people, the spirit of liberality. We have learned to depend upon foreign institutions to support our churches. This should not be so. If, indeed, we have not enough of the Christian religion to induce us to contribute liberally to the cause of the Gospel; if we have not enough zeal for the cause of Christ to make us willing to sacrifice time and money for its good, &c., we

---

[14] The *Official Journal*, dated May 1, 1875, contained intelligence of a conspiracy which had just been suppressed, and a Presidential decree banishing forty of the conspirators.

Mohammedanism and the Negro Race.

had as well give up churches and religion. .... I have known some persons to change a two cent piece so as to get one cent for the church. Alas, for such religion! alas for the churches thus supported![15]

In the recent Ashantee war the most trustworthy Negro troops were the Haussas, who are rigid Mohammedans. The West India Christian Negro troops were not relied on to the same extent.

Now, what has produced this difference in the effects of the two systems upon the Negro race? In reply, we remark generally that the difference must be attributed to the difference in the conditions under which the systems came to those of the Negro race who embraced the one or the other. Mohammedanism found its Negro converts at home in a state of freedom and independence of the teachers who brought it to them. When it was offered to them they were at liberty to choose for themselves. The Arab missionaries, whom we have met in the interior, go about without "purse or scrip," and disseminate their religion by quietly teaching the Koran. The native missionaries—Mandingoes and Foulahs—unite with the propagation of their faith active trading. Wherever they go, they produce the impression that they are not preachers only, but traders; but, on the other hand, that they are not traders merely, but preachers. And, in this way, silently and almost unobtrusively, they are causing princes to become obedient disciples and zealous propagators of Islam. Their converts, as a general thing, become Muslims from choice and conviction, and bring all the manliness of their former condition to the maintenance and support of their new creed.

When the religion was first introduced it found the people possessing all the elements and enjoying all the privileges of an untrammelled manhood. They received it as giving them additional power to exert an influence in the world. It sent them forth as the guides and instructors of their less favoured neighbours, and endowed them with the self-respect which men feel who acknowledge no superior. While it brought them a great deal that was absolutely new, and inspired them with spiritual feelings

---

[15] The Annual Address delivered before the City Council and Citizens of Monrovia, July 27, 1874; by Jehu T. Dimery.

to which they had before been utter strangers, it strengthened and hastened certain tendencies to independence and self-reliance which were already at work. Their local institutions were not destroyed by the Arab influence introduced. They only assumed new forms, and adapted themselves to the new teachings. In all thriving Mohammedan communities, in West and Central Africa, it may be noticed that the Arab superstructure has been superimposed on a permanent indigenous substructure; so that what really took place, when the Arab met the Negro in his own home, was a healthy amalgamation, and not an absorption or an undue repression.

The Oriental aspect of Islam has become largely modified in Negroland, not, as is too generally supposed, by a degrading compromise with the Pagan superstitions, but by shaping many of its traditional customs to suit the milder and more conciliatory disposition of the Negro. As long as Timbuktu, which was but a continuation of Morocco, retained its ascendency, Islam kept up its strictly Arabian aspect; but since the seat of literary activity and ecclesiastical influence has been transferred to Kuka, and since Kano has become the commercial centre—two purely Negro cities grown up under Muslim influence—and since the religion has taken root among the large indigenous communities near the source of the Niger, it has been largely affected by the geographical and racial influences to which it has been exposed. The absence of political pressure has permitted native peculiarities to manifest themselves, and to take an effective part in the work of assimilating the new elements.

Christianity, on the other hand, came to the Negro as a slave, or at least as a subject race in a foreign land. Along with the Christian teaching, he and his children received lessons of their utter and permanent inferiority and subordination to their instructors, to whom they stood in the relation of chattels. Christianity took them fresh from the barbarism of ages, and forced them to embrace its tenets. The religion of Jesus was embraced by them as the only source of consolation in their deep disasters. In their abject miseries, keen anguish, and hopeless suffering they seized upon it

Mohammedanism and the Negro Race.

us promising a country where, after the unexampled sorrows of this life, "the wicked cease from troubling, and the weary are at rest." It found them down-trodden, oppressed, scorned; it soothed their sufferings, subdued their hearts, and pointed them, in its exhaustless sympathy, to the "Man of Sorrows, and acquainted with grief." In their condition of outcasts and pariahs, it directed their aspirations to a heavenly and eternal citizenship; it put new songs in their mouths—those melodies inimitable to the rest of the world—which, from the lips of emancipated slaves, have recently charmed the ears and captivated the hearts of royalty and nobles in Europe by a tenderness, a sweetness, an earnestness, and a solemnity, born of adversity, in the house of bondage. A popular London preacher says:

> The Negro is more really musical than the Englishman. . . . Singing very often merrily with the tears wet upon his ebony cheek, no record of his joy or sorrow passed unaccompanied by a cry of melody, or a wail of plaintive and harmonious melancholy. If we could divest ourselves of prejudice, the songs that float down the Ohio river are one in feeling and character with the songs of the Hebrew captives by the waters of Babylon. We find in them the same tale of bereavement and separation, the same irreparable sorrow, the same wild tenderness and passionate sweetness, like music in the night.[16]

These are great and precious advantages; but, nevertheless, owing to the physical, mental, and social pressure under which the Africans received these influences of Christianity, their development was necessarily partial and one-sided, cramped and abnormal. All tendencies to independent individuality were repressed and destroyed. Their ideas and aspirations could be expressed only in conformity with the views and tastes of those who held rule over them. All avenues to intellectual improvment were closed against them, and they were doomed to perpetual ignorance.

Mohammedanism and learning to the Muslim Negro were coeval. No sooner was he converted than he was taught to read, and the importance of knowledge was impressed upon him. The Christian Negro came in contact with mental and physical proscription and the religion of Christ, contemporaneously. If the Mohammedan Negro had at any time to choose between the Koran

---

[16] Rev. H. R. Haweis in *Music and Morals*, p. 500.—London, 1874.

and the sword, when he chose the former, he was allowed to wield the latter as the equal of any other Muslim; but no amount of allegiance to the Gospel relieved the Christian Negro from the degradation of wearing the chain which he received with it, or rescued him from the political and, in a measure, ecclesiastical proscription which he still undergoes in all the countries of his exile.[17] Everywhere in Christian lands he plays, at the present moment, the part of the slave, ape or puppet. Only a few here and there rise above the general degradation, and these become targets to their unappreciative brethren—

Apparent rari nantes in gurgite vasto.

Is it any wonder, then, that "Christian travellers, with every wish to think otherwise," in commenting upon the difference between Christian and Mohammedan Negroes, with respect to true manliness, must do so to the disadvantage of the former?

Another reason for the superior manliness and *amour propre* of Negro Mohammedans may be found in the fact that, unlike their Christian brethren, they have not been trained under the depressing influence of Aryan art. Deutsch says:—

The Shemites from some strange idiosyncrasy, perpetuated by religious ordinances, abhorred, all of them, at certain stages, the making visible pictures of things they revered, loved or worshipped.[18]

The Second Commandment, with Mussulmans as with Jews, is construed literally into the prohibition of all representations of living creatures of all kinds; not merely in sacred places but everywhere.[19] Josephus tells us that the Jews would not even tolerate the image of the emperor, which was represented on the eagles of the soldiers.[20] The early Christian Fathers believed that painting and sculpture were forbidden by the Scriptures, and that

---

[17] For an interesting discussion of this subject from the pen of a Negro, see Tanner's *Apology for African Methodism in the United States*.
[18] *Literary Remains*, p. 161.
[19] *Mischat ul-Masabih*, vol. ii, p. 368.
[20] *Antiq.* xviii—iii, 1, &c.

Mohammedanism and the Negro Race.

they were therefore wicked arts. Among the Mohammedans of Negroland it is considered a sin to make even the rudest representation of any living thing on the ground or on the side of a house. We shall never forget the disgust with which a Mandingo from Kankan, who was, for the first time, visiting the sea-board at Monrovia, turned from a marble figure in the cemetery through which we were showing him, exclaiming, "*Amâl Shaitân ! amâl Shaitân !*"—the work of Satan.[21]

No one can deny the great æsthetic and moral advantages which have accrued to the Caucasian race from Christian art, through all its stages of development, from the Good Shepherd of the Catacombs to the Transfiguration of Raphael, from rough mosaics to the inexpressible delicacy and beauty of Giotto and Fra Angelico.[22] But to the Negro all these exquisite representations exhibited only the physical characteristics of a foreign race; and, while they tended to quicken the tastes and refine the sensibilities of that race, they had only a depressing influence upon the Negro, who felt that he had neither part nor lot, so far as his physical character was concerned, in those splendid representations. A strict adherence to the letter of the Second Commandment would have been no drawback to the Negro. To him the painting and sculpture of Europe as instruments of education, have been worse than failures. They have really raised barriers in the way of his normal development. They have set before him models for imitation; and his very effort to conform to the canons of taste thus practically suggested, has impaired, if not destroyed, his self-respect, and made him the weakling and creeper which he appears in Christian lands. It was our lot not long since to hear an illiterate Negro in a prayer-meeting in New York entreat the Deity to extend his "lily white hands" and bless the waiting congregation. Another,[23] with no greater amount of culture, preaching from

---

[21] See Koran, v, 92.

[22] See a paper on the Roman Catacombs, &c., read by Dean Stanley before the Royal Institution, May 29, 1874.

[23] The putting forward of thoroughly illiterate men to expound the Scriptures among the Negro Christians has been another great drawback to their proper development.

Christianity, Islam and the Negro Race.

1 John, iii, 2, "We shall be like Him," &c., &c., exclaimed, "Brethren, imagine a beautiful white man with blue eyes, rosy cheeks, and flaxen hair, and *we shall be like him.*" The conceptions of these worshippers were what they had gathered from plastic and pictorial representations as well as from the characteristics of the dominant race around them. The Mohammedan Negro, who is not familiar with such representations, sees God in the great men of his country. The saying is attributed to an ancient philosopher [24] that if horses, oxen, and lions could paint they would certainly make gods in their own image :—

> If oxen or lions had hands, and could work in man's fashion,
> And trace out with chisel and brush their conception of Godhead,
> Then would horses depict gods like horses, and oxen like oxen,
> Each kind the divine with its own form and nature endowing.

This is no doubt true, and the Negro who grew up normally would certainly not be inferior to lions, horses, and oxen. The Christian Negro, abnormal in his development, pictures God and all beings remarkable for their moral and intellectual qualities with the physical characteristics of Europeans, and deems it an honour if he can approximate—by a mixture of his blood, however irregularly achieved—in outward appearance, at least, to the ideal thus forced upon him of the physical accompaniments of all excellence. In this way he loses that "sense of the dignity of human nature" observable in his Mohammedan brother.

A third very important influence which has retarded the development of the Christian Negro may be found in the social and literary pressure which he has undergone. It is not too much to say that the popular literature of the Christian world since the discovery of America, or, at least for the last two hundred years, has been anti-Negro. The Mohammedan Negro has felt nothing of the withering power of caste. There is nothing in his colour or race to debar him from the highest privileges, social or political, to which any other Muslim can attain. The slave who becomes a Mohammedan is free.[25] Mohammedan history

---

[24] Xenophanes of Colophon (six centuries B.C.).
[25] Ockley's *History of the Saracens*, sixth edition.—London, 1871, p. 14.

abounds with examples of distinguished Negroes. The eloquent Azân, or "Call to Prayer," which to this day summons at the same hours millions of the human race to their devotions, was first uttered by a Negro, Bilâl by name, whom Mohammed, in obedience to a dream, appointed the first Muezzin, or Crier.[26] And it has been remarked that even Alexander the Great is in Asia an unknown personage by the side of this honoured Negro. Mr. Muir notices the inflexible constancy of Bilâl to the faith of Islam under the severest trials.[27] Ibn Khallikan mentions a celebrated Negro Khalif, who reigned at Bagdad in the ninth century.[28] He describes him as a man of great merit, and a perfect scholar. None of the sons of Khalifs spoke with greater propriety and elegance, or composed verses with greater ability. The following lines were addressed to him by a contemporary poet:—

> Blackness of skin cannot degrade an ingenious mind, or lessen the worth of the scholar or the wit. Let blackness claim the colour of your body; I claim as mine your fair and candid soul.

The poet Abu Ishak Assabi, who lived in the tenth century, had a black slave named Yumna, to whom he was greatly attached, and on whom he wrote some remarkable verses, which are much quoted by Muslims. Notice the following:—

> The dark-skinned Yumna said to one whose colour equals the whiteness of the eye, "Why should your face boast its white complexion? Do you think that by so clear a tint it gains additional merit? Were a mole of my colour on that face it would adorn it; but one of your colour on my cheek would disfigure me."

Here is another:—

> Black misbecomes you not; by it you are increased in beauty; black is the only colour princes wear. Were you not mine, I should purchase you with all my wealth. Did I not possess you, I should give my life to obtain you.[29]

Ibn Muslimeh, an enthusiastic lover, exclaims, "If a mole be set in an ugly cheek it endows it with beauty and grace; how then

---

[26] Muir's *Life of Mahomet*, vol. iii, p. 54.
[27] *Ibid.*, vol. ii, p. 129.
[28] *Biographies of Ibn Khallikan*, translated by Baron de Slane, vol. i, p. 18.
[29] *Ibn Khallikan*, vol. i, p. 82.

should the heart-stricken be blamed for looking upon his mistress as a mole all over?"[80]

Mr. Gifford Palgrave, whose travels in Eastern countries have no doubt diminished the sensitiveness of his Western prejudices, concludes his brilliant *Essays on Eastern Questions* with a poem composed by a Negress in memory of her celebrated semi-Arab son, who had perished in one of his daring adventures.

Now, it must be evident that Negroes trained under the influence of such a social and literary atmosphere must have a deeper self-respect and higher views of the dignity of human nature than those trained under the blighting influence of caste, and under the guidance of a literature in which it has been the fashion for more than two hundred years to caricature the African, to ridicule his personal peculiarities, and to impress him with a sense of perpetual and hopeless inferiority. Christian literature has nothing to show on behalf of the Negro comparable to Mohammedan literature; and there is nothing in Mohammedan literature corresponding to the Negro—or "nigger," as even a liberal clergyman like Mr. Haweis will call him[81]—of Christian caricaturists. A distinguished American scholar and thinker has noticed this. He says:—

> The black man in literature is either a weakling or caricature. The comic side of him alone comes into view. The single sonnet of Wordsworth upon the chieftain Toussaint, and the "sparkles dire of fierce, vindictive song" from the American Whittier, are almost the only literary allusions to the sublime and tragic elements in the Negro's nature and condition; certainly the only allusions that, without any abatement and introduction of ludicrous traits, ally him *solely* with human
>
> ".... Exultations, agonies,
> And love, and man's unconquerable mind."[82]

No one will charge the Negro Mohammedans with giving ground

---

[80] The *Assemblies of Al-Hariri*. Translated by Thomas Chenery; Williams and Norgate, 1870. This work is also called the *Makamat*, &c.

[81] *Music and Morals*, p. 550.

[82] Professor W. G. T. Shedd, in an Address delivered before the Massachusetts Colonisation Society, Boston, May 27, 1857. The remarkable Address of Wendell Phillips on Toussaint L'Ouverture must not be forgotten. Mr. Phillips is the only American orator who has had the temerity to lavish the flowers of a brilliant rhetoric in adorning the memory of a Negro.

for the notion, put forward recently from a very distinguished source, that the African entertains "a superstitious awe and dread of the white man." Ibn Batoutah, cited before, though a Mohammedan, experienced no greater respect among the Muslims of Negroland on account of his colour, than a Negro in the same position would have received. He complains of the cool and haughty bearing of a certain Negro prince towards himself and a number of European and Arab traders who appeared in the royal presence. "It was then," he says, "that I regretted having entered the country of Negroes on account of their bad education, and the little regard they have for white men." And what was the evidence of this "bad education and little regard for white men?" The chief chose to speak to them through a third party, "although they were very near him." "This was done," observes the sensitive traveller, "solely on account of his contempt" for them. Réné Caillié, the French traveller, who made the journey from West Africa to Morocco, viâ Timbuktu, was compelled to travel in strict disguise as a poor Muslim. His sojourn in Timbuktu was of only fourteen days; and, as he was in constant danger of being discovered, he could neither move about freely nor note down all that he wished. Even Barth was obliged, for a short time, to adopt the character of a Muslim. Of course these things occurred before the days of Sir Garnet Wolseley, who, in a grave official document, thought it necessary to reassure his troops in the following terms:—

It must never be forgotten by our soldiers that Providence has implanted in the heart of every native of Africa a superstitious awe and dread of the white man that prevents the Negro from daring to meet us face to face in combat.[83]

But Sir Garnet also deemed it important to bring to bear against these awe-struck Negroes armed with cheap flint muskets, all the appliances of modern warfare, and, no doubt, bore in mind the Roman poet's advice—*Ne crede colori*. As a *ruse de guerre*—a military expedient—the statement served its purpose, and is one among the many evidences of Sir Garnet's skill and readiness in

---

[83] Notes issued for use of the troops by order of Sir Garnet Wolseley, dated. Cape Coast Castle, December 20, 1873.

not only availing himself of advantageous elements in the situation, but of creating them, if they do not exist. In this case, he adroitly played upon the "superstition" of white men :—

<blockquote>An dolus an virtus, quis in hoste requirat?</blockquote>

A cool and discriminating critic at home, however, at the close of the war assured us that, "without arms of precision, guns and rockets, and English skill and discipline, no invader could have made his way to Coomassie."

Had Sir Garnet, even before his practical experience, read the history of the great Civil War in America, he would have found in the thrilling records of many a desperate encounter, in which the Negro proved himself no mean antagonist when he met the white man "face to face in combat," materials for imposing a check upon that exuberance of imagination which tempted him to so sweeping an assertion. We admit that the Negro in Christian lands, and all along the Coast where he has been under the training of the white man, exhibits a cringing and servile spirit; but this, as we have endeavoured to show, is the natural result of that habit of mind which it was the interest of his masters to impress upon him. Sir Garnet's dogma is only one of the innumerable lessons which the Negro is constantly made to imbibe, even at times from his religious guides and teachers,[34] the tendency of which is to blunt his "sense of the dignity of human nature."

Another very important element which has given the Mohammedan Negro the advantage over his Christian brother is the more complete sympathy which has always existed between him and his foreign teacher. Mr. Bosworth Smith says :—

<blockquote>The Mussulman missionaries exhibit a forbearance, a sympathy, and a respect for native customs and prejudices, and even for their more harmless</blockquote>

---

[34] See an article on the 'Negro' in the *Church Missionary Intelligencer* for August 1, 1878. The special correspondent of the *Daily News* at Cape Coast, under date of October 2, 1878, speaks of the Native Chiefs as follows :—" There is nothing that seems to signify power about their dignity ; and knowing, as we did, that it has been our policy on the Coast for years to deprive these chiefs of all real influence, their very solemnity of manner left on me an impression of the theatrical."

Mohammedanism and the Negro Race.

beliefs, which is, no doubt, one reason of their success, and which our own missionaries and school-masters would do well to imitate.[85]

Long prior to the rise of Islam, as we have seen above, the Arab merchant had been in communication with the interior of Africa, and had opened the way for the Arab missionary. When, therefore, the Muslim missionary came as the propagator of a higher religion than any that had been known, he did not enter the country as a stranger. The political and social institutions of the Arabs had already been tried and found suitable to the wants and tastes of the Negro tribes; indeed, the two peoples, if not of cognate origin, have by protracted intercommunication, and by the similarity of the physical influences which have, for ages, operated upon them, become similar in tastes; and it was not difficult for the Arabs to conform to a great extent to the social and domestic customs of the Africans. The Muslim missionary often brought to the aid of his preaching the influence of social and domestic relationships—an influence which in all efforts to convert a people is not to be entirely ignored. "The conversion of the Russian nation," we are told by Dean Stanley, "was effected, not by the preaching of the Byzantine clergy, but by the marriage of a Byzantine princess."[86] So the Arab missionaries often entered into the bonds of wedlock with the daughters of Negroland;[87] and by their teaching, by their intelligence, by their intermarriages with the natives, by the trade and generosity of their merchants, they enlisted so many interests and such deep sympathies, that they rapidly took abiding root in the country. Some of the brightest names in the annals not only of Islamitic but of pre-Islamitic literature, are those of the descendants of Arabs and Africans. One of the authors of the *Muallakat*, for instance, was half Arab and half Negro.

The sympathy, therefore, between the Arab missionary and the African is more complete than that between the European and the

---

[85] P. 34.

[86] *Eastern Church*, p. 84.

[87] Mr. Palgrave tells us that intermarriages between Arabs and Negroes have been at no period rare or abnormal; to such admixtures, indeed, the East owes not a few of her best celebrities.—*Essays on Eastern Questions*, p. 387.

Christianity, Islam and the Negro Race.

Negro. With every wish, no doubt, to the contrary, the European seldom or never gets over the feeling of distance, if not of repulsion, which he experiences on first seeing the Negro.[88] While he joyfully admits the Negro to be his brother, having the same nature in all its essential attributes, still, owing to the diversity in type and colour, he naturally concludes that the inferiority which to him appears on the surface must extend deeper than the skin, and affect the soul. Therefore, very often in spite of himself, he stands off from his African convert, even when, under his training, he has made considerable advance in civilisation and the arts. And especially is this the case in West Africa, where, living among large masses of his countrymen, the African Christian, who from the pressure of circumstances has been forced into European customs, presents very often to the foreign observer, in contrast with his native brethren, an artificial and absurd appearance. And the missionary, looking from a comfortable social distance, surveys the Europeanised native, sometimes with pity, sometimes with dismay, seldom with thorough sympathy. He

> Back recoils, he knows not why,
> Even at the sound himself has made.

Or, like the stream it Racine, at the sight of the monster it had washed to the shore:—

> Le flot qui l'apportat recule épouvanté.[89]

The African convert, under such practical teaching, looking upon his instructor as superior to himself—or at least *apart* from himself, not only in spiritual and temporal knowledge, but in every other respect—acquires a very low opinion of himself, learns to

---

[88] Bishop Heber, in one of his letters written on his first arrival in India, says: "There is, indeed, something in a Negro which requires long habit to reconcile the eye to him, but for this the features and hair, far more than the colour, are responsible."—*Life of Heber*, by Taylor; 2nd ed., p. 147. And what this distinguished prelate experienced and so candidly avowed, must be experienced in a still greater degree by minds of less calibre and less culture than his. "The more ignorant the whites are," says Dr. Charles Hodge, of Princeton, New Jersey, "the more violent and unreasonable are their prejudices on this subject."—*Hodge's Essays and Reviews*, p. 519.

[89] Racine: *Phèdre*, Acte V, Scène VI.

depreciate and deprecate his own personal characteristics, and loses that " sense of the dignity of human nature" which observant travellers have noticed in the Mohammedan Negro.

The Arab missionary, on the other hand, often of the same complexion as his hearer, does not "require any long habit to reconcile the eye to him." He takes up his abode in Negroland, often for life, and, mingling his blood with that of the inhabitants, succeeds, in the most natural manner, in engrafting Mohammedan religion and learning upon the ignorance and simplicity of the people. Innocent of the scientific attainments of the day, and with no other apparatus than his portable bed and dingy manuscripts, he may be inferior to the theological and classical scholar fresh from College in Europe or America, but he has the advantage of speaking to the people in a sympathetic and perfectly intelligible language.

We will conclude with one more extract from Mr. Bosworth Smith:—

That Mohammedanism may, when mutual misunderstandings are removed, be elevated, chastened, purified by Christian influences and a Christian spirit, and that evils such as the slave trade, which are really foreign to its nature, can be put down by the heroic efforts of Christian philanthropists, I do not doubt; and I can, therefore, look forward, if with something of anxiety, with still more of hope, to what seems the destiny of Africa, that Paganism and Devil-worship will die out, and that the main part of the continent, if it cannot become Christian, will become what is next best to it—Mohammedan.[40]

West Africa has been in contact with Christianity for three hundred years, and not one single tribe, *as a tribe*, has yet become Christian. Nor has any influential chief adopted the religion brought by the European missionary. From Gambia to Gaboon, the native rulers, in constant intercourse with Christians, and in the vicinity of Christian settlements, still conduct their government according to the customs of their fathers, where those customs have not been altered or modified by Mohammedan influence. The Alkali of Port Loko, and the chief of Bullom, under the shadow of Sierra Leone, are *quasi* Mohammedan. The native chiefs of Cape Coast and Lagos are Pagans.[41] So, in the territory ruled by Liberia,

---

[40] P. 40.

[41] See Governor Pope Hennessy's Blue Book Report. Papers relating to Her Majesty's Colonial Possessions. Part II, 1873, 2nd division.

the native chiefs in the four countries—Mesurado, Bassa, Sinou, and Cape Palmas—are Pagans. There is not a single spot along the whole coast, except, perhaps, the little island of Corisco, where Christianity has taken any hold among large numbers of the indigenous tribes.

But we do not believe that these tribes are hopelessly inaccessible to the influence of the religion of the Gospel. We believe that "when mutual misunderstandings are removed;" when the race is better understood; when the effort at indiscriminate Europeanising ceases; when the missionary keeps before his mind—if he knows, or learns if he does not know—that " the idiosyncrasy of a people is a sacred gift, given for some Divine purpose, to be sacredly cherished and patiently unfolded;"[42] there will be nothing to prevent Christianity from spreading among the Pagan tribes, and from eventually uprooting the imperfect Mohammedanism which so extensively prevails. In the meantime, we ought not to grudge the Africans the glimpses of truth which they catch from the Koran; for " a knowledge of a part is better than ignorance of the whole."[43]

A singular anxiety seems to prevail in certain quarters to disparage and depress the character of Mohammedan influence, especially in Africa, by endeavouring to show that wherever it prevails it erects an insurmountable barrier to our further progress —that it produces a far greater than Chinese immobility. We are surprised that a writer, apparently so well informed as the author of the article on Mahomet, in the *British Quarterly Review* for January, 1872, should have put forward the following:—

Islam is a reform which has stifled all other reforms. It is a reform which has chained down every nation which has accepted it at a certain stage of moral and political growth.

In keeping with this is a remarkable statement of Mr. Freeman's is his *History and Conquests of the Saracens*, a work described by a recent subtle and eloquent writer as " more

---

[42] Compare the views of Stopford Brooke in Sermons on *Christ in Modern Life*, p. 58.

[43] Abu-l-Fida.

equitable and conscientious than Gibbon's"! Mr. Freeman says that Mohammedanism has "consecrated despotism; it has consecrated polygamy; it has consecrated slavery;" and Dean Church, to whom we are indebted for the quotation, not only endorses it, but adds, "It has done this directly, in virtue of its being a religion, a religious reform." [44]

A Mohammedan writer, taking the same superficial view of the effects of Christianity, and with the same love for epigrammatic terseness, might say, "Christianity has consecrated drunkenness; it has consecrated Negro slavery; it has consecrated war;" and he might gather ample materials for sustaining his position from the history of Christianity during the last three hundred years, especially in the Western hemisphere. When we see so many evils known to be antagonistic to the Christian religion still, after eighteen hundred years, prevalent in Christian lands, why should Mohammedanism be so fiercely assailed because, during the twelve hundred years of its existence, it has not extirpated from the countries in which it prevails all social evils? Must we not suppose that, as with other creeds so with Islam, its theology is capable of being made subservient to worldly interests? May we not believe that many of the evils in lands under its sway are due, not to its teachings, but to human passions? "As late as the fifteenth century," we are told by Mr. Maclear, "the Church in Europe was engaged in eradicating the remains of Sclavonic Heathenism, and protesting against a rude Fetishism and serpent worship." [45]

It is to be regretted that statements such as those referred to above continue to be made by men whose character, position, and literary ability make them the guides of thousands. They tend to perpetuate in the Christian Church the feeling of distrust in any effort to evangelise the Mohammedan—to keep alive the suspicion that "the successes of the Mohammedan missionary condemn beforehand the labours of the Christian missionary to be in vain"

---

[44] Lectures on the *Influences of Christianity*, &c.; by R. W. Church, M.A., Dean of St. Paul's; p. 8.

[45] *Apostles of Mediæval Europe,* p. 82.

Christianity, Islam and the Negro Race.

—feelings which a closer acquaintance with the facts—we speak especially for Africa—does not justify. We are satisfied, however, that with the light which, increasing every day, is now being thrown upon the religion of Mohammed, writings based more upon the opinions and theories of the Middle Ages—as Mr. Bosworth Smith has so well shown—than upon the demonstrated facts of to-day, are almost sure, in proportion to the growth of a more accurate knowledge and a more thoroughly discriminating and literary appreciation of Islam, to be riddled out into oblivion as inappropriate platitudes and barren superfluities.[46]

We entertain the deliberate conviction—gathered not from reading at home, but from travels among the people—that, whatever it may be in other lands, in Africa the work of Islam is preliminary and preparatory. Just as Ishmael came before Isaac in the history of the great Semitic families, so here the descendant of Ishmael has come before the illustrious descendant of Isaac. The African Mohammedans, as far as we have observed, are tolerant and accessible, anxious for light and improvement from any quarter. They are willing to have Christian Schools in their towns, to have the Christian Scriptures circulated among them, and to share with Christians the work of reclaiming the Pagans.[47]

In view, then, of the work which Islam has already accomplished for Africa and the Negro race, and the work which it may yet accomplish, we may express the belief of Möhler, quoted by the *Guardian*,[48] that "one day the true labourers may find (in

---

[46] See an able discussion of this subject in Syed Ameer Ali's *Life and Teachings of Mohammed*, chap. 15.

[47] Bishop Crowther, in his Report for 1874, says: "I have not met with a stern opposer of Christianity, as far as I had conversation with Mohammedans, up the Niger. . . . . The reception of an Arabic Bible, which was presented to the Emir of Nupe, from the Church Missionary Society, with a childlike glee, in the presence of his courtiers, was a proof that this people desire to hear and search after the truth. Another copy was sent through him to Alihu, the King of Ilorin, who is also an Arabic scholar. . . . . In all our religious conversation with these Mohammedans we never met with an obstinate disputer, or a bigoted denial of what we read or said to them."—*Monthly Reporter* of Church Missionary Society, February, 1875.

[48] November 4, 1874.

Mohammedanism and the Negro Race.

Africa) a harvest ready for their reaping, and the Gospel speed thither on its way rejoicing, and Mahomet prove a servant of Christ." Till then, all earnest Christians may consistently join in the prayer of Abraham, adopted in the liturgy of the Moravian Church, " Oh, that Ishmael may live before Thee!"

Christianity and the Negro Race.

MR. GLADSTONE, in the exordium of his celebrated article on the Church of England, in the *Contemporary Review* (July, 1875), says:—

> To uphold the integrity of the Christian dogma, to trace its working, and to exhibit its adaptation to human thought and human welfare, in all the varying experience of the ages, is, in my view, perhaps the noblest of all tasks which it is given to the human mind to pursue. This is the guardianship of the great fountain of human hope, happiness and virtue. But with respect to the clothing which the Gospel may take to itself, my mind has a large margin of indulgence, if not of laxity, both ways. Much is to be allowed—I can hardly say how much—to national, sectional, and personal divergencies.

This is a view to which the very highest minds in the world—the best cultivated and the most enlightened—would at once readily subscribe. By the word "dogma" Mr. Gladstone evidently means, not the petrified formula of any particular sect or race, deduced according to their view from the Word of God, but the whole system of Christianity itself, as a living organism, in *esse* and in *posse*, in its essence as well as in its capabilities and potentialities; for in the same paragraph he uses the word "Gospel" as synonymous with "dogma." Looking at the Gospel system as a whole, it may be called, with no inconsiderable propriety, the "Christian dogma," or that system of belief which distinguishes the Christian world from all others.

We have said that the very highest minds would readily subscribe to the view of Mr. Gladstone, for only the highest minds would cordially agree with the whole paragraph. A very large number—perhaps the whole Christian Church—would give their

Christianity and the Negro Race.

sanction to the first two sentences; but the number is comparatively small who would read the last two sentences without feeling disposed to brand the author as a latitudinarian and unsafe guide. And yet those sentences contain the lessons which all practical experience teaches must be learned by the aggressive portion of the Church before the Gospel can take root in " all the world," and become the spiritual life of " every creature."

There is, we doubt not, one and only one Prophet for all times and for all nations—the immaculate Son of God; and the teachings which He inculcated contain the only principles that will regenerate humanity of all races, climes, and countries. But the Gospel, though it has been promulgated for eighteen hundred years, has, as yet, taken extensive root only among one race—the Indo-European. It is established in Europe, Asia, Africa, America, and on all the islands of the sea, but, for the most part, in regions and localities occupied by different branches of the same Aryan family.

When Dean Church wishing to illustrate the ' Influences of Christianity on National Character,' had passed in review the Greek, Latin, and Teutonic races, he evidently felt that his subject was exhausted. Dean Merivale went as far afield as the facts would allow him to go, when after concluding his lectures on the ' Conversion of the Roman Empire,' he proceeded to discuss the ' Conversion of the Northern Nations.' Indeed, so convinced was the learned author that his two courses of lectures embraced all he could say on the subject of the spread of Christianity in the conversion of nations, that, in his preface to the second course, he remarks, that if, at some future time, he should print them together, he will probably give them the general title of the " Conversion of the Ancient Heathens." But would such a title be strictly accurate in view of the " Ancient " Semitic, Mongolian, and Negro " Heathens " who have been left out of the lecturer's calculations? The omission of the little word " the " from the proposed new title would probably meet the wish to have a comprehensive title, without transcending the bounds of strict accuracy.

It could not have escaped the distinguished lecturer, that only comparatively small portions of the Semitic, Mongolian, and Negro families of man have as yet embraced the religion of Jesus. And we are disposed to think that one chief reason why the progress of the Gospel among races foreign to the European has been so limited, lies in the fact that the last two sentences of Mr. Gladstone's paragraph quoted above are not yet understood and heeded by those who may be called the missionary nations of the earth, and who, having the vigorous and dominant instincts of the Aryan race, have become providentially the instruments through which the Semitic conceptions of Deity and the Semitic inspirations of Christianity are to be spread through all nations.

The object of this paper is to trace the influence of Christianity upon the Negro Race, and to enquire how far the method of its dissemination has affected their reception of it. And our illustrations will be drawn principally from the Western world, as containing the largest portion of the Negro race who have been brought under the influence of Christianity, and especially from the United States, where the largest number of Negroes live together under the same Christian Government.

Everybody knows how it happened that the Africans were carried in such large numbers from Africa to America; how one continent was made to furnish the labourers to build up another; how the humanity of a Romish priest, while anxious to dry up tears in America, was indifferent to unsealing their fountains in Africa. It was out of deep pity for the delicate Caribs, whom he saw groaning under the arduous physical toil of the Western hemisphere that Las Casas strove to replace them by robust and indefatigable Africans. Hence the innumerable woes which have attended the African race for the last three hundred years in Christian lands. In justice, however, to the memory of Bartolomé de las Casas, it should be stated that, before he died, he changed his mind on the subject, and declared that the captivity of the Negroes was as unjust as that of the Indians,[1] and even expressed a fear that, though he had fallen into the error of favouring the importation of black slaves into America from ignorance and

---

[1] Sot tan injusto el cautiverio de los Negros como él de los Indios.—Ticknor's *History of Spanish Literature;* vol. ii, chap. vi.

goodwill, he might, after all, fail to stand excused for it before the Divine Justice.

But the tardy, though commendable, repentance of Las Casas did not arrest the flow of that blood-red stream which, from the fountain opened by his mistaken philanthropy, poured incessantly, for three hundred years, from East to West. It was not long before the transference of Negroes from Africa to the Western hemisphere assumed the importance of a national policy. Even England, under a contract with Spain, enjoyed the monopoly of the traffic in slaves for thirty years.[2]

The first slaves were landed in North America in 1620, and men whose characters were otherwise irreproachable, were induced by the habits of thought then prevailing, and by the supposed necessity and convenience of slave labour, to purchase the African captives brought to their shores. Some even of the most eminent divines were so far implicated in the error, that, with perfect ease of conscience, they held Negroes in bondage. The distinguished William Penn, the Rev. George Whitefield, of world-wide celebrity, and President Edwards, author of several standard works in theology, were *slave-holders*. Good and conscientious men were led away by the plausible arguments of those who, while they were busy turning to pecuniary account the benighted Africans, alleged, that they were thus being brought under the influence of the Gospel. But, according to Mr. Bancroft, there were among the colonists some far-seeing men who foresaw the mischiefs that would ultimately result from the introduction of slavery into the colonies. Virginia and South Carolina did place some restrictions upon the importation of Negroes. But the British Goverment, listening to her African slave merchants rather than to her American colonists, not only neutralised those restrictions, but obliged the noble-hearted Oglethorpe to relax his determination that in Georgia, the colony which he founded, there should be neither slavery nor slave trade.[3]

---

[2] The Assiento contract stipulated that, from the first day of May, 1713, to the first day of May, 1743, the English should have the Exclusive privilege of transporting Negroes into the Spanish West Indies at the rate of four thousand eight hundred a year.

[3] Bancroft's *History of the United States*, chap. xxiv.

Christianity, Islam and the Negro Race.

Thus, for nearly two hundred years, Negroes were poured into North America without restriction. During six generations, large interests grew up out of the system, giving it in the eyes of those upon whom it had been entailed, a sanction and a sanctity which it was regarded as sacrilegious to question.

Of course, the slaves who were introduced during the first hundred years, we may presume, died Heathens, or with only imperfect glimpses of Christian teaching. For the Christianisation of their descendants, a system was invented which so shocked the feelings of John Wesley that, in view of its resulting enormities, he denounced American slavery as the "sum of all villanies."

That which the early colonists of Virginia, South Carolina, and Georgia had opposed, having now grown into gigantic proportions, was not only apologised for by their descendants, but eulogised as eminently necessary and useful to the proper development of society; and all the religious, political, and scientific teachings of the time were not only tinged, but deeply steeped, in pro-slavery sentiments. Generations descending from Huguenot and Puritan ancestry were trained to believe that God had endowed them with the right to enslave the African for ever. And upon those Africans who became members of the Christian Church, the idea was impressed that it was their duty to submit, in everything, to their masters. Christian divines of all shades of opinion, in the South, taught this doctrine, and embodied it in books prepared specially for the instruction of the slaves—their "oral instruction," for they were not allowed to learn to read.

For example, the Right Rev. William Meade, Bishop of the diocese of Virginia, published a book of sermons, tracts, and dialogues, for masters and slaves, and recommended them to all masters and mistresses to be used in their families. In the preface of the book, the Bishop remarks:—

The editor of this column offers it to all masters and mistresses in our Southern States, with the anxious wish and devout prayer that it may prove a blessing to themselves and their households.

On page 93 he says:—

Some He hath made masters and mistresses for taking care of their children and others that belong to them. . . . Some He hath made servants and slaves,

Christianity and the Negro Race.

to assist and work for their masters and mistresses, that provide for them; and others He hath made ministers and teachers to instruct the rest, to show them what they ought to do, and to put them in mind of their several duties.

On pages 94 and 95 he says, addressing the slaves:—

Almighty God hath been pleased to make you slaves here, and to give you nothing but labour and poverty in this world, which you are obliged to submit to, as it is His will that it should be so. Your bodies, you know, are not your own; they are at the disposal of those you belong to, &c.

Again, on page 132:—

When *correction* is given you, you either deserve it or you do not deserve it. But whether you really deserve it or not, it is your duty, and Almighty God requires that you bear it patiently. You may, perhaps, think that this is hard doctrine, but if you consider right you must needs think otherwise of it. Suppose, then, that you deserve correction, you cannot but say that it is just and right you should meet with it. Suppose you do not, or at least you do not deserve so much, or so severe a correction for the fault you have committed, you perhaps have escaped a great many more, and are at last paid for it all. Or, suppose you are quite innocent of what is laid to your charge, and suffer wrongfully in that particular thing, is it not possible you may have done some other bad thing which was never discovered, and that Almighty God, who saw you doing it, would not let you escape without punishment one time or another?

A clergyman of another denomination wrote a catechism for the use of slaves, in which we find the following:—

Q. Is it right for the servant to run away, or is it right to harbour a runaway?—A. No.

Q. What did the Apostle Paul to Onesimus, who was a runaway? Did he harbour him, or send him back to his master?—A. He sent him back to his master with a letter.[4]

A right reverend prelate tells the slave, in another work written for his "oral instruction," that "to disobey his master is to yield to the temptation of the devil."[5]

It will be noticed that both these works, though written for slaves, carefully conceal on the title-page the unfortunate class for whom they were intended under the softening euphemism, in the one case, of "coloured persons," and in the other of "those who cannot read." That Christian divines should publish books drawn

---

[4] *Catechism of Scripture, Doctrine, and for the Oral Instruction of Coloured Persons;* by C. C. Jones.—Charleston, 1845; p. 120.

[5] *A Catechism to be taught Orally to those who cannot Read;* by Bishop Ives.—New York, 1848; p. 30.

from the Scripture for "slaves," no doubt seemed to clerical educators an incongruity which, even in those days of ardent pro-slavery views, they hesitated to perpetrate.

But the politicians were not so scrupulous. In order to uphold the system, they did not hesitate to brand with folly the founders of the Republic, and to pour contempt upon the judgment of the wisest of their statesmen.

Chancellor Harper, in his *Memoir on Slavery*, takes up the sentence of Jefferson, that "All men are born free and equal, and endowed with certain inalienable rights," &c.; and proceeds in a most elaborate, but false and sophistical discussion, to demonstrate that Jefferson was wrong.

The most audacious utterances we have read on this subject are those by General Hammond in his notorious *Letters to Clarkson*. That gallant and chivalrous gentleman says, under date of January 28th, 1845, writing from Silver Bluff, South Carolina :—

> I firmly believe that American slavery is not only not a sin, but especially commanded by God himself through Moses, and approved by Christ through His Apostles. .... I endorse without reserve the much-abused sentiment of Governor McDuffie, that "slavery is the corner-stone of our Republican edifice;" while I repudiate as ridiculously absurd that much-lauded but nowhere accredited dogma of Mr. Jefferson, that "all men are born equal." . . . Slavery is truly the "corner-stone" and foundation of every well-designed and durable Republican edifice.

Again :—

> If the slave is not allowed to read the Bible, the sin rests upon the abolitionists; for they stand prepared to furnish him with a key to it, which would make it, not a book of hope, and love, and peace, but of despair, hatred, and blood; which would convert the reader, not into a Christian, but a demon.

We wonder what key would be required when such wide doors into the temple of liberty as the following stand so constantly open —Jeremiah xxxiv, 17 ; Matt. vii, 12 ; Luke iv, 18 and 19 ?

Nor was such teaching confined to divines and politicians. Philologists and scientific men, brought contributions from their peculiar fields to strengthen and adorn the infamous fabric whose corner-stone was slavery. John Fletcher, of Louisiana, in *Studies on Slavery in Easy Lessons*, published at Natchez in 1852, brings the resources of the Hebrew language to the support of his idol. He

Christianity and the Negro Race.

gives the public a paradigm of the Hebrew verb עָבַד abad, to slave, in kal, niphal, piel, pual, hiphil, hophal, hithpael; and a declension of the "*factitious, euphonic segholate*" noun עֶבֶד ebed, a slave. Messrs. Nott and Gliddon contributed to the same honourable worship the results of their scientific researches.

But these reasoners have, one and all, been easily beaten on their own fields. Not one of these writers for slavery, whether political, theological, or scientific, ever produced anything with the mark on it of original observation or genius. None of their effusions ever passed the limits of the time or place at which they were produced. Entirely local and temporary, they have added nothing to the sum of human knowledge.

At last, when Charles Sumner was hurling those thunderbolts against the system which made it tremble from its base to its apex —when he was exposing the degenerate departure of the South from every noble American tradition, and when Calhoun, the great "nullifier," was no more, and the voice of Hayne, the brilliant and accomplished orator and politician, was silent—there came on the floor of the Senate a warrior from the South, not to hurl back in impassioned oratory, as Calhoun would have done, the charges of Sumner; not to neutralise their immediate effect by a gorgeous rhetoric, as Hayne would have done; but to appeal to brute force, and by one blow to exile the great Senator from his seat for four years.[o] *Non opus est verbis, sed fustibus.*

Such were the circumstances under which the Negro throughout the United States received Christianity. The Gospel of Christ was travestied and diluted before it came to him to suit the "peculiar institution" by which millions of human beings were converted into "chattels." The highest men in the South, magistrates, legislators, professors of religion, preachers of the Gospel, governors of states, gentlemen of property and standing, all united in upholding a system which every Negro felt was wrong. Yet these were the men from whom he got his religion, and whom he was obliged to regard as guides. Under such teaching and discipline, is it to be wondered at that his morality is awry—that

---

[o] Preston S. Brooks.

his sense of the "dignity of human nature" is superficial—that his standard of family and social life is low and defective?

Not so much by what Christianity said as by the way in which, through their teachers, it said it, were the Negroes influenced. The teachings they received conveyed for them no clear idea or definite impression of the religion of Christ. As regards their religion, they were left less to their intellectual apprehension of the truth than to their emotional impulses. The emotions were their guide on Sunday and on Monday, in the conventicle and in the cornfield. No change was wrought upon their moral nature, for there was nothing to act upon it. Nothing was imparted from without, and nothing was checked and stifled within. The influence of the Church was exerted continually to repress—to produce absolute outward submission. Such influence, even if it had been wholesome, could not penetrate deep or mould with much force the inner working of the soul. It produced an outward conformity to the views and will of their masters, while it left the heart untouched. Or, perhaps, it might be more accurate to say that their whole nature was taken possession of, and all its capacities for thought and feeling, for love and hope, for joy and grief, were completely under the control of their taskmasters.

Nevertheless, by that mysterious influence which is imparted to man independently of outward circumstances, to not a few of them the preaching of the Gospel, defective as was its practical exemplification, opened a new world of truth and goodness. There streamed into the darkness of their surroundings a light from the Cross of Christ, and they saw that, through suffering and affliction, there is a path to perfect rest above this world; and, in the hours of the most degrading and exhausting toil, they sang of the eternal and the unseen; so that while the scrupulous among their masters often with Jefferson "trembled for their country," the slaves who had gained a new language and new faculties were enjoying themselves in rapturous music—often labouring and suffering all day, and singing, all night, sacred songs, which, in rude but impressive language, set forth their sad fortunes and their hopes for the future. No traveller in the South, who passed by the plantations thronged

Christianity and the Negro Race.

with dusky labourers, and listened to their cheerful music, could ever dream that they beheld in that suffering but joyous race the destroyers of the Southern whites. The captive Jews could not sing by the waters of Babylon, but the Negroes in the dark dungeon of American slavery made themselves harps and swept them to some of the most thrilling melodies. From a people who were so full of music no mischief could have been apprehended, excepting by the delinquent of the drama, who "fears each bush an officer." It is the man "who hath no music in his soul" who is fit for stratagems and treasons and all dark deeds. We do not wonder that the *Westminster Review*, some years ago, made the following remark: " Were we forced at this moment to search for the saints of America, we should not be surprised to find them amongst the despised bondsmen."[7]

Saints, no doubt, there were among the bondsmen, but they became so not in consequence, but in default, and often, we may say, in defiance of, instruction. And it cannot be expected that a people brought out of savagery into contact with a new, if a higher life, would, under such circumstances, produce, as a rule, such characters as "Uncle Tom." There have been "Uncle Toms" in the South, but they were the exceptions. As a rule, the Christianity of the Negroes is just such a grotesque and misshapen thing as the system under which they were trained is calculated to produce.

The Africans who were carried to the Western world were, as a general rule, of the lowest of the people in their own country. They did not fairly represent the qualities and endowments of the race. Even the traditions of their country they carried away in the most distorted form. And in the midst of their sorrows in a strange country, they constructed out of their dim recollections of what they had seen at home, a system of religion and government for themselves, which they curiously combined with what they received from their new masters; and so the elements of civilisation and barbarism—of Christianity and Heathenism—not only subsisted side by side, but, so far as the Negro was concerned, were inlaid,

---

[7] January, 1853.

so to say, into each other, in a sort of inharmonious mosaic all over the Western hemisphere.

This accounts for the singular fact that a system of Heathenish worship—now rare among the tribes of West Africa—is found among the Negroes, especially in the West Indies, where, the climate being more congenial and the flora similar to the African, they could produce with greater facility the rites and practices of their native land. Canon Kingsley, in the record of his travels in the West Indies,[e] gives an account of the horrible Obeah system prevalent in some of those islands, which, allowing for the necessary exaggerations into which a writer must fall who gathers his information during a flying trip, conveys a pretty fair idea of a state of things which still lingers among the more ignorant of the Negro population of those islands, and which the Christianity they have thus far received, seems powerless to eradicate.

Since the emancipation in the United States, the defective Christian character of the Negroes of the Southern States is constantly made the theme of essay, lecture, and newspaper article. In the report of Dr. W. H. Ruffner, Superintendent of the Public Schools of Virginia, for 1874, we find the following:—

> Much of the glamour with which the Negro has been covered by philanthropic zeal, acting at a distance, has passed away as knowledge has increased; but the real character of this people can be learned only from those who have long lived among them. The Southern Negroes are polite, amiable, quiet, orderly, and religious; and hence it is hard to believe that as a class they are without moral character. And yet such is the unhappy fact. . . . Occasionally a high type is manifested by individuals; and while there is a great deal of religious sincerity and earnestness among them, and whilst the style of piety is modified by the character of the religious instruction they have received, and whilst families and congregations which have enjoyed special privileges exhibit better results, yet with the masses of those who claim to be Christians, their piety is of an unintelligent, sometimes superstitious, and always spasmodic type, and it covers a multitude of sins.

The *American Missionary* newspaper publishes the following from a Northern teacher who is at work among the Negroes in Louisiana:—

Good teachers and preachers are very much needed in this State. I heard a

---

[e] *A Christmas in the West Indies.*

Christianity and the Negro Race.

preacher telling his hearers that they must go to *hell*, and leave their sins on the *mud-sills of hell* before they can say that they are born again. To prove this, he said that he would quote the fifty-third chapter of Isaiah. Now, what do you think he quoted? Why, Bunyan's *Pilgrim's Progress*, in relation to Christian's leaving the City of Destruction, and the falling-off of his burden at the foot of the cross. The mischief of the thing was that the people appeared to believe that what he was saying was really in the Bible. What it is to be a pure Christian very few of these people understand. They profess to be religious, yet the Ten Commandments are a dead letter to them.

In the *Spirit of Missions* for June, 1875, the organ of the Episcopal Church in the United States, we find the following:—

It is quite time that Christian people at the North should be brought face to face with the fact that the salvation of the nation depends not only upon giving the Negro a secular education, but also upon radically reforming his notions of what religion is . . . The absence from his religion of the ethical element is a radical defect, and one that will bring the Negro and the nation to ruin together, if it be not speedily supplied.

We are less surprised at the existence of such a state of things among a people of savage ancestry who have lived two hundred years as "chattels" in a Christian land, than we are at the apparent surprise of the writers quoted above, when everybody knows the sort of school into which the Negroes were introduced when, wild and untamed, they were brought from Africa. It will not be possible in a generation to correct the results of the radically defective teachings of such popular and influential periodicals as *De Bow's Review*, the *Richmond Examiner, et id genus omne*. They established a system of political and social morality in which the "ethical element," if not "absent," was wholly distorted and caricatured—and to this system the Negro, having no other guide, endeavoured at a humble distance to conform. It will be a long time before the intelligent Negro will be able to forget the injustice done to the moral instincts of his race, while he has access to the thrilling "narratives" of such heroic and eloquent fugitives from slavery as Frederick Douglass, William Wells Brown, Henry Bibb, Roper &c.; and he will be able to understand, if his *quondam* oppressors will not, why it is that, with his less favoured brother, plunder and prayer are not supposed to be incompatible; why, like the Italian brigand, he can be pious without leaving a disreputable profession.

Christianity, Islam and the Negro Race.

But, even now, while white Christians in the North are shocked at the moral character of Southern Christian Negroes, they do not cease, by their practical teaching, to impress upon the minds of the blacks that there is one standard of morality for white and another for black men. The shadow of the slave system still throws such a gloom over the land, that, where the Negro is concerned, right and wrong are only indistinctly seen.

Many prominent Christians in the South still hold to the opinion that it is right to enslave the African,[o] and these exert a degree of influence upon the North which, if it does not lead them to desire a renewal of the slave system, perpetuates among them the old feeling of contempt for the Negro. All the Christianity in the country seems helpless to remedy a state of things in which the following occurrence is possible.

Professor C. H. Thompson, D.D., of Straight University, a graduate of a theological seminary, for several years a beloved pastor in Newark, New Jersey, chosen moderator of the Presbytery, of which he was the only coloured member, and whenever his turn comes appointed to examine candidates for licence in Greek and Hebrew, finds himself excluded from hotel accommodations in travelling to and from a National Congregational Church, which he has been appointed to address, *because he is a Negro*.

We have before us the *American Citizen*, a Negro newspaper, published at Lexington, Kentucky, dated February 27, 1875, containing a most touching Appeal, addressed "to the American People," by the Bishops of the African Methodist Church, craving protection against the impositions and oppressions which they

---

[o] In the *Narrative of the State of Religion* issued by the Southern General Assembly of the Presbyterian Church in the year 1864, is a sentence which declared that it was the mission of the Southern Church to "conserve the system of African slavery." Against this, however, the Northern Presbyterian Church earnestly protested, and still protests. Dr. Charles Hodge, the veteran professor at Princeton, celebrated for his sententious and epigrammatic utterances, embodied the indignant feeling of the North in one memorable sentence: "That since the death of Christ no such dogma stains the record of an ecclesiastical body." Chief Justice Taney's celebrated decision in the Dred Scott case in 1856, that "the Negro has no rights which white men are bound to respect," is the political counterpart of the dogma of the Southern Assembly.

Christianity and the Negro Race.

and their people suffer. They open their pathetic Address as follows:—

> As Bishops of the oldest and most numerous organisation of coloured persons in the country, we beg permission to lay the distress of our people before you. Never were Christian pastors doomed to witness the despoiling of their flocks as we have been. Before freedom, we were the hapless victims of wrong, well characterised by the great Wesley as the "sum of villanies." Since freedom, while we expected our liberty to cost us much, yet did we console ourselves with the belief that the strong arm that had shivered the chains which did fetter us would secure protection throughout the trying ordeal. But, alas, we have been doomed to miserable disappointment.

Now, as long as the sad and practical lessons suggested by the above are still impressed upon the Negro, as long as the Christianity he sees stands in such striking contrast to the Christianity of Christ, how can the "ethical element" be prominent in his religion? How can he be trained to any sense of the "dignity of human nature," to any feeling of human brotherhood? How can he acquire unshaken faith in those great truths about God and man which his teachers would impress upon him? How can he ever rise to the recognition of a high moral ideal? How can he ever conceive a pure and lofty standard of family and social life? How can his general character be strengthened, elevated, expanded, or refined?

The advantages enjoyed by the Negro in the Western world, now that he is free, are hardly greater for the attainment of true manhood than when he was in bondage. And a far more serious difficulty lies in the way of his genuine progress than the mere physical inconveniences which his colour entails, and that is, the impossibility, in the countries of his exile, of securing a proper individual or race development. The Negro in Christian lands, however learned in books, cannot be said to have such a thing as self-education. His knowledge, when brought to the test, often fails him. And why? Because he is taught from the beginning to the end of his book-training—from the illustrated primer to the illustrated scientific treatise—not to be himself, but somebody else. We might illustrate what we mean by some of the most ludicrous and painful incidents—but this is not the place to record them—of the efforts of Christian Negroes of intelligence to force their outward appearance into, as near as possible, a resemblance to Europeans. From the lessons he every day receives, the Negro unconsciously imbibes the conviction that to be a great man he must be like the white man. He is not brought up —however he may desire it—to be the companion, the equal, the comrade of the white man, but his imitator, his ape, his parasite. To be himself in a country where everything ridicules him, is to be nothing—less, worse than nothing. To be as like the white man as possible—to copy his outward appearance, his peculiarities, his manners, the arrangement of his toilet, that is the aim of the Christian Negro—this is his aspiration. The only virtues which under such circumstances he develops are, of course, the parasitical ones. Every intelligent Negro, in the lands of his exile, must feel that he walks upon the face of God's earth a physical and moral incongruity, and as legitimate a subject of laughter as Horace's famous heterogeneous picture, the creation of "a sick man's dream":—

> Humano capiti cervicem pictor equinam
> Jungere si velit, et varias inducere plumas
> Undique collatis membris, ut turpiter atrum
> Desinat in piscem mulier formosa superne.

Imitation is not discipleship. The Mohammedan Negro is a much better Mohammedan than the Christian Negro is a Christian, because the Muslim Negro, as a learner, is a disciple, not an imitator. A disciple, when freed from leading-strings, may become a producer; an imitator never rises above a mere copyist. With the disciple progress is from within; the imitator grows by accretion from without. The learning acquired by a disciple gives him capacity; that gained by an imitator terminates in itself. The one becomes a capable man; the other is a mere sciolist. This explains the difference between the Mohammedan and the Christian Negro.

Since the proclamation of freedom in the United States, however, the effect of the schools which have been thrown open to the Negro is becoming more and more palpable. We observe in the discussions in American newspapers published by Negroes, an incipient movement towards mental emancipation. But the effect of their educational training must, for some time yet, be chiefly negative or preparatory—in removing the pressure of external evils.

Christianity and the Negro Race.

in dissipating the superstitions and prejudices of both races, and so opening a wider sphere for the free play and development of the moral and spiritual nature of the Negro. But as his mind is strengthened and expanded by the wide and inviting prospects which continually open before him, he will feel the need of increasing measures of freedom, social and ecclesiastical as well as political. By the nature of things, he can never enjoy this complete emancipation in the United States. When this period arrives, when the Negro begins to feel the need of wider scope for the full expansion of the inherent energies of his mind, he will seek refuge in his Fatherland, for entrance into which Liberia is the most promising door.

We have followed with deep interest a discussion, which has been going on recently in the leading coloured journals in the United States, on the relative claims of the Roman Catholic and Protestant Churches to the respect and allegiance of the Negro. The Rev. John M. Brown, a Negro of high culture, and a bishop of the African Methodist Episcopal Church, wrote an article, which appeared in the *Independent* newspaper, warning the coloured people against the aggressions upon their ranks of the Roman Catholics. To this article George T. Downing of Washington, said to be "a coloured gentleman of education, property, and influence among his people, and a special friend of the late Senator Sumner," wrote an able and vigorous reply, in which, in the course of a long argument, he says:—

For one, I, as a coloured man, would ask the *Independent* what there is in the Catholic Church to repel me from its communion? I would like to ask also, what there is in monarchy more hideous, more to be dreaded, than this cruel spirit of caste, which thus finds sympathy and protection under a Protestant Republic? . . . The Protestant Church proclaims the doctrine of the brotherhood of man, and then tramples upon that which it professes to revere . . . If I were a Russian subject to-day, I should enjoy more liberty under the Empire of the Czar than I do as a coloured man in Republican America. I should possess more real equality, more justice, more protection for all that constitutes "life," than I now possess as an American citizen. . . . I remember when my own State slammed the door of its schools in the face of my little ones (schools that my taxes helped to support), that the Catholic Church opened wide its school doors to those little ones. I remember gratefully that my children, thus excluded from Protestant schools, partook freely, on terms of equality, of the blessings of education and kindly sympathy thus extended . . . The Catholic Church has to-day in its schools over 800,000 coloured children. It is educating coloured youth at Rome for its missionary work in America and Africa. In the West Indies, Central America, and South America, nearly 9,000,000 of Africans acknowledge its faith.[10]

Whatever may be the ecclesiastical connection of the thoughtful and cultivated Protestant Negro—though he may *ex animo* subscribe to the tenets of the particular denomination to which he belongs, as approaching nearest to the teachings of God's Word—yet he cannot read History without feeling that the Negro race owes a deep debt of gratitude to the Roman Catholic Church. The only Christian Negroes who have had the power successfully to throw off oppression, and maintain their position as freemen, were Roman Catholic Negroes—the Haïtians; and the greatest Negro the Christian world has yet produced was a Roman Catholic—Toussaint Louverture.

In the ecclesiastical system of modern, as was the case in the military system of ancient Rome, there seems to be a place for all races and colours—

Colchus an Assyrius, Thebis nutritus an Argis.

At Rome, the names of Negroes, males and females, who have been distinguished for piety and good works are found in the calendar under the designation of "saints." Protestantism has no Negro saints. Mr. Ticknor tells us of a Negro at Granada, in the sixteenth century, who, brought as an infant from Africa, rose by his learning to be Professor of Latin and Greek in the school attached to the Cathedral of Granada. He is the same person noticed by Cervantes as "el Negro Juan Latino," in a poem prefixed to *Don Quixote*. He wrote a Latin poem in two books. He was married to a lady of Granada, who fell in love with him, as Eloisa did with Abelard, while he was teaching her; and after his

---

[10] Several adverse criticisms have appeared from influential quarters upon Mr. Downing's position, but we find him, in his latest utterances, reaffirming his views as follows:—"I am fully persuaded that a general alliance, on the part of the coloured people of America, with the Catholic Church of America, would be the most speedy and effective agency to break down American caste, based on colour."

Christianity and the Negro Race.

death his wife and children erected a monument to his memory in the church of Sta. Ana, in that city, inscribing it with an epitaph, in which he is styled "Filius Ethiopium, prolesque nigerrima patrum."[11] No such record occurs in the annals of Protestantism. In what Protestant university would a Negro professor be tolerated? The most distinguished Negro produced by a Protestant country, of whom we have read, was Benjamin Banneker; and the only literary recognition he ever received was in an appreciative letter from Thomas Jefferson, the reputed infidel.

It is said that in all the histories of Brazil the name of Henry Diaz, the distinguished Negro general, is extolled. The Portuguese historian, Borros, says that Negroes are, in his opinion, preferable to Swiss soldiers, whose reputation for bravery has generally stood high. In 1708 the blacks took arms for the defence of Guadaloupe, and were more useful than all the rest of the French troops. At the same time they bravely defended Martinique against the English. When and where has there ever been a Negro general in a Protestant army? If it is asked why Protestant Negro soldiers are not equally efficient—why the West India troops did not distinguish themselves in the recent Ashantee war—we have no other reply than the query of the poet:

> Quis enim virtutem amplectitur ipsam
> Præmia si tollas?

The Negro, under Protestant rule, is kept in a state of such tutelage and irresponsibility as can scarcely fail to make him constantly dependent and useless whenever, thrown upon himself, he has to meet an emergency.

The Deputy for the colony of Martinique in the French National Assembly in 1872 was M. Pory-Papy, a Negro. The idea of representing the British colonies in the House of Commons is often discussed. If it should ever be realised, would the people of Jamaica and Barbadoes be as liberal and enlightened as those of Martinique? For the present, we fear not.

We saw published some years ago the "Bill of Sale of an American Clergyman." This clergyman was a Negro, who on

---

[11] Ticknor's *History of Spanish Literature*, vol. ii, p. 582.

Christianity, Islam and the Negro Race.

account of his learning had received from a German university the degree of D.D. He was a minister of one of the leading Protestant denominations in the United States; but he was a "chattel"—a fugitive from slavery. South of Mason and Dixon's line he would have had neither name nor character. His German diploma would have been no more than so much waste paper. His liberty had to be paid for in gold before he could become a man. We question whether such a thing has ever occurred, or could ever occur, under the administration of the Roman Catholic Church.[12]

The American nation, by the force of its peculiar circumstances and the genius of its political institutions, and, perhaps, also from its composite character, is far more advanced in its dealing with the Negro than is the mother country. In Church and State, laws are being passed giving him larger measures of freedom.

The American Episcopal Church has recently consecrated a pure Negro as Bishop of Haïti. A curious but significant circumstance occurred in the Episcopal Convention held in New York in October, 1874, at which it was decided to consecrate this Negro Bishop. The only Episcopal voice raised during the discussion of the subject, in a tone at all dissentient, was that of Dr. Courtenay, the English Bishop of Jamaica, who, in the course of his remarks, among other things said:—

> We have not, as yet, in Jamaica, one priest of purely African race. . . . At the present moment no Negro in Holy Orders could command that respect in Jamaica which a white priest could command. Whether this condition of affairs in Jamaica is to control the position in Hayti is another question.[13]

Now, the question that must arise is: Why is it that, after two hundred years' residence in Christian Jamaica, and after forty years of freedom, the Negro population, so largely outnumbering the whites, have not been able to produce one priest? Why is it that, "at the present moment, no Negro in Holy Orders could command that respect in Jamaica which a white priest could command?" Is this a creditable state of things, after so many

---

[12] The documents connected with the sale and manumission of Rev. J. W. C. Pennington, D.D., are published in an appendix to Theodore Parker's *Additional Speeches*, vol. xi.

[13] *The Church Journal*, New York, Oct. 29, 1874.

Christianity and the Negro Race.

years of Christianising effort? Is not this state of things owing to that peculiar defect in the machinery and administration of the Anglican Church noticed by Lord Macaulay in his review of Ranke's *History of the Popes*, and which he says gives her less elasticity and less assimilating power than her Roman ancestor?

An able writer on Jamaica, in the *Quarterly Review* for July, 1875, reveals the cause of the backwardness of the Negro in that island—it lies in the strong Anglo-Saxon prejudice against his elevation. Though the Reviewer writes with a degree of candour, sobriety, and generosity which it is refreshing to see in these days of sensationalism, yet he could not repress his instinctive Saxon aversion to the full manhood and equality, intellectual and social, of the Negro. He says (p. 72) with remarkable *naïveté*, as if he were writing in the middle of the eighteenth century, or in defence of the Assiento Contract: "The cane-field, the plantation, the provision ground, and the pasture-land, not [even] the work-shop or the engine-room, are the African's heritage."

On page 44 the writer had remarked with justice that "the Negroes have given unmistakable evidence of a notable and constantly increasing amelioration in every respect, moral and intellectual, no less than physical."

Now, we ask, if the Negro is "constantly" improving in those respects, why relegate him to the "cane-field?" Why wish to confine him to menial occupations if he has the ability to perform higher work? Is his colour to be the excuse for always keeping him in a state of degradation? If such be the case—if such is the teaching which is sought to be impressed by able reviewers and by Colonial Bishops upon the British public at home and in Jamaica—then two hundred years more will roll round and the Bishop Courtenay of that day will have again to announce that "there is not, as yet, one priest of purely African race in Jamaica."

But does it not occur to the learned reviewer that the destiny of man, though he be a Negro, may include higher spheres of labour than the "cane-field," and higher purposes than to produce sugars, raise potatoes and rear stock? And may it not be worth while to consider, if only briefly, whether the Negro may not lend something to the intellectual as well as moral resources of an island where, for generations, he has been confined to the labour of the beasts that perish?

This leads us to call attention to another remarkable fact which has struck us in our researches—viz., that the defenders of the Negro during the days of his bondage, and the advocates of his full manhood and equality now that he is free, are, as a rule, found among those who are not regarded as orthodox in the Christian Church. Not the Evangelical churches in the United States, but the Unitarian, have furnished the ablest and most prominent defenders of the slave. The Channings, Theodore Parkers, Garrisons, Wendell Phillipses, Emersons, Longfellows, have preached the most celebrated sermons, written the most brilliant essays, delivered the most stirring lectures, and composed the most touching poems on behalf of the oppressed Negro. American Evangelicalism cannot show such an array of first-class literature in his favour.

In England, not the *Edinburgh*—at least, since the days of Jeffrey, Brougham and Macaulay; not the *Quarterly*, but the *Westminster Review*, has been the constant and uncompromising defender of the Negro. It has never joined in the general merriment of Christian civilisation at his expense. When certain portions of the literary world were in a buzz of gleeful amusement at the attacks made by Mr. Carlyle on the Negro, in 1849,[14] the *Westminster Review* did not participate in the roar of laughter, but, on the contrary, administered the following timely and touching rebuke:—

For the first time in the sad history of his race, the good name of the Negro, his character as a man, had become of value to him—for the "chattel" has neither name nor character. Was it generous, then, of the greatest master of sarcasm of his age—of the first portrait painter of any age—to welcome into civilisation this—its long-excluded guest, with nicknames and caricatures? to brand him with the opprobrium of idleness, to give him a bad character as a servant because his master was wanting in the faculty of mastership—was wanting in wisdom and justice—was himself wanting in industry, in the energy

---

[14] 'Occasional Discourse on the Nigger Question,' *Fraser's Magazine*, December, 1849.

needed to work out the difficulties, and supply the demands of his changed position ?[15]

Who would say that this able review is not entitled to bear on its title-page that noble sentiment of Goöthe—"Wahrheitsliebe zeigt sich darin, dass man überall das Gute zu finden und zu schätzen weiss" (Love of truth shows itself in this, that one always knows how to find and cherish that which is good)—which the Anglo-Saxon, from his peculiar temperament, perhaps, does not, as a rule, exemplify in his dealings with foreign races—a defect which unfits him, in a great degree, as an instrument in the work of reconstructing fallen humanity in distant lands?

On the other hand, professors of orthodox Christianity do not hesitate occasionally to indulge in a chuckle at the expense of "Quashee."

Lord Macaulay has noticed this divorce between precept and practice—however it is to be accounted for—in professing Christians, as contrasted with the proceedings of men who paraded their dislike and opposition to the Christian faith. Speaking of the sect of philosophers which arose in Paris in the last century, Lord Macaulay says :—

> While they assailed Christianity with a rancour and unfairness disgraceful to men who called themselves philosophers, they yet had, in far greater measure than their opponents, that charity towards men of all classes and races which Christianity enjoins. Religious persecution, judicial torture, arbitrary imprisonment, the unnecessary multiplication of capital punishments, the delay and chicanery of tribunals, the exactions of farmers of the revenue, slavery, the slave trade, were the constant subjects of their lively satire and eloquent disquisitions. . . . . The ethical and dogmatical parts of the Gospel were unhappily turned against each other. On one side, was a Church boasting of the purity of a doctrine derived from the Apostles, but disgraced by the massacre of St. Bartholomew, by the murder of the best of kings, by the war of Cevennes, by the destruction of Port Royal. On the other side, was a sect laughing at the Scriptures, shooting out the tongue at the sacrament, but ready to encounter principalities and powers in the cause of justice, mercy and toleration.[16]

Such are the curious facts which history unfolds. And what do they teach? Only that the best and holiest of men are not

---

[15] *Westminster Review*, April, 1853.
[16] Review of Ranke's *History of the Popes.*

infallible—not perfect—only what the Apostle Paul announced eighteen hundred years ago—" We have this treasure in earthen vessels that the excellency of the power may be of God, and not of us."

Nevertheless, because the "treasure" does exist, notwithstanding the base and humble material of the "vessel," the Negro race is largely indebted to instruments who, in spite of themselves, have been the means of conveying to thousands of Africans a knowledge of the true God. The annals of orthodox Christianity are graced with innumerable names of champions of the Negro. The names and brilliant efforts of the Wilberforces, Buxtons, Venns, Gurneys, in England; of the Beechers, Cheevers, Finneys, Whittiers, Stowes, in America, can never be forgotten. And if they could have infused into their adherents and followers the lofty philanthropic spirit which actuated them—if they could have imparted more of their elevated and generous enthusiasm —the condition of the Christian Negro would be far different from what it now is. But notwithstanding all disadvantages, the influences of direct Christian doctrine were silently infiltrating themselves into the Negro minds; and though, in their suffering, comparisons at times glanced through their minds; though they could not help often making contrasts which were not always favourable to their own church; still they understood that the conduct pursued by their teachers towards them was not only not dictated by the religion they professed, but was in opposition to its teachings; hence the singular fact is patent, that, wherever Negroes exist in large numbers, in Protestant countries, they are, for the most part, members of the orthodox denominations. The only ecclesiastical organisation developed among the Negroes in the United States, which nearly copes in numbers, wealth and aggressive power with the most favoured religious sects of the land, is the *African Methodist Episcopal Church*.[17] And we are persuaded that the form of Christianity which will be introduced into Africa by Christian Negroes from abroad will be Protestantism of the orthodox stamp.

---

[17] See Tanner's *Apology for African Methodism in the United States*.

Christianity and the Negro Race.

Whatever, then, the shortcomings of our teachers, they have been the instruments of introducing large numbers of us into the Kingdom of God. The lessons they have taught us, from their uplifting effect upon thousands of the race, we have no doubt contain the elements of imperishable truth, and make their appeal to some deep and inextinguishable consciousness of the soul. While, therefore, we recognise defects—a discrepancy, at times, on their part between precept and practice—we cannot withhold from them the tribute of our respect and gratitude. In no case would we apply the harsh sentence of the great Italian poet towards his teacher, but we may address to them these magnificent and touching words of that great master of song :—

> Chè in la mente m' è fitta, ed or m' accuora
> La cara e buona imagine paterna
>   Di voi, quando . . . .
> M' insegnavate come l' uo m s' eterna:
> E quant' io l' abbo in grado, mentre io vivo
> Convien che nella mia lingua si scerna.[18]

---

[18] *Inferno*, xv. In my memory is fixed, and now goes to my heart, the dear, kind, paternal image of you, when you taught me how man may become immortal. And, while I live, it becomes my tongue to show what gratitude I have for it.

Christian Missions in West Africa.

IT is little more than half a generation since four millions of Africans were held in apparently hopeless bondage in the United States—a condition which determined their status as one of social subordination and inferiority in all Christian lands. The emancipation in the British, French, Danish and Dutch colonies was able, it seems, to effect little towards improving the standing of the Negro. He was bound to a servile position until the supremacy of the cotton empire of the West was overthrown. The proclamation of freedom in the United States gave to the Negro at once a position which he had never before occupied; and, though he is in America numerically weak, and, in a measure, personally insignificant, still the barriers in the way of his progress are rapidly disappearing.

But it is not easy to efface impressions which have been busily taught and cheerfully imbibed during centuries. The Christian world, trained for the last three hundred years to look upon the Negro as made for the service of superior races, finds it difficult to shake off the notion of his absolute and permanent inferiority. Distrust, coldness or indifference, are the feelings with which, generally speaking, any efforts on his part to advance are regarded by the enlightened races. The influence of the representations disparaging to his mental and moral character, which, during the days of his bondage, were persistently put forward without contradiction, is still strong in many minds. The full effect of the new status of the Negro race will not be sufficiently felt during the

Christian Missions in West Africa.

present generation to enable even his best friends to get rid entirely of the pity or contempt for him which they have inherited, and which is, to a great extent, to be accounted for by the fact that the civilised world has hitherto come in contact, for the most part, only with the more degraded tribes of the African continent.

One of the most important of the results of the labours and sufferings of Livingstone is the light which he has been able to throw upon the subject of the African races at home, and which has awakened doubts even in the minds of the most apathetic as to the fairness of the representations disparaging to the Negro's character which have been for so long a time in unimpeded circulation. The whole Christian world has been aroused by that humble missionary to the importance of "healing the open sore of the world," and penetrating "the dark continent" with the light of Christianity and civilisation. Catholics and Protestants—Christians of every name and nationality—are vying with each other in endeavours to promote the work of African regeneration.

One sanguine or sensational letter from Mr. Stanley calling attention to a favourable opening for missionary operations in East Africa fell upon the British public like seed into prepared soil, and, in a short time, a bountiful harvest was reaped, in the shape of thousands of pounds, in response to the more urgent than "Macedonian cry." This prompt liberality shows that there are Christian men and women in England who are deeply in earnest in the work of disseminating the truths of the Gospel in Africa.

It is evident that, at the present moment, there is no mission field in which the Christian public are so anxiously interested for the safety, welfare and success of the missionaries as the African; and there is none, moreover, whose successful working by European missionaries must, in the long run, depend so absolutely upon special and constant study of the mental and moral habits of the people and climatic peculiarities of the country. And yet in the constant necessity which presses upon missionary committees at home, and upon missionaries themselves, to find what may hold the public ear, in the impatient demand for immediate visible results in the unceasing strain after fresh subjects for exciting paragraphs, no leisure or repose is left for quiet thought, for grappling with new facts, or for giving due weight to views out of their accustomed groove of thought.

We do not set before ourselves, in the present paper, the ambitious task of propounding or discussing any new theory of African Missions. To describe accurately or intelligibly how missions in Africa ought to be conducted so as to come nearer than they have yet done to a realisation of the expectations of their supporters in Europe and America—so as in some measure to Christianise the African tribes—would probably be as difficult and impossible a task as any thinking man could well undertake. We are, for our own part, inclined to cut the Gordian knot by expressing the belief that it will not be given to the present generation of foreign workers in this field to solve the problem—or rather, problems—presented by the enormous work of African Christianisation. This is a privilege, we venture to believe, reserved for the "missionaries of the future."[1]

Still, it may not be altogether unprofitable to consider some of the results thus far attained, and the hindrances in the way of more satisfactory achievements.

It is now nearly four hundred years since the first attempt was made to introduce Christianity into the Western portion of Africa. The summary of Christian Missions on this coast may be given in a few words.

The Roman Catholics come first. In 1481 the King of Portugal sent ten ships with 500 soldiers, 100 labourers, and a proper complement of priests as missionaries, to Elmina. The Romish missions thus founded, lingered on for a period of 241 years, till, at last, in 1723, that of the Capuchins at Sierra Leone was given up, and they disappeared altogether from West Africa. They had made

---

[1] The relations of the present generation of Europeans with the African races have not been such as to allow them to be unbiassed workers in the African field. While, like David, they may receive commendation for having conceived the idea of building the great Christian temple in Africa, it may be only given to them to open the way, collect the materials, &c.; other hands may have to rear the superstructure.

Christian Missions in West Africa.

no impression, except upon their immediate dependants; and what little impression they made on them was soon totally obliterated.

Protestant missionary attempts were begun by the Moravians in 1736, and continued till 1770. Five of such attempts cost eleven lives, and were not followed by visible results.

The Wesleyans come next. In the Minutes of the Conference of 1792, we find Africa for the first time included in the list of Wesleyan missionary stations, Sierra Leone being the part occupied, and in the Minutes for 1796, the names of A. Murdoch and W. Patten are set down as missionaries to the Foulah country, in Africa, to which service they were solemnly set apart by the Conference.

The Church Missionary Society sent out its first missionaries in 1804. They established and attempted to maintain ten stations among the aborigines, but they could make no progress owing to the hostility of the natives, who appear to have preferred the slave-traders. The missionaries were forced to take refuge in Sierra Leone, the only place where at that time they could labour with safety and hope.

The Basle Missionary Society—one of the most successful on the coast—had their attention directed to Western Africa as early as 1826; but it was not until 1828 that their first company of missionaries reached Christianborg, near Akra, the place which the Moravians had attempted to occupy more than thirty years previously.

The United Presbyterian Synod of Scotland began a mission on the Old Calabar River, in the Gulf of Benin, in April, 1846.

Five denominations of American Christians—Baptists, Methodists, Episcopalians, Presbyterians, Lutherans—are represented on the coast—in Liberia, at Lagos, the Island of Corisco, and Gaboon. The first American Mission was established on the coast in 1822.

Now, what has been the outcome of these missionary operations? These results thus far achieved are, in many respects, highly interesting and important. At the European settlements established at various points along the coast from Senegal to Loanda, and at the purely native stations, occupied by the Niger

F

(native) missionaries, the Scotch missionaries and the American missionaries, some thousands of natives, having been brought under the immediate influence of Christian teaching, have professed Christianity, and, at the European settlements, have adopted European dress and habits. Numerous churches have been organised, and are under a native ministry, and thousands of children are gathered into schools under Christian teachers.

The *West African Reporter*, a weekly newspaper owned and published at Sierra Leone exclusively by natives, and itself an interesting evidence of the progress of civilisation on the coast, gives, in its issue for January 4, 1876, the following:—

> The Niger Mission and the native pastorate—which latter has received the encomiums of friends and foes—are standing monuments of the [Church Missionary] Society's labours, and proofs of the permanence of results thus far achieved. Bishop Crowther, the first Negro Bishop, the Rev. James Johnson of Lagos, Dr. Africanus Horton, the distinguished physician and author, and numerous others, less widely known but not less useful, sat under the instructions which have been imparted in the Church Missionary College at Fourah Bay, in Sierra Leone.

But other useful men besides preachers have been raised up under the instruction of the missionaries; many able and useful Government officials, skilful mechanics—especially at the Basle Mission—and merchants, who by their intelligence, industry and enterprise have risen to an equality in wealth and influence with the European merchants on the coast.

Still, these results, in their largest measure, are confined almost exclusively to the European settlements along the coast and to their immediate neighbourhood. No mission station of any importance has been established among any of the powerful tribes in the interior, or on the coast at a distance from European settlements. In the evangelistic operations of the Niger Mission, we can hear of no central station of influence among any of the leading tribes. Bishop Crowther's last Report of the "Mission among the Natives of the Bight of Biafra, at Bonny, Brass and New Calabar Rivers,"[2] after ten years' labour, is not particularly encouraging.

---

[2] *Church Missionary Intelligencer*, August, 1875.

Christian Missions in West Africa.

The work done at Sierra Leone and in Liberia cannot be regarded as done upon the indigenous elements of those localities. The native populations of Sierra Leone and Liberia—the Timnehs, Soosoos, Mendis, Veys, Golahs, Bassas, Kroos, &c.—are still untouched by evangelical influence. The visitor at Sierra Leone and at Monrovia is at once struck by the exotic appearance of everything. The whole black population of those settlements who have made any progress in Christian civilisation have been imported—in the case of Sierra Leone, from other parts of Africa, and, in that of Liberia, from America. If everything extraneous or imported were taken away from these settlements to-morrow, the regions they occupy would wear an aspect similar to that which they presented to Sir John Hawkins three hundred years ago, but it is to be feared that the inhabitants would not present the pleasing moral characteristics attributed to them while they were as yet un-Europeanised, by that great pioneer of English-African slave-traders. Nor is even the civilising work done in the settlements without its drawbacks.

In the *African Times* for January 1, 1876, the editor, after the labour of half a generation in the cause of West African progress, opens the year with the following lament:—

> Lagos has grievously disappointed our hopes and expectations. She is not what she ought to be after years of annexation to the British Crown. It is no cause for wonder, therefore, that she has not exercised that influence on the Heathen within her and in the neighbouring countries which we looked for from her. . . . The professed Christians of Lagos ought to be a mighty phalanx against the surrounding Heathenism; but we do not see that they have made any successful attack upon it.

Governor Berkeley, in his Blue Book Report of the Settlement of Lagos for 1872, estimates the population of the entire settlement at 60,221, out of which there were only 92 whites; and he adds:—

> This settlement contributes nothing towards the promotion of religion or education. The Church Missionary Society, the Wesleyan Society, and the Roman Catholics are all represented in the shape of ministers, churches and schools.[3]

---

[3] *Papers relating to Her Majesty's Colonial Possessions*; part i, 1874, p. 138.

Christianity, Islam and the Negro Race.

Sir Charles Adderley, after a full and careful investigation of the subject, says:—

Barbarism survives, for all we expend in lives and taxes to establish what must prove, after all, an ineffectual administration of English power in the West African country.[4]

In the *West African Reporter* (February 1, 1876) we are informed that:—

The Timnehs of Quiah to this day look with wistful eyes to the Peninsula of Sierra Leone, the Bananas Island down to Carmaranca Creek, the Ribbee and Bompeh rivers, and their hearts are burning with revenge against the Powers that wrenched these places from the hands of their ancestors. Their chiefs are dissatisfied with the stipends they receive, as being no equivalent remuneration for the occupation and use of their lands by our Government; and they are only prevented from making any mischievous move by want of power.

The Hon. James S. Payne, the new President of Liberia, in his Inaugural Address, delivered January 3, 1876, refers to the actual state of things in Liberia, which does not exist at Sierra Leone only "from want of power" on the part of the aborigines. He says:—

The war now raging (between the Americo-Liberians and the aborigines of Cape Palmas) has been the subject of consideration for more than three years, of which frequent intimations were given without being accredited. It has for one of its objects the re-possession of the territory at the cost of exterminating the entire civilised population. It is a war against civilisation and Christianity. Upwards of forty years of untiring Christian Mission effort among them as preferred objects of the missions of the Presbyterian and Protestant Episcopal Missions, has made them rather to hate than to admire Christian civilisation.

Now let us see what is the view too often taken of African Mission *protégés* by intelligent Pagan natives. We have heard several expressions in regard to "Christianised" natives made in our hearing by native chiefs in whose country we have travelled; but we prefer to quote the criticism of the King of Dahomey, as given to the world by Commodore Wilmot in a dispatch to Admiral Walker, under date of January 21, 1863. The Commodore was remonstrating with the King against making war upon

---

[4] *Colonial Policy and History*, p. 218.

Christian Missions in West Africa.

the people of Abbeokuta, among whom were many professed Christians:—

> He promised faithfully for my sake (says the Commodore, to spare all the Christians and send them to Whydah, and that his general should have strict orders to this effect. I asked him about the Christians at Ishagga. He said, "Who knew they were Christians? The black man says he is a white man, calls himself a Christian, and dresses himself in clothes: it is an insult to the white man. I respect the white man, but these people are impostors, and no better than my own people." I reasoned with him no longer on this subject (adds the Commodore), because I thought his observations so *thoroughly just and honest*.[5]

Now here is a Christian European of intelligence and influence endorsing the disparaging estimate of Christian Africans as given by a Pagan African of intelligence and influence.[6]

Sir Charles Adderley calls attention to "the strange graft of skill upon barbarous fanaticism which natives acquire who have been played with by dilettante philanthropists in distant unconcerned authority."[7]

The foreign virtues these natives acquire never rise above the parasitical. Their culture is superficial, and its effects artificial, presenting very often an appearance of insincerity and absurdity both to the foreign observer and the Pagan of intelligence. Pagans of discernment know that the black man among them who "calls himself a Christian and dresses himself in clothes" adheres to European habits and customs with a reserved power of disengagement, much as a limpet clings to a rock. These customs seldom strike root in his mind, and grow up as an independent plant. Africans who have been educated even in England, on returning to their own country and among their own people, have again adopted the native dress and habits. And it would show a very slender knowledge of human nature to expect anything else.

Now, why is it that the evangelisation of the tribes of West Africa, after so many years of effort and so vast a sacrifice of life and money, is so backward? The first and most generally admitted

---

[5] *British and Foreign State Papers*, 1863–64; vol. liv, p. 851.

[6] "Educated natives" is often used by Europeans on the coast as a phrase of contempt.

[7] *Colonial Policy and History*, p. 158.

Christianity, Islam and the Negro Race.

cause is the unhealthiness of the climate; and this cause, we may premise, affects injuriously all progress and growth in West Africa to a far greater extent than is generally supposed. No one will undertake to dispute at this day that the moral and intellectual character of a people is very largely dependent upon their physical environments. No great man, physically or mentally, has ever been developed in the inhospitable regions of Greenland or Tierra del Fuego. In some countries a high degree of even material progress is impossible. In Brazil, for instance, Mr. Buckle tells us, "the progress of agriculture is stopped by impassable forests, and the harvests are devoured by innumerable insects. The mountains are too high to scale—the rivers too wide to bridge." A portion of the indomitable Anglo-Saxon race from the southern States of North America have had an opportunity recently of testing these statements. They attempted to found a colony in Brazil, but the obstacles presented by Nature proved insuperable. They have returned to the United States.[8]

Now it is well known that a belt of malarious lands, which are hotbeds of fever, extends along the whole of the West Coast of Africa, running from forty to fifty miles back from the sea-coast. In this region of country neither cattle nor horses will thrive. Horses will not live at all. Sheep, goats and hogs drag out an indifferent existence. At Sierra Leone, Monrovia and other settlements on the coast, fortunes have been expended by lovers of horses in trying to keep them alive, but in spite of all that care and money can do, they pine away and die. The experiment of keeping them constantly housed, like human beings, and imposing upon them the regulation, "early to bed, and early to rise," has, we believe, not yet been tried.[9]

The healthfulness of a country or district, at any given time,

---

[8] The *Times*, January 18, 1876.

[9] In 1871, Dr. McCoy, Colonial Surgeon (of Sierra Leone), sent to the Royal Veterinary College, London, a report on the then so-called "loin disease" (of horses), and the opinion formed thereon by the professor of the College was that the disease arose out of the poisoned state of the blood, the disease being conveyed into the system by means of the atmosphere.—Sierra Leone *West African Reporter*, February 1, 1876.

may generally be determined by the condition of the animals. In pestilential disorders, four-footed animals are said to be first attacked, from their living more in the open air than man, and being, therefore, more exposed to the action of the atmosphere.

Οὐρῆας μὲν πρῶτον ἐπῴχετο καὶ κύνας ἀργούς.
Αὐτὰρ ἔπειτ' αὐτοῖσι βέλος ἐχεπευκὲς, ἐφιεὶς,
Βάλλ'.[10]

In the elevated regions of the interior of West Africa, where there are no dense primeval forests, extensive swamps, and pestilential jungles, cattle and horses show no sign of "infection" or "poisoned state of the blood." They flourish in uncounted herds. And in those regions men are healthy, vigorous and intelligent.

The interior tribes who have, from time to time, migrated to the coast have perished or degenerated. Every child born on the coast is stunted physically and mentally in the cradle by the jungle fever, which assails it a few days after birth. European infants seldom survive such attacks. The Vey tribe, occupying the country about Gallinas and Cape Mount, have traditions that they came to the coast as conquerors, driving before them all the tribal organisations which opposed their march. They were a numerous, intelligent, handsome people. Now, only melancholy traces of what they once were can be discovered in individuals of that waning tribe. "It is to be observed," says the *West African Reporter*,[11] "that the Mendi, as he approaches the sea, becomes more degenerate. Laying aside his innocent, manly exercises, he betakes himself to plundering." It would appear that by a process of natural selection the finest organisations die. Those most capable or "fittest" to endure the pestilential regions, by reason of a coarser or more brutal nature, "survive." We have, then, morally speaking, the "survival" of the "unfittest."

The steady physical, if not mental, deterioration going on among the descendants of re-captives at Sierra Leone is sometimes

---

[10] On mules and dogs the infection first began,
And last the vengeful arrow fixed in man.

[11] February 1, 1876.

attributed by superficial observers to their having enjoyed facilities for European education superior to their fathers. But the same decay is observable among the Mohammedan creoles who have not deviated much from the customs of their ancestors. The Rev. S. W. Koelle, an experienced German missionary, called attention, some years ago, to the important contrast as to salubrity between the coast and the interior. In the preface to his Bornou Grammar, he says:—

> The natives of dry and arid countries, as *e.g.*, Bornou, Hausa, the Sahara, &c., die very fast in Sierra Leone; their acclimatisation there seems to be almost as difficult as that of Europeans.

In the course of thirty years, two hundred Bornouese residents of Sierra Leone had been reduced to thirty. And, as we have said, those who do not die, degenerate, and become dependent upon the tribes of the healthier regions. All the coast tribes, from Senegal to Lagos, where no alien influence interferes, are held under the sway of the inferior tribes. Everybody now knows that the tribes of the Gold Coast are no match in intelligence, enterprise and energy for the Ashantees.

Under such circumstances, unless missionary boards or committees, and the American Colonisation Society in America, are content to repeat the sacrifices they have already made of life and treasure, during another fifty years, with similar inadequate results, would it not be wisdom to try operations in the healthy regions of the interior, where "every prospect pleases," and "man" is *not* so "vile"? As long as the malarious vegetation and deadly mangrove swamps occupy so large a proportion of West African territory, there will be no more probability of making any permanent moral, or even material, progress on the coast, or of developing a great mind, than there is of improving the haunts of the polar bear and the reindeer.[12] Of course, the resources of the philanthropic world

---

[12] Professor Draper, in his *Conflict between Religion and Science*, tells us of a civilisation that had been accomplished in Central America resting on an agriculture that had neither horse nor ox nor plough. If the way could be discovered of accomplishing a civilisation in these days with the slender appliances which such a statement would imply, then there might be hope for West Africa.

Christian Missions in West Africa.

in men and money are inexhaustible, and they have the power of prolonging the experiment indefinitely; and it may be the highest philanthropy to labour to prepare men for the "world to come" in a country where they can have no reasonable hope of enjoying the "world that now is." Many a European visiting this coast returns to his country never to enjoy the vigour of health again. For northern constitutions, the effect of a residence in this country, generally speaking, is similar to that said to have been produced upon the ancients by a visit to the cave of Trophonius—they never smile again.

But another drawback to the success of missions on this coast is the inadequate, not to say contemptuous, view often entertained by European missionaries of the materials with which they have to deal; and this may be assigned as one of the leading causes why no serious effort is made to go to the healthy " regions beyond." They come to the coast imbued with the notions they have derived from books, of the " sanguinary customs " and " malignant superstitions " of the natives. And under the influence of their malarious surroundings they gain more in irritability of temper than in liberality of view, often acquiring greater ignorance of the people than they had before they came. We were startled some time ago by reading a remarkable description of African character, as given by an American missionary from West Africa in the course of an address delivered in the United States. He said:—

The Chinaman meets you with the stolid morality of his Confucianism; the Hindoo with astute logic for his Pantheism. The missionary among those peoples is assaulting strongholds, bristling with guns and bayonets. When I carry my torch into the caves of Africa, I meet only filthy birds of darkness bats, owls, and evil things of night, that, bewildered by the light, know not how to blunder out, or out, blunderingly dash themselves in again.[13]

Similar to this are descriptions we have read from time to time in missionary periodicals.[14] Now, we earnestly protest against such utterances as not only gross exaggerations, but as, to the last

---

[13] Address delivered before the American Colonisation Society, by Rev. R. H. Nassau, M.D., January 21, 1873.

[14] See an article on 'The Negro' in the *Church Missionary Intelligencer* London) for August, 1873.

degree, pernicious in their influence, since they are made to apply not only to the natives of the coast demoralised by their physical surroundings and by European vices, but to all Africans, and they lead young and inexperienced missionaries entirely astray as to the course they should pursue with the people. Coming to the coast under such teaching, they are induced to adopt a method of dealing with the natives, and to maintain a demeanour which, in spite of their educational and other services, inspire the people among whom they labour with feelings of impatience, if not of dislike. And it is not difficult to see that the missionary entertaining such views must labour under very great subjective disadvantages. From his out-look, the work is magnified to enormous proportions. The African mind is regarded as a great blank, or worse than a blank, filled with everything dark and horrible and repulsive. Everything is to be destroyed, and replaced by something new and foreign. Not such were the views entertained of Africans by the Rev. J. Leighton Wilson, who, having been from childhood acquainted with Negroes in the United States, spent twenty years as a missionary in West Africa, where he had opportunities of visiting every place of importance along the sea-coast, and made extensive excursions in many of the maritime districts. He studied and reduced to writing two of the leading languages of the country. In the record of his African experiences, he says:—

Looking at the African race as we have done, in their native country, we have seen no obstacles to their elevation which would not apply equally to all other uncultivated races of men.

We do not expect Africans, under any circumstances, to possess the energy, the enterprise, or the inventive powers of the white man. But there are other traits, quite as commendable as these, in which, if properly trained, he will greatly excel his white compeer. Naturally, the African is social, generous, confiding, and, when brought under the benign influence of Christianity, he exemplifies the beauty and consistency of his religion more than any other human being on the face of the earth. And the time may come when they may be held up to all the rest of the world as examples of the purest and most elevated Christian virtue.[15]

The more slender the outfit as to educational training and experience of those who come as instructors to the coast, the more

---

[15] Wilson's *Western Africa*, chap. xi.

supercilious—as, of course, must be the case—is their bearing. Many and amusing are the instances encountered by intelligent Africans of the very limited qualifications, coupled with large pretensions, of not a few who are sent to the coast as instructors. While sitting on the passengers' deck of one of the African mail steamers, a few years ago, we heard a young Englishman who had been engaged in educational work on the coast, and was returning home on leave, descanting upon the "utter inferiority of the African"—and, by the way, these men who come to guide the "benighted" seldom hesitate (such is their high breeding) to indulge in most contemptuous utterances about the race in the hearing of any member of it who may be a stranger to them. This young man—we say young man, though his hair was slightly sprinkled with grey—overflowing with erudition, and anxious to make known the extent of his researches in African philology, remarked to a comrade, "The stolidity of these Africans is astonishing. Their words are mostly monosyllabic, and even those tribes whose vocabulary is the most copious possess no expressions for abstract ideas." Attracted by the Johnsonese character of the sentence, we turned towards him and said, "Sir, the words in the sentence which you just uttered, that convey any idea at all, are either Roman or Greek. All the purely English words you employed are monosyllabic, expressing no abstract thought." "Oh," he replied, with some surprise, "but that only proves that we possessed the ability to appropriate and apply such foreign terms as we considered serviceable—a feat which your people are unable to achieve." To this second outburst of almost pure Latin we made no reply, but turned away, leaving our learned pedagogue to enjoy the belief that, under the influence of his irresistible argument, we had succumbed; but we noticed that he took care during the remainder of the voyage to indulge, while in our hearing, in no more "high falutin."

We are not of those who deprecate international prejudices; they will exist, probably, until the millennium; for God, "who hath made of one blood all nations of men," hath also "appointed the bounds of their habitation," and within those "bounds" special and divergent tastes will arise among the nations. We remember when, accompanied about six years ago, on a tour in the interior of Monrovia, by Mr. Winwood Reade, we arrived at Boporo,[16] a town about seventy-five miles from the coast, where a white man had rarely been seen, how the women and children fled in every direction at the appearance of Mr. Reade ; and it was not until we had been there several days that the children would venture near enough to speak to him. We are told that a charitable old woman who afforded Mungo Park a meal and lodging, on the banks of the Niger, could not refrain, even in the midst of her kindness, from exclaiming, "God preserve us from the DEVIL!" as she looked upon him.

These deprecatory feelings doubtless arise from the erroneous impressions entertained by Africans of the interior of the mental and moral concomitants of a white skin. The white man, in the imagination of the unsophisticated African, is a cannibal. The Negro of the ordinary traveller or missionary—and perhaps of two-thirds of the Christian world—is a purely fictitious being, constructed out of the traditions of slave-traders and slave-holders, who have circulated all sorts of absurd stories, and also out of prejudices inherited from ancestors, who were taught to regard the Negro as a legitimate object of traffic. And, perhaps, as Bishop Heber has remarked, the "hair and features" of the Negro, "far more than his colour," are responsible for these erroneous conceptions. We entertain no resentment at such feelings on the part of Europeans; but as the object of missionary labour is undoubtedly success, we may venture to suggest that such views, cherished by missionaries, and allowed in a marked manner to influence their demeanour on mission ground, may possibly interfere with the wholesome results at which they aim.

But with regard to all the charges of superstition, &c., made against native Africans, and in consequence of which a hopeless "incapacity of amelioration" is sometimes attributed to the whole race, we may remark, that there is not a single mental or moral

---

[16] This visit is described in Reade's *African Sketch Book*, vol. ii. Mr. Reade correctly represents the impressions of Africans on first seeing a white man. Vol. i, pp. 328–29.

Christian Missions in West Africa.

deficiency now existing among Africans—not a single practice now indulged in by them—to which we cannot find a parallel in the past history of Europe, and even after the people had been brought under the influence of a nominal Christianity. "Out of savages," says Professor Tyndall, unable to count up to the number of their fingers, and speaking a language containing only nouns and verbs, arise at length our Newtons and Shakespeares." [17]

Take *Polygamy*. We are told by Dr. Maclear that—

Nowhere was the Ancient Slavonic superstition more deeply rooted than in Prussia. Every native of the country was allowed to have three wives, who were regarded as slaves, and on the death of their husbands they were expected to ascend the funeral pile or otherwise put an end to their lives. [18]

And Mr. Lecky says:—

The practice of polygamy among the barbarian kings was for some centuries unchecked, or at least unsuppressed, by Christianity. The Kings Caribert and Chilperic had both many wives at the same time. Dagobert had three wives, as well as a multitude of concubines. Charlemagne himself had at the same time two wives, and he indulged largely in concubines. [19]

Take *Slavery*. Slavery and the trade in slaves was almost more difficult to root out than Paganism, and the inhuman traffic was in full activity as late as the tenth century between England and Ireland—the port of Bristol being one of its principal centres. [20] In the canons of a Council in London in 1102, it is ordered that no one from henceforth presume to carry on that wicked traffic by which men in England have hitherto been sold like brute animals. [21]

Take *Human Sacrifices*. Tacitus tells us that the old Teutons, generally sparing in offerings, presented on certain days human victims to Wodan. The old Swedes, every nine years, on the great national festival, celebrated for nine days, offered nine male animals of every chief species, together with one man daily. The Danes, assembling every nine years in their capital, Lederun, sacrificed to

---

[17] Address at Belfast, 1874, p. 52.
[18] *Apostles of Mediæval Europe*, p. 259.
[19] Lecky's *History of European Morals*, vol. ii, p. 368.
[20] Maclear's *Mediæval Europe*, p. 259.
[21] *Influence of Christianity on Civilisation*; by Thomas Craddock.—Longmans, 1856.

their gods, 99 horses, 99 dogs, 99 cocks, 99 hawks, and 99 men. The Prussians, previous to an engagement, offered through their high priest (Criwe) an enemy to their gods, Pikollos and Potrimpos. The Goths thought victory impossible unless they had before offered a human sacrifice. The Saxons, after their war with Charlemagne, killed on the holy Harz-mountain all the Frankish prisoners in honour of their god Wodan.[22] And what shall we say of those human hecatombs offered during a period of three hundred years by Christians to the god of the slave trade?

> Hearest, Thou, O God, those chains,
> Clanking on Freedom's plains
> By Christians wrought?
> Them who those chains have worn
> Christians have hither borne,
> Christians have bought.

We have referred to only a few of the instances we might cite, many of which show that human sacrifices have prevailed most among communities that had advanced in the path of civilisation; and we have quoted these instances not merely as a sort of *tu quoque* argument, but because so many careless writers are fond of dilating upon the "malignant superstitions" and "sanguinary customs" of the Africans, as if these things, owing to some essential inferiority or inherent disposition to wanton cruelty in the Negro, were peculiar to him; and as if, moreover, they could be at once abolished by a few homilies on the stupidity and cruelty of such customs.[23]

Now, as to the "sanguinary customs" of the King of Dahomey. Every candid mind who will take the trouble to read carefully the descriptions of intelligent travellers who have visited the Dahomeyan capital—Norris, Forbes, Wilmot, and even the cynical Burton—will find out that the accounts often circulated of the large numbers killed are gross exaggerations, and that the customs, far from being the result of a wanton desire to destroy human life, are "a practice founded on a pure religious basis, designed as a sincere

---

[22] Kalisch's *Commentary on Leviticus*, Part I.

[23] See a letter addressed to Mr. Winwood Reade by Mr. A. Swanzy on the possibility of effecting important reforms in Dahomey by personal interviews with the King.—Reade's *African Sketch Book*, vol. ii, p. 510.

manifestation of the King's filial piety, sanctioned by long usage, upheld by a powerful priesthood, and believed to be closely bound up with the existence of Dahomey itself." It is not in the power of the King to abrogate the custom. Its gradual extinction must be the result of the increasing intelligence of the people.

Commodore Wilmot had the opportunity of witnessing one of the "annual customs" at the capital of Dahomey, in reference to which the King said to him :

"You have seen that only a few are sacrificed, and not the thousands that wicked men have told the world. If I were to give up this custom at once, my head would be taken off to-morrow. These institutions cannot be opped in the way you propose. By-and-bye, little by little, much may be done : softly, softly, not by threats. You see how I am placed, and the difficulties in the way; by-and-bye, by-and-bye."

Dr. Draper says :—

In vain the Spaniards excuse their atrocities on the plea that a nation like the Mexican, which permitted cannibalism, should not be regarded as having emerged from the barbarous state, and that one which, like Peru, sacrificed human hecatombs at the funeral solemnities of great men, must have been savage. Let it be remembered that there is no civilised nation whose popular practices do not lag behind its intelligence. In America, human sacrifice was part of a religious solemnity, unsustained by passion.[24]

But not only are there exaggerated tales in circulation in foreign countries disparaging to the *Pagan* natives of Africa, there are equally erroneous impressions abroad about the Mohammedans. There is something lamentable—we were going to say grotesque— in the ignorance of some who assume to be authorities and guides on African matters, of the condition of things at even a little distance from the coast. The editor of the *Church Missionary Intelligencer*, in what purports to be an examination of Mr. Bosworth Smith's statements on the subject, informs his readers that "in the waiting-room of Euston Square Station all the Mohammedan Negroes in Africa who have read the Koran, even once, might be most comfortably accommodated. The priests themselves cannot distinguish between 'mumpsimus' and 'sumpsimus' when they jabber the Koran, and do not attempt to understand other Arabic books."[25]

---

[24] *History of the Intellectual Development of Europe*, chap. xix.
[25] *Church Missionary Intelligencer*, August, 1847, p. 247.

Christianity, Islam and the Negro Race.

We read and explained this passage to a young Mohammedan from the interior; his only reply to it was an outburst of uproarious laughter, and he could not, for a long time, suppress his merriment at what seemed to him an extraordinary lack of information on the part of one of the "people of the book," as to the condition of things in Africa. Not by such weapons is Africa to be penetrated. The work requires earnestness and accuracy of information. The day is past for such summary disposition of important and perplexing questions. All efforts which ignore the importance of accurate information of the people and the country must utterly fail, as being behind the times.

> Sic fatus senior, telumque imbelle sino ictu
> Conjecit: rauco quod protenus aere repulsum,
> Et summo clypei nequidquam umbone pependit.[20]

Only a few hours' travel from Sierra Leone—if he would venture to visit the coast—would take the writer of the paragraph quoted above to a Mohammedan town where he would be able to count hundreds of Arabic volumes read and understood by their owners, and where he would find little boys who have read the Koran through.

In January, 1873, the present writer visited, in company with Governor Pope Hennessy, of Sierra Leone, the Mohammedan Literary Institution at Billeh, on the Great Scarcies River, about sixty miles N.E. of Freetown; and in an interview with Fode Tarawally, the venerable head of the institution, we had an opportunity of examining his library. By order of the Governor, the Arabic writer to the Government took down the names of the principal works. In the list submitted were the titles of eighty-nine volumes, among which we noticed the following: *Commentary of Jelaladdin on the Koran, Commentary of Beidhawi, Traditions of Bukhari; Law Book*, by Khalil Ishak (2 vols.); *Rizalat of Imam, Malik, Medical Treatise, Metrical Guide, Grammar, Rhetoric, Prosody, Makamat of Hariri), Ancient History*, &c., written by Arabs. There were also volumes of Prayers, Poetry, Rhetoric, History, composed by Mandingo and Foulah authors. The library of this

---

[20] Virgil's *Æneid*, Book II, pp. 543-545.

distinguished Sheikh, who is considered to be the most learned Mohammedan in this portion of West Africa, embraced well-nigh all the branches of human knowledge and research—theology, medicine, history, astronomy, grammar, &c. He entered into an interesting discussion on the respective merits of the different commentaries on the Koran, and seemed to give the preference to Beidhawi. Among his co-religionists, complete confidence is placed in the exactness of his traditional information, and on all doubtful questions his opinion is final. One of his sons composed *calamo currente*, an acrostic poem in Arabic on the name of Governor Hennessy.[27]

At a town not far from Billeh, a Foulah boy, not more than fourteen years old, was introduced to us as a Hafiz—one who knows the Koran by heart. We tried him on several long chapters, and he recited them *verbatim, literatim, et punctuatim*, without the slightest hesitation. But he was only one of a number of such youths, whom we met in subsequent travels in the interior, who could recite not only the Koran, but many of the standard Arabic poems. Are there many youths in Christian lands who could recite even one book of the Bible from memory?

Every traveller who enters the Mohammedan regions of West and Central Africa with sufficient basis of information to understand what he sees and hears, is forced to admit that the man makes a great mistake who approaches the Negro Muslims with the idea that they are "benighted Africans."

Mohammedanism in Africa, instead of being treated in the off-hand and contemptuous manner adopted by some, who seem to have gathered all their knowledge of the religion from the *Arabian Nights*, ought to be approached with earnestness and respect; for there is much in it which Christians may profitably study, and from which they might glean important lessons. Mr. Bosworth Smith remarks, in his *Lectures on Mohammed and Mohammedanism*, that "Christians have something at least to learn from Mohammedans which will make them not less but more Christian than they were

---

[27] See a paper read by Governor Hennessy before the Society of Arts, April 29, 1873; and Reade's *African Sketch Book*, vol. i, p. 312 (foot-note).

before,"[28] and no one who has seriously studied the subject will deny the truth of the remark. In the pending controversy, for example, about religious and secular education, Christians might profit by the example of Mohammedan communities where the one involves and is inseparable from the other. Their education is religious and their religion educational. The example set by them in the constant and unremitting study of their sacred book, the Koran, is not unworthy of imitation. Sir Wilfred Lawson, again, in his laudable efforts in behalf of temperance, might appeal to the effective Mohammedan legislation on the subject, and gather encouragement from the practical exemplification in all Mohammedan countries of the ultimate result of his theories. The advocates of a "beneficent Erastianism" might study Islam with profit. The Mohammedans have certainly attained, though on a lower ground, a degree of religious unity not yet witnessed in the Christian Church. At all events, those who are engaged in missionary work in Mohammedan countries would not lose anything by heeding the thoughtful and common-sense advice of Barthélemy Saint Hilaire:—

> Il y a aujourd'hui dans trois parties du monde plus de cent millions de Mussulmans, et voilà douze cents ans passés que leur religion règne sur une bonne partie de l'Asie, de l'Afrique et même de l'Europe. A moins de traiter avec une légèreté aveugle cette portion considérable de l'humanité, qui a cependant à peu près les mêmes idées que nous sur Dieu et sa providence, il faut bien prendre aux sérieux un fait aussi vaste et aussi durable. Le Mahométisme n'est pas près de disparaître ; et pour faciliter les rapports qu'on a nécessairement avec lui, il faut tâcher de le comprendre dans tout ce qu'il a de vrai et de bon, et de ne pas l'exclure, malgré ses défauts trop réels, de cette bienveillance universelle que recommande la charité Chrétienne.[29]

Growing out of the general misunderstanding of the people, the first and constant effort of the missionaries is to Europeanise them, without reference to their race peculiarities or the climatic conditions of the country, and this course has been attended with many serious drawbacks, preventing any healthy or permanent result. The missionary, often young and inexperienced, and having

---

[28] *Mohammed and Mohammedanism;* preface to first edition, p. xi.
[29] *Mahomet et le Coran,* p. 218.

no model before him but that which he has left at home, endeavours to bring things in his new field as nearly as possible into conformity to the old. Everything is new and strange to him, and nearly everything he regards with contempt for being so un-European; and with the earnest vigour and sanguine temper which belong to youth he preaches a crusade against the harmless customs and prejudices of the people—superseding many customs and habits necessary and useful in the climate and for the people by practices which, however useful they might be in Europe, become, when introduced indiscriminately into Africa, artificial, ineffective and absurd. The "thin varnish of European civilisation," which the native thus receives, is mistaken for a genuine mental metamorphosis, when, as a rule, owing to the imprudent hurry by which the convert's reformation has been brought about, his Christianity, instead of being pure is superstitious, instead of being genuine is only nominal, instead of being deep is utterly superficial, and, not having fairly taken root, it cannot flourish and become reproductive. And here we cannot do better than quote from the utterances of a native clergyman of ability who, educated on the coast under missionary teaching, has felt the drawbacks of the system, He says:—

> In the work of elevating Africans, foreign teachers have always proceeded with their work on the assumption that the Negro or the African is in every one of his normal susceptibilities an inferior race, and that it is needful in everything to give him a foreign model to copy; no account has been made of our peculiarities—our languages, enriched with the traditions of centuries; our parables, many of them the quintessence of family and national histories; our modes of thought, influenced more or less by local circumstances; our poetry and manufactures, which, though rude, had their own tales to tell; our social habits and even the necessities of our climate. It has been forgotten that European ideas, tastes, languages and social habits, like those of other nations, have been influenced more or less by geographical positions and climatic peculiarities; that what is esteemed by one country polite, may be justly esteemed by another rude and barbarous; and that God does not intend to have the races confounded, but that the Negro or African should be raised upon his own idiosyncrasies. The result has been that we, as a people, think more of everything that is foreign, and less of that which is purely native; have lost our self-respect and our love for our own race, are become a sort of nondescript people, and are, in many things, inferior to our brethren in the interior countries. There is evidently a fetter upon our minds even when the body is

free; mental weakness, even where there is physical strength, and barrenness even where there appears fertility.[80]

Such is the able and pathetic protest of a highly intelligent native, well known as a hard worker for the improvement of his people in the right direction. And as the natives advance in intelligence and culture, they will see things more and more as Mr. Johnson sees them; their views on social questions will diverge in important particulars from those of their European teachers. We regret to notice that there has been an outcry, among some who should rejoice, against those distinctive features and really moral and beneficial results of the contact of the native mind with European culture. The objectors to such deprecatory utterances from intelligent natives seem blind to the embarrassing social problems which must spring up among a distinct race from the new conditions. But it ought to be evident to them that there is no solution to be found in sneering at the aspirations and yearnings of the people and in scorning their "instincts." If there is danger for the future of West Africa, it does not arise from the new aspect which things are assuming, and will, more and more, assume, among the enlightened natives, but from the insufficiency of the agency employed to cope with the new conditions, and to direct and organise the forces evolved.

The attempt to Europeanise the Negro in Africa will always be a profitless task. This is the feeling of the most advanced minds of the race. If it were possible—which, happily, it is not—to civilise and Christianise the whole of Africa according to the notions of some Europeans, neither would the people themselves nor the outside world be any great gainers by it; for the African would then fail of the ability to perform his specific part in the world's work, as a distinct portion of the human race. The warnings of history on this subject are numerous.

Neither Greek science nor Roman culture (says the Rev. Stopford Brooke) had power to spread beyond itself. . . . The fact was that Rome did not try to civilise in the right way. Instead of drawing forth the native energies of

---

[80] From a letter addressed by Rev. James Johnson, native pastor of Sierra Leone (now of Lagos), to Governor Pope Hennessy, dated December 24th, 1872, and published in the *Negro* newspaper, January 1, 1873.

Christian Missions in West Africa.

these nations, while it left them free to develop their own national peculiarities in their own way, it imposed upon them from without the Roman education. It tried to turn them into Romans. Where this effort was unsuccessful, the men remained barbarous; where it was successful, the nation lost its distinctive elements in the Roman elements, at least, till after some centuries the overwhelming influence of Rome had perished. Meantime they were not Britons nor Gauls, but spurious Romans. The natural growth of the people was arrested. Men living out of their native element became stunted and spiritless.[81]

The same mistake is being committed in Africa, and, probably, from the same leading cause which is assigned by Mr. Brooke for the mistake of the Romans: "The Romans," he says, " considered the barbarous Western nations incapable of culture."

There is a solidarity of humanity which requires the complete development of each part in order to the effective working of the whole. To make the African a parasite upon the European would be no gain to mankind. The problem, it appears to us, which the imagination, the wisdom, and the Christian charity of the missionary world has to solve is, how to elevate the African, or enable him to elevate himself, according to the true Christian standard, upon the basis, as Mr. Johnson suggests, of "his own idiosyncrasies." Any progress made otherwise must be unreal, unsatisfactory, precarious, transitory.

If the African is a part of humanity, there need be no fear—if his progress be normal—that he will not eventually come into thorough harmony with the laws of humanity, rejecting whatever may be the result of any distortions or eccentricities in his individuality. We are unwilling, for one moment, to admit the idea that Africans cannot acquire those trusts and convictions and that moral and spiritual development essential to human peace and guidance in this world, and to life everlasting in the world to come, without being cast in the European mould. We believe that Africans can attain to a knowledge of science, receive intellectual culture, acquire skill to develop the resources of their country, and be made "wise unto salvation," without becoming Europeans; "for God is no respecter of persons; but in every nation he that feareth Him, and worketh righteousness, is accepted with Him."

---

[81] *Sermons on Christ in Modern Life*, p. 58.

Christianity, Islam and the Negro Race.

Some of the best European thinkers deprecate any effort to cause the African to part with his special characteristics. A distinguished American writer says :—

When the epoch of the civilisation of the Negro family arrives, in the lapse of ages, they will display in their native land some very peculiar and interesting traits of character, of which we, a distinct branch of the human family, can at present form no conception. It will be—indeed, it must be—a civilisation of a peculiar stamp: perhaps, we venture to conjecture, not so much distinguished by art as a certain beautiful nature, not so marked or adorned by science as exalted and refined by a new and lovely theology—a reflection of the light of heaven more perfect and endearing than that which the intellects of the Caucasian race have ever exhibited. There is more of the child, of unsophisticated nature, in the Negro race than in the European.[82]

With this corresponds the view of Governor Pope Hennessy as stated in his reply to Mr. Johnson's letter quoted above. He says :—

Fortunately, the injurious influences to which you refer have left almost untouched and uninjured the great mass of your race. It is only along the coast that the degenerating effect is seen. Dr. Livingstone bears testimony to the high intelligence and honourable character of your countrymen, as he has met them in the heart of Southern Negroland. Dr. Barth and others have done this for Central Nigritia. The many chiefs and messengers who have come to me from the northern valleys of the Niger have been in themselves witnesses of the same fact. In these times, when sceptical and irreverent inquiries have become the fashion in what are called the leading nations of Europe, it is satisfactory to know that your race is distinguished by a child-like capacity for faith. By keeping your race pure, you will preserve that all-important characteristic. As a student of history and a clergyman, you cannot have failed to see that mixed races are in this respect inferior to your own.[83]

Another drawback—and the last we shall notice at present—to the success of missions on the coast, is the pernicious example of European traders and other non-missionary residents. From the time of the discovery of the Negro country by the Portuguese to the present, Europe has sent to the coast as traders some of its vilest characters.

They (Europeans) spread themselves (says a leading article in the *Times* of December 21, 1872) over the world, following everywhere the bent of their own nature, doing their own will, following their own gain, too generally being and doing nothing that a Heathen will recognise as better than himself. These

---

[82] Alexander Kinmont, quoted by Dr. W. E. Channing in his Works, vol. vi.
[83] Published in the *Negro* newspaper for January 1, 1873.

Christian Missions in West Africa.

preach something, and have their own mischievous mission. They preach irreligion, and the views that go with it. Their gospel does its work, and reaps its fruit.

No stone should be left unturned (says the *Standard*, August 27, 1874) to convince both Mussulman and Brahmin, Caffre and New Zealander, Fantee and Ashantee, that Christianity is the religion of the best men whom Europe boasts of, and that the leaders of science and philosophy, of government and society, profess the same faith as is preached to them by the humble missionary.

The settlements along the coast where it has been thought fit to establish and keep up missionary operations are commercial sea-ports, with all the disadvantages attaching to such localities. The population consists of a heterogeneous crowd—Government officials, itinerant mercantile agents, traders from the interior, and permanent native merchants, all intent upon worldly gains. Mohammedans or Pagans coming from the interior, and forming the larger part of the floating population, do not get the most favourable view of Christianity. But such a view as they get they carry back to their country. The intelligent natives of the interior with whom we have conversed in our travels between Sierra Leone and the head-waters of the Niger, look, with hardly an exception, upon the religion and books of the white man as intended not to teach men the way to heaven, but how to become rich and great in this world.

It is unfortunate for the English and other European languages that, in this part of Africa, they have come to the greater portion of the natives associated with profligacy, plunder, and cruelty, and devoid of any connection with spiritual things; while the Arabic is regarded by them as the language of prayer and devotion, of religion and piety, of all that is unworldly and spiritual.

The Church Missionary Society has wisely devoted a great deal of time and money to the task of reducing to writing some of the leading languages of West and Central Africa. The indigenous tongues will be far more effective instruments of conveying to the native mind the truths of the Gospel than any European language. The Rev. James Johnson—himself an adept in his native tongue, the Aku—in a speech delivered at a recent meeting of the Lagos branch of the British and Foreign Bible Society, made the sagacious remark that " as the African Church failed once in North Africa in days gone by, so it will fail again, unless we read the Bible in our own native tongue." [84]

We need hardly mention that one of the most pernicious elements in the demoralisation of the coast tribes is ardent spirits. It is a very fortunate circumstance for Africa that the Mohammedans of the interior present so formidable and impenetrable a barrier to the desolating flood which, but for them, would sweep across the continent. The abstemiousness of Islam is one of its good qualities which we should like Africans to retain, whatever may be the future fortunes of that faith on this continent. The Negro race, in their debilitating climate, do not possess the hardihood of the North American Indian or of the New Zealander; and, under the influence of that apparently inseparable concomitant of European civilisation, they would, in a much shorter time than it has taken the last-named nations, reach the deplorable distinction of being "civilised off the face of the earth." And Mr. Galton, by a much easier process than he proposed, would have an opportunity of introducing his "hardy and prolific Chinese" *protégés* to take the place of the "lazy, palavering savages," who, according to that accomplished traveller, now "cumber the ground" of a whole continent.[85]

And we cannot help thinking that it would be a step in advance in the intercourse of European Governments with the Pagan tribes along the coast if their agents were discouraged in the injudicious practice of giving ardents spirits as presents to the chiefs—a practice inaugurated by Europeans in the days of the slave trade. The correspondent of the *Daily News* refers to the practice, as he saw it at Cape Coast in 1873, as follows:—

At the end of the speech (Sir Garnet Wolseley's) it was announced by the interpreter that the "usual present" would be made to the kings. This present consisted of a certain quantity of gin, which, according to immemorial usage, appears, on these occasions, to have been issued to the chiefs. It would clearly not have been possible to have broken through the rule at that moment; but as meeting after meeting subsequently took place, at which the chiefs begged for more gin, one began to doubt the advantages of the system.[86]

---

[84] Reported in the *African Times*, January 1, 1876.
[85] The *Times*, June 5, 1873.
[86] *Ashantee War*, by the *Daily News* Special Correspondent: p. 52.

Christian Missions in West Africa.

Commodore Wilmot states in an official despatch that, during his visit to Dahomey, he distributed rum to the people in the way of "dash."[87]

We may remark, in conclusion, that, in view of the great work to be done in Africa, and the innumerable hindrances thereto, it will be seen that a profound conviction of the exclusive truth of the Gospel and an earnest zeal for the conversion of souls—though necessary and indispensable—are not the only qualifications needed by the missionary. The Christian missionaries in Africa should not only be well trained, highly educated, and large-minded men, but they should be men of imagination, logical power, and philosophic spirit, understanding how to set most effectively to work in clearing away what is really evil, in order to lay a durable foundation and erect a permanent superstructure of good. They should be men who understand that it is useless to pour new wine into old bottles, and who will be content to prepare the soil by the painful and judicious husbandry of years, if not of generations.

The following weighty words of Dean Stanley are suggestive and reassuring for the future of missionary work:—

> Above all, it is now beginning to be felt that education is in itself a powerful, almost indispensable, engine, for the introduction of the Gospel. From time to time the truth has been recognised that Christianity depends for its due effect on the condition of those who receive it. It was recognised by Gregory the Great, when he warned the hasty missionary who first planted it amongst our Saxon forefathers, that we move by steps, not leaps. It was recognised by Innocent III, when he warned the first evangelisers of Prussia that they must put new wine into new bottles. It was recognised by the Moravians in their simple phrase that they must teach their converts to count the number *Three* before they taught them the doctrine of the Trinity.[88]

---

[87] *British and Foreign State Papers*, 1863–1864, p. 825.
[88] Sermon on the 'Prospect of Christian Missions.'

THE
Aims and Methods of a Liberal Education for Africans.

A COLLEGE in West Africa, for the education of African youth by African instructors, under a Christian government conducted by Negroes, is something so unique in the history of Christian civilisation, that wherever, in the civilised world, the existence of such an institution is heard of, there will be curiosity as to its character, its work, and its prospects. A college suited, in all respects, to the exigencies of this nation and to the needs of the race cannot come into existence all at once. It must be the result of years of experience, of trial, of experiment.

Every thinking man will allow that all we have been doing in this country so far, whether in church, in state, or in school—our forms of religion, our politics, our literature, such as it is—is only temporary and transitional. When we advance further into Africa, and become one with the great tribes on the continent, these things will take the form which the genius of the race shall prescribe.

The civilisation of that vast population, untouched by foreign influence, not yet affected by European habits, is not to be organised according to foreign patterns, but will organise itself according to the nature of the people and the country. Nothing that we are doing now can be absolute or permanent, because nothing is normal or regular. Everything is provisional or tentative.

The College is only a machine, an instrument to assist in carrying forward our regular work—devised not only for intellectual ends,

Liberal Education for Africans.

but for social purposes, for religious duty, for patriotic aims, for racial development; and when as an instrument, as a means, it fails, for any reason whatever, to fulfil its legitimate functions, it is the duty of the country, as well as the interest of the country, to see that it is stimulated into healthful activity; or, if this is impossible, to see that it is set aside as a pernicious obstruction. We cannot afford to waste time in dealing with insoluble problems under impossible conditions. When the College was first founded, according to the generous conception of our friends abroad, they probably supposed that they were founding an institution which was to be at once complete in its appointments and to go on working regularly and effectively as colleges usually do in countries where people have come to understand, from years of experience and trial, their intellectual, social, and political needs, and the methods for supplying those needs. In their efforts to assist us to become sharers in the advantages of their civilisation, they have aimed at establishing institutions *a priori* for our development. That is, they have, by a course of reasoning natural to them, concluded that certain methods and agencies which have been successful among themselves must be successful among Africans. They have, on general considerations, come to certain conclusions as to what ought to apply to us. They have not, perhaps, sufficiently borne in mind that a college in a new country and among an inexperienced people must be, at least in the earlier periods of its existence, different from a college in an old country and among a people who understand themselves and their work. But, from the little experience we have had on this side of the water, we have learned enough to know that no *a priori* arrangements can be successfully employed in the promotion of our progress. We are arriving at the principles necessary for our guidance, through experience, through difficulties, through failures. The process is slow and sometimes discouraging, but, after a while, we shall reach the methods of growth that are adapted to our wants. The work of a college like ours, and among a people like our people, must be at first *generative*. It must create a sentiment favourable to its existence. It must generate the intellectual and moral state in the community which will give it not only a congenial atmosphere in which to thrive, but food and nutriment for its enlargement and growth; and out of this will naturally come the material conditions of its success.

Liberia College has gone through one stage of experience. We are, to-day, at the threshold of another. It has, to a great extent, created a public sentiment in its favour; but it has not yet done its generative work. It is now proposed to take a new departure and, by a system of instruction more suited to the necessities of the country and the race—that is to say, more suited to the development of the individuality and manhood of the African—to bring the institution more within the scope of the co-operation and enthusiasm of the people. It is proposed also, as soon as we can command the necessary means, to remove the College operations to an interior site, where health of body, the indispensable condition of health of mind, can be secured; where the students may devote a portion of their time to manual labour in the cultivation of the fertile lands which will be accessible, and thus assist in procuring from the soil the means for meeting a large part of the necessary expenses; and where access to the institution will be convenient to the aborigines. The work immediately before us, then, is one of reconstruction, and the usual difficulties which attend reconstruction, of any sort, beset our first step. The people generally are not yet prepared to understand their own interest in the great work to be done for themselves and their children, and the part they should take in it; and we shall be obliged to work for some time to come, not only without the popular sympathy which we think our due, but with utterly inadequate resources.

This is inevitable in the present condition of our progress. All we can hope is that the work will go on, hampered though it may be, until, in spite of misappreciation and disparagement, there can be raised up a class of minds who will give a healthy tone to society, and exert an influence widespread enough to bring to the institution that indigenous sympathy and support without which it cannot thrive. It is our hope and expectation that there will rise up men, aided by instruction and culture in this College, imbued with public spirit, who will know how to live and work and

Liberal Education for Africans.

prosper in this country, how to use all favouring outward conditions, how to triumph by intelligence, by tact, by industry, by perseverance, over the indifference of their own people, and how to overcome the scorn and opposition of the enemies of the race—men who will be determined to make this nation honourable among the nations of the earth.

We have in our curriculum, adopted some years ago, a course of study corresponding, to some extent, to that pursued in European and American colleges. To this we shall adhere as nearly as possible; but experience has already suggested, and will, no doubt, from time to time suggest, such modifications as are required by our peculiar circumstances.

The object of all education is to secure growth and efficiency, to make a man all that his natural gifts will allow him to become ; to produce self-respect, a proper appreciation of our own powers and of the powers of other people; to beget a fitness for one's sphere of life and action, and an ability to discharge the duties it imposes. Now, if we take these qualities as the true outcome of a correct education, then every one who is acquainted with the facts must admit that, as a rule, in the entire civilised world, the Negro, notwithstanding his two hundred years' residence with Christian and civilised races, has nowhere received anything like a correct education. We find him everywhere—in the United States, in the West Indies, in South America—largely unable to cope with the responsibilities which devolve upon him. Not only is he not sought after for any position of influence in the political movements of those countries, but he is even denied admission to ecclesiastical appointments of importance.

The Rev. Henry Venn, late Secretary of the Church Missionary Society, writing in 1867 to the Bishop of Kingston, Jamaica, of the Negro of that island, says :—

> There can be no doubt in the minds of those who have watched the progress of modern missions that a chief cause of the failure of the Jamaica Mission has been the *deficiency of Negro teachers for the Negro race.* [1]

---

[1] *Memoirs of Rev. Henry Venn, B.D.*, p. 215.

Christianity, Islam and the Negro Race.

With regard to the same island, Bishop Courtenay, in an address before the American Episcopal Convention in 1874, said :—

> We have not, as yet, in Jamaica, one priest of purely African race. At the present moment no Negro in holy orders could command that respect in Jamaica which a white man could command.[2]

Bishop Mitchinson, of Barbadoes, at the Pan-Anglican Council in London, in 1878, said with regard to his diocese :—

> Experience in my diocese has taught me to be mistrustful of intellectual gifts in the coloured race, for they do not seem generally to connote sterling work and fitness for the Christian ministry. . . . I do not think the time has come, or is even near, when the ranks of the clergy will be largely recruited in the West Indies by the Negro race.[3]

But this testimony is borne not only by white people, who might be supposed to be influenced by prejudice; it is the experience also of all thinking Negroes who set themselves earnestly to consider the work and disqualifications of the Negro in civilised lands. All along this coast, in the civilised settlements, there is a dissatisfaction with the results, so far, of the training of native Africans in Europe and America, and even with their training on the coast under European teachers.

The *West African Reporter*, of Sierra Leone, complains as follows :—

> We find our children, as a result of their foreign culture (we do not say, *in spite* of their foreign culture, but as a *result* of their foreign culture), aimless and purposeless for the race—crammed with European formulas of thought and expression so as to astonish their bewildered relatives. Their friends wonder at the words of their mouth; but they wonder at other things besides their words. They are the Polyphemus of civilisation, huge but sightless—*cui lumen ademptum*.

This paragraph has been quoted in several American periodicals. *The American Missionary*, the organ of the American Missionary Association, in commenting, adds: "To some extent, the same holds true of Negroes from the South, educated in the North, for work in their old homes." *The Foreign Missionary*, organ of the

---

[2] *The Church Journal*; New York, October 29, 1878.
[3] *The Guardian*, July 3, 1878.

Liberal Education for Africans.

Presbyterian Board of Foreign Missions, referring to the same paragraph, says:—

> We would further add, that Negroes educated anywhere out of Africa labour under certain disadvantages in becoming missionaries to the Heathen of their own race. As *foreigners*, with foreign habits, they fail to exert the influence wielded by Anglo-Saxons. We cannot hand over the evangelisation of Africa to the coloured race, except so fast and so far as they can be trained, like Bishop Crowther's men, on the soil.

To a certain extent—perhaps to a very important extent—Negroes trained on the soil of Africa have the advantage of those trained in foreign countries; but in all, as a rule, the intellectual and moral results, thus far, have been far from satisfactory. There are many men of book-learning, but few, very few, of any *capability* —even few who have that amount, or that sort, of culture, which produces self-respect, confidence in one's self, and efficiency in work. Now, why is this? The evil, it is considered, lies in the system and method of European training to which Negroes are, everywhere in Christian lands, subjected, and which everywhere affects them unfavourably. Of a different race, different susceptibility, different bent of character from that of the European, they have been trained under influences in many respects adapted only to the Caucasian race. Nearly all the books they read, the very instruments of their culture, have been such as to force them from the groove which is natural to them, where they would be strong and effective, without furnishing them with any avenue through which they may move naturally and free from obstruction. Christian and so-called civilised Negroes live, for the most part in foreign countries, where they are only passive spectators of the deeds of a foreign race; and where, with other impressions which they receive from without, an element of doubt as to their own capacity and their own destiny is fastened upon them, and inheres in their intellectual and social constitution. They deprecate their own individuality, and would escape from it if they could. And in countries like this, where they are free from the hampering surroundings of an alien race, they still read and study the books of foreigners, and form their idea of everything that man may do, or ought to do, according to the standard held up in those teachings. Hence, without the physical or mental aptitude for the enterprises which they are taught to admire and revere, they attempt to copy and imitate them, and share the fate of all copyists and imitators. Bound to move on a lower level, they acquire and retain a practical inferiority, transcribing, very often, the faults rather than the virtues of their models.

Besides this result of involuntary impressions, they often receive direct teachings which are not only incompatible with, but destructive of, their self-respect.

In all English-speaking countries the mind of the intelligent Negro child revolts against the descriptions given in elementary books—geographies, travels, histories—of the Negro; but though he experiences an instinctive revulsion from these caricatures and misrepresentations, he is obliged to continue, as he grows in years, to study such pernicious teachings. After leaving school he finds the same things in newspapers, in reviews, in novels, in *quasi* scientific works; and after a while—*sæpe cadendo*—they begin to seem to him the proper things to say and to feel about his race, and he accepts what, at first, his fresh and unbiassed feelings naturally and indignantly repelled. Such is the effect of repetition.

Having embraced, or at least assented, to these errors and falsehoods about himself, he concludes that his only hope of rising in the scale of respectable manhood is to strive after whatever is most unlike himself and most alien to his peculiar tastes. And whatever his literary attainments or acquired ability, he fancies that he must grind at the mill which is provided for him, putting in the material furnished to his hands, bringing no contribution from his own field; and of course nothing comes out but what is put in. Thus he can never bring any real assistance to the European. He can never attain to that essence of progress which Mr. Herbert Spencer describes as *difference*; and therefore, he never acquires the self-respect or self-reliance of an independent contributor. He is not an independent help, only a subordinate help; so that the European feels that he owes him no debt, and moves on in contemptuous indifference of the Negro, teaching him to contemn himself.

Those who have lived in civilised communities, where there are

Liberal Education for Africans.

different races, know the disparaging views which are entertained of the blacks by their neighbours—and often, alas! by themselves. The standard of all physical and intellectual excellencies in the present civilisation being the white complexion, whatever deviates from that favoured colour is proportionally depreciated, until the black which is the opposite, becomes not only the most unpopular but the most unprofitable colour. Black men, and especially black women, in such communities, experience the greatest imaginable inconvenience. They never feel at home. In the depth of their being they always feel themselves strangers in the land of their exile, and the only escape from this feeling is to escape from themselves. And this feeling of self-depreciation is not diminished, as I have intimated above, by the books they read. Women, especially, are fond of reading novels and light literature; and it is in these writings that flippant and eulogistic reference is constantly made to the superior physical and mental characteristics of the Caucasian race, which, by contrast, suggests the inferiority of other races—especially of that race which is furthest removed from it in appearance.

It is painful in America to see the efforts which are made by Negroes to secure outward conformity to the appearance of the dominant race.

This is by no means surprising; but what is surprising is that, under the circumstances, any Negro has retained a particle of self-respect. Now in Africa, where the colour of the majority is black, the fashion in personal matters is naturally suggested by the personal characteristics of the race, and we are free from the necessity of submitting to the use of "incongruous feathers awkwardly stuck on." Still, we are held in bondage by our indiscriminate and injudicious use of a foreign literature; and we strive to advance by the methods of a foreign race. In this effort we struggle with the odds against us. We fight at the disadvantage which David would have experienced in Saul's armour. The African must advance by methods of his own. He must possess a power distinct from that of the European. It has been proved that he knows how to take advantage of European culture, and that he can be benefited by it. This proof was perhaps necessary, but it is not sufficient. We must show that we are able to go alone, to carve out our own way. We must not be satisfied that, in this nation, European influence shapes our polity, makes our laws, rules in our tribunals, and impregnates our social atmosphere. We must not suppose that the Anglo-Saxon methods are final, that there is nothing for us to find out for our own guidance, and that we have nothing to teach the world. There is inspiration for us also. We must study our brethren in the interior, who know better than we do the laws of growth for the race. We see among them the rudiments of that which, with fair play and opportunity, will develop into important and effective agencies for our work. We look too much to foreigners, and are dazzled almost to blindness by their exploits—so as to fancy that they have exhausted the possibilities of humanity. In our estimation they, like Longfellow's Iagoo, have done and can do everything better than anybody else:—

> Never heard he an adventure
> But himself had made a greater;
> Never any deed of daring,
> But himself had done a bolder;
> Never any marvellous story
> But himself could tell a stranger.
> No one ever shot an arrow
> Half so far and high as he had;
> Ever caught so many fishes,
> Ever killed so many reindeer,
> Ever trapped so many beaver.
> None could run so fast as he could;
> None could dive so deep as he could;
> None could swim so far as he could:
> None had made so many journeys;
> None had seen so many wonders,
> As this wonderful Iagoo.

But there are possibilities before us not yet dreamed of by the Iagoos of civilisation. Dr. Alexander Winchell, Professor in one of the American universities—who has lately written a book, in the name of Science, in which he reproduces all the old slanders against the Negro, and writes of the African at home as if Livingstone,

Liberal Education for Africans.

Barth, Stanley and Cameron had never written—mentions it, as one of the evidences of Negro inferiority, that in "Liberia he is indifferent to the benefits of civilisation."[4] I stand here to-day to justify and commend the Negro of Liberia—and of everywhere else in Africa—for rejecting with scorn, "always and every time," the "benefits" of a civilisation whose theories are to degrade him in the scale of humanity, and of which such sciolists as Dr. Winchell are the exponents and representative elements. We recommend all Africans to treat such "benefits" with even more decided "indifference" than that with which the guide in Dante treated the despicable herd—

> Non ragionam di lor, ma guarda, e passa.

Those of us who have travelled in foreign countries, and who witness the general results of European influence along this coast, have many reasons for misgivings and reserves and anxieties about European civilisation for this country. Things which have been of great advantage to Europe may work ruin to us; and there is often such a striking resemblance, or such a close connection between the hurtful and the beneficial, that we are not always able to discriminate. I have heard of a native in one of the settlements on the coast who, having grown up in the use of the simple but efficient remedies of the country doctors, and having prospered in business, conceived the idea that he must avail himself of the medicines he saw used by the European traders. Suffering from sleeplessness he was advised to take Dover's powders, but, in his inexperience, took instead an overdose of morphine, and next morning he was a corpse. So we have reason to apprehend that in our indiscriminate appropriations of European agencies, or methods in our political, educational, and social life, we are often imbibing overdoses of morphine, when we fancy we are only taking Dover's powders!

And it is for this reason, while we are anxious for immigration from America and desirous that the immigrants shall push as fast as possible into the interior, that we look with anxiety and concern at the difficulties and troubles which must arise from their misconception of the work to be done in this country. I apprehend that

---

[4] *Pre-Adamite Man*, p. 265.

in their progress towards the interior there will be friction, irritations and conflicts; and our brethren, in certain portions of the United States, are, at this moment, witnessing a state of things among their superiors which they will naturally want to reproduce in this country, and which, if reproduced here, will utterly extinguish the flickering light of the Lone Star, and close forever this open door of Christian civilisation into Africa.

Mr. Matthew Arnold reminds us[5] that when some one talked to Themistocles of an art of memory, he answered, "Teach me rather to forget." The full meaning of this aspiration must be realised in the life of the Christian Negro before he can become a full man, or a successful worker in his fatherland.

In the prosecution of the work of a college in America for the education of Negro youth, it seems to me, therefore, that the aim should be, to a great extent, to assist their power of forgetfulness—an achievement of extreme difficulty, I imagine, in that country where, from the very action of the surrounding atmosphere, "the interstices with which Nature has provided the human memory, through which many things once known pass into oblivion, are kept constantly closed."

In the prosecution of the work of a college for the training of youth in *this* country, the aim, it occurs to me, should be to study the causes of Negro inefficiency in civilised lands; and, so far as it has resulted from the training they have received, to endeavour to avoid what we conceive to be the sinister elements in that training.

In the curriculum of Liberia College, therefore, it will be our aim to increase the amount of purely disciplinary agencies, and to reduce to its minimum the amount of those distracting influences to which I have referred, as hindering the proper growth of the race.

The true principle of mental culture is perhaps this: to preserve an accurate balance between the studies which carry the mind out of itself, and those which recall it home again. When we receive

---

[5] Preface to Johnson's *Lives of the Poets.*

Liberal Education for Africans.

impressions from without we must bring from our own consciousness the idea that gives them shape; we must mould them by our own individuality. Now, in looking over the whole civilised world I see no place where this sort of culture for the Negro can be better secured than in Liberia—where he may, with less interruption from surrounding influences, find out his place and his work, develop his peculiar gifts and powers; and for the training of Negro youth upon the basis of their own idiosyncracy, with a sense of race-individuality, self-respect, and liberty, there is no institution so well adapted as Liberia College with its Negro faculty and Negro students.

We are often told of the advantages which students of the African race are enjoying in the institutions established for their training in America; but listen to the testimony of Dr. Winchell with regard to the position of the students in one of the best of them, namely, Fisk University, Nashville, Tennessee. He says:—

> I have sometimes, when visiting Fisk University at Nashville, looked with admiration at some magnificently formed heads which are there working, under all the discouragements of social repression, for knowledge, culture, and high respectability. My sympathies have been deeply moved at the evidences of their earnestness and conscious strength, coupled with a keen and crushing perception of the weight of the social ban which their race brings upon them. I will not refrain from expressing here the hope that such cases may receive every encouragement and mark of appreciation.[o]

This testimony, coming from one who is ostentatiously anti-Negro, is peculiarly striking; but one is amused at the *naïveté* exhibited in the expression of the "hope" recorded in the last sentence by a man who has assailed the Negro with every weapon of antipathy which could be drawn from his imagination, and is doing all in his power to swell the Negrophobic literature, and to intensify a public sentiment sufficiently hostile to that class of people.

It has always been to me, let me say in passing, a matter of surprise that there should be found white men who—in spite of this anti-Negro literature, with the Notts and Gliddons and Winchells and Bakers to instruct them, with the prophets of ill on every hand

---

[o] *Pre-Adamite Man*, p. 182 (note).

—are still willing and ready to give their means and their time and their labour for the promotion of the intellectual training of such a race. It is astonishing, not that so little money is spent on African education, but that any at all is spent by men who, from their childhood, have been imbibing from the books they read, and from their surroundings, sentiments of disparagement and distrust of the possibilities of the African race.

We may conclude, then, that there is no field so well adapted for the work of Negro training as Liberia; and it must be our aim to bring Liberia College up to the work to be done in this peculiar and interesting field. Now, what is the course to be adopted in the education of youth in this College?

I have endeavoured to give careful consideration to this important subject; and I propose now to sketch the outlines of a programme for the education of the students in Liberia College, and, I may venture to add, of the Negro youth everywhere in Africa who hope to take a leading part in the work of the race and of the country. I will premise that, generally, in the teaching of our youth, far more is made of the importance of imparting information than of training the mind. Their minds are too much taken possession of by mere information drawn from European sources.

Lord Bacon says that "reading makes a full man;" but the indiscriminate reading by the Negro of European literature has made him, in many instances, too full, or has rather destroyed his balance. "The value of a cargo," says Huxley, does not compensate for a ship being out of trim;" and the amount of knowledge that a man has does not secure his usefulness if he has so taken it in that he is lop-sided.

We shall devote attention principally, both for mental discipline and information, to the earlier epochs of the world's history. It is decided that there are five or six leading epochs in the history of civilisation. I am following Mr. Frederic Harrison's classification. First, there was the great permanent, stationary system of human society, held together by a religious belief, or by social custom growing out of that belief. This has been called the Theocratic state of society. The type of that phase of civilisation was the old

Liberal Education for Africans.

Eastern empires. The second great type was the Greek Age of intellectual activity and civic freedom. Next came the Roman type of civilisation, an age of empire, of conquest, of consolidation of nations, of law and government. The fourth great system was the phase of civilisation which prevailed from the fall of the Roman Empire until comparatively modern times, and was called the Mediæval Age, when the Church and Feudalism existed side by side. The fifth page of history was that which began with the breaking-up of the power of the Church on the one side, and of feudalism on the other—the foundation of modern history, or the Modern Age. That system has continued down to the present; but, if subdivided, it would form the sixth type, which is the Age since the French Revolution—the Age of social and popular development, of modern science and industry.

We shall permit our curriculum the unrestricted study of the first four epochs, but especially the second, third and fourth, from which the present civilisation of Western Europe is mainly derived. There has been no period of history more full of suggestive energy, both physical and intellectual, than those epochs. Modern Europe boasts of its period of intellectual activity, but none can equal, for life and freshness, the Greek and Roman prime. No modern writers will ever influence the destiny of the race to the same extent that the Greeks and Romans have done.

We can afford to exclude, then, as subjects of study, at least in the earlier college years, the events of the fifth and sixth epochs, and the works which, in large numbers, have been written during those epochs. I know that during these periods some of the greatest works of human genius have been composed. I know that Shakespeare and Milton, Gibbon and Macaulay, Hallam and Lecky, Froude, Stubbs and Green, belong to these periods. It is not in my power, even if I had the will, to disparage the works of these masters; but what I wish to say is, that these are not the works on which the mind of the youthful African should be trained. It was during the sixth period that the transatlantic slave-trade arose, and those theories—theological, social, and political—were invented for the degradation and proscription of the Negro. This epoch continues to this day, and has an abundant literature and a prolific authorship. It has produced that whole tribe of declamatory Negrophobists, whose views, in spite of their emptiness and impertinence, are having their effect upon the ephemeral literature of the day—a literature which is shaping the life of the Negro in Christian lands. His whole theory of life, quite contrary to what his nature intends, is being influenced, consciously and unconsciously, by the general conceptions of his race entertained by the manufacturers of this literature—a great portion of which, made for to-day, will not survive the next generation.

I admit that in this period there have been able defences of the race written, but they have all been in the patronising or apologetic tone—in the spirit of that good-natured man who assured the world that—

> Fleecy looks and dark complexion
> Cannot forfeit Nature's claim.

Poor Phillis Wheatly, a native African educated in America, in her attempts at poetry is made to say, in what her biographer calls "spirited lines"—

> Remember, Christian, Negroes, black as Cain,
> May be refined, and join the angelic train.

The arguments of Wilberforce, the eloquence of Wendell Phillips, the pathos of *Uncle Tom's Cabin*, are all in the same strain—that Negroes have souls to save just as white men have, and that the strength of Nature's claim is not impaired by their complexion and hair. We surely cannot indulge, with the same feeling of exultation that the Englishman or American experiences, in the proud boast that—

> We speak the language Shakespeare spoke,
> The faith and morals hold which Milton held;

for that "language," in some of its finest utterances, patronises and apologises for us, and that "faith" has been hitherto powerless to save us from proscription and insult.

It is true that culture is one, and the general effects of true culture are the same; but the native capacities of mankind differ, and their word and destiny differ, so that the road by which one

Liberal Education for Africans.

man may attain to the highest efficiency, is not that which would conduce to the success of another. The special road which has led to the success and elevation of the Anglo-Saxon is not that which would lead to the success and elevation of the Negro, though we shall resort to the same means of general culture which has enabled the Anglo-Saxon to find out for himself the way in which he ought to go.

The instruments of culture which we shall employ in the College will be chiefly the Classics and Mathematics. By Classics I mean the Greek and Latin languages and their literature. In those languages there are not, as far as I know, a sentence, a word, or a syllable disparaging to the Negro. He may get nourishment from them without taking in any race-poison. They will perform no sinister work upon his consciousness, and give no unholy bias to his inclinations.[7]

---

[7] I have noticed a few lines in a poem, by some, attributed to Virgil, describing a Negress of the lower class, which are made to do duty on all occasions when the modern traducers of the Negro would draw countenance for their theories from the classical writers; but similar descriptions of the lower European races abound in their own literature. The lines are the following, used by Nott and Gliddon, and recently quoted by Dr. Winchell:—

> Interdum clamat Cybalen; erat unica custos;
> Afra genus, tota patriam testanto figura;
> Torta comam, labroque tumens, et fusca colorem,
> Pectore lata, jacens mammis, compressior alvo,
> Cruribus exilis, spatiosa prodiga planta;
> Continuis rimis calcanea scissa rigebant.

[Meanwhile he calls Cybale. She was his only (house) keeper. African by race, her whole figure attesting her fatherland; with crisped hair, swelling lip, and dark complexion; broad in chest, with pendant dugs, and very contracted abdomen; with spindle shanks and broad enormous feet; her lacerated heels were rigid with continuous cracks.]

But hear how Homer, Virgil's superior and model, sings the praises of the Negro Eurybates, who signalised himself at the siege of Troy:—

> A reverend herald in his train I knew,
> Of visage solemn, sad, but *sable* hue.
> Short *woolly curls* o'er-fleeced his bending head,
> O'er which a promontory shoulder spread
> Eurybates, in whose large soul alone,
> Ulysses viewed an image of his own.

Christianity, Islam and the Negro Race.

The present civilisation of Europe is greatly indebted to the influence of the rich inheritance left by the civilisations of Greece and Rome. It is impossible to imagine what would be the condition of Europe but for the influence of the so-called dead languages and the treasures they contain.

Had the Western World been left to itself in Chinese isolation, says Professor Huxley, there is no saying how long that state of things might have endured; but happily it was not left to itself. Even earlier than the 18th century the development of Moorish civilisation in Spain, and the movement of the Crusades, had introduced the leaven which from that day to this has never ceased to work. At first, through the intermediation of Arabic translations, afterwards by the study of the originals, the Western nations of Europe became acquainted with the writings of the ancient philosophers and poets, and, in time, with the whole of the vast literature of antiquity. Whatever there was of high intellectual aspiration or dominant capacity, in Italy, France, Germany and England, spent itself for centuries in taking possession of the rich inheritance left by the dead civilisations of Greece and Rome. Marvellously aided by the invention of printing, classical learning spread and flourished. Those who possessed it prided themselves on having attained the highest culture then within the reach of mankind.[8]

Passing over, then, for a certain time, the current literature of Western Europe, which is, after all, derived and secondary, we will resort to the fountain head; and in the study of the great masters, in the languages in which they wrote, we shall get the required mental discipline without unfavourably affecting our sense of race individuality or our own self-respect. There is nothing that we need to know for the work of building up this country, in its moral, political and religious character, which we may not learn from the ancients. There is nothing in the domain of literature, philosophy, or religion for which we need be dependent upon the moderns. Law and philosophy we may get from the Romans and the Greeks, religion from the Hebrews.

Even Europeans, advanced as they are, are every day devoting more and more attention to the Classics. A very recent writer remarks:—

We have not done with the Hellenes yet, in spite of all the labour spent and all the books written on them, and their literature bequeathed to us It has,

---

[8] Inaugural Address at the opening of Mason Science College, Birmingham, September, 1880.

Liberal Education for Africans.

indeed, been said that we know nearly as much about the Greeks and Romans as we shall ever know; but this can only be true of the mass of facts, to which, without some new discoveries, we are not likely to add greatly. It is not in the least true in regard to the significance of Hellenic history and literature. Beyond and above the various interpretations placed by different ages upon the great writers of Greece, lies the meaning which longer experience and more improved methods of criticism, and the test of time declare, to be the true one. From this point of view, much remains, and will long remain, to be done, whether we look to the work of the scholar or to the influence of Hellenic thought on civilisation. We have not yet found all the scattered limbs of Truth; it may be that we are only commencing the search. . . . The *Gorgias* of Plato and the *Ethics* of Aristotle are more valuable than modern books on the same subjects, for the simple reason that they are nearer the beginning. They have a greater freshness, and appeal more directly to the growing mind."[9]

If we turn to Rome, we find equal instruction in all the elements of a correct and prosperous nationality. "The education of the world in the principles of a sound jurisprudence," says Dean Merivale, "was the most wonderful work of the Roman Conquerors. It was complete, it was universal; and in permanence it has far outlasted—at least, in its distinct results—the duration of the empire itself."

"As supernatural wisdom came from God through the mouths of the prophets," said St. Augustine, "so also natural wisdom, social justice, came from the same God through the mouth of the Roman legislators."[10] [*Leges Romanorum divinitus per ora principum emanarunt.*]

Roman civilisation produced not only *great* men but *good* men, of high views of human life and human responsibility, with a high standard of what men ought to aim at, with a high belief of what they ought to do. And it not only produced individuals, it produced a strong and permanent force of sentiment it produced a character shared very unequally among the people, but powerful enough to determine the course of history. . . . Certainly, in no people which the world has ever seen has the sense of public duty been keener or stronger than in Rome, or has lived on with unimpaired vitality through great changes for a longer time. . . . Its early legends dwelt upon the strange and terrible sacrifices which supreme loyalty to the commonwealth had enacted and obtained without a murmur from her sons. They told of a founder of Roman freedom dooming his two young sons to the axe for having tampered with a conspiracy against the state; of great men resigning office because they bore a

---

[9] *Hellenica;* edited by Evelyn Abbott, M.A., LL.D.—London, 1880.

[10] Quoted by Père Hyacinthe in the *Nineteenth Century*, February, 1880.

dangerous name, or pulling down their own houses because too great for private citizens; of soldiers, to whose death fate had bound victory, solemnly devoting themselves to die, or leaping into the gulf which would only close on a living victim; of a great family purchasing peace in civil troubles by leaving the city and turning their energy into a foreign war in which they perished; of the captive general who advised his countrymen to send him back to certain torture and death, rather than grant the terms he was commissioned to propose as the price of his release. Whatever we may think of these stories, they show what was in the mind of those who told and repeated them; and they continued to be the accredited types and models of Roman conduct throughout Roman history.[11]

It is our purpose to cultivate the study of the languages of the two great peoples to whom I have referred as among the most effective instruments of intellectual discipline.

A great deal of misapprehension prevails in the popular mind as to the utility, in a liberal education of the so-called dead languages, and many fancy that the time devoted to their study is time lost; but let it be understood that their study is not pursued merely for the information they impart. If information were all, it would be far more useful to learn the French and German, or any other of the modern languages, during the time devoted to Greek and Latin; but what *is* gained by the study of the ancient languages is that strengthening and disciplining of the mind which enables the student in after life to lay hold of, and, with comparatively little difficulty, to master, any business to which he may turn his attention. A recent scholarly and experienced writer says on this subject:—

Even if it were conceivable that a youth should entirely forget all the facts, pictures, and ideas he had learned from the Classics, together with all the rules of the Greek and Latin grammar, his mind would still, as an instrument, be superior to that of every one who has not passed through the same training. Nay, even the youth who was always last in his class, and who dozed out his nine years on the benches of a classical school, only half attentive to his teacher, and not doing half his tasks—even he will surpass, in mental mobility, the most deligent scholar who has been taught only the modern languages and a quantity of special and disconnected knowledge. One of the first bankers in a foreign capital, lately told me that, in the course of a year he had given some thirty clerks, who had been educated expressly for commerce in commercial schools, a trial in his offices, and was not able to make use of a single one of them; while those who came from the German schools (and had studied the

---

[11] *The Gifts of Civilisation;* by Dean Church.—New edition. London, 1880.

Liberal Education for Africans.

Classics), although they knew nothing whatever of business matters to begin with, soon made themselves perfect masters of them.[12]

The study of the Classics also lays the foundation for the successful pursuit of scientific knowledge. It so stimulates the mind that it arouses the student's interest in all problems of science. It is a matter of history that the scientific study of Nature followed immediately after the revival of classical learning.

But we shall also study Mathematics. These, as instruments of culture, are everywhere applicable. A course of Algebra, Geometry, and Higher Mathematics must accompany, step by step, classical studies. Neither of these means of discipline can be omitted without loss. The qualities which make a man succeed in mastering the Classics and Mathematics are also those which qualify him for the practical work of life. Care, industry, judgment, tact, are the elements of success anywhere and everywhere. The training and discipline, the patience and endurance, to which *each* man must submit in order to success; the resolution which relaxes no effort, but fights the hardest when difficulties are to be surmounted —these are qualities which boys go to school to cultivate, and these they acquire, in a greater or less degree, by a successful study of Classics and Mathematics. The boy who shirks these studies, or retires from his class because he is unwilling to contend with the difficulties they involve, lacks those qualities which make a successful and influential character.

It will be our aim to introduce into our curriculum also the Arabic, and some of the principal native languages—by means of which we may have intelligent intercourse with the millions accessible to us in the interior, and learn more of our own country. We have young men who are experts in the geography and customs of foreign countries; who can tell all about the proceedings of foreign statesmen in countries thousands of miles away; can talk glibly of London, Berlin, Paris and Washington; know all about Gladstone, Bismarck, Gambetta, and Hayes; but who knows any-

---

[12] Karl Hillebrand in *Contemporary Review*, August, 1880.

thing about Musahdu, Medina, Kankan, or Sego—only a few hundred miles from us? Who can tell anything of the policy or doings of Fanfi-doreh, Ibrahima Sissi, or Fahqueh-queh, or Simoro of Boporu—only a few steps from us? These are hardly known. Now as Negroes, allied in blood and race to these people, this is disgraceful; and as a nation, if we intend to grow and prosper in this country, it is impolitic, it is short-sighted, it is unpatriotic; but it has required time for us to grow up to these ideas, to understand our position in this country. In order to accelerate our future progress, and to give to the advance we make the element of permanence, it will be our aim in the College to produce men of ability. Ability or capability is the power to use with effect the instruments in our hands. The bad workman complains of his tools; but, even when he is satisfied with the excellence of his tools, he cannot produce the results which an able workman will produce, even with indifferent tools.

If a man has the learning of Solomon, but, for some reason, either in himself or his surroundings, cannot bring his learning into useful application, that man is lacking in ability. Now what we desire to do is to produce ability in our youth; and whenever we find a youth, however brilliant in his powers of acquisition, who lacks common sense, and who, in other respects, gives evidence of the absence of those qualities which enable a man to use his knowledge for the benefit of his country and his fellow-man, we shall advise him to give up books and betake himself to other walks of life. A man without common sense, without tact, as a mechanic or agriculturist or trader, can do far less harm to the public than the man without common sense who has had the opportunity of becoming, and has had the reputation of being, a scholar.

I trust that arrangements will be made by which girls of our country may be admitted to share in the advantages of this College. I cannot see why our sisters should not receive exactly the same general culture as we do. I think that the progress of the country will be more rapid and permanent when the girls receive the same general training as the boys; and our women,

Liberal Education for Africans.

besides being able to appreciate the intellectual labours of their husbands and brothers, will be able also to share in the pleasures of intellectual pursuits. We need not fear that they will be less graceful, less natural, or less womanly; but we may be sure that they will make wiser mothers, more appreciative wives, and more affectionate sisters.

In the religious work of the College, the Bible will be our text-book, the Bible without note or comment—especially as we propose to study the original language in which the New Testament was written; and we may find opportunity, in connection with the Arabic, to study the Old Testament. The teachings of Christianity are of universal application. "Other foundation can no man lay than that which is laid." The great truths of the Sermon on the Mount are as universally accepted as Euclid's anxioms. The meaning of the Good Samaritan is as certain as that of the forty-seventh proposition, and a great deal plainer.

Christianity is not only not a local religion, but it has adapted itself to the people wherever it has gone. No language or social existence has been any barrier to it; and I have often thought that in this country it will acquire wider power, deeper influence, and become instinct with a higher vitality than anywhere else.

When we look at the treatment which our own race and other so-called inferior races have received from Christian nations, we cannot but be struck with the amazing dissimilitude and disproportion between the original idea of Christianity, as expressed by Christ, and the practice of it by his professed followers.

The sword of the conqueror and the cries of the conquered have attended or preceded the introduction of this faith wherever carried by Europeans, and some of the most enlightened minds have sanctioned the subjugation of weaker races—the triumph of Might over Right—that the empire of civilisation might be extended; but these facts do not affect the essential principles of the religion. We must gather its doctrines not from the examples of some of its adherents but from the sacred records. But even as exemplified in human action, notwithstanding the drawbacks to which I have referred—

> It has so manifested its superiority, says Dr. Peabody, in beneficent action, to all the other working forces of the world combined, that the experimental evidence for it under this head is oppressive and unmanageable from its multiplicity and fulness. . . . It is in the exclusively Christian elements that the great workers of the last eighteen centuries have been of one mind and heart. No matter what their sphere of labour, wherever we see pre-eminent ability and success in a life-work worth performing, we find but the reproduction of the specifically Christian elements of St. Paul's energy, a spirit profoundly moved in grateful sympathy with a loving suffering Redeemer, a strong emotional recognition of human brotherhood, and a merging of self in the sense of a mission and a charge from God. . . . If you were to take away Christian work and workers from the world, and destroy the vestiges of what has been wrought in Christ's name, I doubt whether those who now reject or despise the Gospel would think the world any longer worth living in.[18]

Now this is the influence which is to work that great reformation in our land for which we hope. This is the influence which is to leaven the whole country and to become the principle of the new civilisation which we believe is to be developed on this continent. It has already produced important changes, notwithstanding its slow and irregular growth, notwithstanding the apparent scantiness and meagreness of its visible fruits; and it shall be the aim of this College to work in the spirit of the great Master who was manifested as an example of self-sacrifice to the highest truth and the highest good—that spirit which excluded none from his converse, which kept company with publicans and sinners that he might benefit them, which went anywhere and everywhere to seek and to save that which is lost. We will study to cultivate whatsoever things are true, whatsoever things are honest, whatsoever things are just, whatsoever things are pure, whatsoever things are lovely, whatsoever things are of good report. If there be any virtue, and if there be any praise, we will endeavour to think on these things.

Our fathers have borne testimony to the surrounding Heathen of

---

[18] *Christianity and Science*, by Andrew P. Peabody, D.D., LL.D.—New York, 1875.

Liberal Education for Africans.

the value and superiority of Christianity. They endeavoured to accomplish what they saw ought to be accomplished; and, according to the light within them, fought against wrong and asserted the right. Let us not dwell too much on the mistakes of the past. Let us be thankful for what of good has been done, and let us do better if we can. We, like our predecessors, are only frail and imperfect beings, feelers after truth. Others, let us hope, will come by-and-bye and do better than we—efface our errors and correct our mistakes, see truths clearly which we now see but dimly, and truths dimly which we do not see at all. The true ideal, the proper work of the race, will grow brighter and more distinct as we advance in culture.

Nor can we be assisted in our work by looking back and denouncing the deeds of the oppressors of our fathers, by perpetuating race antagonism. It is natural, perhaps, that we should at times feel indignation in view of past injustice, but continually dwelling upon it will not help us. It is neither edifying nor dignified to be forever declaiming about the wrongs of the race. Lord Beaconsfield once said in the House of Commons that Irish members were too much in the habit of clanking their chains on rising to speak. Such a habit, when it ceases to excite pity, begets contempt and ridicule. What we need is wider and deeper culture, more intimate intercourse with our interior brethren, more energetic advance to the healthy regions.

As those who have suffered affliction in a foreign land, we have no antecedents from which to gather inspiration.

All our traditions and experiences are connected with a foreign race. We have no poetry or philosophy but that of our taskmasters. The songs that live in our ears and are often on our lips are the songs which we heard sung by those who shouted while we groaned and lamented. They sang of their history, which was the history of our degradation. They recited their triumphs, which contained the record of our humiliation. To our great misfortune, we learned their prejudices and their passions, and thought we had their aspirations and their power. Now, if we are to make an independent nation—a strong nation—we must listen to the songs of our unsophisticated brethren as they sing of their history, as they tell of their traditions, of the wonderful and mysterious events of their tribal or national life, of the achievements of what we call their superstitions; we must lend a ready ear to the ditties of the Kroomen who pull our boats, of the Pesseh and Golah men, who till our farms; we must read the compositions, rude as we may think them, of the Mandingoes and the Veys. We shall in this way get back the strength of the race, like the giant of the ancients, who always gained strength, for his conflict with Hercules, whenever he touched his Mother Earth.

And this is why we want the College away from the seaboard—with its constant intercourse with foreign manners and low foreign ideas—that we may have free and uninterrupted intercourse with the intelligent among the tribes of the interior; that the students, even from the books to which they will be allowed access, may conveniently flee to the forests and fields of Manding and the Niger, and mingle with our brethren and gather fresh inspiration and fresh and living ideas.

It is the complaint of the intelligent Negro in America that the white people pay no attention to his suggestions or his writings; but this is only because he has nothing new to say—nothing that they have not said before him, and that they cannot say better than he can. Let us depend upon it, that the emotions and thoughts which are natural to us command the curiosity and respect of others far more than the showy display of any mere acquisitions which we have derived from them, and which they know depend more upon our memory than upon any real capacity. What we must follow is all that concerns our individual growth. Let us do our own work and we shall be strong and worthy of respect; try to do the work of others, and we shall be weak and contemptible. There is magnetism in original action, in self-trust, which others cannot resist. I think we mistake the meaning of the lines of the poet which are so often quoted—

> Lives of great men all remind us
> We can make our lives sublime,
> And, departing, leave behind us
> Footprints on the sands of time.

Liberal Education for Africans.

How shall we make our "lives sublime"? Not by imitating others, but by doing well our own part as they did theirs. We are to study the "footprints" that when we are "forlorn," or have been "shipwrecked," we may "take heart again;" not to put our own feet in the impressions previously made, for by so doing we should be compelled at times to lengthen, and at times to shorten our pace—sometimes to make the strides of Hiawatha, and sometimes to crawl—and thus not only cut a most ungainly figure, but accomplish nothing, either for ourselves or the world.

Whilst I read the poets, says Emerson, I think that nothing now can be said about morning and evening; but when I see the day break, I am not reminded of these Homeric or Shakespearian or Miltonic or Chaucerian pictures. No; but I am cheered by the moist, warm, glittering, budding melodious hour, that takes down the narrow walls of my soul, and extends its life and pulsation to the very horizon. *That* is morning—to cease for a bright hour to be a prisoner of the sickly body, and to become as large as Nature.

We have a great work before us, a work unique in the history of the world, which others who appreciate its vastness and importance, envy us the privilege of doing. The world is looking at this Republic to see whether "order and law, religion and morality, the rights of conscience, the rights of persons and the rights of property," may all be secured and preserved by a government administered entirely by Negroes.

Let us show ourselves equal to the task.

The time is past when we can be content with putting forth elaborate arguments to prove our equality with foreign races. Those who doubt our capacity are more likely to be convinced of their error by the exhibition, on our part, of those qualities of energy and enterprise which will enable us to occupy the extensive field before us for our own advantage and the advantage of humanity—for the purposes of civilisation, of science, of good government, and of progress generally—than by any mere abstract argument about the equality of races. The suspicions disparaging to us will be dissipated only by the exhibition of the indisputable realities of a lofty manhood as they may be illustrated in successful efforts to build up a nation, to wrest from Nature her secrets, to lead the van of progress in this country, and to regenerate a continent.

The Origin and Purpose of African Colonisation.

THERE is not a thinking being, whatever his religious belief, who does not recognise the fact that everything in the physical and moral world proceeds according to some plan or order; that some subtle law, call it by whatever name you please, underlies and regulates the movements of the stars in their courses and the sparrows in their flight. It is also the belief of all healthy minds that that law or influence is always tending towards the highest and best results; that its prerogative and design are to make darkness light, crooked things straight, and rough places smooth; or, in the misty phraseology of modern criticism, it is the "Eternal, not ourselves, that makes for righteousness"—that its fiats are irrevocable and their outcome inevitable. With this understanding, men are now constructing the science of History, the science of Language, the science of Religion, the science of Society, formulating dogmas to set aside dogma, and consoling themselves that they are moving to a higher level and solving the problems of the Ages.

Among the conclusions to which study and research are conducting philosophers, none is clearer than this—that each of the races of mankind has a specific character and a specific work. The science of Sociology is the science of Race.

In the midst of these discussions, Africa is forcing its claims for consideration upon the attention of the world, and science and philanthropy are bringing all their resources to bear upon its

Origin and Purpose of African Colonisation.

exploration and amelioration. There is hardly an important city in Europe where there is not an organisation formed for the purpose of dealing with some of the questions connected with this great continent.

There is "The International African Association," founded at Brussels in 1876, of which the King of the Belgians is the patron; "The Italian National Association for the Exploration and Civilisation of Africa;" the "Association Espanola para la Esploracion del Africa" (the King of Spain has taken great practical interest in this Society); "The German Society for the Exploration of Africa," founded in 1872 by the German Geographical Associations—it receives assistance from the Government; the "Afrikanische Gesellschaft," in Vienna, founded in 1876, also under royal patronage; "The Hungarian African Association," founded in 1877; "The National Swiss Committee for the Exploration of Central Africa." The French Government and the French Chamber of Commerce have made large grants of money to aid in African exploration. Then, there is an African Association at Rotterdam, besides the great Royal Geographical Society of England, which has a special fund for African researches, and has recently sent Thomson to explore the snow-covered mountains of Eastern Africa.

This anxiety to penetrate the mysteries of Africa, this readiness to turn from the subtleties of philosophy and the fascinations of science, in order the better to deal with the great physical fact of an unexplored continent, is not a new experience in the world. It is to be found among the ancients also. With a zealous curiosity, overcoming the promptings of the finer sentiments and the desire for military glory, Cæsar proposed to abandon his ambitious exploits for the privilege of gazing upon the source of the Nile.

The modern desire for more accurate knowledge of Africa is not a mere sentiment; it is the philanthropic impulse to lift up the millions of that continent to their proper position among the intellectual and moral forces of the world; but it is also the commercial desire to open that vast country to the enterprises of trade. Europe is overflowing with the material productions of its own genius. Important foreign markets, which formerly consumed these productions, are now closing against them. Africa seems to furnish the only large outlet, and the desire is to make the markets of the Soudan easily accessible to London, Manchester and Liverpool. The depressed factories of Lancashire are waiting to be inspired with new life and energy by the development of a new and inexhaustible trade with the millions of Central Africa; so that Africa, as frequently in the past, will have again to come to the rescue and contribute to the needs of Europe. Emergencies drove homeless wanderers to the shores of Libya :—

> Defessi Æneadae, quae proxima litora, cursu
> Contendunt potere, et Libyae vertuntur ad oras.

But the plans proposed by Europeans for opening up Africa, as far as they can be carried out by themselves, are felt to be inadequate. Many feel that commerce, science and philanthropy may establish stations and trace out thoroughfares, but they also feel that these agencies are helpless to cope fully with the thousand questions which arise in dealing with the people.

Among the agencies proposed for carrying on the work of civilisation in Africa, none has proved so effective as the American Colonisation enterprise. People who talk of the civilising and elevating influence of mere trade on that continent, do so because they are unacquainted with the facts. Nor can missionaries alone do this work. We do not object to trade, and we would give every possible encouragement to the noble efforts of missionaries. We would open the country everywhere to commercial intercourse. We would give everywhere hospitable access to traders. Place your trading factories at every prominent point along the coast, and even let them be planted on the banks of the rivers. Let them draw the rich products from remote districts. We say, also, send the missionary to every tribe and every village. Multiply throughout the country the evangelising agencies. Line the banks of the rivers with the preachers of righteousness—penetrate the jungles with those holy pioneers—crown the mountain-tops with your churches, and fill the valleys with your schools. No single agency is sufficient to cope with the multifarious needs of the

Origin and Purpose of African Colonisation.

mighty work. But the indispensable agency is the Colony. Groups of Christian and civilised settlers must, in every instance bring up the rear, if the results of your work are to be widespread, beneficial and enduring.

This was the leading idea that gave birth to the Society whose anniversary we have met to celebrate. To-day we have the Sixty-sixth Annual Report of the American Colonisation Society. This fact by itself would excite no feeling, and, perhaps, no remark; but when we consider that, although this is but the sixty-sixth year of its existence, it has been successful in founding a colony which has now been for thirty-five years an independent nation, acknowledged by all the Powers of the earth, we cannot but congratulate the organisation upon an achievement which, considering the circumstances, is unparalleled in the history of civilisation, and which must be taken as one of the most beautiful illustrations of the spirit and tendency of Christianity.

When the Society began its work, its programme was modest, and in the early declarations of its policy, it was found expedient to emphasise the simplicity of its pretensions and the singleness of its purpose. In describing its objects, one of the most eloquent of its early supporters, Dr. Leonard Bacon, said: " The Colonisation Society is not a missionary society, nor a society for the suppression of the slave trade, nor a society for the improvement of the blacks, nor a society for the abolition of slavery: it is simply a society for the establishment of a colony on the coast of Africa."

But, in pursuance of its legitimate objects, its labours have been fruitful in all the ways indicated in Dr. Bacon's statement. It has not only established a colony, but it has performed most effective missionary work; it has suppressed the slave trade along six hundred miles of coast; it has improved the condition of the blacks as no other means have; and it is abolishing domestic slavery among the aborigines of that continent.

Like all great movements which are the outcome of human needs, and have in view the amelioration of the condition of large masses of people, it attracted to its support, at the opening of its career, men of conflicting views and influenced by divers motives. Some of its adherents gave one reason for their allegiance, others gave another; and sometimes, to the superficial observer or to the captious opponent, these different reasons furnished grounds for animadversions against the Society. Though it owed its origin to the judicious heads and philanthropic hearts of some of the best men that ever occupied positions of prominence and trust in this nation, yet there were those who ridiculed the scheme as wild and impracticable. Some opposed it because they loved the Negro; others discountenanced it because they hated the Negro. Some considered that the Society—in wishing to give him an opportunity for self-government—placed too high an estimate upon his ability; others thought that the idea of sending him away to a barbarous shore was a disparaging comment upon his capacity, and a robbing him of his right to remain and thrive in the land of his birth. To not a few, who neither loved nor hated the Negro, but were simply indifferent to him, the idea of transporting a few emancipated slaves to Africa, with the hope of bringing about a general exodus of the millions in this country, or of building up a nation in that far-off land of such materials, seemed absurd and ridiculous.

The Society had hardly been fifteen years in operation when it met with organised opposition in the American Anti-Slavery Society, the founders of which looked upon the work of Colonisation as an attempt to evade the duty and responsibility of emancipation. At this time, Mr. William Lloyd Garrison, a leader of the Abolition movement, was the most eloquent and persistent of the assailants of the Society. He carried the war against it into England, and pursued with unrelenting scorn and invective Mr. Elliott Cresson, who was then representing the cause before the British public. In the interesting life of the great anti-slavery reformer, by Oliver Johnson, it is said that when Mr. Garrison returned to this country from England in 1833, he brought with him a "Protest" against the Colonisation scheme, signed by Wilberforce, Macaulay, Buxton, O'Connell and others of scarcely less weight.[1]

---

[1] *William Lloyd Garrison and his Times*, by Oliver Johnson; p. 180.

Origin and Purpose of African Colonisation.

But Mr. Garrison ought to have known, and probably did know, that it was not the Colonisation scheme as conceived by its founders that these philanthropists opposed, for they were men of a spirit kindred to that which animated Samuel J. Mills, and the Finleys and Caldwells, whose labours brought the Society into being. What they did oppose was the scheme as they saw it under the representations of Mr. Garrison, who, himself benevolent at heart, had been influenced by personal reasons and by the injudicious utterances of certain advocates of Colonisation. They opposed it as they saw it through the glasses of such good old Negroes as Father Snowden, of Boston, who, in those days, offered a prayer for the Colonisation Society so striking in its eloquence as to have deserved a place, in the judgment of Mr. Oliver Johnson, in a serious narrative of the doings of the great anti-slavery leader. "O God," said the simple and earnest old man, "we pray that that seven-headed, ten-horned monster, the Colonisation Society, may be smitten through and through with the fiery darts of truth, and tormented as the whale between the swordfish and the thresher."[2]

I say that the friends of Africa in England did not oppose African Colonisation in itself, for just about the time of Mr. Garrison's visit to England, or very soon after, they adopted, under the lead of Sir Thomas Fowell Buxton, a scheme for the regeneration of Africa by means of her civilised sons, gathered from the countries of their exile, and, at great expense, sent out an expedition to the Niger, for the purpose of securing on that river, a hundred square miles of territory on which to settle the returning exiles. Capt. William Allen, who commanded the first Niger expedition, on his return in 1834, when describing the advantages of a civilised colony, used these words:—

> The very existence of such a community, exalted as it would be in its own estimation, and in the enjoyment of the benefits of civilisation, would excite among its neighbours a desire to participate in those blessings, and would be at once a normal or model society, gradually spreading to the most remote

---

[2] *Garrison and his Times*, p. 4. Mr. Oliver Johnson, throughout his work, shows his own conception of the status and functions of the Negro by never using a capital letter in writing the word that describes the race.

regions, and calling forth the resources of a country rich in so many things essential to commerce, might change the destinies of the whole of Western Central Africa.[3]

In a letter addressed by Stephen Lushington and Thomas Fowell Buxton to Lord John Russell, August 7, 1840, all the arguments used by the American Colonisation Society for settling civilised blacks in Africa, are reproduced.

Thomas Clarkson, writing to a friend, under date September 12, 1842, says:—

I am glad to find that, in the *Friend of Africa*, you lay such stress upon native agency, or the agency of the black people themselves to forward their own cause. Good sense would have dictated this; but God seems to point it out as one of His plans. He has raised up a people by the result of emancipation, qualified, both in intellect and habituation to a hot climate, to do for us the grand work in Africa. You know well that we can find among the emancipated slaves people with religious views and with intellectual capacity equal to the whites, and from these, principally, are we to pick out labourers for the African vineyard. . . . . You cannot send two or three only to a colony. In the smallest colony there must be more; there must be enough to form a society, both for the appearance of safety and for that converse for which man was fitted by the organs of speech to pass the time usefully to himself and others.[4]

The experience of years and the progress of Liberia have only served to illustrate the soundness of these views. European workers for Africa feel more and more the importance of such agencies as the Colonisation Society has been instrumental in establishing for civilising Africa. A writer in the London *Times* for May 31, 1882, says:—

As I have recently returned from Zanzibar, and can speak from some personal experience, may I be allowed to draw the attention of your readers to an attempt to bring about these results (viz., the abolition of the slave trade and civilisation of the people) with remarkable success? It is the formation of self-sustaining communities of released slaves in the countries whence they were originally brought by the slave dealers, in order that, by their example and influence, they may teach to the surrounding people the advantages of civilisation. The sight of a body of men of the same race as themselves, living in their midst, but raised to a higher level by the influence of Christianity and civilisation, has naturally produced in them a desire of raising themselves also.

---

[3] *Narrative of the Expedition to the Niger;* vol. ii, p. 434.

[4] *African Repository;* vol. xvi, p. 397.

Origin and Purpose of African Colonisation.

In an article on 'The Evangelisation of Africa,' in the Dublin *Review*, January, 1879, written by a Roman Catholic Prelate, the writer asks—" Why should not the example given by the American Colonisation Society, in founding Liberia, be followed by us in other parts of Africa?"

In a lecture delivered in 1872, in New York, by the same distinguished author, he says:—

> We have come to evangelise the coloured people in America. But our mission does not terminate with them. We are travelling through America to that great unexplored, unconverted continent of Africa. We have come to gather an army on our way, to conquer Africa for the Cross. God has his designs upon that vast land. . . . . The branch torn away from the parent stem in Africa, by our ancestors, was brought to America—brought away by Divine permission, in order that it might be engrafted upon the tree of the Cross. It will return in part to its own soil, not by violence or deportation, but willingly, and borne on the wings of faith and charity.

It is sometimes supposed and asserted that the efforts of the Colonisation Society stir up a feeling of unrest among the coloured population, and make them dissatisfied with their condition in this country. But this charge is brought only by those who have no idea of the power of race instincts. The descendants of Africa in this country have never needed the stimulus of any organisation of white men to direct their attention to the land of their fathers. Just as the idea of a departure from the "house of bondage" in Egypt was in the minds of the Hebrews long before Moses was born, even when Joseph gave commandment concerning his bones; so, long before the formation of the Colonisation Society, there were aspirations in the breasts of thinking Negroes for a return to the land of their fathers. The first practical Colonisationist was not a white man, but a Negro, Paul Cuffee. This man took thirty Negro emigrants from New Bedford, in his own vessel, to Africa, in 1815. The law of God for each race is written on the tablets of their hearts, and no theories will ever obliterate the deep impression, or neutralise its influence upon their action; and in the process of their growth they will find or force a way for themselves. Those who are working with or for the race, therefore, should seriously consider, in any great movement in their behalf, the steps which the proper representatives deem it wise to take. "March without the people," said a French deputy, "and you walk into night; their instincts are a finger pointing of Providence, always turning toward real benefit."

The Colonisation Society was only the instrument of opening a field for the energies of those of the Africans who desired to go and avail themselves of the opportunities there offered. Boswell, in his life of Samuel Johnson, tells us that when the sale of Thrale's Brewery was going forward, Johnson was asked what he really considered to be the value of the property which was to be disposed of. He replied, "We are not here to sell a parcel of boilers and vats, but the potentiality of growing rich beyond the dreams of avarice." So the founders of this Society looked to the "potentiality" of the few seeds they were planting on the coast of Africa. In their reply to opponents they said :—" We are not here simply to send a few Negroes to Africa, and to occupy with them a few swampy regions on the margin of a distant country, but we are endeavouring to stimulate for a race and a continent their potentiality of unlimited development."

They assisted a few courageous men to go and plant a colony on those distant and barbarous shores, in days when nearly every body doubted the wisdom and expediency of such a step. Who, then, could have divined the results? Considering the circumstances of those pioneer settlers and the darkness of the outlook when they started, no man could have believed, until he learned it as a matter of history that those few men could have established an independent nation on that coast. The story of their trials and struggles and conquests would furnish the material for an exciting novel—many portions of it would resemble chapters, not from Froude or Hallam, but from Thackeray or Scott. The string of episodes in the first thirty years of their history would form the basis of an interesting epic.

Now what is the work thus far accomplished and being accomplished on that coast? If, when those colonists landed on those shores, inexperienced and uneducated ex-slaves as they were, they had had to contend with simple barbarism or the absence of

Origin and Purpose of African Colonisation.

civilisation, their task would have been comparatively easy; but they had to deal with tribes demoralised by ages of intercourse with the most abandoned of foreigners—slave-traders and pirates, who had taken up their abode at various points of the coast, and had carried on for generations, without interruption, their work of disintegration and destruction. When, therefore, the colonists found themselves in possession of a few miles of territory, they very soon perceived that they had more to do than simply to clear up the land, build and cultivate. They saw that they had to contend, not with the simple prejudices of the Aborigines, but with the results of the unhallowed intercourse of European adventurers. But they were brave men. Their spirits, though chastened by the burden of slavery and the sorrows of oppression, were never clouded by any doubt in their destiny. They felt themselves able to build up a State, and they set themselves cheerfully to deal with the new and difficult problems which confronted them. Fierce were the struggles in which they had to engage before they succeeded in expelling the pirates from the neighbourhood of their settlements. And after they had dislodged these demons in human form, the mischievous consequences of their protracted residence in the land continued and still, to a great extent, continue.

In his last Message to the Liberian Legislature, the President of the Republic, referring to the difficulties at Cape Mount, says:— "The native wars which have been going on in the vicinity of Cape Mount have now nearly exhausted themselves. These periodical wars are, for the most part, the results of long-standing feuds arising from the horrible slave trade, that dreadful scourge which distinguished the intercourse of the European world with Africa for more than ten generations."

Having secured an undisturbed footing in the land of their fathers, the next step on the part of the colonists was to conciliate the Aborigines and to enlarge the borders of the Colony by purchase from the native lords of the soil. In this way, the Colony increased in power and influence, until 1847, when it became a sovereign and independent State. As such it has been acknowledged by all the Powers of Europe and by the United States.

The special work which, at this moment, claims the attention of the Republic is to push the settlements beyond the sea-board to the elevated and salubrious regions of the interior, and to incorporate the Aborigines, as fast as practicable, into the Republic. Native chiefs are summoned to the Legislature from the different counties, and take part in the deliberations; but, as yet, only those Aborigines who conform to the laws of the Republic as to the tenure of land, are allowed to exercise the elective franchise. All the other questions which press upon independent nations, questions of education, of finance, of commerce, of agriculture, are receiving the careful attention of the people. They feel the importance of making provisions by judicious laws and by proper executive, legislative and judicial management, for the preservation and growth of the State.

In educational matters, there is daily noticeable improvement. We are developing a system of common schools, with a College at the head as a guarantee for their efficiency. The educational work is felt to be of the greatest possible importance; education, not only in its literary and religious forms, but also in its industrial, mechanical, and commercial aspects.

The effort now is to enlarge the operations and increase the influence of the College.

We have application for admission to its advantages from numerous youths in various institutions of learning in this country, who wish, on the completion of their course, to labour in Africa. Influential chiefs on the coast and in the interior are also anxious to send their sons; and we shall, before very long, have young men from the powerful tribes in our vicinity—Mandingoes, Foulahs, Veys, Bassas, Kroos, Greboes.

A female department has also lately been established in connection with this Institution, and a Christian lady of education and culture, in this country, longing to labour in the land of her fathers, has been appointed as first Principal. She will sail in a few months.

Origin and Purpose of African Colonisation.

In financial matters the Republic is hopeful. The public debt is not so large that it cannot, by the reforms now contemplated, be easily managed and placed under such control as to give no inconvenience to the State. There are evidences of an abundance of gold in the territory of the Republic. The precious metal is brought to the coast from various points in the interior. But the Government is not anxious to encourage the opening of gold mines. We prefer the slow but sure, though less dazzling process, of becoming a great nation by lapse of time, and by the steady growth of internal prosperity—by agriculture, by trade, by proper domestic economy.

In commercial matters, there is also everything to encourage. Three lines of steamers from England and Germany, and sailing vessels from the United States, visit the Liberian ports regularly for trading purposes. And the natural resources of the Republic have, in various portions of it, hardly yet been touched. Palm oil, camwood, ivory, rubber, gold-dust, hides, beeswax, gum copal, may be produced in unlimited quantities. For the enterprising merchants of this country—coloured or white—there is no better field for the investment of pecuniary capital.

The agriculture of the country is rapidly on the increase. Liberia has been supplying the Coffee Planters of Ceylon and Brazil with a new and superior kind of coffee for their agricultural industry. The Liberian coffee is considered among the best in the world, and the people are now turning their attention largely to its cultivation. As immigrants arrive from this country, extensive farms under their persevering industry are taking the place of the dense forests. The new settlements, pushing out to the rich valleys and fertile slopes of the interior, are a marvel to those who, a few years ago, saw the country in its primitive condition; and to the Negro new comer from this country in search of a field for his energy and enterprise, there is no picture which, for inspiration and grandeur, can ever equal the sight of these new proprietors of land and these new directors of labour engaged in their absorbing and profitable pursuits. When he sees the thriving villages, the comfortable dwellings, the increasing agriculture, all supervised and controlled by men just like himself, who had only been more fortunate in preceding him by a few years, a feeling of pride and gratification takes possession of him. Like Æneas, when he witnessed the enterprise of the Tyrian colonists in the building of Carthage, he exclaims,—

O fortunati, quorum jam moenia surgunt.

But, unlike the mythical author of that exclamation, he feels that he has a part in the rising fortunes of the settlements; that what he beholds is not only what he himself may accomplish, but is the promise and pledge of the future greatness of his adopted country.

The nations of the earth are now looking to Liberia as one of the hopeful spots on the continent of Africa. The President of the United States, in his last Message, referred to the interest which this Government feels in that youngest sister of the great international family. To a deputation from the Colonisation Society, which called upon him a year ago, President Arthur said that he "had always taken great interest in the work of the Colonisation Society, which was, in his judgment, eminently practical."

President Gardner, who has for the last five years presided over the little nation, expresses the views entertained by its most enlightened citizens as follows:—

The ship of State which, in 1847, we launched in fear and trembling, is still afloat, with timbers sound and spars unharmed. The Lone Star of Liberia, untarnished, is pushing its way eastward, successfully achieving victories of peace even to the slopes of the Niger, gathering willing thousands under its elevating and hopeful folds. The American Colonisation Society must feel greatly strengthened in its work. It has achieved what no other philanthropic agency in modern times has accomplished, and what, perhaps, no nation could have effected, viz., the giving to the Negro an independent home in the land of his fathers, where he has unlimited scope for development and expansion. Had Liberia been the colony of a powerful government, political and commercial jealousies, and the purposes of party spirit, might have prevented the surrender of the colony to the absolute control of the colonists. Hayti had to fight for her independence. It is not practicable for Great Britain to give up Jamaica, or Barbadoes, or Sierra Leone, or Lagos. But the American Colonisation Society founded a nation, and continues to strengthen it. So God takes the weak things of the earth to confound the things that are mighty.

Origin and Purpose of African Colonisation.

In a letter dated at the Palace of Madrid, February 11, 1882, King Alfonso XII, of Spain, writes to the President of Liberia as follows:—

GREAT AND GOOD FRIEND,
 Desiring to give you a public testimony of my Royal appreciation and my particular esteem, I have had special pleasure in nominating you Knight of the Grand Cross of the Royal Order of Isabel the Catholic. I am pleased by this action also to furnish new proof of the desire which animates me to strengthen more and more the friendly relations which happily exist between Spain and the Republic of Liberia; and with this motive I repeat to you the assurance of the affection which I entertain towards you, and with which I am, Great and Good Friend,

Your Great and Good Friend,
Palace at Madrid, February 11, 1882.   ALFONSO.

The Republic of Liberia now stands before the world—the realisation of the dreams of the founders of the American Colonisation Society, and, in many respects, more than the realisation. Its effect upon that great country is not to be estimated solely by the six hundred miles of coast which it has brought under civilised law. A sea of influence has been created, to which rivulets and large streams are attracted from the distant interior; and up those streams, for a considerable distance, a tide of regeneration continually flows. Far beyond the range of the recognised limits of Liberia, hundreds of miles away from the coast, I have witnessed the effects of American civilisation; not only in the articles of American manufactures, which I have been surprised to see in those remote districts, but in the intelligible use of the English language, which I have encountered in the far inland regions, all going out from Liberia. None can calculate the wide-spreading results of a single channel of wholesome influence. Travellers in Syria tell us that Damascus owes its fertility and beauty to one single stream —the river Abana. Without that little river, the charm and glory of Damascus would disappear. It would be a city in a desert. So the influence of Liberia, insignificant as it may seem, is the increasing source of beauty and fertility, of civilisation and progress, to West and Central Africa.

As time has gone on, and the far-reaching plans of the Society have been developed, its bitterest opponents among the whites have relaxed their opposition. They see more and more that the idea which gave rise to it had more than a temporary or provisional importance; that, as long as there are Christian Negroes in this land who may do a civilising work in Africa, and who desire to go thither, so long will this colonisation enterprise be a necessary and beneficent agency.

Coloured men of intelligence are also taking a more comprehensive view of the question. The coloured people in various parts of the country are not only asserting their independence of party trammels, but are taking higher ground with regard to their relations to Africa. The Colonisation Society no longer stands between them and the land of their fathers as a dividing agency; no longer the gulf that separates, but, for many, the bridge that connects. Liberia is producing the elements which—if they do not, to the minds of the thinking coloured people, vindicate the methods of some colonisationists in days gone by—amply justify the policy of the Colonisation Society. The leading men of colour are recognising the distinction between Liberia as an independent nation, claiming their respect and support, and the Colonisation Society, which, from their standpoint, contemplated their expatriation.

Your speaker has had the honour of being listened to on the various occasions on which, recently, he has spoken in this city, by full houses composed of the most intelligent classes of the coloured population, who, a few years ago, would not have thought of attending any meeting which had the remotest connection with Liberia. He has also had the privilege of being the guest, for several days, at Uniontown, of the leading coloured man of the United States, better known than any other Negro in both hemispheres; and this address was written under his hospitable roof, and, perhaps, on the same table on which, in years gone by, had been forged those thunderbolts which he hurled with so much power and effect against Colonisation; but *tempora mutantur nos et mutamur in illis*—the times are changed, and we are changed with them.

The dawn of a new day in the history of the coloured people is

Origin and Purpose of African Colonisation.

not only inspiring them with new views, but bringing forward new actors or leaders. It is not that those who are coming forward are superior to those who have passed away, or are passing away. No; the giants of former years—the Wards and Garnets and Douglasses—can never be surpassed, or even reproduced. They were the peculiar product of their times. But it is, that the present times require different instruments, and leaders are arising with different purposes and different aspirations. I saw, in large letters, in a prominent part of Mr. Frederick Douglass's residence, the scriptural injunction, "Live peaceably with all men"—a fitting motto, I thought, for the soldier who, after the hard-fought battle and the achievement of the victory, has laid down his arms. The motto in the days of Douglass's greatest activity was, "Fight the good fight." Now the days of peace have come. The statesman's office comes after the soldier's. *Cedant arma togae.* The Negro youth—as a result of the training which he is now so generously receiving in the schools—will seek to construct States. He will aspire after feats of statesmanship, and Africa will be the field to which he will look for the realisation of his desires. Bishop Turner, of the African Missionary Episcopal Church, who enjoys exceptional opportunities for knowing the feelings of the coloured people of this country, said, in a newspaper article published a few days ago:—

> There never was a time when the coloured people were more concerned about Africa, in every respect, than at present. In some portions of the country it is the topic of conversation; and if a line of steamers were started from New Orleans, Mobile, Savannah or Charleston, they would be crowded to density every trip they made to Africa. There is a general unrest and a wholesale dissatisfaction among our people in a number of sections of the country, to my certain knowledge, and they sigh for conveniences to and from the continent of Africa. Something has to be done; matters cannot go on as at present, and the remedy is thought by tens of thousands to be a NEGRO NATIONALITY. This much the history of the world establishes, that races either fossilised, oppressed, or degraded, must emigrate before any material change takes place in their civil, intellectual, or moral status; otherwise extinction is the consequence.[5]

The general practice among superficial politicians and irre-

---

[5] *Christian Recorder;* January 4, 1888.

sponsible coloured journalists in this country, is to ignore and deprecate the craving for the fatherland among the Negro population. But nothing is clearer to those who know anything of race instincts and tendencies than that this craving is a permanent and irrepressible impulse. For some reason the American Government has never seen its way clear to give any practical recognition to these aspirations. In vain, apparently, does the American Colonisation Society, from year to year, present the cries and petitions of thousands and hundreds of thousands who yearn for a home in the land of their fathers. Individual philanthropists may admit that such cries deserve respectful sympathy, but the Government takes no note of them. It must be stated, however, that the Government is ever ready to extend assistance to Liberia, and on the ground, partly, as often urged in their diplomatic correspondence, that Liberia is to be the future home of thousands of American citizens of African descent.

Has not the time now come when an earnest and united effort should be made by all sections of this great country to induce the Government to assist the thousands who are longing to betake themselves to those vast and fertile regions to which they are directed by the strongest impulses that have ever actuated the movements of humanity? While it is true that there are causes of dissatisfaction with his position in this country on the part of the Negro, still he will be carried to Africa by a higher impulse than that which brings millions to this country from Europe. Mr. Bright has said: "There are streams of emigration flowing towards America, and much of this arises from the foolishness of European peoples and European Governments," and he quotes from Mr. Bancroft the statement that "the history of the colonisation of America is the history of the crimes of Europe."

No natural impulses bring the European hither—artificial or economical causes move him to emigrate. The Negro is drawn to Africa by the necessities of his nature.

We do not ask that all the coloured people should leave the United States and go to Africa. If such a result were possible it is not, for the present, at least, desirable; certainly it is not indispensable.

Origin and Purpose of African Colonisation.

For the work to be accomplished much less than one-tenth of the six millions will be necessary. "In a return from exile, in the restoration of a people," says George Eliot, "the question is not whether certain rich men will choose to remain behind, but whether there will be found worthy men who will choose to lead the return. Plenty of prosperous Jews remained in Babylon when Ezra marshalled his band of forty thousand, and began a new, glorious epoch in the history of his race, making the preparation for that epoch in the history of the world, which has been held glorious enough to be dated from forevermore."

There are Negroes enough in this country to join in the return—descendants of Africa enough, who are faithful to the instincts of the race, and who realise their duty to their fatherland. I rejoice to know that here, where the teachings of generations have been to disparage the race, there are many who are faithful, there are men, and women who will go, who have a restless sense of homelessness which will never be appeased until they stand in the great land where their forefathers lived; until they catch glimpses of the old sun, and moon and stars, which still shine in their pristine brilliancy upon that vast domain; until, from the deck of the ship which bears them back home, they see visions of the hills rising from the white margin of the continent, and listen to the breaking music of the waves—the exhilarating laughter of the sea as it dashes against the beach. These are the elements of the great restoration. It may come in our own life time. It may be our happiness to see those rise up who will formulate progress for Africa—embody the ideas which will reduce our social and political life to order; and we may, before we die, thank God that we have seen His salvation; that the Negro has grasped with a clear knowledge his meaning in the world's vast life—in politics, in science, in religion.

I say it is gratifying to know that there are Negroes of this country who will go to do this great work—cheerfully go and brave the hardships and perils necessary to be endured in its accomplishment. These will be among the redeemers of Africa. If they suffer they will suffer devotedly, and if they die, they will die well. And what is death for the redemption of a people? History is full of

Christianity, Islam and the Negro Race.

examples of men who have sacrificed themselves for the advancement of a great cause—for the good of their country. Every man who dies for Africa—if it is necessary to die—adds to Africa a new element of salvation, and hastens the day of her redemption. And when God lets men suffer and gives them to pain and death, it is not the abandoned, it is not the worst or the guiltiest, but the best and the purest, whom He often chooses for His work, for they will do it best. Spectators weep and wonder; but the sufferers themselves accept the pain in the joy of doing redemptive work, and rise out of lower levels to the elevated regions of those nobler spirits—the glorious army of martyrs—who rejoice that they are counted worthy to die for men.

The nation now being reared in Africa by the returning exiles from this country will not be a reproduction of the American. The restoration of the Negro to the land of his fathers will be the restoration of a race to its original integrity, to itself; and working by itself, for itself and from itself, it will discover the methods of its own development, and they will not be the same as the Anglo-Saxon methods.

In Africa there are no physical problems to be confronted upon the solution of which human comfort and even human existence depend. In the temperate regions of the earth there are ever-recurring problems, first physical or material, and then intellectual, which press for solution and cannot be deferred without peril.

It is this constant pressure which has developed the scientific intellect and the thoughtfulness of the European. Africa can afford to hand over the solution of these problems to those who, driven by the exigencies of their circumstances, must solve them or perish. And when they are solved, we shall apply the results to our purposes, leaving us leisure and taste for the metaphysical and spiritual. Africa will be largely an agricultural country. The people, when assisted by proper impulse from without—and they need this help just as all other races have needed impulse from without—will live largely in contact with Nature. The Northern races will take the raw materials from Africa and bring them back in such forms as shall contribute to the comfort and even elegance of life in that country; while the African, in the simplicity and purity of rural enterprises, will be able to cultivate those spiritual elements in humanity which are suppressed, silent and inactive under the pressure and exigencies of material progress. He will find out, not under pressure, but in an entirely normal and natural way, what his work is to be.

I do not anticipate for Africa any large and densely crowded cities. For my own taste, I cannot say that I admire these agglomerations of humanity. For me, man has marred the earth's surface by his cities. "God made the country and man the town."

It is the cities which have furnished the deadliest antagonisms to prophets and reformers. The prophets and apostles are nurtured in the Nazareths and Bethlehems of the world. I cherish the feeling that in Africa there will never be any Jerusalem, or Rome, or Athens, or London; but I have a strong notion that the Bethlehems and Nazareths will spring up in various parts of the continent. In the solitudes of the African forests, where the din of Western civilisation has never been heard, I have realised the saying of the poet that the "Groves were God's first temples." I have felt that I stood in the presence of the Almighty; and the trees and the birds and the sky and the air have whispered to me of the great work yet to be achieved on that continent. I trod lightly through those forests, for I felt there was "a spirit in the woods." And I could understand how it came to pass that the prophets of a race— the great reformers who have organised states and elevated peoples, received their inspiration on mountains, in caves, in grottoes. I could understand something of the power which wrought upon Sakya Muni under the trees of India; upon Numa Pompilius in the retreat of the Nymph Egeria; upon Mohammed in the silent cave; upon Martin Luther, Xavier and Ignatius Loyola in the cloisters. One the sweetest of American poets—Whittier—in his poem on the Quaker Meeting, pictures the beauty and instructive power of unbroken stillness—

> And so I find it well to come
> For deeper rest, to this still room;
> For here the habit of the soul
> Feels less the outer world's control.

Christianity, Islam and the Negro Race.

> And from the silence multiplied
> By these still forms on either side,
> The world that time and sense have known
> Falls off, and leaves us God alone.
>
> So to the calmly gathered thought
> The innermost of truth is taught,
> The mystery, dimly understood,
> That love of God is love of good.

It is under such circumstances that the African will gather inspiration for his work. He will grow freely, naturally unfolding his powers in a healthy progress.

The world needs such a development of the Negro on African soil. He will bring as his contribution the softer aspects of human nature. The harsh and stern fibre of the Caucasian races needs this milder element. The African is the Feminine; and we must not suppose that this is of least importance in the ultimate development of humanity. "We are apt," says Matthew Arnold, "to account amiability weak and hardness strong," but even if it were so, there are forces, as George Sands says, truly and beautifully, "there are forces of weakness, of docility, of attractiveness or of suavity, which are quite as real as the forces of vigour, of encroachment, of violence, of brutality." [o]

Soon after the close of the war it was the favourite cry of some that the Colonisation Society had done its work and should be dropped. But that cry has been effectually hushed by the increasing light of experience, and under the louder cries of the thousands and tens of thousands, who in various parts of the country are asking for aid to reach the land of their fathers. Both white and coloured are now recognising the fact that the Society with its abundant knowledge, with its organised plans, is an indispensible machinery for the diffusion of that special information about Africa of which the American people are generally so destitute, and for the inoffensive creation among the Negro portion of the population of those enlightened opinions about the land of their fathers, and their duty to that land which will lead some at least of them to enter upon it with intelligence and efficiency.

---

[o] *Nineteenth Century*, June, 1881.

Origin and Purpose of African Colonisation.

There is evidently, at this moment, no philanthropic institution before the American public that has more just and reasonable claims upon private and official benevolence than the American Colonisation Society. And the Christian sentiment of the country, as I gather it from the east and from the west, from the north and from the south, is largely in favour of giving substantial and generous aid to that struggling Christian Republic in West Africa, the power of which, it is conceded, it should be the pride of this nation, as it is its commercial interest, to increase and perpetuate.

Ethiopia stretching out her hands unto God;

OR,

Africa's Service to the World.

THERE was, for a long time, in the Christian world considerable difference of opinion as to the portion of the earth, and the precise region to which the term Ethiopia must be understood as applying. It is pretty well established now, however, that by *Ethiopia*, is meant the continent of Africa, and by *Ethiopians*, the great race who inhabit that continent. The etymology of the word points to the most prominent physical characteristics of this people.

To any one who has travelled in Africa, especially in the portion north of the equator, extending from the West coast to Abyssinia, Nubia and Egypt, and embracing what is known as the Nigritian and Soudanic countries, there cannot be the slightest doubt as to the country and people to whom the terms Ethiopia and Ethiopian, as used in the Bible and the classical writers, were applied. One of the latest and most accurate authorities says: "The country which the Greeks and the Romans described as Ethiopia, and the Hebrews as Cush, lay to the south of Egypt, and embraced, in its most extended sense, the modern Nubia, Senaar, Kordofan, &c., and in its more definite sense, the kingdom of Meroe, from the junction of the Blue and White branches of the Nile to the border of Egypt."[1]

Herodotus, the father of history, speaks of two divisions of Ethiopians, who did not differ at all from each other in appearance,

---

[1] Smith's *Dictionary of the Bible*—(sub voce).

Africa's Service to the World.

except in their language and hair; "for the eastern Ethiopians," he says, "are straight haired, but those of Libya (or Africa), have hair more curly than that of any other people."[2] "As far as we know," says Mr. Gladstone, "Homer recognised the African coast by placing the Lotophagi upon it, and the *Ethiopians* inland from the east, all the way to the extreme west."[3]

There has been an unbroken line of communication between the West Coast of Africa, through the Soudan, and through the so-called Great Desert and Asia, from the time when portions of the descendants of Ham, in remote ages, began their migrations westward, and first saw the Atlantic Ocean.

Africa is no vast island, separated by an immense ocean from other portions of the globe, and cut off through the ages from the men who have made and influenced the destinies of mankind. She has been closely connected, both as source and nourisher, with some of the most potent influences which have affected for good the history of the world. The people of Asia, and the people of Africa have been in constant intercourse. No violent social or political disruption has ever broken through this communication. No chasm caused by war has suspended intercourse. On the contrary, the greatest religious reforms the world has ever seen—Jewish, Christian, Mohammedan—originating in Asia, have obtained consolidation in Africa. And as in the days of Abraham and Moses, of Herodotus and Homer, so to-day, there is a constantly accessible highway from Asia to the heart of the Soudan. Africans are continually going to and fro between the Atlantic Ocean and the Red Sea. I have met in Liberia and along its eastern frontiers, Mohammedan Negroes, born in Mecca, the Holy City of Arabia, who thought they were telling of nothing extraordinary when they were detailing the incidents of their journeyings and of those of their friends from the banks of the Niger—from the neighbourhood of Sierra Leone and Liberia—across the continent to Egypt, Arabia and Jerusalem. I saw in Cairo and Jerusalem, some years ago, West Africans who

---

[2] *Herod.* iii, 94; vii, 70.
[3] *Homer and the Homeric Age;* vol. iii, p. 305.

had come on business, or on religious pilgrimage, from their distant homes in Senegambia,

Africans were not unknown, therefore, to the writers of the Bible. Their peculiarities of complexion and hair were as well known to the ancient Greeks and Hebrews, as they are to the American people to-day. And when they spoke of the Ethiopians, they meant the ancestors of the black-skinned and woolly-haired people who, for two hundred and fifty years, have been known as labourers on the plantations of the South. It is to these people, and to their country, that the Psalmist refers, when he says, "Ethiopia shall soon stretch out her hand unto God." The word in the original, which has been translated "soon," is now understood to refer not so much to the *time* as to the *manner* of the action. Ethiopia shall *suddenly* stretch out her hands unto God, is the most recent rendering.

But, even if we take the phraseology as it has been generally understood, it will not by anyone acquainted with the facts, be held to have been altogether unfulfilled. There is not a tribe on the continent of Africa, in spite of the almost universal opinion to the contrary, in spite of the fetishes and greegrees which many of them are supposed to worship—there is not, I say, a single tribe which does not stretch out its hands to the Great Creator. There is not one who does not recognise the Supreme Being, though imperfectly understanding His character—and who does perfectly understand His character? They believe that the heaven and the earth, the sun, moon, and stars, which they behold, were created by an Almighty personal Agent, who is also their own Maker and Sovereign, and they render to him such worship as their untutored intellects can conceive. The work of the Christian missionary is to declare to them that Being whom they ignorantly worship. There are no atheists or agnostics among them. They have not yet attained, and I am sure they never will attain, to that eminence of progress or that perfection of development; so that it is true, in a certain sense, that Ethiopia now stretches out her hands unto God.

And if the belief in a common Creator and Father of mankind is illustrated in the bearing we maintain towards our neighbour, if

Africa's Service to the World.

our faith is seen in our works, if we prove that we love God, whom we have not seen, by loving our neighbour whom we have seen, by respecting his rights, even though he may not belong to our clan, tribe, or race, then I must say, and it will not be generally disputed, that more proofs are furnished among the natives of interior Africa of their belief in the common Fatherhood of a personal God by their hospitable and considerate treatment of foreigners and strangers than are to be seen in many a civilised and Christian community. Mungo Park, a hundred years ago, put on record in poetry and in prose—and he wished it never to be forgotten—that he was the object of most kindly and sympathetic treatment in the wilds of Africa, among a people he had never before seen, and whom he never could requite. The long sojourn of Livingstone in that land in contentment and happiness, without money to pay his way, is another proof of the excellent qualities of the people, and of their practical belief in an universal Father. And, in all history, where is there anything more touching than that ever-memorable conveyance, by "faithful hands," of the remains of the missionary traveller from the land of strangers over thousands of miles, to the country of the deceased, to be deposited with deserved honour in the "Great Temple of Silence"?

And this peculiarity of Africans is not a thing known only in modern times. The ancients recognised these qualities, and loved to descant upon them. They seemed to regard the fear and love of God as the peculiar gift of the darker races. In the version of the Chaldean Genesis, as given by George Smith, the following passage occurs: "The word of the Lord will never fail in the mouth of the dark races whom He has made." Homer and Herodotus have written immortal eulogies of the race. Homer speaks of them as the "blameless Ethiopians," and tells us that it was the Ethiopians alone among mortals whom the gods selected as a people fit to be lifted to the social level of the Olympian divinities. Every year, the poet says, the whole celestial circle left the summits of Olympus and betook themselves, for their holidays, to Ethiopia, where, in the enjoyment of Ethiopian hospitality, they sojourned twelve days.

Christianity, Islam and the Negro Race.

> The Sire of gods and all the etherial train
> On the warm limits of the farthest main
> Now mix with mortals, nor disdain to grace
> The feasts of Ethiopia's blameless race;
> Twelve days the Powers indulge the genial rite,
> Returning with the twelfth revolving night.

Lucian represents a sceptic, or freethinker, of his day, as saying, in his irreverence towards the gods, that on certain occasions they do not hear the prayers of mortals in Europe because they are away across the ocean, perhaps among the Ethiopians, with whom they dine frequently on their own invitation.

It shows the estimate in which the ancients held the Africans, that they selected them as the only fit associates for their gods. And, in modern times, in all the countries of their exile, they have not ceased to commend themselves to those who have held rule over them. The testimonies are numerous and striking, in all the annals of this country, to the fidelity of the African. The newspapers of the land are constantly bearing testimony to his unswerving faithfulness at this moment, notwithstanding the indignities heaped upon him.

But there is another quality in the Ethiopian or African, closely connected with the preceding, which proves that he has stretched out his hands unto God. If service rendered to humanity is service rendered to God, then the Negro and his country have been, during the ages, in spite of untoward influences, tending upward to the Divine.

Take the country. It has been called the cradle of civilisation, and so it is. The germs of all the sciences and of the two great religions now professed by the most enlightened races were fostered in Africa. Science, in its latest wonders, has nothing to show equal to some of the wonderful things even now to be seen in Africa. In Africa stands that marvellous architectural pile—the great Pyramid—which has been the admiration and despair of the world for a hundred generations. Scientific men of the present day, mathematicians, astronomers and divines, regard it as a sort of key to the universe—a symbol of the profoundest truths of science, of religion, and of all the past and future history of man. Though apparently

Africa's Service to the World.

closely secluded from all the rest of the world, Africa still lies at the gateway of all the loftiest and noblest traditions of the human race —of India, of Greece, of Rome. She intermingles with all the Divine administrations, and is connected, in one way or another, with some of the most famous names and events in the annals of time.

The great progenitor of the Hebrew race and the founder of their religion sought refuge in Africa from the ravages of famine. We read in Gen. xii, 10, " And there was a famine in the land ; and Abram went down into Egypt to sojourn there, for the famine was grievous in the land." Jacob and his sons were subsequently saved from extinction in the same way. In Africa, the Hebrew people from three score and ten souls multiplied into millions. In Africa, Moses, the greatest lawgiver the world has ever seen, was born and educated. To this land also resorted the ancient philosophers of Greece and Rome, to gaze upon its wonders and gather inspiration from its arts and sciences. Later on, a greater than Moses and than all the prophets and philosophers, when in infancy, was preserved from death in Africa. " Arise," was the message conveyed by the angel to Joseph, " Arise, and take the young child and his mother and flee into Egypt, and be thou there until I bring thee word ; for Herod will seek the young child to destroy him." When, in his final hours, the Saviour of mankind struggled up the heights of Calvary, under the weight of the Cross, accused by Asia and condemned by Europe, Africa furnished the man to relieve him of his burden. "And as they led him away they laid hold upon one Simon, a Cyrenian, coming out of the country, and on him they laid the Cross that he might bear it after Jesus."

And all through those times, and in times anterior to those, whether in sacred or profane matters, Africa is never out of view, as a helper. Egypt was the granary of Europe, often furnishing relief to starving populations out of her inexhaustible abundance. Then in modern times, when the enterprise and science of Europe had added a fourth continent to the knowledge of mankind by the discovery of America, the discoverers found themselves helpless in their efforts to utilise the richer portions of the vast domain. The Aborigines, who welcomed them to the strange country, were not available for industrial purposes. The imagination of the new comers was dazzled with visions of untold wealth, but they were powerless to avail themselves of it. The feeble frame of the Mexican could not support the burdens of his Spanish taskmaster, and the whole race was passing away, with the throne of Montezuma, before the mailed warriors of Castile. The despairing cries of a moribund population reached the ears of the sympathetic in Europe, when the Negro with his patience, his stronger physical qualities, and his superior powers of endurance, was thought of, and Africa, the grey-haired mother of civilisation, had to be resorted to for the labourers who could work the newly-discovered country, and thus contribute towards the development of modern civilisation, and towards making this almost boundless territory what it now is. The discovery of America without Africa, would have been comparatively useless, but with Africa, the brilliant eulogy recently pronounced upon this country by Mr. Bright, has become appropriate.

"If we examine," says that distinguished orator and statesman, "all those old empires, the Assyrian, the Babylonian, the Parthian or the Roman; or if we go still further back in time and place, and examine what we know of the great empires of India or of China; or if we go to a more modern time and regard the fall of ancient Rome; if we look, in our own time, at the growth of the empire of Russia; if we look at the French Revolution, with all its vast results; if we look at the present power of Germany in Europe; if we look at the vast empire over all the world, of most of which we in this little island are, for a time, the centre, I think we shall admit, after all, that there is nothing, in all these transactions of history, which for vastness and for permanence, can compare with the grandeur there is in the discovery of the American continent by Christopher Columbus."

But in bringing about these great results, in helping to achieve this material and moral grandeur, Africa has borne an important part. He who writes the history of modern civilisation will be culpably negligent if he omit to observe and to describe the black stream of humanity, which has poured into America from the heart

Africa's Service to the World.

of the Soudan. That stream has fertilised half the Western continent. It has created commerce and influenced its progress. It has affected culture and morality in the Eastern and Western hemispheres, and has been the means of transforming European colonies into a great nationality. Nor can it be denied that the material development of England was aided greatly by means of this same dark stream. By means of Negro labour sugar and tobacco were produced; by means of sugar and tobacco British commerce was increased; by means of increased commerce the arts of culture and refinement were developed. The rapid growth and unparalleled prosperity of Lancashire are, in part, owing to the cotton supply of the Southern States, which could not have risen to such importance without the labour of the African.

The countless caravans and dhow-loads of Negroes who have been imported into Asia have not produced, so far as we know, any great historical results; but the slaves exported to America have profoundly influenced civilisation. The political history of the United States is the history of the Negro. The commercial and agricultural history of nearly the whole America is the history of the Negro.

Africa, in recent times, also, has been made, incidentally, to confer an important political benefit upon Europe, and probably upon the whole of the civilised world. When, two generations ago, Europe was disturbed and threatened by the restless and uncontrollable energy of one of whom Victor Hugo has said that he put Providence to inconvenience (*il genait Dieu*); and when the civilisation of the whole world was in danger of being arrested in its progress, if not put back indefinitely, by a prolific and unscrupulous ambition, Africa furnished the island which gave asylum to this infatuated and maddened potentate, and, by confining to that sea-girt rock his formidable genius, gave peace to Europe, restored the political equilibrium, and unfettered the march of civilisation.

And now that Europe is exhausting itself by over-production, it is to Africa that men look to furnish new markets. India, China and Japan are beginning to consume their raw material at home, thus not only shutting Europe out from a market, but cutting off the supplies

L

of raw material. Expedition after expedition is now entering the country, intersecting it from east to west and from north to south, to find out more of the resources of a land upon which large portions of the civilised world will, in no very remote future, be dependant. In the days of the slave-trade, when the man of the country was needed for animal purposes, no thought was given to the country. In those days Africa was not inaptly compared to "An extensive deer forest, where the lordly proprietor betakes himself at times in quest of game and recreation. He has certain beats, which he frequents, where the deer have their tracks, and to which his beaters drive them. Here he takes his stand and watches for his prey, while the deep recesses of the forest remain to him a perfect *terra incognita*. In the same way the nations of Europe had planted their establishments upon that coast, upon those lines which communicated most freely with the interior, and there awaited the approach of their prey, while little thought was given to the country beyond."

But now things have changed. The country is studied with an almost martyr-like devotion, but with a somewhat contemptuous indifference as to the inhabitants. In their eager search, the explorers have discovered that Africa possesses the very highest capacity for the production, as raw material, of the various articles demanded by civilised countries. English, and French, and Germans, are now in the struggles of an intense competition for the hidden treasures of that continent. Upon the opening of Africa will depend the continuation of the prosperity of Europe. Thus Providence has interwoven the interests of Europe with those of Africa. What will bring light and improvement, peace and security, to thousands of women and children in Africa, will bring food and clothing to thousands of women and children in Europe.

Thus, Ethiopia and Ethiopians, having always served, will continue to serve the world. The Negro is, at this moment, the opposite of the Anglo-Saxon. Those everywhere serve the world; these everywhere govern the world. The empire of the one is more wide-spread than that of any other nation; the service of the other is more wide-spread than that of any other people. The

Africa's Service to the World.

Negro is found in all parts of the world. He has gone across Arabia, Persia, and India to China. He has crossed the Atlantic to the Western hemisphere, and here he has laboured in the new and in the old settlements of America; in the Eastern, Western, Northern and Southern States; in Mexico, Venezuela, the West Indies and Brazil. He is everywhere a familiar object, and he is, everywhere out of Africa, the servant of others. And in the light of the ultimate good of the universe, I do not see why the calling of the one should be considered the result of a curse, and the calling of the other the result of special favour. The one fulfils its mission by domination, the other by submission. The one serves mankind by ruling; the other serves mankind by serving. The one wears the crown and wields the sceptre; the other bears the stripes and carries the cross. Africa is distinguished as having *served* and *suffered*. In this, her lot is not unlike that of God's ancient people, the Hebrews, who were known among the Egyptians as the servants of all; and among the Romans, in later times, they were numbered by Cicero with the "nations born to servitude,"[4] and were protected, in the midst of a haughty population, only "by the contempt which they inspired." The lot of Africa resembles also His who made Himself of no reputation, but took upon Himself the form of a servant, and, having been made perfect through suffering, became the "Captain of our salvation." And if the principle laid down by Christ is that by which things are decided above, viz., that he who would be chief must become the servant of all, then we see the position which Africa and the Africans must ultimately occupy. And we must admit that through serving man, Africa—Ethiopia—has been stretching out her hands unto God.

But, if we understand the phrase to mean "suddenly," there is every indication that it will receive literal fulfilment. Men are now running to and fro, and knowledge of Africa is increasing. The downfall of Negro slavery in this country was sudden. The most sanguine philanthropists, thirty years ago, did not dream of

---

[4] Renan's *Hibbert Lectures*, p. 47.

so sudden a collapse of that hoary institution. And more has been learned of Africa in the seventeen years since slavery has been abolished, than was ever known during all the previous period of modern civilisation, or, perhaps, of the world's history. And now, every possible interest that can give impulse to human activity is aroused in connection with that land; and the current which is moving the civilised world thitherward, gains every day in force, in magnitude and in importance. The man of science is interested on account of the wonderful things that must be concealed in that vast continent. The statesman and politician is interested in the possibilities of new states yet to be founded in the march of civilisation. The merchant is interested in the new and promising outlets for trade. The philanthropist is interested in the opening of a career of progress, of usefulness, and of happiness before the millions of that country.

Another indication of the suddenness of Africa's regeneration is to be found in the restlessness of her descendants in this country. There are thousands of Negroes, in comfortable circumstances here, who are yet yearning after the land of their fathers; who are anxious, not so much to be relieved from present pressure, as to obtain an expansive field for their energies; who feel the need not only of horizontal openings—free movement on the plane which they occupy—but a chance to rise above it—a vertical outlet.

Within the last thirty years, the sentiment of race and of nationality has attained wonderful development. Not only have the teachings of thinkers and philosophers set forth the importance of the theory, but the deeds of statesmen and patriots have, more or less successfully, demonstrated the practicability of it. The efforts of men like Garibaldi and Cavour in Italy, of Kossuth in Hungary, of Bismarck in Germany, of the Ashantees and Zulus in Africa, have proved the indestructible vitality and tenacity of race.

Notwithstanding the widespread progress of Mohammedanism in Africa, and though it has largely influenced the organic life of numerous tribes in the vast regions of the Soudan, yet the Arabs, who first introduced the religion, have never been allowed to obtain political ascendancy. None of the Nigritian tribes have ever abdi-

Africa's Service to the World.

cated their race individuality or parted with their idiosyncracies in embracing the faith of Islam. But, whenever and wherever it has been necessary, great Negro warriors have arisen from the ranks of Islam, and, inspired by the teachings of the new faith, which merges all distinctions in one great brotherhood, have checked the arrogance of their foreign teachers, and have driven them, if at any time they affected superiority based upon race, from their artificial ascendancy. In the early days of Islam, when the Moors from the north attempted to establish political supremacy in the Nigritian countries, there rose up a Negro statesman and warrior, Soni Heli Ischia, and expelled the Moorish conquerors. He destroyed the ecclesiastical strongholds, which were fast growing into secular kingdoms, and erected upon their ruins one indigenous empire, having conquered all from Timbuctoo westward to the sea, and eastward to the frontier of Abyssinia, making about three thousand miles in length. Since then, Islam in Africa has been very much modified in its practices by the social peculiarities of the people. And, within the last twenty years, a distinguished native scholar and warrior, Omaru Al-Hajj, suppressed the undue influence of the Arabs at Timbuctoo—attacked that city in 1864, expelled the Arabs, and, with the same troops, confined the French to the western side of the Niger. His son Ahmadu now reigns at Sego, and, both by diplomacy and force, is checking or controlling the renewed operations of the French in the valley of the Niger.

This seems to be the period of race organisation and race consolidation. The races in Europe are striving to group themselves together according to their natural affinities. The concentration and development of the Sclavonic power in deference to this impulse is a menace to other portions of Europe. The Germans are confederated. The Italians are united. Greece is being reconstructed. And so this race impulse has seized the African here. The feeling is in the atmosphere—the plane in which races move. And there is no people in whom the desire for race integrity and race preservation is stronger than in the Negro.

And I may be permitted to add here, that on this question of race, no argument is necessary or effective. Argument may be necessary in discussing the methods or course of procedure for the preservation of race integrity, and for the development of race efficiency, but no argument is needed as to the necessity of such preservation and development. If a man does not feel it—if it does not rise up with spontaneous and inspiring power in his heart—then he has neither part nor lot in it. The man who needs conviction on this subject, had much better be left unconvinced.

The Rev. Henry Venn, the late able Secretary of the Church Missionary Society, frequently dealt with this subject in the "Instructions given to Missionaries at their dismission" from Salisbury Square. In one of these inimitable addresses he says, with large practicality and clearness of judgment:—

> The importance of taking into account national distinctions is forced upon us by the enlargement of our missionary experience. . . . . The committee warn you, *that these race distinctions will probably rise in intensity with the progress of the mission.* The distinctions may be softened down by grace; they may be hid from view in a season of the first love, and of the sense of unity in Christ Jesus; but they are part of our nature, and, as the satirist says, "You may expel Nature for a time by force, but it will surely return." So, distinctions of race are irrepressible. They are comparatively weak in the early stage of a mission, because all the superiority is on one side; but as the native race advances in intelligence, as their power of arguing strengthens, as they excel in writing sensational statements, as they become our rivals in the pulpit and on the platform, long cherished but dormant prejudices, and even passions, will occasionally burst forth.[5]

But to return after this digression. It is no doubt hard for you in this country to understand the strong race feeling in the Negro, or to appreciate the existence of such a feeling. As you glance over this land at the Negro population, their condition is such as to inspire, if not always the contempt, the despair, of the superficial observer, as to their future; and as you hear of their ancestral home, of its burning climate and its fatal diseases, of its sandy deserts and its malarious swamps, of its superstitious inhabitants and degraded populations, you fancy that you see not one glimpse of hope in the dim hereafter of such a race. But let me assure you that, ignoble as this people may appear here, they have brought a blessing to-

---

[5] Instructions of the Committee, June 30, 1868. See *Memoir of the Rev. H. Venn;* by Rev. William Knight, M.A.—Longmans, Green and Co., London, E.C.

Africa's Service to the World.

your shores; and you may rely upon it, that God has something in store for a people who have so served the world. He has something further to accomplish by means of a country of which He has so frequently availed himself in the past; and we may believe that out of it will yet come some of the greatest marvels which are to mark the closing periods of time.

Africa may yet prove to be the spiritual conservatory of the world. Just as in past times, Egypt proved the stronghold of Christianity after Jerusalem fell, and just as the noblest and greatest of the Fathers of the Christian Church came out of Egypt, so it may be, when the civilised nations, in consequence of their wonderful material development, shall have had their spiritual perceptions darkened and their spiritual susceptibilities blunted through the agency of a captivating and absorbing materialism, it may be, that they may have to resort to Africa to recover some of the simple elements of faith; for the promise of that land is that she shall stretch forth her hands unto God.

And see the wisdom and justice of God. While the Africans have been away rendering service their country has been kept for them. It is a very insignificant portion of that continent, after all, that foreigners have been permitted to occupy. Take any good map of Africa, and you will see that it is blank everywhere almost down to the sea. Senegambia, that important country north of the equator, has been much travelled over, and yet it is only on the coast and in spots here and there that it is occupied by Europeans. Going down along the west coast, we find the French colonies of Senegal and Goree, the British settlements at the Gambia, Sierra Leone, the Gold Coast and Lagos, the French colony of Gaboon, the Spanish island of Fernando Po, and the Portuguese colony of Loanda. The most important parts of the coast are still in the hands of the aborigines; and civilised and Christian Negroes from the United States occupy six hundred miles of the choicest territory in Africa, called the Republic of Liberia. All travellers along the Coast pronounce the region of country included within the limits of Liberia, as the most fertile and wealthy along the entire coast, and commanding a back country of untold resources. Europeans tried

Christianity, Islam and the Negro Race.

for centuries to get a foothold in that territory; but the natives would never consent to their settlement in it, while they gladly welcomed their brethren returning from exile in this country.

The exiled Negro, then, has a home in Africa. Africa is his, if he will. He may ignore it. He may consider that he is divested of any right to it; but this will not alter his relations to that country, or impair the integrity of his title. He may be content to fight against the fearful odds in this country; but he is the proprietor of a vast domain. He is entitled to a whole continent by his constitution and antecedents. Those who refuse, at the present moment, to avail themselves of their inheritance think they do so because they believe that they are progressing in this country. There has, no doubt, been progress in many respects in their condition here. I would not, for one moment, say anything that would cast a shadow upon their hopes, or blight, in the slightest degree, their anticipations. I could wish that they might realise to the fullest extent their loftiest aspirations. It is indeed impossible not to sympathise with the intelligent Negro, whose imagination, kindled by the prospects and possibilities of this great country, the land of his birth, makes him desire to remain and share in its future struggles and future glories. But he still suffers from many drawbacks. The stranger visiting this land, and going among its coloured inhabitants, and reading their newspapers, still hears the wail of slavery. The wail of physical suffering has been exchanged for the groans of an intellectual, social, and ecclesiastical ostracism. Not long since the touching appeal of a coloured man, almost in *forma pauperis*, before a great ecclesiastical assembly for equal rights in the Church,[o] was wafted over the country, and sent its thrilling tones into many a heart, but yet the only response has been the reverberation of the echo. And who cannot understand the meaning of the hesitancy on the part of the powers that be to grant the appeal? " He who runs may read."

As a result of their freedom and enlarged education, the de-

---

[o] Rev. Mr. Hammond before the General Conference of the Methodist Episcopal Church, held at Cincinnati, in May, 1880, on the question of the election of a coloured bishop.

Africa's Service to the World.

scendants of Africa in this country are beginning to feel themselves straitened. They are beginning to feel that only in Africa will they find the sphere of their true activity. And it is a significant fact that this impulse is coming from the Southern States. *There* is the great mass of the race; and there their instincts are less impaired by the infusion of alien blood and by hostile climatic influences. There we find the Negro in the almost unimpaired integrity of his race susceptibility, and he is by an uncontrollable impulse feeling after a congenial atmosphere which his nature tells him he can find only in Africa. *And he is going to Africa.*

As long as he remains in this country, he is hampered both in mind and body. He can conceive of no radiance, no beauty, no inspiration in what are ignorantly called " the Wilds of Africa." The society in which he lives in the lands of his exile he supposes, from knowing no other, to be the normal condition of man, and fancies he will suffer if he leaves it. But when he gets home he finds the atmosphere there a part of himself. He puts off the garment which has hampered his growth here, and he finds that he not only does not take cold, but has a chance for healthful development.

There is not a single Negro in the United States on the road to practical truth, so far as his race is concerned. He feels something in him, his instincts point to it, but he cannot act out what he feels. And when he has made up his mind to remain in America, he has also made up his mind to surrender his race integrity; for he sees no chance of its preservation. There is in him neither hope enough to excite the desire to preserve it, nor desire enough to encourage the hope of its preservation. But, in Africa, he casts off his trammels. His wings develop, and he soars into an atmosphere of exhaustless truth for him. There he becomes a righteous man; he casts off his fears and his doubts. There for him is perpetual health; there he returns to reason and faith. There he feels that nothing can happen to the race. There he is surrounded by millions of men, as far as he can see or hear, just like himself, and he is delivered from the constant dread which harasses him in this country, as to what is to become of the Negro. There the solicitude is in the opposite direction. There he fears for the white man, living in a climate hostile, and often fatal to him.

But there are two other facts, not, perhaps, generally known, to which I would like to call attention. The first is, that, notwithstanding the thousands and millions who, by violence and plunder, have been taken from Africa, she is as populous to-day as she ever was; and the other is, that Africa has never lost the better classes of her people. As a rule, those who were exported—nearly all the forty millions who have been brought away—belonged to the servile and criminal classes. Only here and there, by the accidents of war, or the misfortunes of politics, was a leading African brought away. Africa is often called the Niobe of all nations, in allusion to the fact that her children in such vast numbers have been torn from her bosom; but the analogy is not strictly accurate. The ancient fable tells that Niobe clung to her children with warding arms, while the envious deities shot child after child, daughters and fair sons, till the whole twelve were slain, and the mother, powerless to defend her offspring, herself became a stone. Now this is not the fact with Africa. The children who were torn from her bosom she could well spare. She has not been petrified with grief; she has not become a stone. She is as prolific to-day as in the days of yore. Her greenness and fertility are perennial. It was said of her in the past, and it may be said of her to-day, that she is ever bringing forth something new.

And she has not been entirely bereaved even of those who have been torn from her bosom. In all the countries of their exile, severe as the ordeal has been, they have been preserved. It might be said of them as of the Hebrews in Egypt, "the more they afflicted them, the more they multiplied and grew."

No; if we are to gather an analogy to Africa from ancient fable, the Sphinx supplies us with a truer symbol. The Sphinx was said to sit in the road side, and put riddles to every passenger. If the man could not answer, she swallowed him alive. If he could solve the riddle, the Sphinx was slain. Has not Africa been, through the ages, sitting on the highway of the world? There she is, south of Europe, with but a lake between, joined on to

Africa's Service to the World.

Asia, with the most frequented oceans on the east and west of her—accessible to all the races, and yet her secret is unknown. She has swallowed up her thousands. The Sphinx must solve her own riddle at last. The opening up of Africa is to be the work of Africans.

In the Providence of God, it seems that this great and glorious work is reserved for the Negro. Centuries of effort and centuries of failure demonstrate that white men cannot build up colonies there. If we look at the most recent maps of Africa, we see that large tracts have been explored: English, German, Belgian, French and American expeditions have lately described large portions of the continent; but every one must be struck by the enormous gaps that remain to be filled in—the vast portions which the foot of the white man has never trodden. With the exception of the countries south of Egypt, the great lake region, and the strip of country from east to west, containing the routes of Cameron and Stanley, and if we leave out the portion of North Central Africa explored by Barth—the country is still as unknown to foreigners as it has been throughout all history, from the days of Herodotus and Ptolemy to the present. Who knows anything of the mountains of the moon? of all that vast region which lies directly east of Liberia, as far as the Indian Ocean? What foreigner can tell anything of the interior of Bonny, or of Calabar? If we examine the Continent, from the extreme north to the extreme south, from Egypt to Kaffraria or the country of the Zulus, we see very little yet accomplished. The most successful effort yet made in colonising Africa is in Liberia. This will be permanent, because the colonists are of the indigenous stock. There are six hundred miles of coast, and two hundred miles of breadth, rescued for civilisation. I mean, in that extent of country, over a million of people are on the road to self-elevation. They come in contact with an atmosphere of growth.

Now the people who are producing these changes have a peculiar claim upon this country—for they went out from this nation and are carrying American institutions into that Continent. And this great country has peculiar facilities for the work of African civilisation. The nations of Europe are looking with anxious eyes to the "Dark Continent," as they love to call it, probably for the purpose of kindling their religious zeal, or stimulating their commercial instincts. But not one of them has the opportunity of entering that Continent with the advantages of the United States. They cannot send their citizens there from Europe to colonise— they die. France is now aiming at taking possession, by railroads, of the trade of the Soudan, from Algeria and Senegal. But the success of the scheme, through European agency, is extremely problematical. The question has been mooted of transferring their Negro citizens from the West Indies—from Martinique and Guadaloupe— but they cannot spare them from those islands. England would like to transport to the countries of the Niger, and to the regions interior of Sierra Leone, civilised blacks from her colonies in the Western hemisphere : but to encourage such a movement would be to destroy Barbadoes, Jamaica and Antigua. The King of the Belgians, in his philanthropic and commercial zeal for the opening and colonising of Africa, has no population available. The United States is the only country which, providentially, can do the work which the whole world now wants done. Entering on the West Coast, through Liberia, she may stretch a chain of colonies of her own citizens through the whole length of the Soudan, from the Niger to the Nile—from the Atlantic to the Indian Ocean.

This country, said Dr. Storrs, has thousands of liberated and Christianised Africans in it, just at the moment when that dark continent is suddenly opened to the access of the Gospel. God has been building here a power, for the glory of His name, and for His service in the earth. I see the stamp held in the hand, and the liquid wax lying before it ; and I do not doubt that the purpose is to fix the impression on that wax from the engraved brass or stone. I see the men whom man has brought here, and whom God has converted, and before them those vast outstretching realms made ready for the truth ; and I cannot doubt that His purpose is to fix by these men, upon those prepared lands, the inscription of the Gospel and the Cross ! And it seems to me that in the end all men must feel this." [7]

Some have already gone, the pioneers in this great work. Leaving the land of their birth, where they have laboured for

---

[7] Discourse before the American Missionary Association, October, 1879.

generations, they have gone to brave the perils of another wilderness, to cut down forests, to clear away jungles, to make roads, to build towns, to cultivate farms, and to teach regular industry to their less favoured brethren; and they ask you to follow these new settlements, as they push into the heart of the continent, with all the aids and appliances of your advanced civilisation.

In visions of the future, I behold those beautiful hills—the banks of those charming streams, the verdant plains and flowery fields, the salubrious highlands in primæval innocence and glory, and those fertile districts watered everywhere as the garden of the Lord; I see them all taken possession of by the returning exiles from the West, trained for the work of rebuilding waste places under severe discipline and hard bondage. I see, too, their brethren hastening to welcome them from the slopes of the Niger, and from its lovely valleys—from many a sequestered nook, and from many a palmy plain—Mohammedans and Pagans, chiefs and people, all coming to catch something of the inspiration the exiles have brought—to share in the borrowed jewels they have imported, and to march back hand-in-hand with their returned brethren towards the sunrise for the regeneration of a continent. And under their united labours, I see the land rapidly reclaimed—raised from the slumber of ages, and rescued from a stagnant barbarism; and then, to the astonishment of the whole world, in a higher sense than has yet been witnessed, "Ethiopia shall *suddenly* stretch out her hands unto God."

Echoes from Africa.

"THE fate of the Negro," it has been said "is the romance of our age." The events which have transpired in his history, since the great emancipation in the United States, and which are now transpiring, are in the highest degree romantic. There will always gather around the history of the race a pathetic interest, which must kindle the imagination, touch the heart, and awaken the sympathies of all in whom there is a spark of humanity.

The intelligence we have just received from America of large migrations of Negroes from the Southern to the Western States is full of melancholy and suggestive interest. To reflecting minds acquainted with the history of Southern society during the last fifty years these events are not surprising. Retributive justice may linger, but it is sure. A prosperity built up on the wrongs of a race by the unrequited labour of a whole people, ought not to have been expected to be permanent. In 1858, the chivalry of Louisiana passed a law forbidding free blacks to come in; now they would pass a law forbidding them to go out.

Many years ago, we are informed by a writer of Southern birth, an artist of Philadelphia was engaged by the State of South Carolina to paint some national emblematic picture for her State House. Jefferson Davis was requested to act with the South Carolina Committee at Washington in criticising the studies for this work. The most creditable sketch presented was a design representing the North by various mechanical implements; the West by a prairie and plough; while the South was represented by various things, the centre-piece, however, being a cotton-bale with a Negro upon it fast asleep. When Mr. Davis saw it, he said, "Gentlemen, this will never do; what will become of the South when the Negro wakes up?"

The discussions which the reconstruction laws have made

Echoes from Africa.

possible in the South, the circulation of newspapers, the education of Negro youth as preachers and teachers, have roused the Negro, and startled him to his feet. The thunders of the Civil War awoke him from his profound slumber; but he lay on the cotton-bale with his eyes open, uncertain where he was. The man who has been suddenly roused from a long sleep takes some time to recover himself. The Negro is now up—stupid, perhaps, as yet, from a protracted and undisturbed slumber, but he is up, and wants to adjust his relations to the cotton-bale upon an equitable footing, or leave the bale and its owner to their fate. Hence the exodus and migration idea, which menaces the South in every department of its organic life. And this is a specially inopportune moment for the carrying out of such an idea on anything like a large scale. The prosperity of the South has been rapidly returning under free labour, and was being placed on a satisfactory and enduring basis. Mr. Jefferson Davis lately declared that the ex-slaveholders were so far satisfied with the change that they would not, if they could, revert to the former system. And yet the owners of these reviving estates have been so unwise and reckless as to adopt such a system of treatment as has spread dissatisfaction among their hands. And, from all we can gather, this harsh and oppressive treatment has not been of a hap-hazard or isolated character, but the result of a deep-laid scheme. The plan seems to have been so to impoverish their labourers as to make them helplessly dependent, to check by a tyrannical repression the normal impulse of advance, to arrest the people through their elementary needs at a capriciously-chosen point in their progress, and *fix* them in it, and thus bring about a species of serfdom very little better than the former bondage.

The Rev. Joseph Cook, the celebrated Boston lecturer, in an address before the American Association, furnishes the following information:—

Last summer, on Lake Chautauqua, while I had a little leisure, I fell into conversation with one of the acutest members of Washington society—I dare not describe him more definitely—and he said to me : " The Negro is getting in debt. He is a peasant; he rents land; he has only very small wages; he buys his groceries at a store owned by his landlord, and runs up a bill there; and

Christianity, Islam and the Negro Race.

the silent scheme of the South is to get the Negro into debt. Then he cannot very well leave town until his debts are paid. He becomes a fixture, in many cases, because of his indebtedness; and, to make the story short, sir," said my informant, "some of us fear that fifty years hence a considerable portion of the freedmen will be in a state of peonage. They will be bankrupt tenants under the power of landlords. And it is often whispered in the South that this will be the next best thing to the restoration of slavery." [1]

No people having their eyes open and standing on their feet would long submit to such a state of things. But the intelligent among the Negro population do not seem to consider that any migration in the United States will materially affect for the better the social and political *status* of the coloured people.

The *People's Advocate* (Feb. 1, 1879), a coloured paper published at Washington, in an able editorial on the subject, says:—

There has been a very respectable partial migration, and no perceptible change has come over the South in its ideas of Negro citizenship. In 1869–70, 60,000 left Virginia and North Corolina for Alabama, Mississippi, Louisiana, and Arkansas. They left Georgia by the thousands for Arkansas, Mississippi, and Louisiana, and have gone from Eastern Virginia to New York and New England; but the feeling is nearly as bad to-day in Virginia and Georgia as it was years ago,

And they are now fleeing from Alabama, Mississippi and Louisiana.

'Tis but a poor relief they gain
Who change the place but keep the pain.

And it strikes us, viewing matters from this distant standpoint, that the feeling toward the Negro will continue to be "bad" in the United States, if being "bad" means the non-recognition of his social and political equality with the white man. For the Negro, pure and simple, there is no country but Africa, and in America his deeper instincts tell him so. He will never be understood, nor will he ever understand his European guide and teacher, as long as he remains in the countries of his exile. He is often misled by the overflowing and ceaseless generosity of white men into a belief that his benefactors are getting nearer to the idea of practical oneness and brotherhood with him. But among the phenomena in the relations of the white man to the Negro in the house of bondage

---

[1] 'The Three Despised Races,' &c., p. 25.

Echoes from Africa.

none has been more curious than this: that the white man, under a keen sense of the wrongs done to the Negro, will work for him, will suffer for him, will fight for him, will even die for him, but he cannot get rid of a secret contempt for him.

Mr. James Parton, in his article on 'Antipathy to the Negro,'[2] says:—

When Miss Kemble came first to Boston, in 1832, she sat next to the late John Quincy Adams at dinner one day, and the conversation turned upon the tragedy of "Othello." Miss Kemble has since reported one of Mr. Adams' remarks on this subject:—"Talking to me about Desdemona, he assured me, with a most serious expression of sincere disgust, that he considered all her misfortunes as a very just judgment upon her for having married a *nigger*." If this anecdote had not come to us on such respectable authority, we could hardly believe it of a man who, during the last and best ten years of his life, was looked upon as the black man's champion.

Theodore Parker, who, in pleading for the slave, could " stir his hearers to the bottom of their hearts and soften them to tears;" who, in his famous letter to Millard Fillmore (Nov. 21, 1850), could say :—

I would rather lie all my life in jail and starve there, than refuse to protect one of these parishioners of mine. . . . . William Craft and Ellen were parishioners of mine. They have been at my house. I married them a fortnight ago this day. After the ceremony I put a Bible and then a sword into William's hands, and told him the use of each. . . . . There hang beside me in my library, as I write, the gun my grandfather fought with at the battle of Lexington—he was a captain on that occasion—and also the musket he captured from a British soldier on that day, the first taken in the war for independence. If I would not peril my property, my liberty, my life, to keep my parishioners out of slavery, then I would throw away these trophies, and should think I was the son of some coward, and not a brave man's child.[3]

Theodore Parker, who could say, "I should like of all things to see an insurrection of slaves;"[4] who could pronouce that pathetic and touching but terrible discourse over the great Webster; this same Theodore Parker did not think it inconsistent with his high

---

[2] *North American Review*, Nov.-Dec., 1878.

[3] *Biography of Theodore Parker;* by Octavius Brooks Frothingham.—Boston, James R. Osgood & Co., 1875; pp. 410, 411.

[4] Ibid., p. 475.

ideal of human liberty and equal rights to write in a private letter as follows :—

> Last night I could not coax the thermometer down below 79 degrees any way we could fix it. Now, at eight and a-half a.m., I dare not look at it, it is so high. In the midst of the heat, there just came a monstrous African black! O dear, how black he was! Fat! bless me, he looked like a barrel (no, a *sugar hogshead*) of tar, so black, so fat! What an aggravation, with the thermometer at 90 degrees in the shade![5]

We should have taken this for the irrepressible overflow of harmless witticism but for other disparaging references to the Negro. To Miss Hunt he writes, under date November 10, 1857 :—

> There are inferior races which have always borne the same ignoble relation to the rest of men, and *always will*. For two generations what a change there will be in the condition and character of the Irish in New England! But, in twenty generations, the Negroes will stand just where they are now; that is, if they have not disappeared. In Massachusetts there are no laws now to keep the black man from any pursuit, any office, that he will; but there has never been a rich Negro in New England; not a man with ten thousand dollars, perhaps none with five thousand dollars; none eminent in anything except the calling of a *waiter*.[6]

Again: "In respect to the *power of civilisation*, the African is at the bottom, the American Indian next."[7] Again: "When slavery is abolished, the African population will decline in the United States, and die out of the South as out of Northampton and Lexington."[8]

Mr. Parker, after all he said and did for freedom, seems to have had an invincible contempt for weak and oppressed races. He waged uncompromising warfare against the process by which such peoples are degraded, but had no charity toward those suffering from the results of such process. He fought against the parent, and ridiculed the offspring. The abstract to him was hateful ; the concrete examples contemptible or ludicrous. He scorned the Irish and laughed at the Negro. He speaks of the Irish as follows :—

> I don't know but these Paddies are worse than the Africans to the country. We made a great mistake in attracting them here and allowing them to vote under less than twenty-one years of quarantine. Certainly it would take all

---

[5] *Biography*, p. 311.   [6] Ibid., p. 467.   [7] Ibid., p. 327.   [8] Ibid., p. 478.

Echoes from Africa.

that time to clean a Paddy—on the *outside*, I mean; to clean him inwardly would be like picking up all the sands of the Sahara. There would be nothing left when the sands were gone.[9]

It is a pity that in speaking of the "gintleman from Car-r-r-k," as in caricature he describes the Irishman, and of "the poor wretches from Africa," he did not conform to his own canon of criticism. Speaking of Pierpont, he says: "Just now, considering all that he has done and suffered, it would seem a little ungenerous to be quite just. All pictures must be painted in reference to the light they are to hang in and be looked at."[10]

Mr. Parker knew the "light" of prejudice and contempt in which his picture of the Negro was to "hang," and yet, making no allowance for circumstances, and uninfluenced by the laws of moderation, he holds the balance between light and shade with an indifferent hand, paints in the gloomiest possible colours, and thus encourages rather than disarms the falsifying faculty of the observer, predisposed to an unfavourable impression.

Would Mr. Parker have joined Dennis Kearney, and raised a crusade in favour of the inhospitable legislation proposed by the opponents of Chinese immigration? In view of the splendid results in the United States, and in the world generally, of the manly struggle which Mr. Parker maintained for truth and freedom—in view of the large sacrifices which he unquestionably made in the cause of free humanity—many errors of temper and judgment on his part may be forgotten; but the Negro can never forget the slurs upon his race, of which, however, no one, perhaps, more readily than Mr. Parker would now admit the impolicy, if not the injustice. For how do such utterances differ in character and effects from those of the Notts and Gliddons, of the Calhouns and Jeff. Davises? And the fact—which should be suggestive to thinking Negroes in the United States—that they are reproduced in the Biography by Mr. Frothingham, shows that there is a feeling that they are the proper thing to say, even now, about the Negro. Can Congressional legislation remedy the evils produced

---

[9] Ibid., p. 473.   [10] *Biography*, p. 329.

by such caricatures and misrepresentations? Congress may decree civil rights to the "despised" race in America, and the exigencies of party may occasionally bring the Negro to the front; but what progress can he make when a public sentiment against him is fostered in the writings and in the private intercourse of his friends? In the language of the Liberian Declaration of Rights, "Public sentiment, more powerful than law, will never frown him down."

The Negro, pure and simple, may rely upon it that, for him, the most enthusiastic of his benefactors sees nothing but the lowest occupations. In the case of the most liberal of his advocates, he will have occasionally to exclaim, *Et tu, Brute!*

A writer in the *Methodist Quarterly Review* for January, 1875, on 'The Negro,' has the following among the closing sentences of an able and plausible defence of the race:—

> Without the Negro, the top-stone of our national greatness will not be lifted to its predestined lofty altitude for centuries yet to come. Expatriate the Negro, and our cotton-fields whiten no more; our turpentine orchards become silent as the grave; our rice-fields grow up into canebrakes, sheltering the alligator and wild boar.

But does the American conscience ever look forward to the time when, in the United States, the Negro will have any common interest in, or any—the slightest possible—control over, the political and financial elements of the country—when he will be needed as a part of the directing agency in the halls of legislation, in counting-houses, and in banking establishments?

Mr. Parton, in the *North American Review*, says:—

> The South is most happy in possessing the Negro, for it is through his assistance that there will be the grand agriculture in the Southern States, which cannot flourish unless there is a class to labour and individuals to contrive. The Southern farmer, by the black man's help, can be a "scholar and a gentleman," and at the same time secure and elevate the black man's life.

Such utterances "give colour to the idea" that the Negro was made to live and improve only in the service, and under the guidance of, a superior. If this view is correct, then why does not the great Creator allow the elect masters to have free access and safe incursion into the natural home of the created slaves, and

Echoes from Africa.

live in a land where they might hold their predestined *protégés* in unlimited numbers, and in comfortable service? Why did He make for the slaves so magnificent a country, and surround it with a wall of fire, so that if the master comes to the threshold, he either beats a hasty retreat, or perishes in the attempt to penetrate?

> Massa run away,
> Darkee stay, oh oh!

No; the destiny of the Negro and his marvellous country is veiled from the view of the outside world according to the wise and beneficent purposes of Omniscience.

> God is His own interpreter,
> And He will make it plain.

He can wait, if the impatient Caucasian cannot.

The American Missionary Association (whose publications we have added to this paper in the contents page) in their work of lofty and noble purpose throughout the South, are endeavouring to prepare the Negro for higher spheres of labour than "cotton-fields, turpentine orchards, and rice-fields." Every Negro who is at all acquainted with matters in the United States must have the highest admiration for that Association. Almost alone among the benevolent institutions of that land in the days of the great struggle, they never, for one moment, yielded to the imperious dictates of an oligarchical monopoly, but gave expression to the idea which they inscribed upon their banner, that one of the chief purposes of their organisation was to resist the tyranny of the autocracy which doomed the Negro to perpetual servitude. No one could be enrolled among the members of their Society who was a "slave-holder." They have the gratitude of the Negro race.

But history will have a brighter page than even that with which to adorn their annals, when she comes to recount the devotion and sacrifices of the hundreds who have been sent forth, under their auspices, as uplifters of the prostrate host in the South, to whom, left as they were, paralysed by slavery, free movement and real progress were intrinsically impossible without the aid of such agencies as the American Missionary Association. As time rolls

Christianity, Islam and the Negro Race.

on, the romance which clings to those heroes who fought to unfetter the body of the slave will fade beside the halo which will surround those who have laboured to liberate his mind.

We have read, with the deepest interest, the Report and some of the addresses made at the Thirty-second Anniversary of this Association, held in October, 1878, as well as letters from various portions of the field under its supervision. In reading the accounts of the struggles and sufferings of the missionaries, their sorrows and disappointments, their battles and their victories among the lowly in remote and sequestered districts, it is often impossible to repress tears—tears of sympathy, of gratitude, and of joy.

At the Annual Meeting, the Rev. C. M. Southgate said:—

We heard words of hearty praise this afternoon, telling of the success of the work. They tell hardly enough. But these efforts should be redoubled. We want more institutions like those at Atlanta, New Orleans, Charleston, and the other large Southern cities where high culture and intelligence rule. The scholarship can be compared without fear with similar grades at the North. I never heard, in our boasted common schools, such recitations as I have heard from boys as black as the blackest. I know what Yale and Harvard and Dartmouth can show; but, in Greek and Latin, those coloured students can rival their excellence. The culture in morals and manners is at least not inferior, nor the religious instruction less fruitful. The report from the Churches shows as large and as healthy success as we can show here. The young men and women in these institutions have an intense longing to be at work for the Master. The desperate condition of their race rests upon them like a pall. God is making them His prophets, and speaking through them, and sending redemption.

The Rev. Dr. Bascom, in a letter from Alabama, says:—

I see abundant proofs of the beneficent work of your Society here. Could its influence have been exerted in like manner among all our coloured people of the South, the problem so perplexing to politicians and philanthropists, as to the future of this class in our country, would have been already solved.

The Committee on the "Normal Work of the Association" reported that—

The eagerness of the coloured people to obtain at least a rudimentary education has ever been a most encouraging sign. The young man who, last year, walked fifty miles with his trunk upon his back that he might enter school, recalls the zeal of the late Dr. Godell, of Constantinople, who, in his youth, also walked sixty miles with a trunk strapped upon his back, that he

Echoes from Africa.

might enter Phillips Academy, at Andover. The demand for teachers from the normal schools—quite beyond the ability to supply them—is one of the surest indications that the schools are meeting an urgent need.

We regret that Professor Hartranft, in his able address on the "Five Tests of American Civilisation," should have spoken of the "brutality of the Negro." In what portion of the United States has that "brutality" been shown? Such a charge is in flagrant contradiction to all the testimony borne of the Negro by those who know him best.

And here we must venture to enter our earnest protest against the use of such phrases as "The Despised Races," which we see frequently used of late in the publications of the American Missionary Association. The Rev. Joseph Cook addressed the Association on the "Three Despised Races," and he was followed by the Rev. C. M. Southgate on "Puritanism and the Despised Races." Such expressions as "The Despised Race" and "The Dark Continent," applied to the Negro and his ancestral home, have not, we fancy, the most salutary effect either upon those who employ them or upon those to whom they refer; in the one they often beget arrogance; in the other, servility or resentment. They do more than serve the *ad captandum* purposes for which they are probably intended. In using "great plainness of speech" the instructors of humanity should be "wise as serpents and harmless as doves," which, according to a Negro interpreter, means "an ounce of serpent to a pound of dove." Moreover, the whole of the rest of mankind does not hold the European, in view of his past history, in such unqualified admiration as to admit without serious question that he has a right to embody in terse phrases, and to parade in the titles of books, pamphlets, and addresses his contempt for other races. There are those of other races who also sneer and scorn and "despise." Some of the proceedings of Baker and Stanley in Africa must frequently have impressed the natives with the feeling that those energetic travellers came from much "darker continents" than any their unsophisticated imaginations had ever before suggested to them. The African now coming forward through education and culture cannot have unlimited respect for all the qualities of the European races: "A people with a passion for taking away the countries of others and dignifying the robbery as conquests; and whose systematic cruelty has been shown for ages, in chaining, buying, and selling another race." The intelligent Negro feels that the part of the oppressor is not less to be despised than the part of the oppressed—that the part of the man-stealer and man-seller is far more contemptible than the part of the man stolen and sold. And this he will feel more and more. The brilliancy of the universal and prolonged success which has given the European the idea that he has a right to despise others, and to proclaim the fact—the glories which have followed in the wake of his progress and conquests—are getting sadly dimmed in the light of a fuller understanding of the Gospel of Christ. Under the searching criticisms of rising intellects imbued with the essence of a Christian philosophy, and influenced by the spirit of a science properly so called, those brutal instincts which received the eulogiums of the past are finding their proper recognition as elements of character to be reprobated and suppressed. The Bosworth Smiths of to-day are superseding the Carlyles of yesterday. Might no longer makes right. The motto on the British coat-of-arms is being slightly altered—not " God and *my* Right," but " God and *the* Right." Whatever " smacks of saltpetre "[11] is being deprecated and condemned. Says the eloquent author of *Carthage and the Carthaginians* :—

It is equally reprehensible, whether it be the plunder of half of Europe by the representative of one of its most enlightened nations, the arch-robber of modern times, Napoleon; or the sack of a Chinese palace by those whom the Chinese had a right, in this instance at least, to style Barbarians. If good men and great nations have hitherto often followed the example of Cicero in drawing a broad contrast between the extortions of a Verres and the highhanded plunder of Marcellus, a Warren Hastings, or a Napoleon, it is because they have not yet reached the moral standard which condemns the public robber; they look askance only at a thief.[12]

---

[11] Lord Salisbury's Speech in the House of Lords, 1879.

[12] *Carthage and the Carthaginians;* by R. Bosworth Smith, M.A., Assistant Master in Harrow School, &c.—London: Longmans, Green & Co., 1878. When

Echoes from Africa.

History, then, as it is read by the thinking Negro, will not diminish the vehemence of his protest against the injustice of being regarded by the European as belonging to a "despised race," nor lessen the grounds of his desire to reciprocate the disparaging sentiment. His hands are free from the blood of other men. He has not in any way oppressed other races. He has suffered, *and that is all*. He has been scattered and peeled, despoiled and plundered, abused, persecuted, and down-trodden, *and that is all*. The late Professor Tayler Lewis, of Union College, when he was once asked the flippant question, "What shall we do with the Negro?" replied, "And pray, sir, what shall the Negro do with you? It is my logic, with no disrespect to anybody, that one question is as fair as the other." [13]

The Negroes on the African continent who have not read European history are divided into two classes, namely, those who have seen and had intercourse with the Europeans, and those who have never seen but only heard of them. The view taken by the former at this moment was exactly that described by Mungo Park a hundred years ago.[14] A century has made no change. Of the impressions of the latter we have a fair specimen in one of Stanley's amusing anecdotes. That distinguished traveller, describing the people on the south-western shores of Lake Tanganyika, says:—

The conduct of the first natives to whom we were introduced pleased us all. They showed themselves in a very amiable light, sold their corn cheaply and without fuss, behaved themselves decently and with propriety, though their principal men, *entertaining very strange ideas of white men*, carefully concealed themselves from view, and refused to be tempted to expose themselves within view or hearing of us.

Their doubts of our character were reported to us by a friendly young Arab as follows: "Kassanga, chief of Ruanda, says, 'How can the white men be good when they come for no trade, whose feet one never sees, who always go covered from head to foot with clothes? Do not tell me they are good an

---

Dr. Johnson expressed a hope that he might never hear of the Punic Wars again, he never anticipated anything like this brilliant and charming work— this startling investment in flesh and blood of the dry bones of Carthaginian history.

[13] *Methodist Quarterly Review*, Oct. 1878, p. 617,
[14] *Park's Travels*.

friendly. There is something very mysterious about them; perhaps wicked. Probably they are magicians; at any rate, it is better to leave them alone, and to keep close until they are gone.'"

And again :—

> In these people we first saw the mild, amiable, unsophisticated innocence of this part of Central Africa, and their behaviour was exactly the reverse of the wild, ferocious, cannibalistic races the Arabs have described to us.[15]

After the disparaging view of the Negro taken by Professor Hartranft, it is not surprising that he should have exclaimed :—

> As to the African, there are not a few Americans, even in this day, who think a righteous solution of the African question is to ship them all off to the Dark Continent. So far as the American Colonisation Society keeps in view education and other Christian instrumentalities I bid them God-speed; but if they desire to send the Negro out of the country, I say, No !—a thousand times, No ! Let us solve the problem right here where God has placed them.

We cannot help repeating the last words of the paragraph—" right here where *God has placed them* "—and we think of the sanguinary scenes attending the capture and deportation of their fathers from the ancestral land; the devastation of flourishing districts; the desolation and ruin by fire and sword; the pillage, the plunder, the murders, and the horrors of the middle passage.

There was among philanthropists a difference of opinion when these people, or their fathers, were being shipped to America; and Professor Hartranft is not alone in his benevolent scruples about shipping them back to the " Dark Continent."

The Rev. Sylvanus Heywood, who seems to have a higher appreciation of the race and of its work, speaks of the Negro as the " black diamond plucked out of Africa," and advocates for him an education the same in character and completeness as that given to the white man. He says :—

> You may enact laws and hedge them about with penalties for securing the rights of the blacks, but law alone will prove a failure. But give to them the highest Christian culture, and they will not only demand, but command, their rights. Give them a common school education, and it will be a blessing to them; but with nothing more they will remain but hewers of wood and drawers of water. They will be *in* society, but not *of* it. But give them the highest culture among cultured men, and the case will be far different. It is too late in

---

[15] *Through the Dark Continent;* vol. ii, pp. 68, 69.

Echoes from Africa.

the day to raise the question whether they are capable of this. This Association has demonstrated that day by day. I have spent ten years as a teacher among the whites, and two among the blacks, and I must say that I accomplished more in those two years than in ten—more in the way of giving instruction. I say, it is too late to raise that question at all. It is already demonstrated. Let them be educated with broad culture. Let them have the training that will put them in possession of practical skill, such as shall win success. Let them have their own lawyers well trained in legal lore, so that they shall be able—in that natural eloquence in which they excel—to carry conviction to dignified courts. Let them have clergymen, not only earnest and sanctified, but able to cope with the deep things of science and theology—men able to stand before the most learned bodies. Let them have statesmen, well grounded in philosophy, history, and government, so that they will be able, not only to win victories upon the stump, but in the halls of legislation. Let their homes become homes of Christian culture and social refinement. Then, and not till then, will they cease to struggle for their rights and *take* them.

But Mr. Heywood takes also a much broader view of the logical and necessary sequence of all this high culture—of all this effective training. He points to the fatherland. His philosophy is correct. For the Negro, pure and simple, this is the only real solution of his difficulties. He says:—

The ways of God are mysterious. We must walk by faith, and not by sight. We hear His voice saying, "This is the way; walk ye in it." In this darkness we see His hand. In the raising of this Society and the doing away with slavery, we can see almost visibly the hand of God displayed upon the midnight sky, pointing to that dark continent, saying we should send these freemen forth as the apostles of light to purify and make glad their ancestral homes.

No man who has any proper conception of the capacities and work of the Negro, and has caught anything like a glimpse of his ultimate destiny, can fail to arrive at Mr. Heywood's conclusion. To the intelligent and earnest Negro in America, there is, as he rises in culture, an ever-widening horizon of duty and of liberty—Home, or rather the place of his birth, gets too narrow for liberty, too circumscribed for work, and he looks to Africa as the field for both.

In an able article in the London *Times* for May 19, on the Negro migration in the United States, the following words occur:—

The truth is, that the Negro is not a migratory being. He did not come of his own accord to Virginia, or any other Southern State; nor will he willingly leave it again now that he is acclimatised there. He has found an Africa in the South which is quite as congenial to him as that from which his forefathers were transported.

Christianity, Islam and the Negro Race.

On the subject of the Negro, *The Times* and everybody else, not African, are utterly in the dark. An acknowledged mystery hangs about him and his destiny. Foreigners do not know the Negro. They have never had an opportunity of knowing him. Foreign slavery on the one hand, and aboriginal barbarism on the other, are the only circumstances under which they have had an opportunity of contemplating him. It is true that the " Negro is not a migratory being." He would never have appeared on American soil, if he had not been taken thither by violence. And the restlessness he now shows is among the strongest proofs of his freedom. He is now free to think and act for himself, and the consciousness of being a stranger in a strange land is beginning to operate upon him. *The Times* admits that " this is not the first symptom of a desire for change among the coloured citizens; " and yet it fancies that the Negro has found " an Africa in the South which is quite as congenial to him as that from which his forefathers were transported." The fact is, that the Negro is getting, every day, more and more into a position to show himself no longer a dormant, but an active, factor among the forces of civilisation, and the European will witness, almost daily, new developments in his character—the exhibition of qualities never suspected. Next to ridicule, one of the most repulsive things to a sensitive mind is sympathy unduly extended, especially when the sympathiser has no means of correctly estimating the situation which he imagines should call forth his sympathy. There are very few Europeans who are qualified either to guide or to sympathise with the Negro in the countries of his exile; and gratuitous advice, even from these, in vital questions of his race, has no practical influence upon him.

" The enthusiasm for Liberia " has not died out, as *The Times* imagines. The American Colonisation Society has at this moment five hundred thousand applicants for passage to Liberia. Dr. A. L. Stanford, a Negro of culture, who was sent last year as Commissioner to Liberia from his people in Arkansas, returned with a favourable report, in which he says:—

> After travelling extensively in Liberia and observing the prosperous condition of the colony which the American Colonisation Society has planted—

Echoes from Africa.

and, I am convinced, firmly established—I am prepared to lend my aid in disabusing the public mind in regard to the noble efforts put forth by that Society in elevating the downtrodden Negro race. I entertain very different views from what I held before. I verily believe that Africa is the natural home of the Negro, and that ere long the remnant of her descendants, wherever dispersed, will return to that land. I favour a gradual emigration of the more enterprising, hard-working, and intelligent class of American Negroes. I believe such a course would prove a blessing to Africa and to the race.[10]

It is admitted by all travellers to the coast that Liberia occupies five hundred miles of the finest and most picturesque portion of West Africa, with an interior extending two hundred miles or indefinitely back, abounding in everything necessary for the growth and prosperity of a people. The whole valley of the Niger is accessible to this Republic, teeming with a population everywhere hospitable and friendly, ready and anxious to welcome to their salubrious, prolific, and picturesque home, their brethren returning from the countries of their exile.

In the trade and commerce of this country there seems to be a special interest, not only for the Negroes in the United States, but for the whole American people. There would be unlimited demand for American productions in that vast region now almost untouched. Gold, and hides, and beeswax, and rubber, as well as the finest coffee, might be had in unlimited quantities. Not far from Liberia are the unvisited but easily accessible and wealthy countries north and west of Ashantee and Dahomey, possessing the very highest capacity for the consumption of manufactured articles and for the production of raw material—from which a prodigious trade, struggling for an outlet, filters through, in very small quantities, to the Gulf of Benin.

Viewing the subject in this light, it becomes a practical business question whether there are no large capitalists in the Northern or Southern States willing to invest in an entirely virgin country, so much nearer to the United States than many of those countries from which at great expense tropical productions are now obtained for the American market—a field where agriculture may find

---

[10] *African Repository*, April, 1879 ; pp. 40, 41.

unobstructed scope; where so many results, moral, political and pecuniary, may be at once achieved; and where a Christian nation, with its multifarious agencies for diffusing civilisation, may be built up. If American capitalists desired to engage in agriculture, and to produce the far-famed Liberia coffee, or any other tropical product, they could themselves select and send out able hands from America for this work, who, while building up a congenial home for themselves and their children, and making "the wilderness and solitary place glad" for their presence, would be also enlarging the wealth of their patrons.

At a banquet given in Paris on the 19th of May, 1879, in commemoration of the abolition of slavery, M. Victor Hugo said: "In the nineteenth century, the white man has made the Negro a man, and, in the twentieth century, Europe will make Africa a world."

We admire the epigrammatic form of this sentence, but we venture to disagree with the sentiment it contains. As philosopher and prophet, the great poet is in this instance mistaken. Poetical inspirations do not always suggest sound political lessons. But what he said further on in his speech should be carefully pondered by all intelligent Negroes everywhere. He said:—

The day had come for the vast continent which alone among the five parts of the world had no history, to be reformed by Europeans. The Mediterranean was a lake of civilisation, and it was the duty of Greece and of Italy, of France and of Spain, the four countries that occupied its northern shores, to recollect that a vast territory lay unredeemed on the opposite coast. England was also worthy to take part in the great work. She, like France, was one of the great free nations of the globe; and, like France, she had begun the colonisation and civilisation of Africa. The latter held the north and east, the former the south and the west. America had joined in the task, and Italy was ready to do so. This showed the unity of spirit which pervaded the people of the world. M. Victor Hugo then described the magnificent scenery, the fertility, and the navigable rivers of Central Africa in eloquent language, and concluded by exhorting the European nations to occupy this land offered to them by God, to build towns, to make roads, to cultivate the earth, to introduce trade and commerce, to preach peace and concord; so that the new continent should not be the scene of strife, but, free from princes and priests, should enjoy the blessings of fraternity.[17]

---

[17] *Daily Telegraph*, May 20.

Echoes from Africa.

It is really high time that a "unity of spirit should pervade the peoples of the world" for the regeneration of a continent so long despoiled by the unity or consent of these same peoples. Thinking Negroes should ask themselves what part they will take in this magnificent work, the work of reclaiming a continent—*their own continent*. In what way will they illustrate their participation in the "unity of spirit" which pervades the peoples for the redemption of their fatherland? Compared to this, most of the questions with which they are endeavouring to grapple in the United States, sink into insignificance. The local can bear no comparison to the universal, nor the temporary to the eternal.

Victor Hugo exhorts the European nations to "occupy this land offered to them by God." He has forgotten the prudent advice of Cæsar to the ancestors of those nations against invading Africa. The Europeans can hold the domain "offered to them" by only a precarious tenure. But it already belongs to the exiled Negro. It is his by creation and inheritance. Every man, woman, and child of the Negro race out of Africa ought to thank God for this glorious heritage, and hasten to possess it—a field for the physical, moral, and spiritual development of the Negro, where he will live under the influence of his freshest inspirations; where, with the simple shield of faith in God and in his race, and with the sword of the spirit of progress, he will grow and thrive; where, with his sympathetic heart, he will catch stray, far-off tones, inaudible to the foreigner, which, penetrating through the local air, will waken chords in his nature now unknown to the world, and unsuspected even by himself. He will come under the influence of powers which will haunt him with strange visions, and indicate the way he should go. Emerson says:—

<blockquote>
A man's genius, the quality that differences him from every other, the susceptibility to one class of influences, the selection of what is fit for him, the rejection of what is unfit, determines for him the character of the universe. A man is a method, a progressive arrangement, a selecting principle, gathering his like to him wherever he goes. He takes only his own out of the multiplicity that sweeps and circles round him. He is like one of those booms which are set out from the shore on rivers to catch drift-wood, or like the loadstone among splinters of steel. . . . . . A few anecdotes, a few traits of character, manners, face, a few incidents, have an emphasis in your memory out of all
</blockquote>

proportion to their apparent significance, if you measure them by the ordinary standards. They relate to your gift. Let them have their weight, and do not reject them and cast about for illustrations and facts more useful to literature. What your heart thinks great is great. The soul's emphasis is always right.[18]

When Professor Hartranft says, "Let us solve the Negro problem right here," in America, to what "problem" does he refer? and how does he propose to solve the great questions of the African race in the United States? There are certain problems at times set before a people by accidental and temporary circumstances; these may admit of solution by extraneous help. There are others which grow out of their natural, inherent, and unchangeable relation to the outside world, or the universe; these are to be solved by the people themselves under favouring circumstances; the trusts and responsibilities which these impose are special, incommunicable, and inalienable. But probably Professor Hartranft means the problem pressing upon the white man in his relations to the Negro; the problem of his duty toward the "despised" race—his power to arrive at a satisfactory solution being a "test" of his civilisation. In regard to this, of course, we can suggest nothing. But, from all we can gather, it appears that the chief problem held up to the Negro for *his* solution by his friends in America is that of "conquering the caste prejudices of the whites" around him; of becoming, as the usual phrase is, "a man among men" (white men); of "wiping out the colour line," &c. Now, we beg most respectfully, with all the earnestness and deference becoming the subject, and with the serious emphasis which we know the enlightened of the race would authorise us to employ, to assure our white friends that these are matters for which the Negro, when cultivated up to Mr. Heywood's standard, will care very little. He will then feel that, in his own race-groove and on his own continent, he has a work to accomplish equal to that of the European, and that caste or race prejudices are as natural to him as to the white man. The passion for equality does not always exert an elevating influence on the character, but may be positively mischievous where, to produce or sustain it, certain sentiments in the

---

[18] The Prose Works of Ralph Waldo Emerson; vol. i, p. 292.

Echoes from Africa.

mind are flattered by holding the higher attributes in abeyance, or brought into prominence at the expense of judgment and love of truth.

Ripe scholarship and disciplined thought, even under the training he is receiving in America, will give to the Negro a freshness, a manliness, a hopefulness, and a faith which will deliver him from the tyranny of his surroundings, widen his view of his own capabilities, make him conscious of belonging to a race which has rich things in store for the world, and glorify his heart with a thousand strange and fruitful sympathies, and with endless heroic aspirations.

The Negro who is really restless on the subject of caste in America is he who, from defective culture or lack of culture, has not half found out the calling of his race; who, consequently, unduly impressed by his surroundings, is eager for immediate success, and anxious to play his part well amid the circumstances in which he finds himself—aiming at technical skill, which is popular or fashionable, rather than artistic life, which may be unique and unpopular. Fascinated by the present, he cannot conceive anything else, and harasses himself with the ever-recurring and ever-unsatisfying and unsatisfactory task of imitating imitators. The Negro, raised to Mr. Heywood's standard, will feel the force of Emerson's words:—

> We like only such actions as have already long had the praise of men, and do not perceive that anything man can do may be divinely done. We think greatness entailed or organised in some places, or duties in certain offices or occasions, and do not see that Paganini can extract rapture from a catgut, and Eulenstein from a jew's-harp, and a limber-fingered lad out of shreds of paper with his scissors, and Landseer out of swine, and the hero out of the pitiful habitation and company in which he was hidden. What we call obscure condition or vulgar society is that condition and society whose poetry is not yet written, but which you shall presently make as enviable and renowned as any.[10]

Recognising the force of these truths, the cultivated Negro will have insight enough to discover his exact relation to surrounding superficial phenomena, and self-respect and independence enough

---

[10] Prose Works, vol. ii, p. 291.

to acknowledge the fact that his peculiar work cannot be done under the overshadowing influence of a foreign race; that there he cannot "communicate himself to others in his full stature and proportion;" and, feeling this, he will turn to the fatherland, to "the one direction in which all space is open to him," and under the conviction that "he has faculties inviting him thither to endless exertion."

The teachers of the Negro in America cannot have failed to observe that there seems always to be in the mind of their pupils some reservation which they cannot overcome—some hesitancy which they cannot explain, but which they attribute to a sort of modesty growing out of a sense of inferiority in the pupil. But the fact is, that, under the influence of the means of culture to which he has access, his race-consciousness is kindled into active and sensitive life, and he receives, under mental protest, many a dogma, which for European growth and development is orthodox and inspiring. Not only the physical and metaphysical teachings often puzzle and contradict his deepest feelings, but even the Scriptures are, at times, a perplexity to him; and as he becomes acquainted with the original languages in which they were written, he feels that there is in them a temporary and local element which must be separated from the permanent and universal, before the sacred records can utter what, in the depths of his being, he wants to say. But, in America, he will never be able to make the discrimination that will be useful to him. He will never be able to translate the letter, which is often adapted to another age and race, into the spirit of his own times and race. He is, therefore, lonely with his secret, with which nothing around him seems to sympathise. Development is denied him; he cannot expand. He fills his belly with theories and dogmas which to him are like the dry, hard husk. He cannot digest them, and they afford him no nourishment. Nearly everything he produces comes from the memory; very little flows fresh from the heart. The African Methodist Episcopal Church in the United States is the result, in part, of just such experiences on the part of the Bishop Allens of a former day. They found that the waters flowing from the fountain

Echoes from Africa.

which God had opened in their soul were slackened and half-choked by being forced through the pent-up and artificial channels provided for them in the white Churches, and they established that noble organisation—the admiration of Negroes everywhere, which during the last fifty years has attained such wonderful growth—that the living streams of their unfettered nature might wind their own sweet way along the meadows of an ecclesiastical Liberia. If the fare with which they were furnished in the new religious Republic was ridiculed by their enemies as "ash cake," it was to them more than the wheat bread upon which they were starved in their previous connection. The food now dispensed to them was to their souls the very bread of life.

But there are many drawbacks to this *imperium in imperio*. It grew out of a temporary and local necessity, and, like all such products, must be partial and limited in its influence. Does it not become this most honourable and useful body—this first-born of African Churches—this pledge and proof of Africa's future evangelisation—to inquire whether they may not increase their efficiency and even develop their central strength by taking a wider, deeper, and more practical interest in the land of their fathers, in their kith and kin in Africa? Their system is capable of indefinite development in the vast and unoccupied field which this continent presents. The message to them, as a Church of Christ is, "Go ye into all the world"—not only over the United States, from California to New York and from New England to Texas, but to "regions beyond," especially to the lost sheep of their own race. Their talents, it occurs to us, are not as useful and as profitable as they might be made. This is a drawback and a mistake. If it be sinful to wrap our talent in a napkin and hide it in the earth, it is only one degree less sinful so to handle it as to make it yield twofold only where it might yield ten. We are persuaded, however, that it is not the courage they lack for the work, but conviction. The same self-control and self-reliance, the same energy and independence, which led to the founding of the African Churches in the United States would readily, if there were earnest conviction on the subject, sacrifice the charms of home, the comforts of civilisation, the æsthetic and sensuous attractions of an enlightened country, for the labours and toils and privations of the wilderness. They are quite equal to, and have shown themselves worthy of, the great achievement of taking possession of the whole valley of the Niger for Christ. Let them arise and come, and they will find in the home of their widowed parent that "the barrel of meal will not waste, nor will the cruse of oil fail." Freedom from restraint ought not to be our ultimate and final object, but FREEDOM TO WORSHIP GOD; and the desire for such freedom is, in certain aspects of the subject, among the happiest of the popular instincts of the Negro race.

It is remarkable that the message which Moses was commanded to bear to the tyrant Pharaoh was not "Let My people go that they may be *free*," but "Let my people go that they may *serve* ME." As long as they remained in a strange country under a foreign race they could not render that service for which they were fitted, and which God requires of every man. They could not serve the Lord with their "whole heart," the undiminished fulness of their nature, in carrying out the purposes of their being. "How could they sing the Lord's song in a strange land?" Their race-impulses and instincts were hampered, confused and impaired. So with the Negro in America. Although their gatherings, of whatever nature, are usually marked and enlivened by a stream of religious feeling which continually flows with a rapid, and sometimes boisterous, current, still they cannot fully know God in that land, for they see him through the medium of others. Here and there there may be a "Caleb, who has another spirit within him, and follows the Lord fully;" but the masses are distracted by the disturbing *media*. The body, soul, and spirit do not work in harmony. The religious passions are predominant in their influences among them, and they show a co-operative and successful energy in ecclesiastical organisations; but, in their political struggles, there is no attempt at any logical or reasoned solution of their difficulties. "The Negro," says Rev. Joseph Cook, "has gone to the wall in Mississippi, in spite of having a majority there and the suffrage. And he is likely to go to the wall in South Carolina. He is going to the wall even where he has a majority; and his inferiority in politics results from his lack of education "—such an education as he can never receive in America. But let him be delivered from the restraints of his exile; let him be set free from the stocks that now confine him, and he will not only arise and walk, but he will point out the way to the eminent success, which, in his particular line, only *he* can find out, and which he *must* find out for himself. He will discover the central point from which the lines may be easily and infallibly drawn to all the points of the circle to which he is to move effectively, in the true work of his race, for his own elevation and the advantage of the rest of mankind. He will prove that what in African history and character seems nebulous confusion is really a firmament of stars. There are stars, astronomers tell us, whose light has not yet reached the earth; so there are stars in the moral universe yet to be disclosed by the unfettered African, which he must discover before he will be able to progress without wandering into perilous seas and suffering serious injury. Let him, then, return to the land of his fathers, and ACQUAINT HIMSELF WITH GOD, AND BE AT PEACE.

Philip and the Eunuch.

THERE is no people, except the Hebrews and other ancient inhabitants of Palestine, more frequently mentioned in the Scriptures of the Old and New Testaments than the Ethiopians; and there is no country more frequently referred to than Ethiopia; and the record of no people, whether in sacred history or in ancient secular history, has less of the discreditable than the record of the Ethiopians.

Let us see what is said of them in sacred history.

The first time that we meet with any distinct mention of the Ethiopian is in the account given in the twelfth chapter of Numbers, of the disagreement between Moses and his brother and sister in the matter of his marriage with an Ethiopian woman. The next mention of this people is in 2 Chron. xiv, where we read of Zerah, the Ethiopian general, who commanded an army of a thousand thousand men and three hundred chariots. The next mention is in Jeremiah xxxviii, where we learn of Ebedmelech, who, having deeper spiritual insight, and understanding more the ways of the Lord than the king and all the other Hebrew inhabitants of Jerusalem, believed the unpopular utterances of the prophet Jeremiah, and rescued him from his unpleasant and perilous condition in the dungeon of Zedekiah. For his faith and spiritual perception he was rewarded, in the time of trouble.

A singular passage in 1 Chron. iv, 40, gives an important clue to the opinions entertained in those days, and by the sacred writers, of the character of the descendants of Ham. Describing a certain district to which the children of Simeon had migrated, the chronicler

Philip and the Eunuch.

says: "They found fat pasture and good, and the land was wide and *quiet* and *peaceable*, for they of Ham had dwelt there of old."

The secular poets and historians of those times also bear witness to the excellence of the Ethiopian character. Homer, the prince of poets, and Herodotus, the father of history, both speak in praise of them.

In the earliest traditions of nearly all the more civilised nations of antiquity, the name of this distant people is found. The annals of the Egyptian priests were full of them ; the nations of inner Asia, on the Euphrates and Tigris, have interwoven the fictions of the Ethiopians with their own traditions of the conquests and wars of their heroes; and, at a period equally remote, they glimmer in Greek mythology. When the Greeks scarcely knew Italy and Sicily by name, the Ethiopians were celebrated in the verses of their poets; they spoke of them as the "remotest nation," the "most just of men," the "favourites of the gods." The lofty inhabitants of Olympus journey to them, and take part in their feasts; their sacrifices are the most agreeable of all that mortals can offer them. And when the faint gleam of tradition and fable gives way to the clear light of history, the lustre of the Ethiopians is not diminished. They still continue the object of curiosity and admiration; and the pen of cautious, clear-sighted historians often places them in the highest rank of knowledge and civilisation.[1]

When Cambyses, the Persian monarch, had spread his conquests over Egypt, had gratified the impulses of national envy and jealousy in the destruction of the magnificent city of Memphis, had disfigured the Sphinx with his battering-rams; and had failed, after two years' effort, to demolish the mysterious Pyramids, he turned his covetous eyes to Ethiopia, and was anxious to pluck and wear the inaccessible laurels, never before nor since his day worn by European or Asiatic brow, as the conqueror of Ethiopia. Before entering upon this dazzling enterprise, he took the precaution of sending his spies to examine the country and report to him. The account which Herodotus gives, of the interview between the spies and the Ethiopian monarch, has forever embalmed Ethiopian character in history. The fragrance of the name, despite the distance of time and the counter-currents in the literary atmosphere, has floated over the fields of history, triumphantly lingering in the hostile air, and has come down unimpaired to us.

---

[1] *Heeren's Historical Researches*, vol. i, pp. 293, 294.

Christianity, Islam and the Negro Race.

When the spies of Cambyses arrived before the king of Ethiopia, they offered the treacherous gifts from their master of which they were the bearers, and delivered the following address :—

Cambyses, king of the Persians, desirous of becoming your friend and ally, has sent us, bidding us confer with you; and he presents you with these gifts, which are such as he himself most delights in.

But the Ethiopian, knowing that they came as spies, spoke thus to them :—

Neither has the king of the Persians sent you with presents to me because he valued my alliance, nor do you speak the truth; for ye are come as spies of my kingdom. Nor is he a just man; for if he were just, he would not desire any other territory than his own, nor would he reduce people into servitude who have done him no injury. However, give him this bow, and say these words to him: "The king of the Ethiopians advises the king of the Persians, when the Persians can thus easily draw a bow of this size, then to make war on the Macrobian Ethiopians with more numerous forces; but, until that time let him thank the gods, who have not inspired the sons of the Ethiopians with a desire of adding another land to their own."[2]

---

[2] Dr. George Ebers, the German novelist, has woven this incident into one of his popular romances, entitled *An Egyptian Princess*. A superficial criticism, guided by local and temporary prejudices, has attempted to deny the intimate relations of the Negro with the great historic races of Egypt and Ethiopia. But no one who has travelled in North-eastern Africa, or among the ruins on the banks of the Nile, will for a moment doubt that there was the connection, not of accident or of adventitious circumstances, but of consanguinity between the races of inner Africa of the present day, and the ancient Egyptians and Ethiopians. To get rid of the responsibility of brotherhood to the Negro, an American professor, in an elaborate work, claims for the tropical African a pre-Adamite origin, and ignores his relation with Ham. His arguments, however, are, as yet, beneath the level of scientific criticism. *Stat pro ratione voluntas*. The impressions of Volney, the great French traveller, after visiting the magnificent ruins of Egypt, are expressed as follows: " When I visited the Sphinx, I could not help thinking the figure of that monster furnished the true solution of the enigma; when I saw its features precisely those of a Negro, I recollected the remarkable passage of Herodotus, in which he says: ' For my part, I believe the Colchi to be a colony of Egyptians, because, like them, they have black skins and frizzled hair (lib. ii); that is, that the ancient Egyptians were real Negroes, of the same species with all the natives of Africa. . . . . This historical fact affords to philosophy an interesting subject of reflection. How are we astonished when we reflect that to the race of Negroes, at present our slaves, and the objects of our extreme contempt, we owe our arts, sciences, and even the very use of speech!" (*Volney's Travels*, vol. i, ch. iii.) Catafago, in his Arabic and English Dictionary, under the word *Kusur* (palaces), says :—

Philip and the Eunuch.

This reply of the Ethiopian monarch expresses the characteristic of the African as seen even to this day. In a recent account, given of some European missionaries in East Africa, it is said: "They are much respected by the people, who say of them, 'These are men who do not covet other people's goods;' the highest praise in their eyes, as the other white men they had seen came among them only to enrich themselves at their expense."[3]

If we come down to New Testament times, we find, again, Africans and their country appearing in honourable connections. When the Saviour of mankind, born in lowly circumstances, was the persecuted babe of Bethlehem, Africa furnished the refuge for his threatened and helpless infancy. African hands ministered to the comfort of Mary and Joseph while they sojourned as homeless and hunted strangers in that land. In the final hours of the Man of Sorrows, when His disciples had forsaken Him and fled, and only the tears of sympathising women, following in the distance, showed that His sorrows touched any human heart; when Asia, in the person of the Jew, clamoured for His blood, and Europe, in the Roman soldier, was dragging Him to execution, and afterwards nailed those sinless hands to the cross, and pierced that sacred side—what was the part that Africa took then? She furnished the man to share the burden of the cross with the suffering Redeemer. Simon, the Cyrenian, bore the cross after Jesus. "Fleecy locks and dark complexion" thus enjoyed a privilege and an honour, and was invested with a glory in which kings and potentates, martyrs

---

"The ruins of Thebes, that ancient and celebrated town, deserve to be visited, as just those heaps of ruins, laved by the Nile, are all that remain of the opulent cities that gave lustre to Ethiopia. It was there that a people, since forgotten, discovered the elements of Science and Art at a time when all other men were barbarous, and when a race, now regarded as the refuse of society, explored among the phenomena of Nature those civil and religious systems which have since held mankind in awe." A more recent investigator, Dr. Hartmann, in an 'Encyclopædic Work on Nigritia' (*Saturday Review*, June 17, 1876), contends for the strictly African extraction of the Egyptians, who, he seems to consider, may have dwelt upon the shores of the inner African sea, whose desiccation has formed the existing Sahara.

[3] *Dublin Review*, April, 1881.

and confessors in the long roll of ages, would have been proud to participate.

But what of the country of the Africans? What of Ethiopia itself? It has always worn a forbidding aspect to foreigners. Although the ancients, on account of the amiable qualities of the inhabitants, made the country frequently the scene of Olympic festivities, with Jupiter as the presiding genius, yet they had the most curious notions of the country. And it may be that, in keeping with a well-known instinct of human nature, to surround sacred things with mystery, the land was invested with repellent characteristics because it was the occasional abode of the gods. Herodotus (iv, 91), in describing the interior of Africa, says:—

> This is the region in which the huge serpents are found, and the lions, the elephants, the bears, the aspicks, and the horned asses. Here, too, are the dog-faced creatures, and the creatures without heads, whom the Lybians declare to have their eyes in their breasts; and also the wild men, and the wild women, and many other far less fabulous beasts.

And from that day onwards, the ideas of Africa, entertained by the outside world, were calculated to produce only fear and abhorrence. Dante, the classic poet of Italy, has preserved the opinions of his day in one of the cantos of the *Inferno*, in the comparison he makes of an indescribable region, which he saw in Malebolge, with Africa. After picturing the horrors of the place, that master of Italian song says:—

> I saw within a fearful throng of serpents, and of so strange a look that even now the recollection scares my blood. Let Libya boast no longer with its sand; for though it engenders chelydri, jaculi and pareæ, and cenchres with amphisbæna, plagues so numerous or so dire it never showed, with all Ethiopia, nor with the land that lies by the Red Sea.[4]

---

[4]   E vidivi entro terribile stipa
    Di serpenti, e di si diversa mena,
    Che la memoria il sangue ancor mi scipa.
    Più non si vanti Libia con sua rena:
    Che, se chelidri, jaculi, e faree
    Produce, e cencri con anfesibena;
    Nè tante pestilenzie, nè sì ree
    Mostrò giammai con tutta l' Etiopia,
    Nè con ciò che di sopra 'l mar Rosso ee.
              (*Inferno*, Canto xxiv., lines 85–90.)

Philip and the Eunuch.

Shakespeare makes Othello win Desdemona by the horrible tales he tells of interior Africa:—

> Of antres vast and deserts idle.
> * * *
> And of the cannibals that each other eat,
> The Anthropophagi, and men whose heads
> Do grow beneath their shoulders.

And these notions cannot be said to have been entirely dispelled until within our own day—within the last five-and-twenty years. Those who dealt, even forty years ago, with African geography, are now proved to have been wrong in every detail. They denied the existence of great lakes and broad rivers flowing from the centre to the coast. They spoke of the great mass of Central Africa as consisting of vast deserts, bare of vegetation, bare of animal life, and, above all, bare of men. There was so much of uncertainty and indefiniteness in the maps constructed by those writers on Africa as to justify the witty lines of Swift:—

> Geographers in Afric's maps
> With savage pictures fill their gaps;
> And o'er *un*habitable downs
> Place elephants, for want of towns.

But what physical glories, what mountains and lakes, and rivers, and what a wealth of population have been unfolded to the astonished gaze of the present generation! In the former years all was gloomy and mysterious and forbidding. The country seemed to the ancients to have been created only as the scene of the happy residence of the gods and of the native races. And it is a noticeable fact that no other race than the Ethiopian, in its different varieties, has ever had permanent or extensive foothold in that land. To-day, whether in its northern or southern extremities, the tenure of foreigners might be described simply as an "armed occupation."

Let us, for a moment, glance at the history of foreign efforts in Africa. Of the secular agencies which have operated from abroad, the Egyptian power—if we take for granted the modern notion that the Egyptians were an alien race—has been, perhaps, the most important. But even this has been subject to such vicissitudes and changes as to have left no distinct or wide-spread impression upon the country. Dynasty after dynasty has arisen and disappeared; and these, while they lasted, have prospered only when in alliance with the undoubtedly indigenous and interior races. And even with these alliances, they have not been able to push their power beyond the alluvial regions—the country called, from its geological origin, "The gift of the Nile." The natives beyond have always held their own; and, even to this day, the indigenous power neighbouring to Egypt is a source of constant anxiety and concern to the Albanian rulers of that "house of bondage." Recent intelligence informs us that King John of Abyssinia is using the present crisis in Egypt to take possession again of those provinces which Egypt had taken away from Abyssinia, *i.e.*, Mensa and Bagos. The so-called False Prophet of the Soudan, emerging with uncounted warriors from the regions of the Sahara, has been lately spreading alarm among the adherents of the Khedive.

The next important secular influence, planted by foreigners in Africa, was the Carthaginian Empire. That empire flourished for seven hundred years, and its people were the most enterprising of the nations of their day. They sent out exploring expeditions by sea and by land. They circumnavigated the continent and penetrated its interior. Their sway extended from the coast of the Mediterranean down towards the Niger. They collected by traffic the valuable products of the Soudan; the elephants and their ivory answered their purposes for war and for commerce; but with all these advantages, they disappeared without having produced any impression upon the inner portions of the continent. It is certain that when their cities fell before the military energy of the Romans, many of them fled to the regions south of their country, but they were soon lost in the boundless forests of the Soudan and in the oblivion of the Desert.

The Romans next essayed to colonise and conquer Africa. They could overpower Carthage, after years and even generations of persistent warfare; they could destroy her cities, overthrow her monuments, and, with the wanton indifference of a cruel jealousy, scatter her literary treasures; but they could construct no lasting

Philip and the Eunuch.

power in that land. They could not even rival the African glories of Carthage. Their boasted power, and the weight of their crushing influence, availed them little here. They disappeared from the continent like a shadow and a dream; and one of their rulers, in the last moments of his life, solemnly deprecated the invasion of Africa by the Romans.[5]

A modern European power, of great military reputation, has been recently, and is now, endeavouring to force its way inward by arms, by railways, by commercial expeditions, by diplomatic *finesse;* but its successes so far warn us that what the conquerors of ancient Gaul could not accomplish, there is no evidence that the descendants of the conquered will ever achieve. In spite of all the efforts made in that quarter, the state of things at the head-waters of the Niger, around Lake Chad, and throughout the Western Soudan, is not very different from what it was when Hannibal marshalled his legions against Rome, and drew many of his warriors, with their trained elephants, from the regions south of the Great Desert. Many have been the plans adopted, both in ancient and modern times, for taking possession of that continent; and all, whether military, commercial, or philanthropic, as conducted by Europeans or Asiatics, have had but temporary success. With regard to all, history has been obliged to write, sooner or later, the words with which Herodotus closes his account of the disastrous expedition of Cambyses into Ethiopia: "Thus ended the expedition."

Among the foreign *Christian* agencies which have operated in Africa, may be noticed: first, the Church in Egypt, with its ten thousand anchorites; the Church of North Africa, with its three

---

[5] The Romans appear to have penetrated to the Niger; for Pliny mentions that, like the Nile, it swelled periodically, and at the same season, and that its productions were also the same. He likewise relates that Suetonius Paulinus, the first of the Romans who crossed Mount Atlas, made an expedition during winter into the interior parts of Africa, and marched through deserts of black dust and places uninhabitable from excessive heat, where the very rocks seemed to be scorched. (I saw such rocks in the neighbourhood of Timbo and Falaba, about three hundred miles north-east of Sierra Leone; but their appearance has not been caused by heat.) It does not appear, however, that the Romans formed any settlements among the aboriginal tribes.

Christianity, Islam and the Negro Race.

thousand towns and villages, and its five hundred and sixty episcopal sees—the Church that produced Tertullian, Cyprian and Augustine. These, after flourishing for a time, fell away without affecting the continent—like the morning cloud and the early dew.

Later on in history came the extensive missionary efforts of the Roman Catholic Church. The great missionary movement set in with the Portuguese conquests in the fifteenth century, and it continued during the sixteenth and into the seventeenth, with great success. In the Portuguese possessions in Africa, and their neighbourhood, such were the zeal and energy of the Roman Catholic missionaries, that the conversion of all Africa seemed at one time to be at hand. The Rev. H. Rowley, of the Society for the Propagation of the Gospel, pays the following tribute to the zeal and earnestness of the first Catholic missionaries to Africa:—

> As the Portuguese were, at first, as zealous for the extension of God's kingdom as for their own aggrandisement, it seemed as though they would be equal to their opportunity, and build up great Christian empires on either side of the continent. The missionary zeal of the Portuguese at this, the best period of their history, was great. No ship was permitted to leave their coasts without being accompanied by one or more priests, and no nation ever had more devoted missionaries. They made the kingdom of Congo the field of their principal efforts, but they also laboured zealously to convert the natives of Loango and Angola. For a time it appeared as though nothing could withstand the religious energy of the good men who strove for the conversion of Congo. The King was among the first of their converts. No danger appalled them; they shrank from no suffering; and they died willingly in the performance of their duty. This, indeed, may be said of almost all the missionaries who, for nearly one hundred years, laboured amongst the Heathen in those parts of Africa which were brought under the power and influence of Portugal. Though many of them quickly succumbed to fatigue, privation, and disease—others, nothing daunted, filled their places. Within fifty years of its discovery, the population of Congo had become nominally Christian. The success obtained in Loango and Angola was almost as great.

But there is very little trace now of the results of the great missionary work done by those zealous and self-denying men. We have it, on the testimony of Roman Catholic writers, that "At present, not only are the Portuguese settlements in the lowest state of degradation, but that they are positively hostile to the

Philip and the Eunuch.

missionary operations of the Church, whose presence they will not tolerate within their frontiers."[6]

It is not yet one hundred and fifty years since the first Protestant missionary efforts commenced in Africa, and while a great deal has been accomplished within European colonies, and in their neighbourhood on the coast, very little indeed has been effected among the aborigines of the country away from the settlements. Protestant missionary efforts, in purely native regions, have been undertaken, on anything like a large scale, only within the last twenty years. They are the Universities' Mission, established between Lake Nyassa and the East Coast; the Mission of the London Missionary Society, near Lake Tanganyika; the Church Missionary Society's Mission, near the Victoria Nyanza; and the Missions of the American Board of Commissioners for Foreign Missions, recently opened in West Central Africa. These missions, excepting that of the American Board, are all manned by white men, and the usual mortality has prevailed. The nineteenth death among the missionaries of the Universities' Mission at Lake Nyassa was, a few months ago, reported, and, very recently, the death of Bishop Steere has been announced.

In view of the serious obstacles which have so far confronted the work of African evangelisation and civilisation through European agency, it is a matter of serious concern among Christian workers as to how the work should be done. There is, perhaps, not one of the members of missionary boards or committees, whose experience in the African work extends over ten years, who does not feel a measure of discouragement.

Now, in view of these melancholy experiences, what is to be inferred as to the will of Providence? It is evident that the Gospel of Jesus Christ is designed for all countries and climes—for all races and nations; but it is also evident that we have this "treasure in earthern vessels," which subjects it to human conditions and limitations. The constitutions of mortal men, who are to be instruments of proclaiming the glad tidings, are not

---

[6] *Dublin Review*, January, 1879.

adapted to all countries and climates; yet the command is, "Go ye into *all the world* and preach the gospel to *every creature.*" This was the parting injunction of the Saviour to His disciples. But He had told them before, that the Spirit of Truth, whom He would send to them after His departure, would explain what He had said unto them, and guide them into all truth. Now, after the Spirit had come, and had filled the disciples with power for their mission, and they began to organise for aggressive work, it was found necessary to add to the number of evangelistic agents. Accordingly, under the direct inspiration of the Holy Spirit, seven men were chosen as evangelists, among whom was Philip. This man, after the murder of Stephen, went away from Jerusalem, and preached with great success in the city of Samaria. The injunction not to enter into any city of the Samaritans had been withdrawn, and the whole world was now opened to the preachers of the gospel. They went over into Europe, penetrated farther eastward into Asia, went south to Arabia. But there lay Ethiopia, with its inhospitable climate and difficulty of access. What was to be done? The Spirit which was to guide them into all truth met the emergency. An African had come up in search of truth to Jerusalem, and, having completed his mission, was returning to his home, and was so far on his journey as to have reached the southern confines of the Holy Land, when Philip the Evangelist received a message from Heaven concerning him : "The angel of the Lord spake unto Philip, saying, Arise and go toward the south, unto the way that goeth down from Jerusalem unto Gaza, which is desert. And he arose and went, and behold a man of Ethiopia, an eunuch of great authority under Candace, queen of the Ethiopians, who had the charge of all her treasure, and had come to Jerusalem for to worship, was returning ; and, sitting in his chariot, read Esaias the prophet. Then the Spirit said unto Philip, Go near and join thyself to this chariot."

Now, this incident I take to be a symbolic one, indicating the instruments and the methods of Africa's evangelisation. The method, the simple holding up of Jesus Christ; the instrument, the African himself. This was the Spirit's application and explication

Philip and the Eunuch.

of the command, "Go ye into all the world," &c.—giving the gospel to a man of Ethiopia to take back to the people of Ethiopia.

We are told that after the singular and interesting ceremony, "the Spirit of the Lord caught away Philip, that the eunuch saw him no more; and he went on his way rejoicing." Philip was not to accompany the eunuch, to water the seed he had planted, to cherish and supervise the incipient work. If he desired to do so—and perhaps he did—the Spirit suffered him not, for he "caught him away."

The eunuch "went on his way rejoicing." Strange must have been his delight as he listened to the wonderful words which fell from the lips of Philip. Strange must have been his joy—strange the exulting rush of his heart, in this, his first communion with God through Jesus Christ our Lord. A member of a race separated by indelible physical characteristics from the people among whom he had been to worship, and thinking of the millions, like himself, who would be blest by the new revelation, who can tell the dreams of the future which he cherished in his soul, kindling the hope of a total revolution in his country through the words he had heard? The vision of communities regenerated and saved, through the sufferings and death of Him whom the prophet had described, loomed up before him and filled his soul with joy.

And there was something symbolic, also, of the future sad experience of his race—and at the same time full of consolation—in the passage which he read. It was holding up Christ as the "man of sorrows and acquainted with grief," as if in anticipation of the great and unsurpassed trials of the African. These were to be the words of comfort and uplifting to these people in their exile and captivity. They were to remember that if they were despised and scorned, a far greater than themselves had had a similar experience. Christ was to be held up to the suffering African not only as a propitiation for sin, and as a Mediator between God and man, but as a blessed illustration of the glorious fact that persecution and suffering and contempt are no proof that God is not the loving Father of a people—but may be rather an evidence of nearness to

God, seeing that they have been chosen to tread in the footsteps of the first-born of the creation, suffering for the welfare of others.[7]

Tell me, now, ye descendants of Africa, tell me whether there is anything in the ancient history of your African ancestors, in their relation to other races, of which you need to be ashamed. Tell me, if there is anything in the modern history of your people, in their dealings with foreign races, whether at home or in exile, of which you need be ashamed? Is there anything, when you compare yourselves with others, to disturb your equanimity, except the universal oppression of which you have been the victims? And what are suffering and sorrow but necessary elements in the progress of humanity? Your suffering has contributed to the welfare of others. It is a part of the constitution of the universe, that out of death should come life. All the advancement made to a better future, by individuals or races, has been made through paths marked by suffering. This great law is written not only in the Bible, but upon all history. "Without the shedding blood there is no remission." We may say, then, in the language of the poet—

> In all the ills we bore,
> We grieved, we sighed, we wept—
> We never blushed.

We could not blush physically, and we had no need to blush mentally or morally.

Among the beautiful legends which are scattered throughout ancient Jewish literature is the following, which is not less applicable to us than to the Hebrew race.

When the Decalogue was given, the Israelites said to the Lord; "Thou forbiddest us to attempt the life, the honour, or the interest,

---

[7] In Mrs. Stowe's inimitable novel we read the following. It was after her principal character had suffered most unjust and brutal treatment: "I saw 'em," said Uncle Tom, "throw my coat in that ar corner, and in my coatpocket is my Bible; if Missis would please get it for me."

Cassy went and got it. Tom opened it at once, to a heavily-marked passage, much worn, of the last scenes in the life of Him by whose stripes we are healed.

"If Missis would only be so good as to read that ar'—it's better than water."—*Uncle Tom's Cabin*, ch. xxxiv.

of our fellow-man. Thou forbiddest us to lie, to covet, to return evil for evil, blow for blow. But if this prohibition is not addressed also to the other nations of the earth, we shall become, alas! their victim." The Lord answered: "My children, when I created the lamb it came to me and said, 'O, Lord! Thou hast given me neither claws to tear with, nor teeth to bite with, nor horns to strike with, nor even swift feet with which to flee away. What will become of me in the midst of other animals if I am thus weak and defenceless? And I answered the lamb, 'Would'st thou, then, prefer to thy feebleness the cruelty of the tiger or the venom of the serpent?' 'No, Lord,' answered Me the lamb; 'I prefer my feebleness and my innocence, and I thank Thee that Thou hast made me rather the persecuted than the persecutor.' So thou, O my people Israel. Thou shalt be a lamb in the midst of the nations. Let them tear thee; let them sacrifice thee; thy triumph shall be in thy calmness, in thy resignation, in thine innocence."

Two characteristics of the African are brought out in the narrative before us. Firstly his teachableness. The eunuch was reading with an earnest desire to understand—to arrive at the knowledge of the truth—but, at the same time, with a dim consciousness that he was only imperfectly apprehending it. "How can I, except some one should guide me?" Secondly, his courtesy and hospitality. "He desired Philip that he would come and sit with him." Though a man of great power and influence, he did not distain to invite the wandering pedestrian to a seat in his chariot; giving him a real and unaffected welcome, and placing himself at his feet; becoming the guest and pupil, and giving the stranger the place of host and instructor. All truthful travellers in Africa testify to the courteous disposition of the interior natives—those who have never been tampered with by either Arabs or Europeans. They are confiding, unsuspicious, childlike, hospitable, honest, peaceable, and anxious to learn. Thomson, the youthful explorer, who has written one of the best of the recent books on Africa, says: "Of the natives, I have for the most part nothing but good to say. In the majority of places I found them peaceable. Rarely did they attempt to throw any obstacles in my way.

Almost everywhere, I was received with genuine hospitality and friendship."[8]

The eunuch returned to his country with his heart full of joy and peace and love—with a new-born and unquenchable enthusiasm, and became the founder, it is believed, of the Abyssinian Church, which, through various trying vicissitudes, continues to this day. It has resisted all attacks from Paganism on the one hand, and Mohammedanism on the other. In one hundred and fifty years after the death of Mohammed, the victorious banners of Islam had been carried from Arabia into Judea and Palestine; had wrested Egypt and North-western Africa out of the hands of Christians; had pushed its conquering way to Constantinople, and had taken possession of Spain; but it was unable to transcend the limits of Abyssinia. The Abyssinian Church is the only real African Church yet founded whose priests and people are all of the African race.[9]

It is a curious fact that historians, in speaking of the African Church, seldom meant by that phrase the Abyssinian Church, which is far more entitled to that description than any other. Some mean the Church of North-eastern Africa—the Church of Clement of Alexandria, and Origen; others mean the Church of North-western Africa—the Church of Tertullian and Cyprian.

---

[8] In the 'Annals of the Propagation of the Faith,' a Roman Catholic missionary describes his reception by the natives of Southern Kordofan as follows; "On the evening of the 21st September, 1875, I was extremely surprised to find, at half a day's journey from the station of Delen, the great chief of the Noubas coming to meet me, followed by fifty Noubas armed with firearms and lances. He had scarcely seen me, when he dismounted, approached my camel, kissed my hand, saluted me profoundly several times, and said to me in good Arabic, in the dialect of Kordofan, ' God has sent you amongst us; and behold—we, our little children, our wives, our young daughters, our oxen, cows, sheep and goats, our houses and lands, all are now placed at your disposal. You are our father, and we are your children; we will do all you command us, and we shall be happy.' "--*Dublin Review*, April, 1881, p. 418.

[9] The growing system of indigenous missionary work under Bishop Crowther—the nascent Church of the Niger—if left to struggle through the difficulties incident to youthful life, without the hampering influence of unsympathetic alien oversight, and the injury of misplaced praise or censure, will, in the next generation, be a second Abyssinian Church in aboriginal vigour and permanence.

Philip and the Eunuch.

And here I cannot avoid pointing out the fact that the continent of Africa comes into view again, in the case of these two Churches, as contributing to the enlightenment and welfare of humanity. The two most wonderful and productive of all the primitive Christian Churches were both located in Africa, namely, the Greek-speaking Church in North-eastern Africa, and the Latin-speaking Church in North-western Africa. The Latin-speaking Church produced those three great Latin-Africans—Tertullian, Cyprian, and Augustine. Through them the north-western African Church has permanently affected all Western Christendom—Protestant as well as Roman Catholic, the New World as well as the Old World. The African Tertullian Latinised the theological and ecclesiastical language of the West; and in all controversies on the constitution of the Church, the appeal has been by Western Christians to the African Cyprian; while no one has contributed so much to Western theology as the African Augustine. "Africa, not Rome," Dean Milman has said, "gave birth to Latin Christianity."

Yet this Church was extinguished before the energy of the Saracens. Why? It is sometimes said that these Greek and Latin Churches fell away because they were not missionary churches—because they were not aggressive. But the reason lies more on the surface than that. They withered away because they had not much depth of earth. They had not taken root among the people of the country. Neither the Western Church of Carthage, nor the Eastern Church of Alexandria, was ever a national Church—had ever become indigenous. The Church of Tertullian and St. Augustine was Latin, not Punic; the Church of Origen and St. Athanasius was Greek, and not Egyptian.

The case has been far different with the third African Church—the Abyssinian or Ethiopian. Founded by a native, it took hold of the inhabitants of the country, and struck its roots deep into the soil. And we have had very recent illustrations of the vigour and activity of that Church. Only last year the Abyssinian monarch told certain Catholic and Protestant missionaries, who sought to establish themselves in this territory, that he did not want either of them, because the Ethiopians were already Christians, and had held fast their faith under a strain which had destroyed that of more prosperous and civilised peoples. He boasted that his own community was the only African Church which had held fast its Christian faith, century after century, against the successive onslaughts of Heathenism and Mohammedanism. Even the Mohammedans believe in the irrepressible and aggressive vigour of the Abyssinian Church. There is an old prediction among them that from Abyssinia—not from Russia, or any part of Europe—will come the conquerors of Arabia and the destroyers of the Holy City of Mecca. This may be taken as representing the idea that the power of Islam will disappear in Africa, under the influence of African Christians led by African teachers.

The 105th chapter of the Koran is devoted to celebrating the deliverance of Mecca from the Christian king of Abyssinia, who, in the year that Mohammed was born, with a large army and some elephants, marched upon Mecca for the purpose of destroying the Kaaba. And yet it was Abyssinia that afforded shelter to the persecuted Muslims, who, in the early days of Islam, had to fly from Arabia for their lives. When Mohammed found that his few followers were likely to be crushed by the opposition at Mecca, he advised their flight into Abyssinia; and there, when the refugees proved to the king, from the Koran, that they were worshippers of the true God and believed in Jesus, they were protected from the destruction which would have extinguished Islam.[10] If then, the two

[10] This was the first Hijra, or Flight. Abu'l Feda, the Mohammedan historian, gives the following account of it: "In the year 626, when Mohammed was forty-five years old, the Koreish became more severe in their persecutions. Mohammed therefore gave permission to those who had no family, to betake themselves to the land of the Ethiopians. The first who went forth were twelve men and four women. Amongst these, Othman, the son of Affan, and his wife Rakia, the daughter of the Apostle of God; and Zobeir, the son of Awami; and Othman, the son of Matani; and Abdullahi, the son of Masadi; and Abdul Rahman, the son of Awsi. All these betook themselves to the sea, sailing across the sea, and dwelt with him. Then Iafar, the son of Abu Talib, went forth an exile, whom other Muslims followed, one after another. All who took flight into the country of the Ethiopians were eighty-three men and eighteen women, besides children and those who were born there. The Koreish sent two men to demand them—Abdu Mahun, son of Abu Rabia, Amru, son of Al-Asi. They both came, therefore, to Al-Nagashi, and demanded of him the fugitives.

Philip and the Eunuch.

principal religions had not their origin in Africa, yet Africa was the cradle which cherished their helpless infancy.

Now, what are the lessons to be gathered from the preceding discussion? I conceive that they are: *First*, That Ethiopia and Ethiopians have ever been connected with the Divine administration and manifestations, and that that great country and its people are not left out of the beneficent purposes of the Almighty. *Second*, That the Gospel, to be successfully carried into Africa, must be carried by Africans. To "a man of Ethiopia" must be entrusted the message to Ethiopians. This truth, I believe, is being recognised now by all foreign workers in Africa. The Mohammedans have acted upon it from the beginning, and this is the chief secret of their widespread and increasing influence on that continent. The finest University for training the propagators of their faith is in Africa. This is established at Cairo, in Egypt. Ten thousand students are to-day gathered under its roof, preparing to go out as missionaries of the Muslim faith. A celebrated traveller has given the following description of this great institution, the educational pride and glory of Islam :—

This University is nine hundred years old (older than Oxford), and still flourishes with as much vigour as in the palmy days of the Arabian conquest. There I saw collected ten thousand students. As one expressed it, "There were two acres of turbans" assembled in a vast enclosure, with no floor but a pavement, and with a roof over it supported by four hundred columns, and at the foot of every column a teacher surrounded by his pupils. As we entered, there rose a hum of thousands of voices reciting the Koran. These students are not only from Egypt, but from all parts of Africa—from Morocco to Zanzibar. They come from far up the Nile, from Nubia and the Soudan, and from Darfour, beyond the Great Desert, and from the Western Coast of Africa. . . . . They live on the charities of the faithful; and when their studies are ended, those who are to be missionaries mount their camels, and, joining a caravan, cross the desert and are lost in the far interior of Africa,

where they become the effective propagators of Islam."

But he did not yield them. Then Amru, son of Al-Asi, said, 'Ask them what they have to say about Jesus.' And Nagashi asked them. And they replied with the words which God the Exalted told them, among which is the address which God, through Gabriel, addressed to the Virgin Mary."—*Koran*, iii, 40-45.

[11] It is a mistake to suppose that Mohammedanism is conquering Africa merely or mainly by arms. The school and the mosque are the most common

Christianity, Islam and the Negro Race.

And this plan of propagating religion in Africa, through indigenous agency, is followed by no Christian Church with greater zeal and determination than the Church of Rome. That Church, ever ready to recognise and utilise those elements in human nature which can be made subservient to her interests, is now everywhere educating Africans for the African work. The *Dublin Review*, an able exponent of Roman Catholic thought, said not long since :—

> We are convinced that the only hopeful, promising, and effective way of procedure in respect to Africa is that which may be summed up in the words, *the conversion of Africa by the Africans*. Christian black settlements ought to be attempted—all over Africa, even, if need be, as among the Mohammedans—after the difficult and costly manner followed by Monsignore Comboni. The task is full of hardship, but *no other system will avail*. . . . Whether it will be practically possible to organise bands of the Catholic Africano-Americans for the settlement and conversion of Africa—as their Protestant brethren, who sail to Liberia in numbers varying annually from two hundred to five hundred, are organised for that very purpose—remains to be proved. Large funds are required—hard heads and generous hearts to direct and carry out such an enterprise; but genuine Faith, Hope and Charity are Divine and creative forces, and we must look for great results where they exist and are brought into energetic action.[12]

The Roman Catholic Church now possesses a number of native black priests; other natives are pursuing their theological studies under the auspices of that Church, in Africa; and a community of over thirty Sisters is rendering immense service to the cause of religion on the West Coast.

A *third* lesson which we gather from the narrative of the text is that, in carrying the Gospel into Africa, the favour of men of influence is not to be despised. While it is true that "not many noble are called," it is also true that, in all ages, the nobles of the earth have been pillars of the Church. The "man of Ethiopia" was "an eunuch of great authority under Candace, queen of the

---

agencies. Richardson, the African traveller, says: "I was generally called a *marabout* (*i.e.*, a religious teacher) in the Desert. This arose from the people seeing me without arms, and occupied in reading and writing."

[12] The regions in the vicinity of the Congo River, now about to be occupied by De Brazza, under the auspices of the French government, would be a capital field for the settlement and energies of "Catholic Africano-Americans."

Philip and the Eunuch.

Ethiopians, who had the charge of all her treasure." Christianity in Africa, so far as brought by Europeans, has only to a very limited extent affected the higher classes; and this is why, wherever it seems to have been established, its hold has been so precarious. It is true that Jesus Christ humbled himself, and took upon himself the form of a servant, but he did not spring from the servile classes. He came of the ruling tribe of Judah, and of David's royal line. No great reforms can be effected without enlisting members of "the household of Cæsar." Reforms, after all, come from above. "The conversion of the Russian nation," says Dean Stanley, "was effected, not by the preaching of the Byzantine clergy, but by the marriage of a Byzantine Princess."[18] Notwithstanding the violent persecutions suffered by the Church in her earlier history, it still remains true that "kings have been her nursing fathers and queens her nursing mothers," sitting at her cradle and fostering her helpless infancy.

A *fourth* point to be noticed in the narrative is the fact that the teacher received patronage from the taught. The evangelist was offered, and accepted, the hospitality of the eunuch. The first preachers of the gospel were received as guests, and were taken care of by those to whom they ministered. They were the labourers worthy of their hire. They were not the dispensers of worldly patronage. They imparted of their spiritual things, while they received of the temporal things of those among whom they laboured.

When Stanley wrote his famous letter from Uganda, which appeared in the London *Daily Telegraph* for November, 1875, asking for missionaries to be sent to Mtesa, he suggested such an outfit for the missionary as would suit a trading expedition. It may be that everything he recommended was necessary for Europeans going to a new, difficult, and unhealthy country; but many of the articles hardly seemed in keeping with that spirit which enjoined it upon the first missionaries to take "neither purse nor scrip."

It is possible that where the gospel has taken root, and the Church has been established, it is not incompatible with its spirit,

---

[18] *Eastern Church*, p. 34.

or with the service of God, that outward magnificence should be an accompaniment of worship. It may be, at times, a duty to bring of our best, and lay it in that form at the feet of our Maker. David would not offer unto the Lord of that which cost him nothing. It was among the excellent qualities of the early Romans, as noted by one of their historians, that they were magnificent in the worship of their gods (*magnifici suppliciis deorum*). And when the stranger from distant and primitive countries visits this land, he cannot help admiring the wonderful triumphs of architecture as displayed in the splendid and costly structures you have erected for the worship of God.

But these are not the conditions of the spread of eternal truth among a primitive people. We must go practically without purse or scrip; and, after the truth pure and simple has made its way, then, in the process of its growth, and in the course of its development, it may take to itself æsthetic forms according to the genius of its recipients.

The true principle is simplicity in those who bring the glad tidings. Herein lies another secret of the success of the Mohammedan missionaries in Africa. In going from town to town and village to village, they go simply as the bearers of God's truth. They take their mats or their skins, and their manuscripts, and are followed by their pupils, who, in every new Pagan town, form the nucleus of a school and congregation. These preachers are the receivers, not the dispensers, of charity. I have met, in my travels in the interior of Liberia and Sierra Leone, missionaries from Kairwan, Cairo, Morocco, with *nothing*—dependent for their daily food upon those whom they instructed; and I have had the humiliating privilege of being benefactor to some of these self-denying men, as missionary to missionary.

The other system—that now pursued by foreign Christian missionaries, and which is perhaps unavoidable—of being the patrons of their disciples, is beset with dangers and temptations. There is the danger on the one hand, of injudiciously patronising —not in the sense of assisting, simply, but in the sense of pauperising—the native converts, and begetting in them a spirit of depen-

Philip and the Eunuch.

dence and servility; and there is, on the other hand, the temptation to the missionary to become proud, supercilious and dictatorial. There was sound philosophy, founded upon an absolute knowledge of human nature, in the direction given by Christ to the first missionaries, when he commanded them to take " neither purse nor scrip." But how is it possible for the European missionary to practise this sort of self-denial, when, to keep his health, energy and life on that continent, he must not be too far from his base of supplies? This, again, shows the necessity of "the man of Ethiopia" for the working the country of the Ethiopians. The Negro missionary, born and brought up in foreign countries, is, to a large extent, in the position of the foreigner; but he has the advantage of physical adaptation, which gives the opportunity for protracted labour; and, from the unfailing and indelible instincts of race, he can more fully enter into sympathy with the people; and, meeting with an unsuppressed and untrammelled response, can arrive at effective methods of dealing with novel questions, as, from time to time, they arise. Thus he is enabled to train the thoroughly indigenous elements which will rise up, and lay deeper foundations, and give more continuous impulse to the truth which he has introduced. It is in this way that American Negroes, who have gone to Africa from this country, have been able to do a great and permanent work there; and it is in this way, and even more effectively, that the thousands now being trained in this country—at Lincoln, Fisk, Hampton, Atlanta, Biddle, and other institutions—will accomplish wonders for the evangelisation and civilisation of the land of their fathers.

A *fifth* point, to be observed in the narrative, is the absence of all forms, the freedom from pomp and circumstance, which attended the conversion of the eunuch. He had been up to Jerusalem, the city of sacred associations, and was probably there during the exciting times of the crucifixion, of the Pentecostal manifestation, and of the accusation and murder of Stephen; but his attention was not drawn to the new revelation. He was, perhaps, too much engrossed by the novel sights he was daily witnessing in the metropolis of Judea, to pay any attention to the execution of felons, the demonstrations of fanatics, or the stoning of a blasphemer. Or, perhaps, his earnest and enquiring mind had been perplexed by the endless discussions of the Sadducees and Scribes: the one denying the existence of everything spiritual, of everything which could not be demonstrated by the senses—the agnostics of their day; the other spending their time in investigating the letter of the Scripture, and failing to catch its spirit; while another party made broad their phylacteries, lengthened their prayers, and multiplied their fasts, insisting that that was the true religion. And, no doubt, bearing in mind the disputations he had heard concerning the Law and the Prophets, he availed himself of those hours of silence, while passing through the desert, to read for himself the sacred pages, and "he read the prophet Esaias." Here was a mind anxiously seeking the truth, and his effort was not to be in vain. "Wherever a great problem of the human spirit is growing towards its solution, and the soil of humanity is prepared for new seed from heaven, God sends his chosen creature to proclaim the truth which brings the light." Philip was directed to "arise and go toward the south, unto the way that goeth down from Jerusalem unto Gaza, *which is desert.*" And there, in that solitude, the truth was revealed to the inquiring eunuch. There was nothing to distract the mind or distort the impression received. When he reached his home there would be only the three things to remember—the *Word*, the *Evangelist*, the *Desert*. With nothing but the air around them, the freedom of whose motion represented the Spirit's influence, blowing where it listeth—and the sunlight, emblem of the Sun of Righteousness, which was rising to illumine the new way on which the eunuch was entering—Philip "preached unto him Jesus." There was no form, no ritual, no liturgy, no action, no rites. A new spirit was coming upon Ethiopia, and it would create new forms for itself. This I take to be the significance of the peculiar circumstances of the eunuch's admission into the Christian Church; and the incident furnishes a most instructive commentary on the words of Christ, that the Kingdom of God "cometh not with observation" or outward show. The hour had come when the worship of the

Philip and the Eunuch.

Father was to be confined neither to holy mountain nor holy city; therefore the new religion was imparted to him, who was to represent it in a new country, divested of forms and elaborate ceremony, in the freedom and silence of the desert.

The next lesson we gather from this interesting narrative is that the preaching of Christ, and Him crucified, is the regenerating power by which Africa is to be reclaimed—the simple story of the Cross.

Observe now, in conclusion, the simplicity of the confession required of the eunuch. "What doth hinder me to be baptized?" he asked, in his anxiety to take upon himself the obligation of membership in the new Church. The reply of the evangelist was, "If thou believest with all thine heart thou mayest." We have no hard condition there, no insisting upon difficult dogmas. Well, what was he to believe? We have it in the prompt answer of the eunuch: "I believe that Jesus Christ is the Son of God." This is the sum and substance of the requirements of the Gospel. This is the faith which, Jesus said to Peter, flesh and blood do not reveal, and upon which the Church is founded. This was the one essential article of faith in the Apostolic Church. It is the radical idea, the central truth, of the Christian system; and it is the only influence that has power to reform the world.

I need not pause here to remark that one of the chief hindrances to the progress of the truth in Africa has been the constant desire to give prominence to deductions made by men from the great facts of revelation, instead of lifting up Christ, and believing the words that He spake unto His disciples: "I, if I be lifted up, will draw all men unto Me;" "Learn of Me, for I am meek and lowly in heart, and ye shall find rest to your souls;" "Come unto Me, all ye that labour and are heavy laden, and I will give you rest." These are the words that bring light and beauty and encouragement and strength to the benighted. Instruct them by the simple teachings of Christ—the Sermon on the Mount, and the Lord's Prayer. Instruct them by the simple method of Christ. He moved through the ordinary life of men, and drew His teachings from everything He saw—the sower and the seed, the field, the fisherman, the boat, the rain that fell, the ways of the sheep, the vine and the branches. Through all these He taught His disciples, and brought instruction and refreshment to their souls, illustrating by His surroundings—by the birds of the air and the lilies of the field—the tender care of God the Father over all His children. This is the teaching that will save men of all races and climes—adapted to men in the lowest stages of society, and adapted to men in the highest walks of life. "For God so loved the world that He gave His only begotten Son, that whosoever believeth in Him should not perish, but have everlasting life."

Mohammedanism in Western Africa.

GEORGE SALE has prefixed to the title-page of his able translation of the Koran the following motto from St. Augustin: "*Nulla falsa doctrina est, quæ non aliquid veri permisceat.*" Recent discussions and investigations have brought the subject of Mohammedanism prominently before the reading public, and the writings of Weil, and Noldeke, and Muir, and Sprenger, and Emanuel Deutsch have taught the world that " Mohammedanism is a thing of vitality, fraught with a thousand fruitful germs;" and have amply illustrated the principle enunciated by St. Augustin, showing that there *are* elements both of truth and goodness in a system which has had so widespread an influence upon mankind, embracing within the scope of its operations more than one hundred millions of the human race; that the exhibition of gems of truth, even though "suspended in a gallery of counterfeits," has vast power over the human heart.

The object of the present paper is to inquire briefly into the condition and influence of Mohammedanism among the tribes of Western Africa. Whatever may be the intellectual inferiority of the Negro tribes (if, indeed, such inferiority exists), it is certain that many of these tribes have received the religion of Islam without its being forced upon them by the overpowering arms of victorious invaders. The quiet development and organisation of a religious community in the heart of Africa has shown that Negroes, equally with other races, are susceptible of moral and spiritual impressions, and of all the sublime possibilities of religion. The history of the progress of Islam in this country would present the same instances of real and eager mental conflict, of minds in honest transition, of careful comparison and reflection, that have been found in other communities where new aspects of truth and fresh considerations have been brought before them. And we hold that it shows a stronger and more healthy intellectual tendency, to be induced by the persuasion and reason of a man of moral nobleness and deep personal convictions to join with him in the introduction of beneficial changes, than to be compelled to follow the lead of an irresponsible character, who forces us into measures by his superior physical might.

Different estimates are made of the beneficial effects wrought by Islam upon the moral and industrial condition of Western Africa. Some are disposed to ignore altogether any wholesome result, and regard the Negro Moslems as possessing, as a general thing, only the external appendages of a system which they do not understand. But such a conclusion implies a very superficial acquaintance with the state of things among the people. Of course cases are found of individuals here and there, of blustering zeal and lofty pretensions—qualities which usually exist in inverse proportion to the amount of sound knowledge possessed—whose views, so far as they can be gathered, are no more than a mixture of imperfectly understood Mohammedanism and Fetichism; but all careful and candid observers agree that the influence of Islam in Central and West Africa has been, upon the whole, of a most salutary character. As an eliminatory and subversive agency, it has displaced or unsettled nothing as good as itself. If it has introduced superstitions, it has expelled superstitions far more mischievous and degrading. And it is not wonderful if, in succeeding to a debasing Heathenism, it has, in many respects, made compromises, so as occasionally to present a barren, hybrid character; but what *is* surprising, is that a religion quietly introduced from a foreign country, with so few of the outward agencies of civilisation, should not, in process of time, have been altogether absorbed by the superstitions and manners of barbarous Pagans. But not only has it not been absorbed—it has introduced large modifications in the views and practices even of those who have but a vague conception of its teachings.

Mungo Park, in his travels seventy years ago, everywhere remarked the contrast between the Pagan and Mohammedan tribes of interior Africa. One very important improvement noticed by him was *abstinence from intoxicating drinks*. " The beverage of the Pagan Negroes," he says, " is *beer and mead*, of which they often drink to excess; the Mohammedan converts drink *nothing but water*." [1] Thus, throughout Central Africa there has been established a vast *Total Abstinence Society*; and such is the influence of this society that where there are Moslem inhabitants, even in Pagan towns, it is a very rare thing to see a person intoxicated. They thus present an almost impenetrable barrier to the desolating flood of ardent spirits with which traders from Europe and America inundate the coast, and of which we have recently had so truthful and sadly suggestive an account from a missionary at Gaboon.[2]

Wherever the Moslem is found on this coast, whether Jalof, Foulah, or Mandingo, he looks upon himself as a separate and distinct being from his Pagan neighbour, and immeasurably his superior in intellectual and moral respects. He regards himself as one to whom a revelation has been "sent down" from heaven. He holds constant intercourse with the "Lord of worlds," whose servant he is. In his behalf, Omnipotence will ever interpose in times of danger. Hence he feels that he cannot indulge in the frivolities and vices which he considers as by no means incompatible with the character and professions of the Kafir or unbeliever. Nearly every day his Koran reminds him of his high privileges, as compared with others, in the following terms:—

> Verily those who believe not, among those who have received the Scriptures, and among the Idolators, shall be cast into the fire of hell, to remain therein for ever. These are the worst of creatures. But they who believe and do good works, these are the best of creatures; their reward with their Lord shall be gardens of perpetual abode.[3]

---

[1] *Park's Travels*, chap. ii. [2] Mr. Walker, in *Missionary Herald*, Feb., 1870.
[3] Sura, xcviii.

Christianity, Islam and the Negro Race.

Whoso taketh God and His apostle and the believers for friends, they are the party of God, and they shall be victorious.[4]

But there are no caste distinctions among them. They do not look upon the privileges of Islam as confined by tribal barriers or limitations. On the contrary, the life of their religion is aggressiveness. They are constantly making proselytes. As early as the commencement of the present century, the elastic and expansive character of their system was sufficiently marked to attract the notice of Mr. Park. "In the Negro country," observes that celebrated traveller, "the Mohammedan religion has made, *and continues to make*, considerable progress." "The yearning of the native African," says Professor Crummell, "for a higher religion, is illustrated by the singular fact that Mohammedanism is rapidly and *peaceably* spreading all through the tribes of Western Africa, even to the Christian settlements of Liberia."[5] From Senegal to Lagos, over two thousand miles, there is scarcely an important town on the seaboard where there are not at least one mosque, and active representatives of Islam, often side by side with the Christian teachers. And as soon as a Pagan, however obscure or degraded, embraces the Moslem faith, he is at once admitted as an equal to their society. Slavery and the slave trade are laudable institutions, provided the slaves are Kafirs. The slave who embraces Islam is free, and no office is closed against him on account of servile blood.

The Pagan village possessing a Mussulman teacher is always found to be in advance of its neighbours in all the elements of civilisation. The people pay great deference to him. He instructs their children, and professes to be the medium between them and Heaven, either for securing a supply of their necessities, or for warding off or removing calamities. It must be borne in mind that people in the state of barbarism, in which the Pagan tribes are usually found, have no proper conceptions of humanity and its capacities. The man, therefore, who by unusual strength or cunning achieves something which no one had achieved before him, or of which they do not understand the process, is exalted into an

---

[4] Sura, v.   [5] *Future of Africa*, p. 805.

extraordinary being, in close intimacy with the mysterious powers of Nature. The Mohammedan, then, who enters a Pagan village with his books, and papers, and rosaries, his frequent ablutions and regularly-recurring times of prayers and prostrations, in which he appears to be conversing with some invisible being, soon acquires a controlling influence over the people. He secures their moral confidence and respect, and they bring to him all their difficulties for solution, and all their grievances for redress.

To the African Mussulman, innocent of the intellectual and scientific progress of other portions of the world, the Koran is all-sufficient for his moral, intellectual, social and political needs. It contains his whole religion, and a great deal besides. It is to him far more than it is to the Turk or Egyptian, upon whom the light of European civilisation has fallen. It is his code of laws, and his creed, his homily, and his liturgy. He consults it for direction on every possible subject; and his Pagan neighbour, seeing such veneration paid to the book, conceives even more exaggerated notions of its character. The latter looks upon it as a great medical repository, teaching the art of healing diseases, and as a wonderful storehouse of charms and divining power, protecting from dangers and foretelling future events. And though the prognostications of his Moslem prophet are often of the nature of *vaticinia post eventum*, yet his faith remains unshaken in the infallibility of "Alkorona." He therefore never fails to resort, in times of extremity, to the Mohammedan for direction, and pays him for charms against evil. These charms are nothing more than passages from the Koran, written on slips of paper and inclosed in leather cases about two or three inches square—after the manner of the Jewish phylactery—and worn about the neck or wrist. The passages usually written are the last two chapters of the Koran, known as the "Chapters of Refuge," because they begin, "Say, I take refuge," &c. In cases of internal complaint, one or both of these chapters are written on certain leaves, of which a strong decoction is made, and the water administered to the patient. We have seen these two chapters written inside a bowl at Alexandria for medicinal purposes.

Christianity, Islam and the Negro Race.

The Moslems themselves wear constantly about their persons certain texts from the Koran, called *Ayat-el-hifz*, verses of protection or preservation, which are supposed to keep away every species of misfortune. The following are in most common use: "God is the best *protector*, and He is the most merciful of those who show mercy."⁶ "And God compasseth them behind. Verily it is a glorious Koran, written on a *preserved* tablet."⁷ Sometimes they have the following rhymed couplet:—

> Auzu billahi min es-Shaytan arrajim,
> Bismi illahi arrahim.⁸

This couplet is also employed whenever they are about to read the Koran, as a protection against the suggestions of Satan, who is supposed to be ever on the alert to whisper erroneous and hurtful constructions to the devout reader.

The Koran is almost always in their hand. It seems to be their labour and their relaxation to pore over its pages. They love to read and recite it aloud for hours together. They seem to possess an enthusiastic appreciation of the rhythmical harmony in which it is written. But we cannot attribute its power over them altogether to the jingling sounds, word-plays, and refrains in which it abounds. These, it is true, please the ear and amuse the fancy, especially of the uncultivated. But there is something higher, of which these rhyming lines are the vehicle; something possessing a deeper power to rouse the imagination, mould the feelings, and generate action. Gibbon has characterised the Koran as a "tissue of incoherent rhapsodies."⁹ But the author of the *Decline and Fall* was, as he himself acknowledges, ignorant of the Arabic language, and therefore incompetent to pronounce an authoritative judgment. Mr. Hallam, in a more appreciative vein, speaks of it as "a book confessedly written with much elegance and purity," containing "just and elevated notions of the Divine nature and

---

⁶ Sura xii, 64. ⁷ Sura lxxxv, 20.

⁸ I take refuge in God from Satan, whom we hate,
In the name of God, the Merciful, the Compassionate.

⁹ Chap. i.

Mohammedanism in Western Africa.

moral duties, the gold ore that pervades the dross."[10] The historian of the Middle Ages, a most conscientious investigator, had probably read the book in the original—had been charmed with its *sense* as well as its *sound*. Only they who read it in the language of the Arabian author can form anything like an accurate idea of its unapproachable place as a power among unevangelised communities for moulding into the most exciting and the most expressive harmonies the feelings and imaginations. A recent able and learned critic says :—

> The Koran suffers more than any other book we think of by a translation, however masterly. The grandeur of the Koran consists, its contents apart, in its diction. We cannot explain the peculiarly dignified, impressive, sonorous mixture of Semitic sound and parlance ; its *sesquipedalia verba*, with their crowd of prefixes and affixes, each of them affirming its own position, while consciously bearing upon and influencing the central root, which they envelop like a garment of many folds, or as chosen courtiers move round the anointed person of the king.[11]

The African Moslem forms no exception among the adherents of Islam in his appreciation of the sacred book. It is studied with as much enthusiasm at Boporo, Misadu, Medina and Kankan,[12] as at Cairo, Alexandria, or Bagdad. In travelling in the interior of Liberia, we have met ulemas, or learned men, who could reproduce from memory any chapter of the Koran, with its vowels and dots, and other grammatical marks. The boys under their instruction are kept at the study of the book for years. First, they are taught the letters and vowel marks, then they are taught to read the text, without receiving any insight into its meaning. When they can read fluently, they are taught the meaning of the words, which they commit carefully to memory; after which they are instructed in what they call the "Jalaleyn," a running commentary on the Koran. While learning the Jalaleyn, they have side studies assigned them in Arabic manuscripts, containing the mystical traditions, the acts of Mohammed, the duties of fasting, prayer,

---

[10] *Middle Ages*, chap. vi.

[11] Emanuel Deutsch, in the *Quarterly Review* (London) for October, 1869.

[12] Mohammedan towns, from seventy-five to three hundred miles east and north-east of Monrovia.

alms, corporal purification,[13] &c. Young men who intend to be enrolled among the ulemas take up history and chronology, on which they have some fragmentary manuscripts. Before a student is admitted to the ranks of the learned, he must pass an examination, usually lasting seven days, conducted by a Board consisting of imáms and ulemas. If he is successful, he is led around the town on horseback, with instrumental music and singing. The following ditty is usually sung:—

Allahumma, ya Rabbee,
Salla ala Mohammade,
Salla Allahu alayhe wa Sallama.[14]

After this, the candidate is presented with a sash or scarf, usually of fine white cloth, of native manufacture, which he is henceforth permitted to wind round his cap, with one end hanging down the back, forming the Oriental turban. This is a sort of Bachelor of Arts diploma. The men who wear turbans have read through and recited the Koran many hundred times; and you can refer to no passage which they cannot readily find in their apparently confused manuscripts of loose leaves and pages, distinguished not by numbers, but by catchwords at the bottom. Carlyle tells us that he has heard of Mohammedan doctors who have read the Koran seventy thousand times.[15] Many such animated and moving concordances to the Koran may doubtless be found in Central and West Africa.

But the Koran is not the only book they read. We have seen, in some of their libraries, extensive manuscripts in poetry and prose. One showed us at Boporo, the *Makâmat* of Hariri, which he read and expounded with great readiness, and seemed surprised that we had heard of it. And it is not to be doubted that some valuable Arabic manuscripts may yet be found in the heart of Africa. Dr. Barth tells us that he saw, in Central Africa, a manuscript of those portions of Aristotle and Plato which had been

---

[13] The student at this stage is called "Talib," that is, one who seeks knowledge.

[14] O God, my Lord, bless Mohammed! God bless him, and grant him peace!

[15] *Heroes and Hero Worship*, p. 80.

translated into Arabic, and that an Arabic version of Hippocrates was extremely valued. The splendid voweled edition of the New Testament and Psalms recently issued by the American Bible Society, and of which, through the kindness of friends in New York, we have been enabled to distribute a few copies among them, is highly prized.

We have collected, in our visits to Mohammedan towns, a number of interesting manuscripts, original and extracted. We will here give two or three specimens as translated by us. We should be glad if we could transfer to these pages the elegant and ornamental chirography of the original.

The first is from a talismanic paper written at Futa Jallon, copies of which are sold to the credulous as means of warding off evil from individuals and communities, to be employed especially during seasons of epidemics. It is as follows:—

In the name of God, the Merciful, the Compassionate. O God, bless Mohammed and save him, the seal of the prophets and the imám of the apostles, beloved of the Lord of worlds!

After the above is the conveying of health, and the completing of salutation and honour:

Verily, the pestilence is coming upon you, beginning with your wealth, such as your cows, and after that with yourselves; and verily if all of you provide water and bread, namely, of your men and your women, and your man-servants and your maid-servants, and all your youths, they shall not endure it. And after that write out the Chapter, 'Opener of the Book'[16] and the 'Verse of the Throne,'[17] and from "God is light" to "Omniscient,"[18] and from "God created

---

[16] 'Fatihat el-Kitab,' the first chapter of the Koran.

[17] 'Ayet el-Kursee,' Sura ii, iv, 256. This verse is repeated by the pious Moslem nearly every time he prays. It is as follows: "God! there is no God but He; the Living, the Eternal. Nor slumber seizeth Him, nor sleep; His, whatsoever is in the heavens and whatsoever is in the earth! Who is he that can intercede with Him but by His own permission? He knoweth what hath been before them, and what shall be after them; yet nought of His knowledge shall they grasp, save what He willeth. His throne reacheth over the heavens and the earth, and the upholding of both burdeneth Him not; and He is the High, the Great.—*Rodwell's Translation.*

[18] Sura xxiv, 35.

every," the whole verse, to "Omnipotent,"[10] and the 'Two Chapters of Refuge'; and write, "They who, when they have done foully and dealt unjustly by their own souls, shall remember God, and seek forgiveness for their sins, (and who forgives sins but God?) and shall not persevere in what they have done while they know it."[20] And if you do this, God shall certainly turn back the punishment from you, if God will, by this supplication. . . . . Because that is the way of escape obligatory on every Moslem man and woman. This document is by a man of wealth, who travelled, travelling from Futa to Mecca on pilgrimage, and stayed three months, and departed to El-Medina, and settled there three years, and returned to Futa. Written by me, Ahmad of Futa, to-day. O God, bless Mohammed and save him! The end.

The next paper professes to be a history of the world. Beginning thousands of years before Adam, it gives account of the successive epochs through which the earth passed before man was created. But we omit all those periods, which might, perhaps, be of interest to the enthusiastic geologist, and come down to the account given of the first meeting of Adam and Eve. Says our author:

When Adam first met Eve he was walking upon the sea, and he said to her, "Who art thou?" And she said, "I am the destroyer of mercies." And Adam said, "*Who* art thou?" And she said, "I am the destroyer of wealth; he who finds wealth finds me, and he who does not find wealth does not find me." And Adam said, "*Who* art thou?" And she said, "I am one in whom no faith is to be reposed—*I am Eve.*" And Adam said, "I believe thee, O Eve." And Adam took her, and she conceived, and brought forth forty twins, a male and a female at each birth, and all died except Seth, who was the father of Noah," &c.

The author then proceeds to trace the descendants of Noah, assigning to Shem, Ham and Japheth the countries in which it is commonly understood that they respectively settled.

The next paper is a very elaborate and accurately written manuscript, styled "The Book of Psalms which God sent down to David." We have been puzzled to account for the origin and purpose of this paper. Whencesoever it comes, it is certain it does not come out of the Psalms of David. It contains, however, some excellent moral teachings, written not in Koranic language, but, on the whole, in very good Arabic, singularly free from those

---

[10] Sura xxiv, 44.

[20] Sura iii, 129. An item in a list of classes of persons who shall be blessed in this world and go to Heaven when they die.

omissions and misplacements of diacritical points which are so troublesome in some Arabic writings. The arrangement of the vowels reveals a thorough acquaintance with the niceties of classical Arabic. It was copied for us from an old manuscript brought by a scribe from Kankan, but he could give no information as to its original source. The statement that it *is* the Psalms is probably a mere freak of the compiler or copyist, unless we suppose the existence of some Mohammedan pseudo-psalmist in the interior. Moreover, the word *anzala*, used in the manuscript, which we have translated "sent down," is not the word applied in the Koran to David's revelations. The word there used is *ata*, signifying to "commit," to "give," etc. The paper is divided into six chapters or parts. We will give, with the introductory formula and blessing, the first, fourth, and fifth parts:

In the name of God, &c. God bless our lord Mohammed, His prophet, and his family, and his wives, and his descendants, and his friends, and keep them safe.

This is the Book of Psalms, which God sent down to David. Peace upon him!

Part the First.

I wonder at him who has heard of Death, how he can rejoice.

I wonder at him who has heard of the Reckoning, how he can gather riches.

I wonder at him who has heard of the Grave, how he can laugh.

I wonder at him who grieves over the waste of his riches and does not grieve over the waste of his life.

I wonder at him who has heard of the future world and its bliss and its enduringness, how he can rest when he has never sought it.

I wonder at him who has heard of the present world and its transitoriness, how he can be secure about it when he has never fled from it.

I wonder at him who is knowing in the tongue, and ignorant in the heart.

I wonder at him who is busy with people's faults, and forgets his own faults.

I wonder at him who knows that God considers him in all places, how he can rebel against Him.

I wonder at him who has purified himself with water, and is not pure in his heart.

I wonder at him who knows that he shall die alone, and enter the grave alone, and render account alone, how he can seek reconciliation with men, when he has not sought reconciliation with his Lord.

There is no God but God, in truth; Mohammed is the Envoy of God. God bless him and save him!

Christianity, Islam and the Negro Race.

PART THE FOURTH.

Son of Man! Be not of them who are long of repentance and long of hope,[21] and look for the last day without work, and say the say of the servants, and work the work of the hypocrite, and are not satisfied if I give to you, and endure not if I keep from you; who prescribe that which is approved and good, and do it not, and forbid that which is disapproved and evil, and forego it not, and love the faithful and are not of them, and hate the hypocrites and are of them—exacting and not exact.

Son of Man! There is not a new day but the earth addresses thee, and thus says she her say unto thee:
Son of Man!
Thou walkest on my back, but thy return is to my belly;
Thou laughest on my back, and then thou weepest in my belly;
Thou art joyful on my back, and then thou art sorrowful in my belly;
Thou sinnest on my back, and then thou sufferest in my belly;
Thou eatest thy desire on my back, and then the worms eat thee in my belly;
Son of Man!
I am the house of desolation, I am the house of isolation;
I am the house of darkness, I am the house of straitness;
I am the house of question, I am the house of terrors;
I am the house of serpents, I am the house of scorpions;
I am the house of thirst, I am the house of hunger;
I am the house of disgrace, I am the house of fires;
Then cultivate me, and burn[22] me not.

PART THE FIFTH.

Son of Man! I did not create you to get greatness by you instead of littleness, nor to get companionship by you instead of desolation, nor to borrow by you anything I wanted; nor did I create you to draw to me any profit, or to thrust from me any loss (far be it from Him the Exalted!). But I have created you to serve me perpetually, and thank me greatly, and praise me morning and evening.[23] And if the first of you and the last of you, and the living of you and the dead of you, and the small of you and the great of you, and the male of you and the female of you, and the lords of you and the servants of you, and the men of you and the beasts of you, if they combine to obey me, this will not add to my dominion the weight of a grain of dust. "Whoever does good service, does good service only for himself; and whoever is unthankful—why, God is independent of the three worlds."[24]

---

[21] That is, waiting on Providence, without attempting to "work out one's own salvation."

[22] This is probably a warning against the practice among the natives of denuding the earth by burning the wood when preparing to plant.

[23] Compare Psalm i, 7-14.

[24] *Koran*, xxix, 5.

Mohammedanism in Western Africa.

Son of man!
As thou lendest, shalt thou borrow;
As thou workest, shalt thou be recompensed;
As thou sowest, shalt thou reap.

We have been surprised to notice that the manuscripts which we receive generally from Boporo, Misadu, and Kankan are much better written, and of a much more edifying character, than those we have seen from the Gambia and that region of country. Some of the latter, consisting of childish legends and superstitious details, are often curious philologically, being mixtures of Arabic and the vernacular dialect. It is said also by those who have seen Mohammedan worship conducted by the Jalofs and Foulahs about the Gambia and Senegal, and have witnessed similar exercises among the Mandingoes in the region of country east of Liberia, that the latter exhibit in their bearing and proceedings during their religious services greater intelligence, order, and regularity than the former.

During a visit of three weeks made to Boporo in the Mohammedan month of Ramadhan (December and January, 1868-69), we had an opportunity of seeing the Mandingo Moslem at home. It being the sacred month of fasting and religious devotedness, we witnessed several religious ceremonies and performances.

As in all Moslem communities, prayer is held five times a-day. When the hour for prayer approaches, a man appointed for the purpose, with a very strong and clear voice, goes to the door of the mosque and chants the *adhan*, or call to prayer. This man is called the Muëddin.[25] His call is especially solemn and interesting in the early hours of the morning. We often lay in bed between four and five o'clock listening for the cry of the Muëddin. There was a simple and solemn melody in the chant at that still hour, which, after it had ceased, still lingered pleasantly on the

---

[25] The first Moslem crier was an Ethiopian negro, Bilah by name, "a man of powerful frame and sonorous voice." He was the favourite attendant of Mohammed. Mr. Irving informs us that on the capture of Jerusalem he made the first *adhan*, "at the Caliph Omar's command, and summoned the true believers to prayers with a force of lungs that astonished the Jewish inhabitants."—Irving's *Successors of Mahomet*, p. 100.

ear, and often, despite ourselves, drew us out to the mosque. The morning *adhan*, as we heard it at Boporo, is as follows: *Allāhu Akbar* (this is said four times). *Ashhadu an la ilāha ill' Allah* (twice). *Ashhadu anna Mohammadu rasoolu 'llah* (twice). *Heiya ala Salāh* (twice). *Heiya alal-felāh* (twice). *Salātu kheiru min a-naumi* (twice). *Allāhu Akbar* (twice). *La ilāha 'ill Allāh* (once).[26]

Says Mr. Deutsch:

May-be some stray reader remembers a certain thrill on waking suddenly in the middle of his first night on Eastern soil—waking, as it were, from dream into dream. For there came a voice, solitary, sweet, sonorous, floating from on high, through the moonlight stillness—the voice of the blind Mueddin, singing the "Ualh," or first call to prayer.... The sounds went and came—"*Allahu Akbar, Allahu Akbar*"—and this reader may have a vague notion of Arabic and Koranic sound, one he will never forget.[27]

At Boporo and other African towns we have visited, this call is made three times within the half-hour immediately preceding worship. Before the third call is concluded the people have generally assembled in the mosque. Then the Imám proceeds with the exercises, consisting usually of certain short chapters from the Koran and a few prayers, interspersed with beautiful chanting of the Moslem watch-word, "*La ilaha ill' Allah, Mohammadu rasoolu 'llahi*"—"There is no God," etc. We may remark, by the way, that their tunes are not set in the minor key, as is almost always the case among the Arabs. Their natures are more joyful. They exult in the diatonic scale of life, and leave their Oriental co-religionists to wail in the sad and mournful chromatics of the desert

The Mandingoes are an exceedingly polite and hospitable people. The restraints of their religion regulate their manners and control their behaviour. Both in speech and demeanour, they appear always solicitous to be *en regle*—anxious to maintain the strictest propriety; and they succeed in conforming to the natural laws of

---

[26] The English is, "God is more great" (four times). "I testify that there is no deity but God" (twice). "I testify that Mohammed is the apostle of God" (twice). "Come to prayer" (twice). "Come to security" (twice). "Prayer is better than sleep" (twice). "God is most great" (twice). "There is no deity but God" (once).

[27] *Quarterly Review*, October, 1869.

Mohammedanism in Western Africa.

etiquette, of which they seem to have an instinctive and agreeable appreciation. In their salutations they always try to exceed each other in good wishes. The salutation "*Salaam aleikum*"—" Peace be with you"—common in Oriental Mohammedan countries, is used by them very sparingly, and, as a general thing, only on leaving the mosque after early morning worship. The reply is, "*Aleikum-e-Salaam, wa rahmatu 'llahi wa barakatuhu*"—" With you be peace, and the mercy of God and His blessing." If " *Salaam Aleikum* " is addressed to them by a Kafir or Pagan they seldom reply; if by a Christian, the reply is, " *Salaam ala man taba el-huda*"—" Peace to him who follows the right way."

Those who speak Arabic speak the Koranic or book Arabic, preserving the final vowels of the classical language—a practice which, in the hurry and exigencies of business life, has been long discontinued in countries where the language is vernacular; so that in Egypt and Syria the current speech is very defective, and clipped and corrupted. Mr. Palgrave informs us, however, that in North-east Arabia the "grammatical dialect" is used in ordinary conversation. "The smallest and raggedest child that toddles about the street lisps in the correctest book Arabic that ever De Sacy studied or Sibaweeyah professed."[28] So among the Arabic scholars whom one meets in the interior of Liberia. In proper names we hear Ibraheema, Aleeu, Suleimana, Abdullahi, Dauda, etc.; in worship Allahu, Akbaru, Lailaha, ill'Allahu, etc.; and it is difficult for the mere tyro in Arabic pronunciation either to understand or make himself understood unless he constantly bear in mind the final vowels in nouns, verbs, and adjectives. A recent number of the *Saturday Review*,[20] in a notice of General Daumas's new work on *Arabic Life and Mussulman Society*, remarks, " One comfort for the learner will be, that the oft-pressed distinction between what is termed the learned and the vulgar (Arabic) tongue is a mere fiction of European growth. It has no foundation in native usage." We fear that the theoretical comfort which the

---

[28] Palgrave's *Arabia*, vol. i, p. 311.
[21] March 26, 1870.

soothing reviewer attempts to administer to the learner of Arabic will be found of no practical avail when applied to the intercourse of daily life in Syria and Egypt. Only such learned natives as Mr. Bistany, of Beyroot, and Dr. Meshakah, of Damascus, speak the language so as to be understood by one versed only in Koranic inflections. And even they generally avoid that style as stilted, pedantic, and absurd. Says a high authority:—[80]

> Les populations Arabes, en general, etant fort ignorantes, par leur misère d'abord, et ensuite par l'extreme difficulté de l'etude et de l'application de leur idiome, le langage usuel des diverses regions est soumis à bien des variétés, soit de prononciation, soit de *denomination* des idées et des choses.

Among the Moslems of West Africa there are some peculiarities in the sounds of the letters. The fourth letter of the alphabet is generally pronounced like *s*; the seventh like the simple *k*; the ninth like *j* in jug; *seen* and *sheen* have both the sound of *s*. The fifteenth letter is sounded like *l*; the nineteenth, whose guttural sound is so difficult to Western organs, is sounded like *k*; the twenty-first like *g* hard.

The introduction of Islam into Central and West Africa has been the most important, if not the sole, preservative against the desolations of the slave trade. Mohammedanism furnished a protection to the tribes who embraced it by effectually binding them together in one strong religious fraternity, and enabling them by their united effort to baffle the attempts of powerful Pagan slave-hunters. Enjoying this comparative immunity from sudden hostile incursions, industry was stimulated among them, industry diminished their poverty; and, as they increased in worldly substance, they also increased in desire for knowledge. Gross superstition gradually disappeared from among them. Receiving a degree of culture from the study of the Arabic language, they acquired loftier views, wider tastes, and those energetic habits which so pleasingly distinguished them from their Pagan neighbours.

Large towns and cities have grown up under Mohammedan energy and industry. Dr. Barth was surprised to find such towns

---

[80] M. Bresnier, professor of Arabic in the Normal College of Algiers, in his *Cours Pratique et Theorique de Langue Arabe*.

Mohammedanism in Western Africa.

or cities as Kanó and Sokoto in the centre of Africa—to discover the focus of a complex and widely-ramified commerce, and a busy hive of manufacturing industry, in a region which most people had believed to be a desert. And there are towns and cities nearly as important farther west, to which Barth did not penetrate, still affording scope to extend the horizon of European knowledge and the limits of commercial enterprise. Mr. Benjamin Anderson, the enterprising Liberian traveller, who has recently visited Misadu, the capital of the Western Mandingoes, about two hundred miles east of Monrovia, describes that city as the centre of a considerable commerce, reaching as far north as Senegal and east as far as Sokoto.

The African Moslems are also great travellers. They seem to travel through the country with greater freedom and safety than any other people, on account, probably, of their superior intelligence and greater usefulness. They are continually crossing the continent to Egypt, Arabia, and Syria. We met a few weeks ago at Toto-Coreh, a town about ten miles east of Boporo, a lad who informed us that he was born at Mecca while his parents were in that city on a pilgrimage. We gave him a copy of the New Testament in Arabic, which he read with unimpeded fluency, and with the Oriental accent and pronunciation.

The general diffusion of the Arabic language[m] in this country, through Mohammedan influence, must be regarded as a preparatory circumstance of vast importance for the introduction of the Gospel. It may be—

The plan of Providence that these many barbarous nations of Africa are to be consolidated under one aggressive empire of ideas and faith, to prepare the way for evangelisation through the medium of one copious, cultivated, expressive tongue, in the place of leaving to the Church the difficult task of translating

---

[m] The natives love and revere the language. All documents of a serious character must be written in that language. Bishop Crowther, of the Niger, in a letter dated October 30, 1869, tells us of his visit to King Masaba, a distinguished Mohammedan sovereign, with whom he entered into a written agreement with reference to the establishment of a Christian mission in his capital. "I drew up his promise," says the Bishop, "in English, which he handed over to his Maalims *to be translated into Arabic.*"—*Christian Observer,* January, 1870.

and preaching in many barbarous languages, incapable of expressing the finer forms of thought.[82]

Already some of the vernaculars have been enriched by expressions from the Arabic for the embodiment of the higher processes of thought. They have received terms regarding the religion of one God, and respecting a certain state of civilisation, such as marrying, reading, writing, and the objects having relation thereto, sections of time, and phrases of salutation and of good breeding; then the terms relating to dress, instruments, and the art of warfare, as well as architecture, commerce, &c.[83]

Mohammedanism, in this part of the world, could easily be displaced by Christian influence, if Christian organisations would enter with vigour into this field. The Rev. G.W. Gibson, Rector of Trinity Church, Monrovia, in a letter published in the *Spirit of Missions* for April, 1869, says :—

> Whatever may have been the influence of Mohammedanism on races in other parts of the world, I think here, upon the African, results will prove it to be merely preparatory to a Christian civilisation. In this country, and almost immediately in our vicinity, it has recovered millions from Paganism, without, I think, having such a grasp upon the minds of the masses as to lead them obstinately to cling to it in preference to Christianity, with its superior advantages. The same feelings which led them to abandon their former religion for the Moslem will, no doubt, lead them still further, and induce them to embrace ours when properly presented. I express this opinion the more readily from several interviews I have had lately with prominent parties connected with some of these tribes.

We are persuaded that, with the book knowledge they already possess, and their love of letters, many of them would become ready converts of a religion which brings with it the recommendation of a higher culture and a nobler civilisation. And, once brought within the pale of Christianity, these Mohammedans would be a most effective agency for the propagation of the Gospel in remote regions, hitherto impervious to European zeal and enterprise, and the work of African regeneration would proceed with uninterrupted course and unexampled rapidity.

---

[82] Prof. Post, of Syrian Protestant College, Beyrout.
[83] See Barth's *Collection of Central African Vocabularies*, part i, p. 29.

Sierra Leone and Liberia:
Their Origin, Work, and Destiny.

THERE is historical evidence that the portion of Africa where are situated the Colony of Sierra Leone and the Republic of Liberia was known to the ancients. The earliest authentic account we have, however, of any visit to this coast by foreigners is contained in a fragment of Carthaginian literature, called the Periplus of Hanno, which shows that five hundred years before Christ, or more than two thousand years ago, Sierra Leone was visited. This document is said to be "the one relic of Carthaginian literature which has come down to us entire." It has been preserved, however, not in the Carthaginian original, but in a Greek translation.[1]

In modern history, the Portuguese claim to have discovered Sierra Leone about 1415, and they are said to have planted a settlement here in 1463, twenty-nine years before the discovery of America by Columbus. The priority of discovery is, however, disputed by the French, who pretend that the merchants of Dieppe visited these coasts in 1346, seventy years earlier. Two of their authors, Villault and Robbé, detail at some length the origin and progress of the French settlements at Sierra Leone, Cape Mount, River Sestos, and Elmina.

The object of these early establishments was legitimate commerce—no thought of carrying the people away into slavery had at that time occurred. The discovery of America in 1492 was the fountain and source of that transatlantic traffic in men which, for

---

[1] Bosworth Smith's *Carthage and the Carthaginians*, p. 48.

more than three hundred years, entailed woes innumerable upon the people of this country. The slave trade was regularly established by Spain twenty-five years after the great exploit by Columbus.

The first Englishman who engaged in the odious traffic was Sir John Hawkins, and the first scene of his disastrous labours was Sierra Leone. He sailed from England for this port in October, 1562. Here he found the aborigines living in peace and quietness, producing by agriculture and trade all that their necessities required. By the sword and other means, he obtained possession of three hundred persons, sailed with them to St. Domingo, where he exchanged them for hides, ginger, sugar, and a good quantity of pearls, returning to England in September, 1563. He subsequently obtained the sanction of Queen Elizabeth, and a grant of two of Her Majesty's ships for his nefarious expeditions. It must be stated in justice to the Queen, however, that she strongly objected to the traffic, and remonstrated against it; but she was assured that none were transported from Africa but those who voluntarily offered themselves as labourers; that their religious condition was improved by being taken away from their native superstitions. The Queen seems to have contented herself with issuing some stringent injunctions against the employment of force, with which those interested in the trade promised to comply.[2]

The principle of African colonisation in modern times, with a view to the improvement of the country and the people, must be attributed to the Swedes. To them belongs the glory of forming the first specific plan for alleviating the evils which the inhuman traffic had caused and was causing to this country; and to the Danes must be assigned the credit of first carrying into execution the idea of an agricultural establishment for instructing the natives in the cultivation of their fertile soil.

A society formed in Sweden, in 1779, obtained a charter from His Swedish Majesty, Gustavus III, empowering forty families to settle on this coast under the protection of Sweden, to organise

---

[2] Walker's *History of the Slave Trade*, p. 87.

Sierra Leone and Liberia.

their own government, to enact their own laws, and to establish a community entirely independent of Europe. In the report of those who were sent out to examine the coast, Cape Verde appeared the most eligible situation; but it was claimed by the French, who had twice purchased the whole peninsula. After Cape Verde they fixed upon Cape Mount and Cape Mesurado, where now stands the capital of the Republic of Liberia. Cape Mount was represented as the Paradise of New Guinea.[a]

The idea of restoring free blacks as colonists, from the countries of their exile in the West to the land of their fathers, originated in England with Granville Sharp and a few others of like philanthropic spirit. Through the efforts of Sharp, a decision was obtained from Chief Justice Mansfield in 1772, laying down the principle that "as soon as any slave sets foot on English ground he becomes free." At that time, there were in England numerous slaves who had been carried from the West Indies and America by their masters. When this decision was published, they were either driven from the houses of their masters or they left of their own accord. Several hundreds of this class of persons were, therefore, found wandering about London homeless and starving, and Sharp and his friends made themselves responsible for their unprotected and suffering condition.

To provide means for their relief a society was organised. In the meanwhile, Granville Sharp conceived the idea of sending them back to Africa, and sketched the outline of a plan for a settlement for all such persons. In July, 1783, while this plan was under serious consideration, Dr. Smeatham, who had spent several years on the coast of Africa, wrote an interesting letter to Dr. Knowles, which came to the notice of Sharp, suggesting the idea of a free Negro settlement at Sierra Leone, "for the purpose of checking and putting down the slave trade, and of diffusing the principles of the Christian religion among the natives."

---

[a] Villault, who saw Cape Mount in 1667, said: "L'Afrique serait preferable à l'Europe, si toutes les parties de cette vaste region resemblait aux environs du Cap Monte."

Christianity, Islam and the Negro Race.

A commercial company, called St. George's Bay Company, organised about 1756, had established its operations at Sierra Leone.[4] Through this company Granville Sharp and his associates secured a considerable district of land for the purpose of settling the emancipated slaves. In the year 1787, a subscription of a few thousand pounds having been raised for assisting the destitute blacks to reach Africa, the Government very liberally seconded these views by taking upon itself the expense of transporting them to their destination, and of supplying them with necessaries during the first six or eight months of their residence in Africa. The number that left England was four hundred and sixty, of whom eighty-four died during their detention in the Channel or on the passage; and near a hundred more fell victims to the hardships to which they were exposed during the first rainy season. They landed here in May, 1787. In May, 1887, three years hence, we shall have reached the centennial anniversary of the settlement. It is to be hoped that it will be duly celebrated by all the inhabitants, and that the occasion will be marked by some suitable memorial.

In the year 1791, the St. George's Bay Company was incorporated by Act of Parliament under the name of the Sierra Leone Company. In consequence of this recognition by the Government, the capital of the company rapidly increased, and the Directors had the opportunity of sending to the colony an additional number of black colonists acquainted with the English language and accustomed to labour in hot climates. In relation to this matter I take the following from the first Official Report of the Directors of the Sierra Leone Company, made in 1793:—

> When the Act of Parliament had passed for incorporating the Sierra Leone Company, a delegate from a body of blacks in Nova Scotia, supposed to amount to a few hundred, who was then in England, represented that the persons who sent him hither had migrated to Nova Scotia at the end of the American war, having received from Government certain promises of lots of land which had never been strictly fulfilled; that both the soil and the climate of Nova Scotia,

---

[4] This was not the earliest English establishment. Villault found an English factory on Bunce Island in 1666.

Sierra Leone and Liberia.

as well as many other circumstances in their situation, were complained of by them, and that many of them were desirous of becoming colonists at the settlement which they understood was likely to be made at Sierra Leone.

The Directors concurred with the delegate in applying to His Majesty's Ministers for a passage for them at the expense of Government, and having obtained a favourable reply, they immediately availed themselves of the services of Lieutenant Clarkson, who very handsomely offered to go to Nova Scotia in order to make the necessary proposals, and to superintend the collecting and bringing over of such free blacks to Sierra Leone as might be willing to migrate.[5]

The Nova Scotians were a portion of those slaves, who, during the American War of Independence, ran away from their masters and took refuge in the King's army. They were born in North America of African progenitors.

The number of Nova Scotians, the Report continues, who were willing to embark for Sierra Leone proved, to the great surprise of the Directors, to be no less than 1,196. In the month of February, 1792, the Company sent out the Nova Scotians in a fleet of sixteen vessels, from which there were landed in Sierra Leone, on the 28th of March, 1,131 blacks, many of them labouring under the effects of a fever first contracted in Halifax, of which 65 had died during the passage.

About this same time, a few gentlemen in the United States, headed by the Revs. Drs. Hopkins and Stiles, of Rhode Island, having several years previously conceived the idea of a missionary settlement in Africa of Christian blacks, were endeavouring to induce merchants to send out a vessel with a few emigrants, and with goods, the profits on which would diminish the expense of the enterprise, and enable them to procure lands on which to make a beginning. But this plan did not succeed from want of funds.

On the 15th of January, 1789, two years after Granville Sharp's first emigrants had been sent out, Dr. Hopkins wrote to him enquiring whether, and on what terms, and with what prospects, blacks from America could join his colony. But it appears that no satisfactory answer was received.

In 1800 and 1801 the colony received another accession of

---

[5] An account of the colony of Sierra Leone, from its first establishment in 1793, being the substance of a Report delivered to the Proprietors. Published by order of the Directors, London, 1795.

emigrants from Jamaica, called Maroons, 550 in number. On their arrival they found the Nova Scotians in rebellion against the Company, on account of a ground-rent or quit-tax which had been imposed upon their farms. They contended that the lands had been granted to them by the Crown. The Maroons joined the Company in the effort to restore order, and the rebellion was put down. This was the cause of bitter alienation of feeling between the settlers and the Maroons. But hostile and powerful attacks made upon the colony by the natives forced the two parties together, and made them feel that their cause was one, and that their only safety was in union and co-operation.

About this time, a charter of justice was obtained from the Crown, authorising the Directors of the Sierra Leone Company to make laws, not repugnant to those of England, and to appoint a Governor and a Council with a similar power of making laws subject to the revision of the Court of Directors. It placed the criminal jurisdiction in the hands of the Governor and Council, the determination of civil suits in a Mayor's court, and the recovery of small debts in a court of requests, and, in civil and criminal cases, the right of a trial by jury.[6]

Though Dr. Hopkins died (December 20, 1803) before his philanthropic plan could be carried out, yet his ideas had been gradually spreading in the United States. In 1800, James Monroe, then Governor of the State of Virginia, was authorised by the Legislature of his State to correspond with the President of the United States, on the subject of the removal of free blacks from the limits of the United States. President Jefferson, whose sagacious and humane mind had led him to say, in view of the sufferings of the Negro in America, "I tremble for my country when I consider that God is just," seized at once upon the idea, and recommended Africa as the country to which the free blacks should be removed. Having heard of the colony of Sierra Leone, he corresponded with the British Government concerning the transfer of blacks to the new settlement, but without success,

---

Report of Dr. Madden, Her Majesty's Commissioner to Western Africa, 1840.

Sierra Leone and Liberia.

the British Government having at that time no control over the colony.

The spirit which had been evoked in England in favour of freedom by the legal question raised by Granville Sharp, and decided by Lord Mansfield, led, after twenty years of struggle and conflict, to the abolition of the slave trade. British vessels, taken in the horrible traffic, were to be seized and their captives released. This Act passed the English Parliament in 1807. As a convenient place for landing and sheltering recaptives, Sierra Leone was fixed upon, and it was transferred by the Company to the Government in 1808. Henceforward the resources of a great nation were to be devoted to making the colony what it was designed to be—namely, an establishment for the suppression of the slave trade, and the religious and moral improvement of the natives.

It is a very interesting fact that on the spot where Englishmen first began the work of African demoralisation, Englishmen should begin the work of African amelioration and restoration. England produced Sir John Hawkins, known to Sierra Leone by his fire and sword policy. Two hundred years later, England produced Granville Sharp, known by his policy of peace, of freedom, and of religion. The land of Pharaoh was also the land of Moses. Alone, amid the darkness of those days, stood Sierra Leone—the only point at which the slave trade could not be openly prosecuted—the solitary refuge of the hunted slave. The geographical position of the peninsula might be taken as an emblem of its moral status. For hundreds of miles on either side of the colony the coast is low and swampy; but here the land rises into mountains of considerable height, and a bold promontory stretches out into the sea, forming an excellent natural harbour for ships pelted by the storm—beautiful emblem of the sublime moral attitude of the principles upon which the colony was founded, and of the rest and protection which the persecuted slave might find here.

Quorum sub vertice laté Aequora tuta silent.[7]

Sierra Leone—" mountain of the lion "—was a prophetic appellation, for it is the mount of moral elevation from which the roaring

---

[7] Virgil's *Æneid*, i, 163, 164.

Christianity, Islam and the Negro Race.

of the lion of the nations has saved hundreds of thousands from an untimely death, or a protracted and cruel bondage worse than death.

The slave trade was a serious interference with African life. Early travellers to this coast describe the pacific character of the people, and their quiet and successful industry. Had the traffic between the natives and Europeans continued regular and normal —such a trade, for instance, as there has been between China or Japan and Europe, a trade in which men did not form a commodity—this country would not now be behind any other tropical country in productive capacity. Before the demand for Negro labour in the Western hemisphere taught the people of the coast districts to make war upon each other, there was continuous intercourse between Sierra Leone and the interior. An extensive agriculture beautified the landscape on every hand. There was gradual, regular growth in the elements of civilisation. But when the necessities of the slave trade spread confusion and disorder through all the maritime regions, legitimate trade retired from this part of Africa, and found its way across the desert to the Mediterranean.

In the sixteenth century, about the same time that John Hawkins was conducting his unhallowed operations, John Leo, or Leo Africanus, was travelling in the interior, about the headwaters of the Niger, where he witnessed a degree of civilisation which could not have failed to develop, by this time, into considerable importance. He thus describes the Kingdom of Melli, which is probably the modern Masina or Bambarra:—

> In this kingdom there is a large and ample village, containing to the number of six thousand or more families, and called Melli, whereof the whole kingdom is so named. And here the king hath his place of residence. The region itself yieldeth great abundance of corn, flesh and cotton. Here are many artificers and merchants in all places; and yet the king honourably entertaineth all strangers. The inhabitants are rich, and have plenty of wares. Here are great store of temples, priests and professors, which professors read their lectures in the temples. The people of this region excel all other Negroes in wit, civility, and industry.[8]

---

[8] *A Geographical Historie of Africa, written in Arabicke and Italian.* By John Leo, a Moor, born it Granada and brought up in Barbary. Translated by John Pory, of Gonville and Caius College, Cambridge.—London, 1600.

Sierra Leone and Liberia.

This was three hundred years ago. But one hundred years ago Bornou was described as follows:—

> Bornou is a very extensive and powerful monarchy. The capital thereof is so large that travellers, in describing its magnitude, state that Cairo, which contains half-a-million of people, "is a trifle to it." Kashna, which is subject to Bornou, is said to contain one thousand towns and villages. The country is represented as being very pleasant, beautifully diversified with hill and dale, very fertile, well cultivated, abounding in flocks and herds, and very populous.[o]

Residents of Sierra Leone, who know, by experience, something of the activity and value of the trade from the interior, even now, after all the waste of the slave trade, can find no difficulty in crediting the accuracy of these descriptions.

Mungo Park tells us that the Mandingo manufacturers furnished the Moors with clothing. Perhaps some present will be surprised to learn that large quantities of ready-made clothing are imported into the settlement from Sego and other places on the Niger. These articles are made by native tailors, of stuff manufactured in the interior. The material is sold at three and four times the price charged for the blue baft from England, which is an inferior imitation of the Mandingo article.

The ancestors of these people understood the use of the cotton-plant, and the manufacture of cotton, when Julius Cæsar found the Britons clothing themselves in the skins of wild beasts. Visitors to the British Museum may see, in the Egyptian department, cloth of the very same material and texture wrapped around the mummies. This cloth was made by those who understood the lost art of embalming, but who, when they retired by successive revolutions, into the interior—the heart of the Soudan, where the conditions of climate forbade the practice of embalming—lost that valuable art, but never forgot the manufacture of the cloth used in the process. Another proof, this, of the connection of the Nigritian tribes with the ancient Egyptians.

Between sixty and seventy years ago Sir Charles McCarthy, then Governor of Sierra Leone, set his heart upon developing the interior traffic of which he had heard so much, and again attracting

---

[o] McQueen's *Central Africa*. p. 219.

it to the coast. His able and zealous efforts met with no little measure of success. In a letter to the Secretary of State for the Colonies, under date May 17, 1814, he depicts the state of things before he began his labours, as follows:—

> Three-fourths of the produce of the very rich mines of Bambouk was allowed to find its way to the Barbary States, from whence the Bambarra Kingdoms derived all their articles of commerce, and even for several years back these mines have been almost totally neglected.

On the eve of his departure from Senegal, where he had been administering the Government (Senegal being then a British colony), he wrote to the Secretary of State, under date May 6, 1814:

> I have great pleasure in reporting to your Lordship that I leave this colony in a perfect state of tranquillity. I have received from the Moors and Negro Princes every possible assurance of a wish on their part to cultivate a good understanding with the British Government and encourage trade. The imports into the colony have exceeded double the amount of last year, and the exports of gum and gold will be in the same proportions.

Here I must crave your indulgence while I digress for a moment, to say a few words on the injurious notion which largely prevails among civilised Negroes, chiefly in foreign lands, gathered from the books they read, that the Negro has had no past, and that all his ideas of civilisation and all his tendencies to growth have been obtained from European instruction and example.

Now it is not surprising that this impression should prevail among white people, who see the Negro only in exile or along this coast, which still suffers from the demoralisation of centuries. But it is not for intelligent Negroes to allow themselves to imbibe this poisonous misrepresentation, especially those in this portion of Africa, who have the opportunity, by only a few days' journey from the coast, to learn the truth about their people. It is this false conception of what Africa has been, and of its actual and possible condition away from the coast, which misleads so many who come for philanthropic and other work from Europe and America.

There is such a thing as the poetry of politics, what is sometimes called sentiment. It is the feeling of race—the aspiration after the development on its own line of the type of humanity to which we belong. Italians and Germans long yearned after such

Sierra Leone and Liberia.

development. The Slavonic tribes are feeling after it. Now, nothing tends more to discourage these feelings, and check these aspirations, than the idea that the people with whom we are connected, and after whose improvement we sigh, have never had a past, or only an ignoble past—antecedents which were "blank and hopeless," to be ignored and forgotten.

We have then nothing upon which to base any hopes for the future, or from which to derive a sense of obligation to posterity. We have a feeling that those who have gone before us have done nothing for us, and why should we do anything for posterity? Under such circumstances, there can be no such thing as a real national history—no continuity or transmission of organic feeling; but without such a feeling there can be no progress. A true respect for the past—a consciousness of a real national history—has not only a binding force but a stimulating effect, and furnishes a guarantee of future endurance and growth. That which has been achieved in the past is a prophecy of what may be done in the future. You may call this poetry if you like, but it is the kind of thing on which nations thrive. Mr. Matthew Arnold has recently told us that "more and more mankind will discover that we have to turn to poetry to interpret life for us, to console and sustain us." When Napoleon on the burning plains of Egypt called out to his soldiers, "Forty centuries look down upon you from the summit of those Pyramids," it was not only the military but the poetic instinct that suggested the words. He borrowed from the past achievements of an alien race inspiration for his exhausted troops. They connected themselves with humanity and took courage from the past deeds of the despised African.

While Sir Charles McCarthy was earnestly labouring in every way to bring the colony up to the performance of the work it was intended to achieve, the idea of transferring free blacks from the United States to Africa was assuming definite and practical shape. In the year 1815, Captain Paul Cuffee, a Negro of some means, brought out to Sierra Leone, in his own vessel, thirty emigrants. (I have been able to find no mention in the records of the colony of this arrival.) This philanthropic and patriotic deed was suggestive and instructive. What the white people had been thinking and talking about for thirty years was thus carried into effect by one of the oppressed class whose condition they were considering—thus showing that the project in contemplation was in harmony with the instincts and desires of the Africans in America.

Two years after Paul Cuffee's enterprise, the American Colonisation Society was organised (January 1, 1817). In November of that year Samuel I. Mills and Ebenezer Burgess were sent to this country as commissioners of the Society to select a site for a colony. Arriving in England in December, on their way out, they were courteously received by His Royal Highness, the Duke of Gloucester, patron and president, and by the other officers of the African Institution. Mr. Wilberforce introduced them to Earl Bathurst, then Secretary of State for the Colonies, who gave them letters to Sir Charles McCarthy, the Governor of Sierra Leone and other officers of the Colony, directing them to aid the explorers in their explorations. But before they could reach the colony, Sir Charles McCarthy, having already heard of the enterprise, addressed the following despatch to the Secretary of State:—

> Government House,
> Sierra Leone, January 2, 1818.
>
> My Lord,—Understanding that it is in the contemplation of the Government of the United States of America to form an establishment of their people of colour in some part of Africa near this place, and being thoroughly convinced that such a measure would not only prove highly prejudicial to the interest of this Colony, but ultimately prevent all commercial intercourse with Great Britain, I beg leave to solicit your Lordship to adopt such measures as you may deem most advisable to prevent an establishment of that nature being formed either to the north of Sierra Leone, or nearer to the south than Cape Palmas. . . .
>
> I have the honour, &c.,
> (Signed) C. McCarthy.
>
> The Right Honourable
> Earl Bathurst, K.G., &c., &c., &c.

Messrs. Mills and Burgess arrived at Sierra Leone March 22nd, 1818, a little less than three months after the letter was written, and were received by the Governor with great personal kindness. He gave them every facility for prosecuting their enquiries, though he did not conceal his unwillingness that an American Negro

Sierra Leone and Liberia.

colony should be established in the vicinity of Sierra Leone. They examined the coast as far as Sherbro, and obtained promises that on the arrival of colonists suitable land should be furnished for their settlement. They then returned to Sierra Leone, and on May 22nd, embarked for England on their homeward voyage.

It appears that nothing more was heard at Sierra Leone of the projected colony until March 9th, 1820, two years after the departure of the explorers, when the ship *Elizabeth*, having sailed from New York, February 6th, arrived in the harbour of Freetown with the first settlers for the new colony—eighty-eight in number—from Virginia, Maryland, Pennsylvania and New York.

Sir Charles McCarthy, three days after their arrival, wrote to Earl Bathurst as follows :—

Government House,
Sierra Leone, March 12, 1820.

My Lord,—I have the honour to inform your Lordship that the merchant ship *Elizabeth*, having left New York on the 6th February, arrived in this harbour on the 9th inst., having on board as passengers, four Agents from the United States of America, with Government stores, tools, provisions, and eighty-eight people of colour—men, women and children, labourers and mechanics—for the purpose (as their senior Agent, the Rev. Samuel Bacon, states to me) of commencing an asylum for liberated Negroes in the River Sherbro, or in such other place to the leeward of this as they may find most convenient. I understand that the *Elizabeth* was to have sailed under the convoy of the American sloop-of-war *Cyane*, but lost sight of her in getting out of the harbour. She (the *Cyane*) is intended to afford the settlement or settlements protection, and at the same time to cruise on this coast. I hear also the *Cyane* is authorised to detain all American slave-vessels, to land the slaves at the new establishment, and send the vessels, for disposal, to America.

Although I am willing to give due credit to the humane and benevolent intentions which have led to the present measure, and that the superintendents are strongly recommended to me by the Honourable Bushrod Washington, and I may add that I trust I shall ever be found anxious to give my weak support and good wishes to any establishment of that description, yet I conceive it my duty, as Governor of this colony, to state that I fear any colonisation of a foreign power so immediately in our neighbourhood may be productive of considerable inconvenience, and even losses, in the trade of the colony. I had the honour of addressing your Lordship to the same purport on the 9th of May, 1818 (No. 144) and 20th same month (No. 150) ; and as your Lordship had been pleased to state in your answer dated 30th September, same year, that you concurred in my opinion, I had been led to hope that the Government of the

Christianity, Islam and the Negro Race.

United States would have paid some deference to your advice. I have not yet seen sufficiently of the gentlemen entrusted with the commission of the United States to be able to state positively that they will not attend to my own suggestions of forming their establishments farther to leeward. I shall transmit to your Lordship a copy of the documents they have communicated to me. The *Cyane* is not yet arrived. I scarcely need to observe that I shall show to the superintendents those marks of attention and civility to which they are entitled.

I have the honour, &c.,

Right Honourable Earl Bathurst, K.G.   (Signed) C. McCARTHY.

For the opportunity of perusing and copying these letters, I am indebted to the courtesy of His Excellency Governor Havelock, who kindly allowed me access to the archives at Government House for the purposes of this lecture. These despatches not only illustrate the very inadequate conception of that day as to the laws of trade, but also furnish one of the proofs, which are everywhere found in the records of that period, of the zeal and solicitude of Sir Charles McCarthy for the future welfare of the colony. It appears that four years after the American settlers had occupied Cape Mesurado, in 1825, opinion had so far advanced that General Turner attempted, by treaties with the native chiefs, to extend the colony of Sierra Leone to the Gallinas River in the direction of Liberia. Sir John Jeremie subsequently attempted the same thing, with a view chiefly to the suppression of the slave trade, but the untimely death of these energetic Governors caused the project to fail.

The progress of events—the growth of the two countries—has shown that not only has Liberia not interfered prejudicially with Sierra Leone, but it has presented a field for the energies, industrial and commercial, of many a native of the settlement. An interesting fact in the present history of Liberia, which Sir Charles McCarthy could hardly have foreseen, is this, that a native of Sierra Leone, brought up amid the institutions of the colony, is a successor of Messrs. Mills and Burgess, as agent of the American Colonisation Society, having charge of the location and rationing of all emigrants arriving in Liberia from America. This native of Sierra Leone is also the Mayor of the city of Monrovia, the capital of the Republic. On the other hand, a citizen of Liberia was, not

Sierra Leone and Liberia.

very long ago, entrusted with the interior matters of this settlement, and executed—by appointment from the Governor-in-Chief—important diplomatic missions to powerful chiefs, for which he received the commendation and thanks of the Secretary of State for the Colonies. These things, I take it, are only indications of the future relations of the two countries. The two peoples are one in origin and one in destiny; and, in spite of themselves, in spite of local prejudices, they must co-operate.

For some years past, a strong desire, just the reverse of that entertained by Sir Charles McCarthy, has prevailed among the Governors of this colony—a desire to carry out the policy of General Turner and Sir John Jeremie. It has been felt that the cause of civilisation and commerce would be subserved not by widening the gulf between the two countries, but by bringing them more closely together. And this desire has been recently realised by making the boundaries of the two countries conterminous. The Liberians, however, have protested against the manner of this junction. "Mohammed has gone to the mountain," but the mountain has shrunk at his approach. The lion has lain down with the lamb, but a part of the lamb has been absorbed.

The present feeling at Government House here on the subject of Sierra Leone and Liberia is expressed in a recent unofficial communication from the Governor-in-Chief as follows: "It is perfectly obvious that cordial and close relations between Liberia and the British Colonies adjoining her would be beneficial to both parties."

Governor Havelock in 1884, and Sir Charles McCarthy in 1818, are two generations apart. The spirit of both is the same—intent upon the welfare of the colony under their rule; but the one utters *vaticinia post eventum*, while the other, through the difficult mists of probabilities, puts forth his prophecies at a venture. After what has already happened in the history of the two countries, who will undertake to say that they will not be brought into even closer connection than the mere physical one? Lord Derby, Secretary of State for the Colonies, said, in a speech a few weeks ago, that "Experience of public life had taught him that the words 'Never' and 'Forever' ought to have no place in a statesman's vocabulary." [10]

A few days after the arrival of the *Elizabeth* at Sierra Leone, the emigrants were taken to Sherbro Island, at the mouth of the Sherbro River. Here the agents were discouraged in their attempts to purchase land for a permanent settlement. The hardships, sickness, and deaths which the colonists had to undergo, compelled their return to Sierra Leone, and they found temporary residence at Fourah Bay, where some now lie buried. The remnant subsequently removed to Cape Mesurado, 260 miles to the south-east, where, after they had occupied for three months a small island at the mouth of the Mesurado River, they were permitted to obtain a permanent foothold.

Thus it will be seen that the British Colony of Sierra Leone and the American Colony of Liberia are one in origin, not only as respects the philanthropic purpose that gave them birth, but as to the materials of the first settlement. Both were planted by Negroes who, having passed through the baptism of slavery on American soil, brought with them as spoils from the land of their captivity the elements of Anglo-American civilisation, finding their first shelter in the land of their fathers, under the shadow of the "lion mountain," and getting refreshed during their first fevers from the brooks of King Jimmy and King Tom. Both colonies were founded by private enterprise and for philanthropic purposes. Both received the same name. *Freetown* is the Saxon for the idea of which *Liberia* is the Latin. Both were given up by their original founders, one after twenty-five years of supervision, and the other after twenty-seven years.

Sierra Leone entered upon effective colonial existence, having the care, attention and guidance of the mother country, drawing within the circle of its influence representatives of the different tribes, and giving the Negro the opportunity for rest from the persecutions of slave-traders. Benign agencies from Europe overshadowed the settlement to protect it from malignant agencies from

---

[10] *Times*, March 4th, 1884.

Sierra Leone and Liberia.

the same quarter. A succession of able philanthropic representatives of the Queen has furnished continuous impulse to civilisation.

Liberia continued a colony of the American Colonisation Society until, as it began to grow and extend along the coast, questions of trade and territorial rights arose which could be adjusted only between sovereign powers. The United States Government, owing to its peculiar institutions, and, perhaps, to the view then taken of the Monroe doctrine, could not assume the direction of the colony.

The Liberians found that if they were to retain their existence at all they must become an independent community, with the right of final legislation for themselves, the power to enter into treaty relations with foreign powers, to regulate and restrict trade, &c.

Therefore the people voted—October 27, 1846—in favour of assuming the entire responsibility of their government. The Legislature, at its next session, ordered a Convention of Delegates to form a new Constitution. The Convention assembled, and after twenty-one days of deliberation, adopted—on the 26th day of July, 1847—their new Constitution and Declaration of Independence. In September, the Constitution was ratified by the almost unanimous vote of the people in their primary assemblies.

The Governor, Joseph Jenkins Roberts, was elected the first President. On the 3rd day of January, 1848, he delivered his inaugural address, and the new Government went into operation. In the course of that year, the Independence of the Republic was formally acknowledged by the Governments of Great Britain and France. It has since been acknowledged by all the leading States of Europe and America. In 1850, when the Republic was two years old, Her Britannic Majesty's Government presented the youthful nation with a gunboat, to act as a revenue cutter and *guarda costa*, with a view to assist the infant State in her efforts to suppress the slave trade. When that vessel, named the *Lark*, became unseaworthy, the British Government gave to Liberia another war schooner called the *Quail*.

Sierra Leone, in the meanwhile, and for fifty years after it was taken over by the Home Government, grew rapidly in population by accessions of recaptives from various parts of the coast. On their arrival these strangers received instruction in the ways of civilisation from the American and West Indian settlers whom they found here. The new comers at first turned to the soil for support, but found, with their limited means and want of skill in systematic agriculture, that it was impossible to do anything in that line with the barren, rocky and mountainous country with which they had to contend. The fact of the inferior quality of the soil had been noticed when the Sierra Leone Company first attempted to settle their emigrants on it. After several unsuccessful experiments at farming on this side, the Governor and Council, towards the end of 1792, purchased a small tract of land on the Bullom shore for enlarged agriculture, but they met with no better success there. Very recently a native member of the Legislative Council has made expensive outlays in the same region with a view to extensive agricultural operations, but his prospects of success, he informs me, are not very cheering. With a soil so unfavourable, the people turned naturally to trade, for which the situation of Sierra Leone furnished splendid opportunities. By strict attention to business, by persevering diligence and economy, many very soon rose to respectability and influence.

The settlers gradually died out, and there being no further accession from America, the recaptives[11] and their descendants naturally and properly came to the front, until they now own most of the valuable property in the colony; and by their enterprise, intelligence, and energy, are successfully competing with European commercial houses on the coast. But this element, which has

---

[11] The word *recaptive*, which I have just employed, like the word *Negro*, seems to some to convey the idea of contempt and degradation; but both are good words, and express important facts—one a fact of nature, the other a fact of history. "Negro" means a man of certain physical characteristics, whose colour and hair differentiate him from other races of men. In America it is applied indiscriminately to all persons of whatever colour who have Negro blood in their veins. "Recaptive" means one captured again. In the case before us it was the stronger saving the weaker from unscrupulous oppression. It was an intervention to suppress intervention. The word embodies the history not only of the sad dealings of Europeans with our people on this coast, but of the "fruits meet for repentance" which they brought forth when the iniquity of the nefarious traffic dawned upon them.

Sierra Leone and Liberia.

superseded the Nova Scotians and Maroons is not exactly indigenous. As the Negroes from across the sea gave place to them, so they, receiving no accessions, will give place to the indigenous tribes. But this fading away will be less marked if, by judicious intermarriages, the Creoles' blend with the surrounding tribes. And I am glad to learn that this process is gradually going on, especially in the villages. Timnehs, Susus, and Mendis are now uniting in marriage with Eboes, Akus, and Congoes, so that in the course of time the tribal peculiarities, which have often been a source of misunderstanding and disunion, will be happily effaced.

Notwithstanding the reports sometimes put forward of the indisposition of the natives to work, they have won, even from the soil of this barren, rocky, and mountainous country, astounding victories. There are very few places in the world where the vegetable market is better stocked than in Sierra Leone. When one looks at the arid and parched character of the soil, and sees the attractive variety of fruit, greens, and vegetables which appears every morning, one wonders by what magic power such pleasing results are produced. It is almost like the miracle of bringing honey out of the rock and oil out of the flinty rock. But not only mere garden products, but the heavier articles of agriculture are exported from the colony. The large quantity of ginger brought to market this season has been something marvellous—marvellous in view of the possibilities, or rather *impossibilities* of the soil.

Some of the leading natives are expending of their means accumulated in other business for the purposes of agricultural industry, not merely for the pecuniary results in the future, but for the sake of the example, and to prove that by diligence, enterprise, and industry, agriculture, which is the only reliable basis of national prosperity, can be successfully pursued in Sierra Leone. Your leading barrister has been, for the last three years, giving his spare time to an enterprise on Bunce Creek, about 17 miles from Freetown, which promises well for the future, but has not yet risen above the character of a most costly experiment. This patriotic and self-denying effort must be remunerative in its moral and industrial results. And here I must beg your indulgence, and I am sure you will all sympathise with me while I pause and drop a tear over the memory of our dear friend, William Grant, whose foresight and anxiety for the welfare of his country led him to forsake another walk of life, in which he had been eminently successful in a pecuniary sense, to take the lead in this most important and difficult work, and to suffer the fate of all pioneers in every noble cause—to die that others might live. The remembrance of my personal loss in the death of that African patriot is one of the shadows in my existence that will depart only when its earthly career ceases.

The trade of the colony has seldom, within recent years, presented so encouraging an aspect as during the current season. The influx of "gold and hide strangers" has been almost unprecedented. In the months of January, February, and March, there arrived 3,726 persons with products seeking a market—Mandingoes, Foulahs, Seracoulies, Bundukahs, and Soosoos. From the 1st to the 15th of April, 738 arrived. This number is exclusive of traders from the Limba, Loko, Timneh, and other countries within two hundred miles of the coast. It was, indeed, an inspiring sight a few weeks ago, while walking the streets, to meet those stalwart men, with flowing robes and majestic tread, from every important city in Nigritia for a thousand miles from the sea. The streams poured into the settlement, sometimes hundreds a day, from the golden hills of Bouré, the shining plains of Wasulu, the pasture grounds of Futah, and the populous districts of Bambarra, from Timbuctoo, from Jenne, from Sego, from Kankan. And we heard, on every hand, the same vocal sounds which may be heard in the streets of Cairo and Alexandria, of Morocco and of Tunis. This was a proof that the obstructions to trade are being rapidly removed. The Hooboos, those renegade Foulahs, who for thirty years have been a terror to caravans passing through the districts which they infested, have been scattered by the military energy of Samudu, a Mandingo chieftain from the Konia country, due east of Liberia. Abal, the chief of the Hooboos, has been captured and banished to a distant region.

An important event, fraught with significance to this colony and

Sierra Leone and Liberia.

to Liberia, took place in the early part of last month. I refer to the arrival of the special embassy to the Governor-in-Chief from the King of Sego. I do not know that any such delegation has ever visited a British Governor on the coast since the days of Sir Charles McCarthy. And it is gratifying to know that prompt measures were taken by the authorities to encourage and develop the relations which their visits ought to establish.

An incident in connection with Sego, published by the great traveller, Mungo Park, ought to make that city an object of special interest to all intelligent Africans. The incident has been repeated for nearly a hundred years, in all parts of the civilised world, as an evidence of the thoughtful hospitality of the African.

It appears that when Mr. Park arrived in the vicinity of Sego, a white man not having been seen there before, he was regarded by the people with fear and astonishment. He had to cross a river before he could get to the king, but no one would cross him; and, moreover, the king had sent word that he could not possibly see the strange traveller until he had learned his object in visiting the country. But let the author recount the story in his own words. He says:—

> I was obliged to sit all day without victuals, in the shade of a tree; and the night threatened to be very uncomfortable, for the wind rose, and there was great appearance of rain; and the wild beasts are so very numerous in the neighbourhood that I should have been under the necessity of climbing up the tree and resting among the branches. About sunset, however, as I was preparing to pass the night in this manner, and had turned my horse loose that he might graze at liberty, a woman, returning from the labours of the field, stopped to observe me, and perceiving that I was weary and dejected inquired into my situation, which I briefly explained to her. Having conducted me into her hut, she lighted up a lamp, spread a mat on the floor, and told me I might remain there for the night. Finding that I was very hungry, she said she would procure me something to eat. She accordingly went out, and returned in a short time with a very fine fish, which, having caused to be half-broiled upon some embers, she gave me for supper. The rites of hospitality being thus performed towards a stranger in distress, my worthy benefactress (pointing to the mat, and telling me I might sleep there without apprehension) called to the female part of her family, who had stood gazing on me all the while in fixed astonishment, to resume their task of spinning cotton, in which they continued to employ themselves a great part of the night. They lightened their labour by songs, one of which was composed extempore, for I was myself the subject of

it. It was sung by one of the young women, the rest joining in a sort of chorus. The air was sweet and plaintive, and the words, literally translated, were these:—

> The wind roared, and the rain fell.
> The poor white man, faint and weary, came and sat under our tree.
> He has no mother to bring him milk; no wife to grind his corn.
>
> CHORUS.
> Let us pity the white man;
> No mother has he to bring him milk;
> No wife to grind his corn.

Trifling as this recital may appear to the reader, adds the author, to a person in my situation the circumstance was affecting in the highest degree. I was oppressed by such unexpected kindness, and sleep fled from my eyes. In the morning I presented my compassionate landlady with two of the four brass buttons which remained on my waistcoat, the only recompense I could make her.[12]

The name of the woman, and the alabaster box of precious ointment; the nameless widow, who, giving only two mites, had given more than all the rich; and this nameless woman of Sego, form a trio of feminine beauty and grandeur of which the sex in all ages may be proud.

An English lady, who was not more distinguished for her rank than for her beauty and accomplishments,[13] to whom this incident was communicated, was so gratified and thought so highly of the improvised song that she made a version of it with her own pen, and caused it to be set to music by an eminent composer.

Her version is as follows:—

> The loud wind roar'd, the rain fell fast;
> The white man yielded to the blast;
> He sat him down beneath our tree,
> For weary, sad, and faint was he;
> And oh, no wife or mother's care
> For him the milk or corn prepare.
>
> CHORUS.
> The white man shall our pity share;
> Alas, no wife or mother's care,
> For him the milk or corn prepare.

---

[12] *Travels in the Interior Districts of Africa, performed in the years* 1795, 1796 *and* 1797; by Mungo Park, Surgeon (chapter xv).
[13] The Duchess of Devonshire.

Sierra Leone and Liberia.

The storm is o'er, the tempest past,
And mercy's voice has hush'd the blast;
The wind is heard in whispers low,
The white man far away must go—
But ever in his heart will bear
Remembrance of the Negro's care.

CHORUS.

Go, white man, go—but with thee bear
The Negro's wish, the Negro's prayer;
Remembrance of the Negro's care.

The following is the description which Mr. Park gives of Sego as it was one hundred years ago:—

Sego, the capital of Bambarra, at which I had now arrived, consists, properly speaking, of four distinct towns; two on the northern bank of the Niger, called Sego Korro and Sego Boo; and two on the southern bank, called Sego Soo Korro, and Sego See Korro.[14] From the best enquiries I could make, I have reason to believe that Sego contains altogether about thirty thousand inhabitants. The view of this extensive city, the numerous canoes upon the river, the crowded population, and the cultivated state of the surrounding country, formed altogether a prospect of civilisation and magnificence which I little expected to find in the bosom of Africa.

It is to be hoped that we shall soon witness regular and uninterrupted intercourse between Sego and this settlement. The recent difficulties with the French have closed up Senegal and Dakar as outlets for the trade of that region of the country, and the king is anxious that it should take this direction. But the effects of the disorders introduced by the slave trade are still felt in the maritime districts. The feuds created through generations of intertribal wars, the habits engendered, and the tendencies impressed upon the people, still show themselves in the periodical interruptions to trade which so perplex civilised governments on the coast, anxious for the progress of civilisation and the development of commerce. These troubles do not extend further than two hundred miles from the coast. Beyond that, the powerful tribes have the habits of order and of work; they possess valuable property and other interests which cannot be endangered by petty

---

[14] These names are still retained.

jealousies and rivalries. The ambassadors from Sego, the other day, gave assurance that the only difficulty in the way of an abundant and uninterrupted trade between their country and this part of the coast is that which arises from the wars on this side of the hills. They said if the Government could keep the roads on this side safe, they could manage the difficulties, such as they are, on the other side.

Liberia will also take a part in this work, and share in the results of this new direction of the interior trade. There is not, however, the amount of capital in that little republic which this settlement enjoys, and which is necessary for the attraction and development of the interior trade.

There have been, ever since the arrival of the first settlers, at least two immigrations a-year from the United States, averaging 250 a-year; but the people are chiefly mechanics and farmers. Besides being thrown upon their own resources, they suffer the inconvenience of a national policy which restricts the intercourse of foreigners with the country. This has kept away foreign capital and foreign enterprise. The restrictive law was to allow the colony to grow up in keeping with the original idea of its foundation. To prevent the fatal interference with this idea, which must have occurred, had Europeans been allowed to take part in the political arrangements of the country, a similar policy was adopted by the Sierra Leone Company in the early history of the colony, "for they had conceived," so the Directors say, in their report published in 1795, "the first success of their colony essentially to depend on the exclusion of all Europeans, those alone excepted who, being in the regular pay of the Company, were entirely subject to them." They were afraid that even a few men from hence (England) of an improper cast, in the situation of independent settlers, might materially prejudice or endanger the undertaking; that they might corrupt the morals of the colony, refuse due obedience to the Government, as well as excite a spirit of general discontent; and if, for any of these causes, they should be excluded from the settlement, that they might then be driven—especially if they had left debts in England—to seek a precarious livelihood, by various

Sierra Leone and Liberia.

improper means, among the neighbouring natives, and perhaps even to turn slave-traders.[15]

The reasons that led to the restrictive laws of Liberia could not be better stated. The ideal Liberia has, of course, not yet been realised. The Liberia of the self-denying and courageous pioneers, of the impassioned Lot Cary, and the statesman-like Elijah Johnson, has not yet been quite organised; but the restrictive clause in the constitution has not suffered the *raison d'être* of the Republic to be lost sight of or obscured. At first, the Liberians, driven by their necessities, generally engaged in trade as yielding quicker results; but, fortunately for them, the soil was fertile, and the country well watered everywhere. They were thus allured to agriculture, and they have, with commendable diligence, improved their advantages. Within the last few years, the production of coffee, sugar, and cocoa is bringing the Republic into American and European markets. Besides these articles, Liberia exports largely palm oil, camwood, ivory, rubber, and palm kernels. Every week the steamers of each of the three English companies touch at the ports of entry of the Republic, of which there are now ten. German steamers call twice a-month, going and returning; and there are American and Dutch sailing vessels engaged in the trade.

In Sierra Leone there are not now any legal enactments restricting the intercourse of foreigners. The law of Nature has put barriers in the way of their multiplication here. The mountains are lofty, the air on their summits salubrious, but the soil is forbidding, in many places as arid as the nether millstone; so that those breezy heights have not, like the mountain slopes of Madeira, invited the establishment of European quintas, and the skilful cultivation of European farmers. The settlement has, therefore, continued to grow as a distinctly Negro colony. According to Koelle, the German missionary, 100 different African tribes were, in 1849, represented here. Mr. Griffith, the Colonial Secretary of the colony, stated in his excellent paper, read before the Royal Colonial Institute, in 1881, that no less than 60 languages were

---

[15] Report of Directors of the Sierra Leone Company; read May, 1798, pp. 14, 15.

spoken in Freetown. Sierra Leone possesses, in fact, what Liberia possesses in theory and possibility—a Negro nationality. This colony is on a small scale what India is on a large scale—an indigenous nation under a foreign protectorate. As soon as a man, alien to the African, lands here, he finds himself at once a stranger. He looks around, and everywhere he sees men unlike himself:—

> Negroes on the right of him;
> Negroes on the left of him;
> Negroes in front of him;
> Negroes in the rear of him;

until the whole land seems to him the very blackness of darkness, and he himself, and all he represents, appear to dwindle into comparative insignificance. No wonder that in some there is a revulsion of feeling which makes them retaliate by contemptuous utterances about the place and people. This is the revenge which brooding and irregular minds take when suddenly confronted with the inevitable. "I soon discovered," says Winwood Reade, "that Sierra Leone is a true paradise of blacks." Captain Ellis begins one of his glowing paragraphs with the remark, "Sierra Leone is a very nice place—for Negroes." Not knowing what to say, they swear. "Come, curse me this people," said Balak to Balaam, when he saw the surging multitudes of Hebrews filling the plains of Moab. Sierra Leone has been over and over again cursed, and the prejudice still continues, owing, mostly, to representations which proceed from persons oppressed by the presence of a strange race and unusual customs.

But this vituperation of the colony must come to an end, because the English language is limited in its vocabulary. The stock of adjectives in the Queen's English, though extensive, has yet a limit; and as only a certain percentage of them are uncomplimentary, an end must come to this sort of thing at last. After denouncing a man as an idiot, and a liar, and a villain to begin with, you cannot very well, at a later stage, produce an effect by saying that his conduct is not thoroughly sagacious and moral. You have to keep on calling him a fool, a liar, and a rogue, until you become a bore. And this is what we see in the disparaging

Sierra Leone and Liberia.

writings of those who find amusement in abusing the settlement. Reade follows Burton, and Ellis follows Reade, and smaller men follow these. Like a flock of sheep, all tread in the path of their leader. Notwithstanding the love of originality which men possess, yet it would seem that the passion for ridiculing and abusing others is stronger in a certain class of minds than the desire to be original; so that rather than strike out a new line in describing Sierra Leone, which must, of course, be complimentary and respectful, they prefer to ring the changes with dull and tiresome monotony upon those words of contempt and vituperation, of which only a limited number can be found in the English dictionary. If I were to collect instances I could fill this page with adjectives, and even substantives, in the use of which these writers seem to revel, bringing to mind the reputation (I believe the ancient reputation) of Shoreditch and Billingsgate. It is of course an economy of argument to prove by misrepresentation that the objects of our hatred or contempt are odious or ridiculous. Happily for the race, those who are fond of employing those contemptuous epithets are generally men who from excessively defective training have not a full acquaintance with even the limited vocabulary of vituperative terms. And this we have noticed also, that the men who take pleasure in dilating upon their race superiority, and in emphasising their connection with the ruling race, are not the men who rise into power, or ever have the opportunity of ruling.

Destiny seems to have forbidden the extension of Sierra Leone to the northward, and to have favoured her growth to the southeast, so that now that her territory adjoins that of Liberia, we have a continuous English-speaking Negro State from the Sierra Leone River to the San Pedro River—a distance of over 800 miles. For 200 years, the Portuguese language was spoken along this coast. Villault says when he landed here, at Cape Mount and at Cape Mesurado in 1666, "all the Negroes who came to trade spoke the Portuguese language." But the English language has everywhere driven it out. The English language and English laws assist and regulate the intercourse of the tribes of this whole region and for hundreds of miles inland. French is confined to the countries

Christianity, Islam and the Negro Race.

north of the Gambia; Portuguese to the region of the Congo. English is, undoubtedly, the most suitable of the European languages for bridging over the numerous gulfs between the tribes caused by the great diversity of languages or dialects among them. It is a composite language, not the product of any one people. It is made up of contributions by Celts, Danes, Normans, Saxons, Greeks and Romans, gathering to itself elements from all peoples, from the Ganges to the Atlantic. In this respect, the Sierra Leone vernacular resembles it. The speech of the Sierra Leone streets cannot be called a *patois* of English. It is not the pigeon English of China nor the unintelligible lingo of the West Indies. It is not the dialect of Quashee nor the humourous slang of Uncle Remus. It is a transfusion, so to say, of numerous African idioms and phrases. Words from the Timneh, Eboe, Aku, Mandingo, Foulah, Soosoo, and Arabic, are blended with words from the English language, which is itself a mixture—so that the proper designation of the Sierra Leone vernacular would be—*mixture of mixtures, all is mixture.* It has become something more than the only medium of communication known to the masses. It has acquired a sacredness of its own. There are certain ideas which have been expressed in it—certain images created—which lose their full flavour if rendered into other words.

Mr. Lewis assures me that it has an unwritten but recognised syntax, and he gave me an amusing specimen of verbal inflection by going over the verb " to go " in its various moods and tenses, according to the unwritten grammar of the vernacular.

Its idioms are Oriental. It has grown up of itself. It has had no grammarian to formulate its rules, nor can it be known how the common agreement among the people was attained. But the fact remains that it exists, and it will linger long among them. It is the language of the domestic life, of courtship, of marriage, of death, of intensest joy and deepest grief. The people will not consent to speak of the private matters of the heart—to discuss matters affecting their domestic well-being in any other tongue, any more than they would discuss such things in company with strangers. To those acquainted with it, it has a convenient flexibility and

Sierra Leone and Liberia.

certain picturesque aspects. It is easily acquired by natives from the interior, and forms a convenient bridge from their dialects to the English language. It cannot be used for descriptions of occult causes; but it is by no means unadapted for comparison of physical things, for descriptions of sensations, for parables and proverbs drawn from visible objects. It has no capacity for fine subtleties; but it has sometimes a terse expressiveness, which, in one single sentence, will convey an amount of satire or irony which would require a whole paragraph of English. What can surpass the concentrated contempt of such a question as the following? Referring to the abuse heaped upon Sierra Leone in a recent publication, I asked an acquaintance why there had been no formal reply. He answered, in one of the picturesque metaphors of the vernacular, "Who dat go wase powder pon condo?"[10]

In the political features of their life, Sierra Leone and Liberia seem to have diverged; but the main purpose of that life has not been defeated. Although Sierra Leone continues a colony under a powerful Imperial Government, and Liberia is a nation still struggling with the problems of independent nationality, yet our political institutions have the same origin. The same jurisprudence which contributes to the prosperity and elevation of Sierra Leone, which protects property, maintains order, and punishes crime here, has been adopted by Liberia, upholds the majesty of the law there, and guards us in the exercise and enjoyment of the rights of freemen. The form of government is a mere incident, and does not interfere with the original idea and special work of the colony. Like the great streams of this part of Africa, taking their rise in the same watershed, some flow eastward and some westward, but all contribute to the fertility and wealth of the same vast region. So, if the paths of the two countries seem to be divergent, they diverge only that they may the more effectually perform their work, by taking within the circle of their influence wider interests, and bringing together larger contributions for the upbuilding and honour of the race.

---

[10] "Condo" is the local name for the red-headed lizard.

Christianity, Islam and the Negro Race.

Before the American Civil War, which gave the *coup de grâce* to the transatlantic slave trade, Sierra Leone was kept in a constantly unsettled state, owing to the frequent accessions of individuals of different tribes and languages, who, soon after their arrival, found out the persons belonging to their particular tribe, and, from the convenience which a common language and the same tribal instincts and prejudices afforded, easily formed themselves into separate clans, and gathered around leaders whom they felt to be their natural organs. The chief work of the Government and of missionary societies for years was to infuse into these incoherent masses the unifying ideas of British law and of the Christian religion—to effect the fusion of many disconnected atoms into one organic whole. But the clannish tendencies of the people furnished to adventurers from abroad, who were for the most part only partially allied to the Negro race, but whose superior educational advantages gave them influence over the minds of the uninformed and unsuspecting men, the opportunity to stimulate, whenever their own ends could be subserved thereby, the tribal prejudices and antipathies of the people.

Passing travellers of superficial mental habitudes, looking at this state of things, which, under the circumstances, would have been considered natural in any other country and among any other race, attributed it to the ignorance and dishonesty of the Negro, and fastened upon the jury system as one of the instruments in the political arrangements of the colony which fostered and encouraged the clannishness of the people, in consequence of which, it was alleged, some sections of the community could never obtain justice. Trial by jury in civil cases was—through repeated attacks upon it in newspapers, pamphlets, and books of travel—lost to the settlement. It could hardly have been otherwise. The people at that time had to rely for representation in judicial matters, in cases of public or private grievances, upon aliens or half-aliens, who did not and could not express the will and feelings of the people, and were, in many important respects, misrepresentatives. It was evident that the whole arrangement was artificial, unstable and unreliable. Trial by jury in civil cases was

Sierra Leone and Liberia.

abolished; but, in the natural course of events, it is becoming clearer and clearer that the alleged abuses were only temporary, due to the peculiar circumstances of those times.

For more than twenty years, now, there has been no accession of new comers of conflicting tribal characteristics. A new generation is appearing on the stage; and the pecuniary advancement of the people has enabled them to give their children an education suitable to the requirements of an enlightened government. The result is, that the population becoming more and more homogeneous, with one language as the medium of communication, and represented at the bar and in the Legislative Council, in the schools and in the church, by their natural organs, two conditions of social and political confidence have been reached which must obliterate all tribal distinctions and organisations, if any such still exist. An indication of this wholesome tendency in the public feeling is the desire on the part of some of the members of the Native Association to change the descriptive part of their title to one less local and restrictive.

The communication made by Lord Derby a few months ago to the people of Jamaica should be suggestive and instructive to the inhabitants of this colony. His lordship did not give an absolute refusal to the request of the people of that colony for popular suffrage and increased representation, but said that, in the judgment of the Government, the time for these things had not yet arrived, intimating that when the time arrived the Government would not withhold the privileges they craved. It is not the business of a Crown Government to develop the liberties of the people—it is their business to recognise and protect what is established. It is their part to give safety, and quietness, and repose; to inspire confidence in the people, and thus give them time for growth.

The original idea of the colony has been gradually realised under the influence of British law. Notwithstanding the frequent changes in the colonial administration, the tendency of the procedure of the Imperial Government has been in keeping with the original idea—in accordance with a desire to promote the educational, social, moral, and political improvement of the natives. And under that enlightened system of government which protects the rights, the liberty, the life, and the property of every individual, of whatever race or religion, the people have been advanced in civilisation and well-being. They have been educated up to the position, the duties, and the privileges of British citizens; and they have not, as we have seen, been slow to avail themselves of the opportunity for material growth, and for educational advancement. The bulwarks of political strength have thus been provided before their political self-consciousness has been stimulated.

The strong objection to direct taxation does not arise simply from the fact that there was sometimes oppressive, not to say cruel, enforcement of the law—the cause of the opposition lay deeper than that. It was because the people who paid the taxes felt no identification of interests between those who imposed the taxes and themselves. They did not attribute any representative character to those who controlled the proceeds of these taxes. Now, everywhere, taxation without representation is considered tyranny. But even where there is representation, people do not enthusiastically, or even cheerfully, welcome impositions laid upon them by government, though they know that the people must bear the burdens of government. A strong feeling of inborn loyalty is necessary to reconcile men everywhere to the inevitable frictions and burdens of government.

Now, this feeling of inborn loyalty will be secured when a city corporation shall be organised, composed chiefly of natives, and whatever honour or fame they may achieve will carry a thrill of exultation to the hearts of the people. The Government will be their own. They will share in its beneficial results as well as bear the odium of mal-administration. The feeling of responsibility will produce internal and domestic improvements never yet witnessed in the colony. When we look back upon what has been achieved in the colony, we cannot allow ourselves to find any fault, so far, with the action of the Government in details of administration, or even upon what are called constitutional questions.

The question of municipal government now before the people is one of great importance to the stability and prosperity of the institutions of the country; and while great care should be taken at every step of the movement, yet it is evident that a city corporation, with its burdens and responsibilities, its duties and its privileges, is necessary to the proper growth and full development of the people. It is essential to their training in self-reliance and self-respect. In the days of Sir Charles McCarthy, as I gather from the books at Government House, a Municipal Council existed in the colony, with its Mayor, and Aldermen, and Magistrates. It may interest you to hear the following :—

When the Prince Regent lost his only daughter (Princess Charlotte, I think), Sir C. McCarthy forwarded an address of condolence from the people of the colony to His Royal Highness, accompanied by the following note to Earl Bathurst :—

Government House, Sierra Leone, March 4th, 1818.

My Lord,—At the request of the Members of His Majesty's Council, Mayor and Aldermen, Magistrates, Clergy, Freeholders, and principal inhabitants of the Colony of Sierra Leone, I have the honour to forward herewith enclosed the humble and dutiful Address of Condolence to His Royal Highness the Prince Regent, and I beg leave to solicit your Lordship's favour to lay the same at the foot of the Throne.

I have, &c.,

To the Right Honourable Earl Bathurst, K.G.　　(*Signed*)　　C. McCARTHY.

But this was before the influx of the heterogeneous tide of uninstructed people which made it the prime function of the Government to deal with the very elements of civilisation and with the rudiments of government, to instruct the consciences of the people, and to superintend the elevation of the whole moral and intellectual standard; and a great deal has been effected when tribal antipathies, narrowness and exclusiveness, which prevented growth, have been broken up. The people are now in a condition to move for themselves as a working social organisation. Their political future is greatly in their own hands; and it is an encouraging sign that young men are rising up who grasp the situation, and are making themselves equal to the necessities of the country. Activity, change, development, aspiration—these are the end of man's being on earth. Apart from them his destiny is frustrated. Such is the law of progress. Whatever others may do for us, there are some things we must do for ourselves. No outward protection, no friendly intervention, no deed of gift can give those personal virtues—those attributes of manhood—self-reliance and independence, without which all past efforts in behalf of the colony will be in vain; and the Negro's part in the political future of Sierra Leone will be extremely doubtful. It has been observed with gratification by friendly foreigners that many of the natives show a power and a breadth of capacity in managing their business—a shrewdness and far-sightedness in dealing with the difficulties of trade which prove that they are fitted for the conduct of some of the details of their political life.

At present their whole activity, physical and mental, is absorbed in the business of the shop; and some who have no inconsiderable accumulations, sit down and simply feel the gratification of looking at a golden heap, not even thinking of the methods by which that heap, so industriously and carefully piled up, shall be preserved. It is said that when the boa-constrictor has over-gorged itself, it lies in a state of torpidity or stupefaction; but man's life on earth was not made to be like that of the boa-constrictor.

It is clear that if in some respects the natives of this colony continue in a position of social or political disadvantage, it is because they choose themselves to acquiesce in it, and to foster those conventional opinions which suspect every attempt to push them a step forward in self-government, and to place upon them the responsibilities which that government involves.

But God has bestowed certain gifts upon the natives of this community, as upon others, and He will not allow those gifts to remain unused. If the talent is laid up in a napkin or buried in the earth, He will resume that talent or give it to those who have power and disposition to use it. The gifts of God are not ours to do as we please with. If we prevent their application or diffusion for the good of others, or for the benefit of our country, He will remove us from them or them from us. We may have our plans for ourselves—for our individual gratification, but God has *His* plans, which are for the country, for the race, for humanity; and His plans will be carried out. The agents for carrying them out

Sierra Leone and Liberia.

are on every hand, in the air, in the water, in the fire. In the operation of the laws of Providence, "The individual dwindles, while the race is more and more." And when we have reached a certain stage of progress, and the next step which that degree of progress necessitates is pointed out to us, it is not ours to say, "Let things remain as they are." There is no such thing as standing still in this life. The law is either forward or backward; if there is no conscious movement forward, there is an unconscious movement backward.

There is no bitterer satire passed upon us, no graver injustice done to the race than by those of its members who assume that they are unfit for higher duties than that which consists in the comparatively unintellectual work of barter. And it is but a refined remnant of the institution of slavery, which we profess so much to dread and abhor, when we attempt to cramp the stature of our people, and to forbid by persecution their advance beyond the narrow limits which we have prescribed for ourselves.

All communities of thinking men naturally divide themselves into two parties—conservative and liberal—the party of stability and the party of movement, as they have been called. We find two such parties in Sierra Leone. We see men who are not sure that what *is* really exists; who are ever trying to secure the past, to clench the nail that has been driven, rather than attempting to open the future. But there are others who feel a deep, an insatiable thirst for something beyond; who are anxious to open roadways for the people and for themselves where before only unbroken and undisturbed forest existed.

These men are often discouraged by the difficulties in the way raised by a conscientious and dogged conservatism. They sometimes fall into despair, and declare that the problems which they set before themselves cannot be worked, much less solved, under the actual conditions and by the available agencies.

But every now and then some sudden emergency arises and becomes what may be called a dynamic element independent of human control or management, which introduces unexpected movement. Some sudden disaster comes upon the community—

an epidemic, a storm, a flood, a fire—which arouses into activity the energies of the most dormant. The liberal influence receives an accession of strength—a momentum—that forces the whole community into new and original directions, and the road is made through the forest, or the causeway thrown up across the swamp.

There is some show of reason on the side of the conservatives. They are apprehensive that any apparent progress will be only *apparent*, and may lead to a reaction that will be worse than the present state. They fear to act the part of the dog in the fable, who threw away the substance to grasp at the shadow. But these nervous individuals should be reminded that revolutions never go backward. The course of things will rather resemble what one sees when one goes from the alluvial and swampy lands of this coast to the beautiful countries of the interior. On the eastern or north-eastern frontier of the Loko country, the traveller is suddenly confronted with lofty hills, which, if he could, he would avoid by some circuitous route; but there is no other way, the road lies over those rugged mountains. He is, therefore, obliged to nerve himself for the task of ascending; but after toiling up those weary heights, he finds to his surprise that instead of a corresponding declivity on the eastern side, he has reached the level of a grand plateau, where the air is purer and cooler. He has reached an elevated region, which slopes gradually to the rich valley of the Niger. So will it be after the people have climbed the heights of political progress, which look so precipitous and threatening. They will have a wider view and a healthier atmosphere, and the advance will be by easier stages to a well-watered and fertile region of political freedom and self-reliance. But at first the progress must be slow and gradual. "*Chi va piano va sano, chi va sano va lontano.*"

> We have not wings, we cannot soar;
> But we have feet to scale and climb
> By slow degrees, by more and more,
> The cloudy summits of our time.

But the question of all others upon the solution of which will depend the character of the political future of the colony, is the

Sierra Leone and Liberia.

educational one. We sometimes wonder why the efforts for the higher education of our people on this coast seem to meet with so many drawbacks. But the reasons, if we look below the surface of things, will be clear and satisfactory. Happily, the educational work, both here and in Liberia, has hardly got beyond its initial stage. The people are getting educated first to the life of the country before the education of books comes. It is not without its providential purposes that hindrances have so frequently arisen in the way of the only two colleges on the coast—Fourah Bay College and Liberia College. Had these institutions gone on and succeeded on the line which their founders had marked out for them, numbers of our people would have passed through a course of discipline which would probably have impaired their natural powers, and aroused on the part of foreign observers hopes, or awakened antagonisms, which would have been based upon artificial and unstable phenomena. The drawbacks and interruptions are giving us time to find out the system of regulation and instruction which will best fit us for the work we have to do.

What is needed in the education of the Negro on this continent is not so much a change in the subjects, for everywhere the instruments of culture, in their better forms at least, must be the same, but a change in the whole method is required. In our contact with the Christian world, our teachers have of necessity been Europeans, and they have taught us books too much, and things too little—forms of expression, and very little the importance of thought. The notion, still common among Negroes— educated Negroes I mean—is, that the most important part of knowledge consists in knowing what other men—foreigners—have said about things, and even about Africa and about themselves. They aspire to be familiar, not with what really is, but with what is printed. Very few among us have got past this step. Hence, some of us are found repeating things against ourselves, which are thoroughly false and injurious to us, and only because we read them in books, or have heard them from foreign teachers. The idea never seems to occur to such persons that there are subjects of enquiry, especially in this large and interesting country of theirs, about which the truth is yet to be found out—people and customs and systems about which correct ideas are to be formed. We have neglected to study matters at home because we were trained in books written by foreigners, and *for a foreign race*, not *for us*—or for us only so far as in the general characteristics of humanity we resemble that race; and from some of these books we learned that the Negro at home was a degraded being—a Heathen, and worse than a Heathen—a fool; and we were taught everything excellent and praiseworthy about foreigners. Therefore, we turned our backs upon our brethren of the interior as those from whom we could learn nothing to elevate, to enlighten, or to refine. A result of this is that we have not yet acted for ourselves. We have had history written for us, and we have endeavoured to act up to it; whereas, the true order is, that history should be first acted, then written. It is easy to account, then, for the want of genuine life and spontaneous activity in the people.

It would be a melancholy outlook for Africa, with its vast territories and countless tribes, if its development and prosperity were altogether contingent upon the labour of foreigners, or even upon the genius and life of a few natives, educated on foreign models and in foreign ways of thinking, to be produced and brought upon the stage of action by the machinery of an alien people. I say the prospect would indeed be dark if we had no security from the law, by which nations and races are controlled, that the men to lead and guide in the affairs of this race shall appear among the people at the right time and place, and with aptitudes for the needful work.

It is a very interesting fact that the main body of the settlers who planted civilisation on these shores in both colonies were men deeply imbued with the religious spirit. Like the puritans of America, the Bible was their code of laws, for civil and religious life. The following graphic and suggestive description is given by Mr. J. B. Eliott of the circumstances attending the first arrival of the Nova Scotians, on the 28th of March, 1792:

> The colony was then quite a forest, thickly populated with wild and ferocious animals, without any passage of approach to the new, beautiful, and principal

Sierra Leone and Liberia.

town, Freetown. Pioneers, from the number of these Nova Scotians, were despatched on shore to clear or make a roadway for their landing; which being done, they all disembarked and marched towards the thick forest, with the Holy Bible and their preachers (all coloured men) before them, singing the hymn taken from the late Countess's Hymn Book, commencing—

> Awake and sing the song
> Of Moses and the Lamb;
> Wake! every heart and every tongue
> To praise the Saviour's name.

They proceeded immediately to worship God, thanking Him for His goodness and mercy in bringing them in safety to the land of their forefathers. . . . . They were anxious to procure an altar, or place of worship, for the God of Jacob. This they did. The place fixed upon was under the shade of a large gree-gree tree, then standing in George Street, now one of the most populous in Freetown, containing the Church of England, the Colonial Office, &c. There they continued in social worship of Almighty God, with their brethren of the Methodist and Baptist Societies—who all arrived together from Nova Scotia—until they were able to provide better accommodation. This they lost no time in doing, for each Society was able, after a short time, to build a hut as a chapel for itself.

The Directors of the Sierra Leone Company, in their Report for 1794, bear the following testimony to the character of the settlers:—

From that class of vices which comes less under the cognisance of a public court, the Nova Scotians are in some respects remarkably free; marriage is extremely general among them, and all those evils which more particularly result from its being in disuse, are therefore in a great measure avoided. Drunkenness is by no means common, swearing is hardly ever heard; their attention to the Sabbath is also great; they, on that day, abstain entirely from work, dress themselves in very good (and some of them even in very gay) attire, and repair, together with their children, to church, where their deportment during the service, and their whole appearance, are represented to be such as form a very striking spectacle. There are five or six black preachers among them, raised up from their own body, who are not without a considerable influence; and it is supposed that the discipline which they preserve in their little congregations, has contributed materially to the maintenance of the general morals which have been spoken of.[17]

Thirty years after, Mr. Ashmun, one of the earliest Governors of Liberia, writes of the colonists as follows:—

It deserves record that religion has been the principal agent employed in laying and confirming the foundation of the settlement. To this sentiment—

---

[17] Report, pp. 78–80.

ruling, restraining, and actuating the minds of the colonists—must be referred the whole strength of the civil government.

In Sierra Leone, excepting, perhaps, Lady Huntingdon's Connexion, there was no regular organisation for religious worship until the plans set on foot by the Church Missionary Society, with the aid of the Government, were carried out in 1817.

The English Baptist Missionary Society sent out two missionaries in 1795; but owing to indiscretion on the part of one, and the failure of health on the part of the other, the mission was speedily abandoned. In the following year, an united attempt was made by the Scottish, the Glasgow, and the London Missionary Societies to form a station, but owing to sickness and dissension among the agents, this effort was attended with no better success.[18]

The opening of the present century witnessed the organisation of the Church Missionary Society for Africa and the East. No Englishman being found to undertake missionary work on this unhealthy coast, the Society sent out in 1804, as their first missionaries, two Germans, Revs. Messrs. Renner and Hartwig. They were, however, appointed not to labour in the colony, but among the Soosoos to the north. It was evident from the beginning that, in view of the state of the country and the character of their machinery, they could not accomplish very much in that direction. In 1816, the Society sent out Rev. Edward Bickersteth to look into their work. His report influenced the committee to turn its attention to Sierra Leone, although Sir Charles McCarthy, two years before, had, without apparent success, suggested to the Society to employ their missionaries in labours among the recaptives. In the Seventeenth Annual Report of the Church Missionary Society they say:—

> After Mr. Bickersteth's return, the committee lost no time in laying the substance of his communication before His Majesty's ministers. A deputation accompanied his lordship the President in presenting a memorial to Earl Bathurst, in which a plan formed by His Excellency, Governor McCarthy, for dividing the colony of Sierra Leone into parishes, was recognised; and offers were made, on the part of the Society, to assist in bringing that plan into full execution. His lordship received the deputation with his accustomed courtesy,

---

[18] Moister's *Africa and the West Indies*, p. 93.

Sierra Leone and Liberia.

and expressed his cordial wish to support the designs of the Society for the benefit of the colony. By a subsequent communication from his lordship, your committee learnt with pleasure that measures would be immediately taken for the erection of two churches in Freetown, and afterwards churches in the several country parishes of Sierra Leone.

Thus began that series of operations in this colony, conducted by the Church Missionary Society, at first with Government aid, which has given to Africa and the Negro race the Sierra Leone Native Church, with its magnificent institutions of the Native Pastorate and Grammar Schools, whose influence is felt all along the coast and far up the Niger.

Dr. Coke, who has been called the father of the Wesleyan Missions, had devised a scheme in 1769, eighteen years before the arrival of the first settlers sent by Granville Sharp, for missionary work among the Foulahs interior of Sierra Leone; but the undertaking proved an entire failure, chiefly for want of adaptation in the agents employed.

The beginning of Wesleyan work in the settlement dates from 1811, when the Rev. G. Warren and three school teachers were sent out. The results of the self-denying labours of these men are seen on every hand throughout the settlement. Its Training Institution, under a native principal, is giving satisfaction, and furnishing interesting proof of the reality of the work which has been accomplished,

The educational and religious training of the people of Sierra Leone, for fifty years, devolved almost wholly upon the Church Missionary Society and the Wesleyans. The effects of their self-denying labours are visible in the intellectual, moral, and religious progress of the people. Whatever Sierra Leone is, she owes mainly to the fostering care of those two great bodies of Christians.

In 1864 came the Roman Catholic Church, and met with no little difficulty in establishing itself in a town where two strong Protestant bodies and other smaller ones had apparently occupied the whole ground. The Catholic priest, with his mediæval dress, supposed alien sympathies, and celibate life, was an object of antagonism; but by patience and perseverance they have so far overcome the opposition as to have now in process of erection, to answer their actual demands, a magnificent cathedral, with the prospect of a resident bishop in Freetown. Negroes will prove that among them, as among other races, there are sympathies broad as the variety of the human mind and comprehensive as the diversity of human temperament; that the ecclesiastical landscape among them will be as diversified in appearance as elsewhere.

Whatever may be thought by some of the Roman Catholic Church, there are four things which can be said in its favour, and which it behoves us carefully to consider:—

1. The Romish Church presents an uncompromising front in the warfare against infidelity in all its forms. Evolution, Agnosticism and Positivism find no place within its fold.

2. The Church of Rome has always been and is now a protesting power—a conservative force—against the onslaughts of Socialism—against those attacks upon constituted authority which are now perplexing true patriots and statesmen in Europe and America.

3. Catholicism sets its face, especially in America, against the freeness and facility of divorce. It respects the integrity of the family, and, through the much-abused confessional, it exercises a watchful care over childhood. Catholics are wiser than Protestants as to the children of the Church.

4. The Roman Catholic Church respects races. It holds to the belief that those words of St. Paul, which declare that "God hath made of one all nations of men to dwell upon the face of the earth," are words of inspiration.

They recognise in their calendar Negro saints, and have in their cathedrals the statues and representations of holy men of the African race. In Roman Catholic countries Negroes have always had a fair chance. I have read of Negroes in Brazil, in Peru, and even in Cuba, and I have seen them in Venezuela, occupying civil, military, and social positions to which they aspire in vain in Protestant countries. This, however, it is sometimes said, is owing not so much to the teachings of the religion as to the peculiar disposition of the Celtic races, who are largely Roman Catholics. The caste feeling, it is alleged, is not so strong in Celt as in Anglo-

Sierra Leone and Liberia.

Saxon. I do not know whether that distinguished nobleman, the Marquis of Bute, has Celtic blood in his veins, but he has recently selected a Negro sculptress to execute for him an important piece of artistic work.

These are facts in the history of Roman Catholics—not eulogies of the Church of Rome. They are great truths to be recognised in all the estimates we may form of the relations of that Church to the work to be done on this great continent, and to the race to which we belong. We may say that Romanism has its faults; but Protestantism also has its faults. We may say that the Romish Church has its irregularities; but so has the Protestant Church. We have, in this country, nothing to lose by welcoming all the agencies which have contributed to the civilisation and upbuilding of Europe, Asia, and America.

Now, these two great systems of Christianity—Protestant and Roman Catholic—are endeavouring to extend their operations among the interior tribes, to subvert and supersede Paganism and Mohammedanism. Let us take a brief view of the Paganism and Mohammedanism which have to be confronted and overcome.

We are sometimes discouraged by what appears to us the obstinacy of Paganism—the stubbornness of a hoary superstition; but when we consider how large tribes, both here and in other parts of Africa—Jaloonkas, Korankos, Limbas, Ashantees, Zulus—are kept in subordination, and fulfil many a national function without any knowledge of letters or written revelation, it must appear that there is something in the Paganism of Africa as in the Paganism of other lands—some subtle, indefinable, inappreciable influence which operates upon the people and regulates their life. And this religion of the imagination, or of the fancy, if you like, has had its influence upon some of the greatest minds, whose words or deeds have graced the annals of history. Socrates, with his measured, settled, and logical intellect, in his last moments ordered a cock to be sacrificed to Æsculapius. The ancient Greeks and Romans had their sacred groves and "mysteries"—their Porroh and Bundo rites. There exists a very touching letter from Plutarch to his wife, written at the time he lost his only daughter, and when they were in the deepest affliction and desolation. He writes to his wife, who was away from him at the time, a very kind and loving letter, trying to give her comfort and hope. He says to her, "Remember the beautiful things we have seen together in the Mysteries of Bacchus." Some people believe that the Mysteries of Bacchus were nothing but drunkenness and disorder; they were something else. They were like the Mysteries of Ceres—the Goddess of Corn—and like the representations, in other cases, of the immortality of the soul. And owing to the hold which these things have upon the minds of those brought up to believe in them, and who get comfort from them, it is impossible suddenly to uproot them. In fact, superstitions are never thoroughly eradicated from any country. In many parts of Europe the rural superstitions of the old mythology are alive to-day. The peasant holds to rites and ideas that his ancestors practised while they were still savages. We must believe that time, and contact with others who have enjoyed superior advantages for information, will remove from the minds of our Pagan brethren many of the objectionable things in their belief.

But in the evangelistic efforts of Christians, as they push to the interior, they will have to meet also the great Mohammedan religion, which has come across the continent from the deserts of Arabia. Between Sierra Leone and Egypt the Mohammedans are the only great intellectual, moral, and commercial power. The tribes intervening have for more than three hundred years been under the influence of Islam. It has taken possession of, and has shaped the social, political, and religious life of the most intelligent tribes. Its adherents control the politics and commerce of nearly all Africa north of the Equator. From their great cities on the Niger and the Volta they send caravans to every point of the compass—to Abyssinia and Egypt, Algiers and Morocco, Sierra Leone and the Gambia, Liberia and Cape Coast. No one can travel any distance in the interior from this settlement without finding that Islam is the ruling influence. In my journeys a few years ago to Falaba, the capital of the great Pagan kingdom of Soolimia, I passed through the Timneh, Loko, Limba, and Koranko

Sierra Leone and Liberia.

countries, which are also Pagan states; and when, subsequently, I went to Timbo, the capital of Futah Jallo, a Mohammedan power, I passed again through several Pagan districts; but I did not pass through a single town on the two routes—going and returning—where I did not find Mohammedans taking a leading part, and where I did not hear the name of Mohammed and his mission publicly proclaimed at least once a-day. I observed that no public speech was delivered without being preceded and followed by the words—" Alla humma, Salla ala Mohammadi, wa ala áli Mohammadi;" and the audience responded—" Salla Allàhu alayhi wa sallam." The meaning is—" O God, bless Mohammed, and the people of Mohammed." Answer—" God bless him and grant him peace." This has become, all through the country, not only a religious, but a political formula, like " God save the Queen." Thus the distinguishing dogma of Islam, that Mohammed is the Apostle of God, is held up and proclaimed every time an assembly meets.

It is sometimes said by some who, anxious not merely to disparage the intellectual influence of Islam upon the mind of the African, but the intellectual capacity of the Negro, that there is no correct knowledge of Arabic possessed by these people. But this is never said by anyone having the slightest knowledge of the language. A hundred years ago, Mungo Park found considerable knowledge of Arabic among the natives in whose country he travelled. He was astonished on perceiving the encouragement which was given to learning. He says that the vessel in which he returned from Africa contained 127 slaves, most of them from the neighbourhood of the coast, but some from the interior of the country; and that out of this number there were seventeen or eighteen who could read and write Arabic fluently; but the master of the ship, he adds, threw the books belonging to the slaves into the sea, for fear a perusal of them " would make them sick at heart." He calculates that one seventh part of the slaves in the West Indies were, in his day, able to read the Arabic Bible, were it put into their hands. In another place he says:—

> The poor Africans, whom we affect to consider as Barbarians, look upon us, I fear, as little better than a race of formidable but ignorant Heathens. When

Christianity, Islam and the Negro Race.

I produced Richardson's *Arabic Grammar* to some Slatees (native merchants), on the Gambia, they were astonished to think that any European should understand and write the sacred language of their religion. One of them offered to give me an ass and sixteen bars of goods if I would part with the book.

When on the expedition to Timbo, I spent a day and a-half at the town of Telico, two days' journey on this side of the Foulah capital. As I sat writing my diary on the evening after my arrival, just after the sunset prayer, having at my side Momodo Waka, who is now the Assistant Government Arabic Interpreter, I heard a melodious voice at the door reciting, in chant-like style, some Arabic verses. I recognised some of the words as from the Makamat of Hariri. I said to Momodo, "Open the door and see who that is, and ask him in." It was one of the wandering minstrels, or itinerant teachers, who live on the alms of the faithful. These minstrels travel from town to town, and village to village. Crowds gather around and hang on their lips while they recite in glowing terms some episode in the Prophet's life, or some exploit of one of their own warriors or poets. These men go from Africa and travel through Arabia and Syria, drawing crowds just as eager to listen to them. When I was at Beirut, in 1866, there was a celebrated "rawi," or minstrel, from the Soudan, of jet black complexion, drawing crowds every evening by the eloquence of his recitals. The object of my visitor on this occasion was to solicit a gift from the stranger. The words he recited were from the Fifth *Assembly of Hariri*, called 'Koufa,' and were the following, according to the late Professor Preston's translation:—

> Inmates of this abode, all hail! all hail!
> Long may you live in plenty's verdant vale!
> O grant your aid to one by toil opprest,
> Way-worn, benighted, destitute, distrest;
> Whose tortured entrails only hunger hold
> (For since he tasted food two days are told);
> A wretch who finds not where to lay his head,
> Though brooding night her dreary wing hath spread,
> But roams in anxious hope a friend to meet,
> Whose bounty, like a spring of water sweet,
> May heal his woes, a friend who straight will say,
> "Come in! 'Tis time thy staff aside to lay;
> A welcome and a meal are thine to-day!"

Sierra Leone and Liberia.

I should like you to hear the words in the original Arabic by a Mandingo native, who is only one of thousands acquainted with the *Makamat of Hariri*, one of the most difficult of the poems of Arabia. It consists of fifty books, and there are many who have committed to memory the whole. The Arabs have a harsher, or more strongly guttural accent. In general, the Soudanic languages —excepting, perhaps, the dialects of Timbuctoo and Bambarra— are devoid of strong gutturals. The Mandingoes, Foulahs, and the Nigritian tribes generally, who use Arabic, soften the sound of the harsher letters—*shin, kha, hha, ghain, ain, gaf;* the reason being that they have a softer and more effeminate intonation in their speech, suited to their genius and physical constitution.[19]

There are young men born in Freetown, children of recaptives, who can not only read and write, and with ease and propriety converse, in the language of Arabia, but can translate readily from Arabic into Aku and English, and from English into Arabic and Aku. When I passed here in June last, there was a brilliant Arab youth, from the schools of Bagdad, on a missionary visit to the Mohammedans of the settlement. He called upon me with one of the Sierra Leone creoles, who astonished me by the fluency with which he could converse with the stranger from the East in the tongue of the Prophet. The other day, when the ambassadors from Sego were leaving, and the Administrator wrote an important letter to the king, it was a creole youth who put it into the Arabic. I have been surprised that while Mohammedan youth are practically acquainted with three languages, which would make them at home in any part of the Soudan, Christian young men content themselves with only one. I am astonished that they have not long since realised the advantages of their contact with this great Oriental language, and with the treasures of its literature, in which the Negro so largely shares.

It is not the part of wisdom to ignore a fact—not only an irrepressible, but an aggressive fact. The Mohammedans must always

---

[19] See *Observations on the Touarick Alphabet*, by James Richardson.—London 1847.

have a powerful influence in Africa. They have given the initiative of intellectual progress to the tribes of the interior. It is through them that the natives have acquired all they have of knowledge of the outside world, or of past history, sacred or profane. They have given unity to the great tribes of the continent, and have placed millions of Africans—by means of their language, letters, and books—under the same inspiration. Suppose Africa had been obliged to wait till now for knowledge of letters and books from Europeans, what would have been the condition of things, at this moment, in the interior?

But it is not simply the religion of the Arabs, but the race of the Arabs which has given them such influence over the tendencies of the great tribes. They belong to a cognate race. Before the days of Mohammed, Negroes shared in the learning and politics of Arabia. Herodotus, in those early days, discovered the relationship of the two peoples. He represents them as belonging to the same great race. His description of the country of the Eastern Ethiopians corresponds to Southern Arabia; while his description of the region inhabited by the Western Ethiopians takes in Nigritia as far as Sierra Leona and Liberia.

Before the rise of Islam, it was customary to hold in Arabia, once a-year, a national gathering, at which tribes made up their dissensions, exchanged prisoners of war, and competed with one another in extempore poetic contests. The poems which were successful were transcribed in letters of gold and suspended on the wall of the Kaaba, where they would be seen by every pilgrim who might visit the most sacred place in the country. These poems were honoured with the title of Moâllacat, or "suspended." Seven of them have been deemed worthy of preservation, and are much admired by European students of Arabic for the beauty of the language and wild richness of the imagery. One of the prize poems was composed by the warrior and poet Antarrah, the son of a negress slave. He was so black that he was nicknamed "Gharab," crow. When some of the members of his clan, who early embraced Islam, went as deputies to Medina to visit Mohammed, and make profession of faith on the part of their brethren, the prophet told them that the warrior whom he most desired to have seen was the Negro Antarrah.[20]

For twelve centuries the Adzan, or call to prayer, has been sounded five times a-day from every mosque in the Mohammedan world. The traveller from Fourah Bay to North-western China is startled in his sleep at early dawn by Muezzins crying aloud from their various minarets, the words "Allahu Akbar," &c. (God is great, &c.).

These self-same words are used by Muslims of every nationality. Turks, Persians, Hindoos, Chinese, Foulahs, Mandingoes, Akus, &c., all use the same Arabic words. Now, it ought to be interesting to us to know that these words were first uttered and composed, in part, by a Negro, named Bilal.[21] Sir William Muir says, "He was tall, dark, and gaunt, with Negro features and bushy hair." He was among the earliest converts to Islam. Mohammed distinguished him as "the first-fruits of Africa"; and on account of his physical and moral qualities, appointed him the first Muezzin, or crier to prayer. After crying the Adzan, Bilal would come to the door of Mohammed and rouse him thus: "To prayer, oh, Apostle of God! to salvation." Then Bilal would take his stand in the first row of worshippers, who used strictly to follow his example in the prayers and genuflexions.[22]

So that the forms of daily worship now used throughout the Mohammedan world were fixed by a Negro.

This distinguished man, like many other Moslem warriors, was granted landed property at Damascus, where he died, A.H. 20, aged 60 years; and where his tomb is still shown. There is not a Christian country governed by Europeans where the tomb of any Negro, whatever his merit, has been preserved for even a hundred years. The Negro came into contact with Christianity as a slave and a follower at a distance. He came into contact with Mohammedanism as a man, and often as a leader. Whatever men of other races may do, can the Negro turn contemptuously upon a

---

[20] The words, "Prayer is better than sleep," were introduced by Bilal.
[21] Chenery's *Assemblies of Hariri*, vol. i, p. 818.
[22] Muir's *Life of Mahomet*.

religion in which he *has* had a part, and listen without protest to the statement of those who, while bringing him Christianity, tell him that his past has been " blank and hopeless ? "

Mohammed not only loved the Negro, but regarded Africa with peculiar interest and affection. He never spoke of any curse hanging over the country or people. When in the early years of his reform, his followers were persecuted and could get no protection in Arabia, he advised them to seek an asylum in Africa. " Yonder," he said, pointing towards this country, " yonder lieth a country wherein no man is wronged—a land of righteousness. Depart thither; and remain until it pleaseth the Lord to open your way before you."[23] This recalls to us Homer's " blameless Ethiopians," and the words of the Angel to Joseph : " Arise and flee into Egypt, and be thou there until I bring thee word again."

You can understand why it is then that Islam has such a hold upon the African tribes who have embraced it. They gather under the beams of the Crescent not only for religious, but for patriotic reasons; till they are not only swayed with one idea, but act as one individual. The faith becomes a part of their nationality, and is entwined with their affections. Arguments from outsiders have no weight with them. There are names and phrases which have such effect upon their minds, and so thrill them as to supersede and transcend all argument: and many of these names and phrases are names and phrases held in reverence by Christians. All the great tribes are held under the same inspiration. Europeans who speak to them speak as outsiders. They listen with the consciousness that they know things altogether hidden from the European propagandist of the Christian religion. It is impossible to ignore, even in religious matters, the fundamental distinctions of race. That theory which attributes the success of Islam in Africa to what are frequently denounced as the sensual aspects of the religion is based upon ignorance, not only of the system, but of the elementary facts of human nature. No religion could exert so powerful a sway over two hundred millions of people—of all races and climes

---

[23] Muir's *Life of Mahomet*, p. 74.

Sierra Leone and Liberia.

—for more than a thousand years, which appealed chiefly to the lower passions. But in our discussion of the Mohammedan question we do not consider the *theology* of the system, but its *anthropology*: those practical features of it which affect man—the natural man, and especially the African man. And in viewing it in this manner, as we become acquainted with its history and literature, we cannot but feel a deep personal interest in the system.

Notwithstanding the copiousness of the Arabic language and its exhaustless fertility, it has no forms of expression to describe any race, which are contemptuous or insulting.

The late Professor Palmer, Arabic Professor at Cambridge, made a translation of the beautiful poems of Beha-ed-din into English, in which he ventured to degrade the language and idea of the original Arabic by using the word "Nigger" to represent the respectable and harmless word "aswad" used by the poet, which simply means "black." These are the things in English literature which repel the Negro student. If, in modern English poetry, the word "Nigger" is the most suitable phrase by which to describe the Negro, I for one must eliminate modern English poetry from the subjects taught to Negro youth.

There is now in one of the adjoining Mohammedan villages a work in manuscript, composed in Egypt or Nubia, describing the exploits of distinguished Negroes in the early history of Mohammedanism; so that the Mohammedan youth, from the books they read, have a far better opportunity of becoming acquainted with the great men of their race than the Christian youth, and therefore of acquiring deeper self-respect, and an earnest attachment to a religion in which their own people have performed such achievements.

It is interesting to feel that the religion of Isaac and the religion of Ishmael, both having their root in Abraham, confront each other on this continent. Japheth introducing Isaac, and Shem bringing Ishmael, Ham will receive both. The moonlight of the Crescent, and the sunlight of the Cross, will dispel the darkness which has so long covered the land. The "Dark Continent" will no longer be a name of reproach for this vast peninsula, for there shall be no darkness here. Where the light from the Cross ceases

Christianity, Islam and the Negro Race.

to stream upon the gloom, there the beams of the Crescent will give illumination; and as the glorious orb of Christianity rises, the twilight of Islam will be lost in the greater light of the Sun of Righteousness. Thus Isaac and Ishmael will be united, and rejoice together in the faith of their common progenitor—*Ibrahim Khalil Allah*—Abraham, the Friend of God.

Let us now enquire what are the advantages of the Colony and the Republic over each other? Perhaps it may be well to review briefly here their financial status. I regret that I have not at present accessible the financial statistics of Liberia; but, through the kindness of the Governor-in-Chief, I am able to furnish a few facts with regard to Sierra Leone.

It is interesting and instructive to contrast the present position of Sierra Leone, as a contributor to the world's well-being, with its position a hundred years ago, when the chief articles of export were human beings.

The total value of articles exported from Sierra Leone during the year 1882 was	£420,015	2 8
Total value of articles imported	398,814	19 9
Excess of exports	£21,200	2 11

These exports and imports were distributed chiefly as follows:—

The exports to Great Britain amounted in value to	£189,120	11 6
The imports from Great Britain amounted in value to	272,195	6 2
Excess of imports from Great Britain	£83,074	14 8
Exports to America amounted in value to	£23,354	8 6
Imports from America amounted in value to	34,436	16 8
Excess of imports from America	£11,082	8 2
Exports to France	£77,861	2 11
Imports from France	15,790	3 1
Excess of exports to France	£62,070	19 10
Exports to Germany amounted in value to	£23,152	17 0
Imports from Germany	20,639	19 6
Excess of exports to Germany	£2,512	17 6
Exports to Belgium	£217	4 0
Imports from Belgium	......	
Excess of Exports	£217	4 0

Sierra Leone and Liberia.

I have mentioned the chief places out of Africa which carry on trade with Sierra Leone, and you will notice that Anglo-Saxon influence largely predominates. England and the United States together send articles to the value of £223,556 17s. 2d., while France and Germany together send only £36,430 2s. 7d., just a little over what America alone sends. Sierra Leone supplies France with produce to the value of £77,861 2s. 11d., and receives in return £15,790 3s. 1d.

It may be, however, that a large portion of the articles going to and coming from France and Germany are shipped *via* Liverpool and London; and yet there are steamers going direct from here to Hamburg and Marseilles.

Let us look now at the traffic between Sierra Leone and places on the coast.

The total value of the articles exported from Sierra Leone to Gambia, in 1882, was	£26,909 10	11
Value of articles imported	5,892 14	7
Excess of exports	£20,016 16	4
Value of articles exported to Windward Coast	£63,451 7	3
Value of articles imported	11,135 13	8
Excess	£52,315 13	7
Exports to Leeward Coast	£4,743 11	4
Imports from Leeward Coast	£1,568 7	3
Excess	£3,175 4	1
Exports to Liberia	£1,220 10	7
Imports from Liberia	203 12	5
Excess	£1,016 18	2
The total revenue of the colony, for 1882, was	£65,537 8	8
The total expenditure of the colony, for 1882, was	62,912 19	5
Excess of revenue	£2,624 9	3
The revenue from imports was	£36,251 18	7
,, ,, exports was	7,788 15	0
,, ,, wharfage was	4,880 5	1
,, ,, tonnage dues was	2,814 5	6
,, ,, light was	1,246 16	9
,, ,, harbour was	547 16	9
,, ,, warehouse rent was	809 19	2
,, ,, auction dues was	2 2	2
	£53,841 19	5

The balance was made up from licenses and other local impositions.

The revenue for 1883 was £62,282 8s. 11d., less than the revenue of the preceding year by about £3,000. The average monthly income of the colony is about £5,000. I was surprised to find that, while the revenue for January and February, 1883, was £5,658 14s. 11d. and £6,359 4s. 3d. respectively, the revenue for the month of August, which is considered one of the dullest months of the year, was £7,948 3s. 7d. Only one month last year yielded less than £4,000, and that was the month of March, when the revenue was £3,969 1s. The months of January, February, May, August and December, yielded each over £5,000.

The impression to be gathered from this statement I take to be that there is a regular and steady improvement in the trade of the colony; and now, with the prospect of open roads and enlarged intercourse with the distant interior, we may safely predict that, within a comparatively brief period, the colony will be able not only to pay off its debts, but to carry on with ease many much-needed internal improvements.

The average annual expenditure for the Civil Service may be set down at about £60,000. A similar amount may be laid down as the expenditure for the Military Service. I find from the Blue Book for 1882 that the expenditure for the military was £38,829 2s. 9d. But this amount did not include—

1. The value of provisions, clothing, accoutrements, arms, ammunition and stores sent out from England.
2. The pay of regimental officers, which is paid in England.
3. The pay of departmental officers on leave.
4. The cost of passages of officers to and from England.
5. Transport of troops to and from the West Indies.
6. The whole proportionate expense of the naval squadron.
7. The Imperial grant in aid of the Colonial steamer, *Prince of Wales*.

The colony contributes nothing on account of its military defence.

The idea of a local force for the defence of the colony is not altogether lost sight of by the Government. Colonel Ord, the Commissioner of Inquiry on the West Coast of Africa, sent out in 1865, in his recommendations on this subject, made the following remark:—

Sierra Leone and Liberia.

Protected as the West Coast Settlements have been hitherto by a body of regular troops, it would not be expedient to make suddenly the experiment of confiding their security entirely to a local force, but as a sufficient number of Haussas can be organised, a reduction may be effected in the strength of the garrisons, especially of the minor settlements.

In the trade of the colony of Sierra Leone there is a large consumption of European manufactures. The most sanguine anticipations of Clarkson and Wilberforce as to the beneficial results of abolishing the slave trade have been more than realised. In the days of the slave trade England exported £1,000,000 to the whole of Africa. Now she exports one-fifth of that amount to Sierra Leone alone. For the first three years after she had abolished the slave trade, British exports for lawful trade to Africa, the Cape of Good Hope included, averaged £88,000 annually,[21] less than one-half the value of her present exports to Sierra Leone. And, even as late as 1840, the total value of British and Irish produce and manufactures exported from the United Kingdom to Sierra Leone and the coast, from the River Gambia inclusive to the River Mesurado, was only £93,640.[23]

The annual revenue of Liberia may be stated at £25,000. The sources of this revenue are—customs, import and export duties; tax on real estate one-half per cent. on the assessed value; poll-tax on all the inhabitants of one dollar per head; military fines.

Liberia, of course, makes no pretensions to defend herself against any foreign power; but she has been able, by her simple military arrangement, which is only a militia system, not only to hold her own against aboriginal aggression, but to exercise, from half-a-dozen effective settlements, along five hundred miles of coast and a considerable distance inland, a very wholesome influence. In the days of the slave trade, that little Republic succeeded in completely suppressing the external operations of that nefarious traffic.

She exercises a useful jurisdiction among the neighbouring tribes, and affords facilities for safe and peaceful traffic between the interior and the coast.

---

[21] McQueen's *Commercial View of Africa*.
[23] Report from the Select Parliamentary Committee on the West Coast of Africa, 1842; part ii, p. 509.

Christianity, Islam and the Negro Race.

Only a few weeks ago hordes of predatory Kossohs were expelled from the region of Little Cape Mount, and their chief captured by the Liberian forces. This great warrior is now in confinement at Monrovia, awaiting trial. The actual material advantages of Sierra Leone over Liberia are that it possesses the finest harbour on the coast; that by means of the large rivers in its neighbourhood it has great facilities of intercourse with the interior; that it is protected and upheld by a strong government; that its extensive trade gives it a large revenue, and puts money in circulation. On the other hand, the advantages of Liberia are a larger area of territory; a soil of far greater fertility, and adapted to the production of every tropical article demanded by commerce; a population thrown, in the earlier stages of their growth, upon their own resources, and therefore possessed of greater self-reliance and individual independence. If Sierra Leone can count more English sovereigns, Liberia can count broader acres. If Sierra Leone can boast of a more extensive commerce, Liberia may be proud of its larger agriculture. It is, perhaps, natural that those who are able to entertain such angels as are stamped at the Royal Mint should have a good opinion of themselves; but they must not be surprised if those who are able to sit under the vine and fig-tree of their own planting are disposed to think rather highly of their own advantages.

In the moral, and even political, possibilities of the two countries, I do not see that one has any advantage over the other. The possibilities of Sierra Leone, in one direction, may be limited and defined by the regulations for Crown Colonies; in another, those possibilities are boundless. The limitations imposed in one direction need not be dwelt upon, when we consider that the possible achievements in the other case are, as I have pointed out, real ethnic or race independence and commercial ascendancy in this part of the continent. There need not be, between the Sierra Leoneans and Liberians, any present or prospective jealousy. That community of the two, will, in the long run, rule more widely which rules more wisely; and superior energy, enterprise and skill will carry off the advantages of trade, and draw the prizes from the interior.

Sierra Leone and Liberia.

The true policy of Liberia is to direct its energies to the improvement of internal administration, both of the country and general governments, to the extension of education, and to the development of the vast natural resources. The same, *mutatis mutandis*, seems to be the proper policy of Sierra Leone. The slow growth of capital is the great drawback of Liberia; the drawback of Sierra Leone is the frequent changing of rulers, which it seems the necessities of the colonial service, not to say the perils of this climate, require.

Now, what guarantee have we that these two countries will be allowed to grow and develop on their own line?

It has been predicted that the Negro race will die out of Africa. Within three hundred years, we have been told, there will not be a Negro left. The suggestion has been made to supersede them by Chinese. Winwood Reade, in closing his book on *Savage Africa*, draws a brilliant picture of the future of this country when Europeans, or their descendants, shall occupy the great centres of the Niger. In the amiable task of spreading civilisation over Africa, the natives may be exterminated.

> But (says Mr. Reade) a grateful posterity will cherish their memories. When the cockneys of Timbuctoo have their tea-gardens in the oases of the Sahara; when hotels and guide-books are established at the sources of the Nile; when it becomes fashionable to go yachting on the lakes of the Great Plateau; when noblemen, building seats in Central Africa, will have their elephant parks and their hippopotami waters; young ladies on camp-stools, under palm-trees, will read with tears—*The Last of the Negroes;* and the Niger will become as romantic a river as the Rhine.[20]

It is a curious thing that, notwithstanding the experience of thousands of years, men seem so slow to learn that in forming plans for carrying out their theories as regards countries and races —especially as regards this country and this race—there are certain invisible barriers that confront them like the angel in the path of Balaam, which cannot be descried by the most piercing sagacity, and which therefore cannot be taken into their most careful calculations. It was a solemn and suggestive piece of

---

[20] Reade's *Savage Africa*, p. 587.

advice that one of the Roman rulers, in his last moments, gave when he warned his people against attempting the invasion of Africa.

No earnest effort yet made by foreigners to take possession of this continent has ever met with permanent success. Something has always happened to divert them from their purpose. Persians, Carthaginians, Greeks and Romans, have all tried, and failed. Alexander the Great, conqueror of Europe and a great part of Asia, sat down, in a fit of despondency, and wept for worlds to conquer.

But here was Africa, with her vast territory and teeming population. He tried his energy and skill in a small section of the country. But after his famous journey to the oracle of Jupiter Ammon, he looked only askance at this magnificent field for military exploits—

> Nor felt the joy that warriors feel
> In foemen worthy of their steel.

When, in modern times, Portugal had magnificent schemes for the colonisation and occupation of Africa, and had built up extensive establishments, her attention was called away by the discovery of America and the demand for labour in that new country. The spirit, strength, and influence of her African enterprises received a check from which she has never since recovered. Her extensive colonies were lost, and dwindled into marts for carrying on the slave trade.

The desire of the French to own large possessions in Africa, is no new idea born of the teachings or inspired by the discoveries of Livingstone and Stanley. No; near the close of the last century, or in the beginning of this, France had large plans for possessing Africa. The plan of Talleyrand and of the first Napoleon was to make Africa the great field for cultivating tropical produce, and this cultivation was to be carried on by means of the native population. But the ambition of Napoleon diverted his energies to European wars, and finally he was confined a prisoner to an African island—sorry ending this of his magnificent schemes of occupation. Instead of holding Africa, a small sea-girt rock near Africa held him till his death. But his plans are not yet lost sight

Sierra Leone and Liberia.

of by the French. They have vast schemes for taking charge of Senegambia, and controlling the trade of the Upper Niger, and have made large expenditure in that direction; but, after years of preparation and effort, their energies are at this moment diverted to other regions. And I have not the slightest doubt, judging from the past, that when the efforts now making on the Congo become serious and really threatening to the true interests of the people, some unseen emergency—some distant or neighbouring complications—will draw them off, and another generation will have to wrestle anew with the African problem. It may be said that the facts I have referred to are mere accident, and that it is superstitious to base conclusions upon fortuitous circumstances. Well, African students of history must be excused—in view of the hard lot of the race—if they are disposed to attach significance to any event, or concourse of events, which indicates the future preservation of their people.

But besides the invisible agencies, there is another guarantee against future oppression of the tribes of this country by foreigners, and that lies in the progress of liberal sentiments in Europe. England, which, in the extent and power of her sway, resembles the Roman Empire, is careful of her proceedings in dealing with Africa. The rising elements of power in that great country are transferring their political homage from tradition to principles, from men or families to rights and duties, from the privileges of the few to universal justice and right. "Rescue and retire" is the modern principle of intervention. And this will be the motto in future of all England's operations in Africa. It should be, and no doubt ere long will be, inscribed upon the banners of all organisations, whether political or philanthropic, at work in Africa.

In conclusion, I may remark that these two countries may be said to represent the true principle or method by which civilisation is to be introduced into Africa. There is no part of West Africa where the openings and opportunities for introducing civilisation and Christianity into this continent are greater than these contiguous states present. The attractions which they offer to the efforts of the philanthropist and African Colonisationist (in the American sense of that phrase) are not without just grounds. For whether we look to the origin and purpose of these settlements, or to their bearing upon the future civil and religious condition of these tribes, or to the influence they have already exerted upon thousands, it is scarcely possible to estimate too highly their importance to the continent as inlets of wholesome impressions from without, or to Europe and America as outlets of a valuable commerce. While they will gather—when the proper policy is pursued by the respective governments—into their bosom, as into a capacious gulf, the main streams, and even the lesser tributaries, of a commerce which only for want of proper facilities has poured its treasures into other regions, they will send up those streams by the returning tide the lessons and principles of order and law, of religion and liberty, of science, literature, and art. And it is not difficult to predict the effect of all this upon the general interests of civilisation, upon the welfare of the Negro race, and upon the great cause of humanity.

Islam and Race Distinctions.

IF the divinity of a religion may be inferred from the variety of races among whom it has been diffused, and the strength of its hold upon them, then there is no religion that can prefer greater claims than Islam. Of the three missionary religions— we adopt the classification of Max Müller [1]—none has in so marked a degree overstepped the limits of race as the religion of Mohammed.

Christianity is more widespread than either Buddhism or Mohammedanism, having made its way across oceans and over continents to distant islands of the sea; but it has followed chiefly the migrations and settlements of members of the Aryan race. In no case has it taken possession of whole races or communities belonging to non-Aryan races, if we except the Sandwich Islands, the inhabitants of which, we now learn, are fast passing away under the influence of the new civilisation they have received.

It is remarkable that the eight distinct religions of which history gives account all had their origin in Asia, and the three highest religions—the Jewish, the Christian, the Mohammedan— took their rise among Semitic peoples. And it is equally remarkable that since Christianity left the place of its birth it has seemed to be the property exclusively of the European branch of the human family. And, so far as it has become the possession of the Western Aryans, it has shared the fate of that other great

---

[1] *Lecture on Missions*, delivered in Westminster Abbey on December 3, 1873.

religion which arose among the Eastern branch of the Indo-European family, viz., Buddhism, as being for the most part confined to one or two races.

It would be interesting to inquire why the religions of the Indo-Europeans—whether we take those which arose among themselves, Brahminism, Buddhism and Zoroastrianism; on the one, incomparable and Divine, which they derived from the Shemites—seem, under their administration, to transcend with difficulty the limits of race; why the grand Semitic idea of the conversion to Divine truth of all the races of mankind, and their incorporation into one spiritual family, seems, under European propagandism, to make such slow progress. If Judaism, as Professor Max Müller holds, was, in its practice, non-missionary, yet it contained the germs of which Christianity is an outgrowth and development, and the missionary idea must be regarded as, after all, a Semitic conception.

Can we refer the want of Aryan success among foreign races to the original idiosyncracy impressed upon the races in their cradles, and fitting each for a specific work? It would seem that the tendency of West Aryan genius is ever to divorce God from His works, and to lay great stress upon human capability and achievement. Man is an end, not a means. The highest man is the highest end to which all things else must bow. The aggregate must bend to the individual if he is superior to other individuals in intellectual or pecuniary might. The more favoured race must dominate and control the less favoured race. Religion is to be cherished as a means of subserving temporal and material purposes. Those of the Aryans, therefore, who have received the Semitic religion look upon it as complete, perfect and final, given to mankind, ages ago, through chosen and exceptional instrumentalities, and once for all. There is now no more direct communion with or inspiration from God necessary or possible. Everything now depends upon man. Everything else is within his grasp. He may even by searching find out God. Material progress is the end of the human race. The speculation of those intellects who are in one direction pre-eminent in their generation—the Darwins, Tyndalls and Huxleys—are typical of the spirit and tendencies of the Indo-

Islam and Race Distinctions.

European mind. What their ancient relatives, the Greeks, strove to express in material forms, they strive now to indicate by scientific theories; we have "atoms" and "protoplasms," "evolution" and "natural selection," instead of exquisite statues and paintings.

And as far back as we know anything of the great Indo-European race we find the same underlying principles, unlike as the surface may be. The Hindoo sees God in all material things, and is content with a dreamy Pantheism which centres in no clear conceptions of Right and Truth, and prompts to no effort to realise them objectively, while the growth of society is arrested by the blighting spirit of caste—and what the Brahmins are to the other tribes of India that the Anglo-Saxons hold themselves with respect to other nations and races. The Greeks materialised their Gods, clothing them in human bodies, and with human feelings and attributes. With them the divine and æsthetic were identical: *Kalos* might be taken to mean the physically beautiful or the morally good. The Romans, who, in certain respects, might be regarded as the ancient representatives of the Anglo-Saxon race, directed their attention to government and law, politics and jurisprudence. Their constant effort was to secure power and supremacy. And the deities whom they invented were striking exemplifications of their materia aims and tendencies. Their highest achievements, therefore, were individual and Roman.

> Tu regere imperio populos, Romane, memento;
> Hæ tibi erunt artes; pacisque imponere morem,
> Parcere subjectis, et debellare superbos.[2]

When a people possessing the peculiarities described above received the Semitic religion they gave it, in a great degree, the colouring of their own minds. The first and most striking departure from the original simplicity of Christianity in deference to national or race instincts may be seen in the mediæval Church, which bore a striking resemblance, in its worship and organisation, to Buddhism. The religion became a great objective mass of rites and dogmas, more stress being laid upon the material and visible than upon the unseen and spiritual. But even after the Reforma-

---

[2] Virgil's *Æneid*, vi, 851-53.

tion, brought about by men of cold Northern temperaments, who protested against the peculiarities which Greeks and Italians had imported into the Church, Aryan genius still asserted itself. Wherever these Protestants went, their aim was to realise a kingdom of God in the civil constitutions of men, and to confine it by a system of caste almost Brahminical to their own people. Presbyterians from Scotland, Episcopalians from England, Puritans who supported Cromwell, all went to foreign shores with high and earnest purpose, but they were hampered in the attainment of any philanthropic result by their race-intolerance and impracticable narrowness. They aimed at securing material aggrandisement at any cost. Indian and Negro must be made, willing or unwilling, tools in the prosecution of their design. The human soul—the immaterial—was of secondary and subordinate importance.

The Semitic mind, on the other hand, destitute, it has been alleged, of the scientific instinct,[3] looks upon man—every man—as standing in direct relation to God, who has not ceased His communications with His creatures, still speaking to them at times in dreams and visions, and at other times by the ordinary events of life. Nature is regarded as inanimate; her powers proceed from and are moved by the will of God. "Pantheism, in the Greek sense, is utterly unknown to the Shemites."[4] By its very nature, the Semitic mind will ever throw itself confidently upon those primal intuitions which, if they do not admit of scientific or logical proof, are yet superior to scientific or logical disproof. Its inquiries, in spite of Tyndallism or Darwinism, will never go beyond the simple truth, that "In the beginning God created the heaven and the earth." The government of the world offers to the Shemite an infinite problem which man can never solve; and hence the greatest aim of man should be the cultivation of those qualities in which he may most resemble God. The Shemite lays most stress, in religion,

---

[3] A part la supériorité de son culte, le peuple juif n'en a aucune autre ; c'est un des peuples les moins doués pour la science et la philosophie parmi les peuples de l'antiquité.—M. Renan, quoted by Max Müller, in *Chips from a German Workshop;* vol. i, p. 350.

[4] Deutsch, *Literary Remains.*

Islam and Race Distinctions.

upon prayer; the Aryan upon preaching. Among the Hebrews there were no adepts in science or art; no architects; no city builders; no sculptors; no painters. Development among them was not in material, but in moral and intellectual, forms. Hence, while the Greek or Indo-European paid more attention to physical than to moral excellence, to the Shemite, the spirit, the mind of man, was the great object of development and culture—the inward character rather than the outward form. And this devotion to external forms—this respect for appearances—is the great drawback to the Aryan in disseminating a religion which was meant for, and is adapted to, all mankind.

The Mohammedan religion, on the other hand, an offshoot from the Semitic mind, disregarding all adventitious circumstances, seeks for the real man, neglects the accidental for the essential, the adventitious for the integral. Hence it extinguishes all distinctions founded upon race, colour, or nationality. "I admonish you to fear God," said Mohammed to his followers, "and yield obedience to my successor, although he may be a black slave."[5] And, therefore, throughout the history of Islam, in all countries, race or "previous condition" has been no barrier to elevation. Frequent are the instances in which proud Arabs have submitted to the rule of aliens, even if those aliens were Negro slaves. Mr. Talboys Wheeler, in his *History of India*, speaks in the highest terms of Kutb-ud-din, the first of the "Slave Kings" in the Mohammedan dynasty in that country, and classes him among the four Sultans whom he thinks the only ones deserving of remembrance in the course of three centuries. One of the most distinguished of the Mohammedan rulers of Egypt was Kafur, "a Negro of deep black colour, with a smooth, shining skin," who rose to be Governor of Egypt, from the position of a slave. He had shown himself equally great as a soldier and a statesman. His dominion extended not only over Egypt, but Syria also; and public prayers were offered up for him, as sovereign, from the pulpits of Mekka, Hijaz, Egypt and the cities of Syria, Damascus, Aleppo, Antioch, Tarsus, &c.[6]

---

[5] *Mischat-al-Masabih*.
[6] *Biographies of Ibn Khallikan;* translated by Baron de Slane, vol. ii, p. 524.

Christianity, Islam and the Negro Race.

An American missionary, resident in Egypt, calls attention to the entire absence of all colour or race-prejudice in that country, which seems to have struck him the more from his experience of the unreasonable and superstitious caste-prejudices in the land of his birth.[7] This liberality, so far as the Negro is concerned, may be chiefly the result of Muslim rule, but it is partly also the result of the traditional respect for the race which has never disappeared from that country since the days of its ancient glory, in which it is now certain that the Negro took a leading part.[8]

In noticing the absorbing influence which, in consequence of its democratic spirit, Islam has exercised over foreign races, Ibn Khaldun, a celebrated Mohammedan author, makes the following observations:—

> It is a curious circumstance that the majority of the learned amongst the Muslims belonged to a foreign race; very few persons of Arabian descent having obtained distinction in the sciences connected with the law, or in those based upon human reason; and yet the promulgator of the law was an Arab, and the Koran—that source of so many sciences—an Arabic book.

The above remarks have been suggested by the title and scope of Major Osborn's *Islam under the Arabs*. This book is, as the author informs us, to be followed by two other volumes which will deal with Islam under the Persian and Indian races. Works might be written also on Islam under the Mongolians, and Islam under the Negroes; for the religion, originating at Mekka, has

---

[7] Lansing's *Egypt's Princes*.

[8] Catafago in his *Arabic and English Dictionary*, under the word "Kusur" (palaces), says: "The ruins of Thebes, that ancient and celebrated town, deserve to be visited, as just those heaps of ruins, laved by the Nile, are all that remain of the opulent cities that gave lustre to Ethiopia. It was there that a people, since forgotten, discovered the elements of science and art, at a time when all other men were barbarous, and when a race, now regarded as the refuse of society, explored among the phenomena of Nature those civil and religious systems which have since held mankind in awe." A more recent investigator, Dr. Hartmann, in an 'Encyclopædic work on Nigritia' (*Saturday Review*, June 17, 1876), contends for the strictly African extraction of the Egyptians, who he seems to consider, may have dwelt upon the shores of the inner African sea, whose desiccation has formed the existing Sahara. See a remarkable passage bearing upon this subject in Volney's *Travels*, vol. i, chap. iii.

Islam and Race Distinctions.

extended west, across Africa, to the Atlantic, and east to North-Western China, north to Constantinople, and south to Mozambique, embracing men of all the known races; and embracing them not as occasional and individual converts, but as entire communities—whole nations and tribes—weaving itself into the national life, and giving colour to their political and social, as well as ecclesiastical existence.

The religion of Jesus, after eighteen hundred years, nowhere furnishes such practical evidence of cosmopolitan adaptation and power. "Christianity is not to blame for this," to use the suggestive words of Mr. Bosworth Smith, "but Christian nations are."[º]

One of the most signal and melancholy instances of the failure of Aryans, in possession of the highest religion, to convert or save a foreign race, is that presented by the history of the Europeans in America, who, for more than three hundred years, have been in contact with large portions of the Mongolian race with very meagre beneficial result. Within the last few months, the military disaster suffered in an attack upon the Indians has sent a thrill of horror through the United States. Theodore Parker, in his *Thoughts on America*, unveils the reasons of the difficulty in his characteristic and incisive style. He says:—

> The Anglo-Saxon disdains to mingle his proud blood in wedlock with the "inferior races of men." He puts away the savage—black, yellow, red. In New England, the Puritan converted the Indians to Christianity, as far as they could accept the theology of John Calvin; but made a careful separation between white and red, "my people and thy people." They must dwell in separate villages, worship in separate houses; they must not intermarry. The General Court of Massachusetts once forbade all extra-matrimonial connection of white and red, on pain of death! The Anglo-Saxon has carefully sought to exterminate the savages from his territory. The Briton does so in Africa, in Van Diemen's Land, in New Zealand, in New Holland—wherever he meets them. The American does the same in the Western world. In New England the Puritan found the wild woods, the wild beasts, and the wild men; he undertook to eradicate them all, and he has succeeded best with the wild men—there

---

[º] It will be understood, of course, that we are not here instituting a comparison between the two systems of religion, but only between the methods and proceedings of their respective professors and propagators.

Christianity, Islam and the Negro Race.

are more bears than Indians in New England. The United States pursues the same destructive policy. In two hundred years more there will be few Indians left between the Lake of the Woods and the Gulf of Mexico, between the Atlantic and Pacific Oceans.[10]

Whatever may be the exaggerations in the above paragraph, no one can deny that, on the whole, there is too much truth in it; yet, in the face of this heartrending truth, some American writers on the Indian question talk flippantly and unfeelingly of a "law of decay," and console themselves with the superficial theory of the "inferior race vanishing before the superior." But a thoughtful writer in a recent number of one of the leading American quarterlies takes a far more serious view of the subject:—

> Those who give but little attention (he says) to Indian affairs, take it for granted that the race is doomed to utter extermination, without thinking of the fact that until they came in contact with white civilisation, they were rapidly increasing in numbers. . . . The story of the Creeks, Cherokees, Choctaws, and Chickasaws has been often told, and only one conclusion has ever been reached by any Christian giving it serious attention, and that is, that the United States Government committed a grievous wrong and crime in removing these tribes from their old home "by force," and placing them on a "reservation" in the far south-west . . . The great error we commit toward the Indian is failing to recognise in him that common humanity which should lead us to call all men brothers *and citizens*. They are men and women like ourselves; they have the same hearts to touch by kindness and warm by friendship, and the same love for home that is common to all mankind, in a greater or less degree.[11]

We venture to express the belief that no such appeal would have been necessary had that interesting race of men been in contact with thirty millions of Mohammedans, instead of thirty millions of Christians. The wars fought against them would have been wars not of extermination but of proselytising. They would have been repetitions, probably in their manner, but certainly in their results, of the Syrian wars of Omar and Ali, the African wars of Amru and Akbah, and the Spanish wars of Musa and Tarik. The millions who were found on the continent would now be alive in their descendants, and absorbed in the national life. The

---

[10] *Additional Speeches*, vol. ii.
[11] *Presbyterian Quarterly and Princeton Review*, January, 1876.

"bears in New England" would have been extirpated, and the Indians would have been saved.[12]

But let us turn more particularly to the works before us.

Mr. Grant-Duff enumerates ten ways in which British influence is leavening India. Major Osborn proposes an eleventh way, namely, that the dominant race should familiarise themselves with the history and traditions of the various peoples whom they govern. And the object which he set before himself in the important work he has undertaken is to put within the reach of his countrymen, and especially of his fellow-officers, "historical sketches of the races from which the native army in India is chiefly recruited."

Islam under the Arabs, the first instalment of Major Osborn's work, is written in a remarkably clear and lively style. There is very little danger of misunderstanding the author's meaning. He has brought together in a small compass some of the most important facts in the early history of Islam, not a few of which will, no doubt, be entirely new to a large majority of readers. It is evident that he has given considerable attention to the external history of Islam; and had he confined himself to a narrative of events, for which his qualifications seem eminently adapted, his book would have taken its place among those valuable works on Oriental subjects for which the world is largely indebted to the literary tastes and industry of British soldiers, and, as a repertory of facts, would have always been referred to with confidence; but his reflections and comments on the theological aspects of the subject are so far behind the enlightened and tolerant spirit of the age, and, in many instances, so contrary to the view taken by Christian writers acquainted with Mohammedan history and literature, and of course by enlightened Mohammedans, that his book will not only be read, even in its most accurate parts, with a constantly hesitating, if not dissenting spirit, by those who are even partially acquainted with the facts, but will mislead those wholly ignorant of the subject, for whose benefit it is professedly

---

[12] A portion of another race—the Negro—carried to that land by force, has grown and multiplied in spite of repressive laws and regulations in Church and State.

written, by inciting them to a contemptuous intolerance; and thus the lofty and praiseworthy object of the writer will fail to be secured.

As the contribution, however, of an industrious and skilful delineator of the course of Mohammedan history in its earlier periods, the work will repay careful perusal; and, in spite of its laboured effort to place the theology of Islam in an unfavourable, and often ridiculous light, it will add its quota to the general enlightenment on that irrepressible faith which, after all that may be said, has attained a majestic stability and permanence in the history of India. When the series is finished, the general reader, anxious to get a clear and connected account of the leading facts of early Mohammedan history, without referring to original and not always accessible sources, will have at his disposal a convenient little library of the annals of Islam. But unless the two volumes to follow are written with a clearer insight into the system of which the author treats, unless, by further research, he becomes imbued with a more thorough appreciation of the facts which he collects, and a more liberal spirit in dealing with them, we need expect no fresh views respecting the secret of the power of Islam, and no livelier prospect as to the conciliatory and harmonising influence of the work.

Dr. Badger, in the *Contemporary Review* for June, 1875, gives us the following information :—

The first English translation of the Kurân was made from the French of André du Ryer, by one Alexander Ross, and published in London in 1649. It is accompanied by an introduction styled ' A needful Caveat or Admonition,' which runs thus: "Good reader, the great Arabian impostor, now at last, after a thousand years, is, by the way of France, arrived in England, and his Alcoran, or Gallimaufry of Errors (a Brat as deformed as the Parent, and as full of heresies as his scald head was of scurf), hath learned to speak English."

The education of two centuries (adds Dr. Badger) has chastened the style of our national literature, and added much to our knowledge of Eastern subjects generally; nevertheless, there is good ground for presuming that the foregoing description of the Kurân and of its reputed author is in accordance substantially with the views still held by the great majority of Englishmen.

Aye, and of Englishmen who have lived in Mohammedan countries, and who profess to have an acquaintance with the

Islam and Race Distinctions.

literature of Islam. Major Osborn does not seem to have come within the influence of "the education of two centuries." He repeats, with the credulity and confidence of those who have gathered their information mainly from Gibbon and Prideaux, the opinions entertained of Islam in the Middle Ages. So far as he is concerned, the labours of Sprenger, Muir, Deutsch, and the host of recent investigators, seem to have been in vain. This, however, he warns us in his preface, is no fault of his, but a "misfortune inseparable from writing history in a remote country like India." The following summary may be given of the system of Islam as it is described in Major Osborn's pages: Its creed is a bald monotheism, absolute and unchanging decrees, introduced by a prophet who felt it to be his Divine mission to exterminate all professors of a religion different from his; a Hell of material fire depicted with Dantesque realism; a Heaven of sensual indulgences and delights. The ideal man of Islam—the saint of the religion—is he who can say, "There is no God but God, and Mohammed is his Prophet," and who for this creed is ready to sacrifice relatives, friends, country—even life itself. He may be ignorant, treacherous, cruel, sensual, anything, so far as character is concerned, and yet look forward to the highest reward of the faithful. Any and every true and noble element of manhood may be left out, and yet, if faithful to his creed and system, the beautiful houris await him in his paradise above.

Such will be the impressions of the system of Islam which will be gathered from Major Osborn's pages by the majority of uninformed readers; and this is, no doubt, the view entertained of that religion by the generality of Christians. We cannot refrain from pronouncing *Islam under the Arabs*, so far as its theological aspects are concerned, a retrogression in Oriental literature. It does not come up to the standard which the critical and historical power of the age—the extension of thought and information on Oriental subjects—now require. Major Osborn surely cannot believe that the representations which he makes of Islam will further the objects he has in view. The natives of India are, no doubt, gratified by seeing foreigners—especially the foreigners who rule over them

—take a lively interest in their religion, literature, and antiquities, in "the memories which still thrill them with pleasure or pride." But to treat these subjects profitably, to make the knowledge of them "a potent magnet for winning the hearts of the native soldiers," a little more is needed than mere reading and superficial observation; the writer must possess, in no small degree, that quality which Mr. Gifford Palgrave, in the dedication of his *Essays on Eastern Questions* to the Earl of Derby, recognised as marking the foreign policy of that distinguished statesman, namely, "a statesmanlike insight into character and race," a quality which both by experience and observation, Mr. Palgrave must have found to be very rare among his countrymen.

We will now give a few specimens of the results of Major Osborn's reading and observation. He tells us on pp. 26 and 301:

Fatalism is the central tenet of Islam. In the Koran, the root conception is the idea of God as an immovable fatality. This is the tenet that has been burned indelibly into the heart and brain of the Mohammedan world. And, under its withering shadow, the idea of "order" has been unable to strike root downwards or bear fruit upwards.

And yet Major Osborn, on p. 70, mentions prayer as one of the "five pillars" on which the religion of Islam is sustained. What where the utility of prayer in a system which regarded the object of it as inflexible and inexorable—"an immovable fatality"? But how do the following passages from the Koran agree with Major Osborn's idea of the Mohammedan's God?

Whoever shall turn him to God after his wickedness, and amend, God truly will be turned to him; for God is "forgiving and merciful."—(Sura v, v. 43) *Rodwell's Translation*, p. 638.

Your Lord hath laid down for Himself a law of mercy; so that if any one of you commit a fault through ignorance, and afterwards turn and amend, He will surely be gracious, merciful.—(Sura vi, v. 54) *Rodwell*, p. 406.

Then was He turned to them, that they might be turned to Him, for God is He that turneth, the Merciful.—*Rodwell*, p. 629.

Know they not that when His servants turn to Him with repentance, God accepteth it, and that He accepteth alms, and that God is He who turneth, the Merciful?—*Rodwell*, p. 626.

God turned to him, for He loveth to turn, the Merciful.—*Rodwell*, p. 483.

But as for those who turn to Me, and amend and make known the truth, even unto them will I turn Me, for I am He who turneth, the Merciful.—*Rodwell*, p. 451.

Islam and Race Distinctions.

We might adduce numerous other passages which prove the absolute fallacy of the notion that Fatalism is a doctrine of the Koran; it teaches the very contrary doctrine. "Mohammed's whole system," says Mr. Deutsch, "is one of faith built on hope and fear."

The following is the estimate which Major Osborn has formed of the founder of Islam (p. 91) :—

At Medina, the religious teacher is superseded by the ambitious politician, and the idols of the Kaaba fall before the mandate of the successful chieftain, not under the transforming influences of a spiritual regenerator. To achieve worldly dominion, he has recourse to assassination; he perpetrates massacre; he makes a Heathen superstition the keystone of his faith; and delivers to his followers, as a revelation from God, a mandate of universal War. With every advance in wordly power he disencumbers himself of that spiritual humility which was a part of his earlier faith. *He associates himself with God on a footing approaching to equality.*

The italics are ours. We have emphasised the passage because of the shocking impiety which such a notion would convey to the most undevout Muslim; and we cannot conceive it possible that Major Osborn could be ignorant of this. We would commend to him the following philosophical and accurate view of M. Barthélemy St. Hilaire :—

On n'a point remarqué suffisamment cette circonstance dans la carrière de Mahomet. Oui, personnellement il s'est cru prophète; il a cru de toute l'impétuosité de son âme à sa mission, et il a eu raison de se prendre parmi ces peuples barbares pour un instrument de Dieu. Mais ce n'est pas sa volonté propre, ce n'est pas la convoitise de son ambition qui en a fait un général et un conquérant. Des événements extérieurs plus forts que lui, et qu'il ne pouvait prévoir, l'ont précipité. Il s'est trouvé sans le savoir, sans le vouloir, le plus grand homme de guerre de son pays, le politique le plus habile, et il a fondé un empire presque malgré lui. . . . Le Coran, qui révèle toute la pensée morale de Mahomet, ne porte pas trace, pour ainsi dire, d'une pensée politique. . . . Et il faut l'imagination d'un poëte tel que Voltaire pour lui prêter, a mille ans de distance, des desseins qu'il n'a conçus.[13]

But we can refer to Mohammed's own utterances, as recorded in the authorised traditions. The Prophet said :—

I am no more than a man; when I order you anything respecting religion

---

[13] *Mahomet et le Coran;* preface.

receive it; and when I order you about the affairs of this world, then I am nothing more than a man.[14]

Again, Major Osborn gives us the following dissertation on the Jihâad :—

> The one common duty laid upon the faithful is to be the agents of God's vengeance on those who believe not. These are to be slaughtered till they pay tribute, when they are to be allowed to go to hell in their own way without further molestation. . . . When Mohammed interdicted the faithful to prey upon each other, he was compelled to find occupation for their swords elsewhere. Out of this necessity sprang the command to inherit heaven by fighting on the path of God. This is the doctrine which has rendered Islam so fascinating a faith to savage and barbarous races. It exacts from them no endeavours after a higher life. It tells them that they can win an immortality of sensual bliss by merely giving free scope to their most imperious passions. . . . The Mohammedan still conceives himself to be the elect of God. He regards not with compassion—that word is too humane—but with contempt unspeakable, as "logs" reserved for "hell fire," the votaries of all other creeds. Wherever he has the power, he holds it to be his mission to trample upon and persecute them.
>
> The ninth sura is that which contains the Prophet's proclamation of war against the votaries of all creeds other than that of Islam.—Pp. 27, 52, 290, 380.

The ninth sura of the Koran contains no such proclamation. Even Mr. Rodwell's translation, upon which Major Osborn relies, does not justify such inference. Those against whom war is declared in that chapter are described in the original as *Mushrikun*—a term in which the radical idea is that of association—the associating one thing with another—and it cannot in strictness be rendered by the comprehensive phrase of "Polytheists," employed by Rodwell, or of "Idolaters," as used by Sale. The sura is addressed to Arabs who believed in and worshipped only the true God, and refers to the treatment to be accorded by them to those Arabs who joined the worship of idols with that of the true God, as Mr. Rodwell explains in a parenthesis in the first verse. In the opening sentences of his book Major Osborn truly says :—

> There is one remarkable assumption that runs through all the warnings, denunciations and appeals of the Koran. The God of whom the Prophet speaks is not an unknown God. The guilt of his fellow-tribesmen, the justification of their impending doom, are deduced from the fact that they did know this God, while they honoured dumb idols.

---

[14] *Mishkat-al-Masabih*, vol. i, p. 46.

Islam and Race Distinctions.

It is strange that, with knowledge so clear and accurate, Major Osborn should have failed to catch the real drift of the ninth sura of the Koran. Nowhere in the Koran are Muslims enjoined to make indiscriminate war upon Christians or Jews. On the contrary, there are numerous passages that inculcate an enlightened tolerance, which writers of the temper of Major Osborn would do well to emulate. The following are among the Koranic utterances on this important subject:—

> Dispute not, unless in kindly sort, with the people of the Book; save with such of them as have dealt wrongfully with you: And say ye, " We believe in what hath been sent down to us, and hath been sent down to you. Our God and your God is one."—*Rodwell*, p. 328.
>
> God is your Lord and our Lord; we have our works and you have your works; between us and you let there be no strife; God will make us all one; and to Him shall we return.—*Rodwell*, p. 337.
>
> Among the people of the Book are those who believe in God, and in what He hath sent down to you, and in what He hath sent down to them, humbling themselves before God.—*Rodwell*, p. 521.
>
> Verily Muslims and they who follow the Jewish religion, and the Christians, and Sabeites[15]—whoever of these believeth in God, and the Last Day, and doeth that which is right, shall have their reward with their Lord; fear shall not come upon them, neither shall they be grieved.—*Ib.*, p. 437.

There is nothing in the original teachings of the Mohammedan religion that requires hostility to Christians. There are, no doubt, bigots and fanatics among Muslims, as there have been and are now, bigots and fanatics among Christians; but the spirit of the religion, as taught in its original records, is tolerant. And here we cannot but protest against the unwarrantable emphasis with which Christians generally persist in calling themselves "Infidels" when professing to represent the light in which they are held by Muslims. No such term is ever applied to Christians either in the Koran or by intelligent Mohammedans. And for Christian controversialists to insist upon such a use of it is only to foster prejudices which, in this enlightened age, ought to be entirely eliminated from the popular instincts of Christian countries.

---

[15] The Sabeites are identical with the Mendaites, or so-called Christians of St. John, residing in the marshy district at the mouth of the Euphrates, but are not the same with star-worshipping Sabians of Harran, in Mesopotamia.—*Rodwell* (*Note*).

Christianity, Islam and the Negro Race.

Under the Moorish Governments of Spain, when Islam enjoyed political ascendency, the large masses of native Christians were protected by a wide toleration, not as a political expedient, but according to the laws of Islam. The Christians were permitted to have their bishops, churches and monasteries, and to be judged by their own laws and tribunals, whenever the question at issue was one that related only to themselves.[16]

But we can refer to modern instances of more immediate interest to the British public, and bearing directly upon the objects which Major Osborn has in view. During the startling crisis through which the British Indian Empire passed about twenty years ago, many and touching were the illustrations of Mohammedan toleration and friendship towards Christians, which it is singular that a man of Major Osborn's profession should so soon have forgotten.

From the outbreak to the suppression of the Mutiny, and from one end of India to the other, thousands upon thousands of Mohammedans, high and low, rich and poor, princes and servants, soldiers and civilians, not only refrained from lifting a finger against the British Government or any Christian individual, but rendered active and most useful service—at the hazard often of their lives and fortunes—to both it and them. Of native princes, the Nawab of Rampore—a Mohammedan of the Mohammedans—and the Begum of Bhopal, were not merely faithful but signally helpful. The Nawab of Tonk, son of the celebrated Ameer Khan, a formidable leader in the Pindaree war, who probably ruled over more Mohammedan fanatics than any prince in India, stood by the British Government with exemplary firmness.[17]

"In a word," says the *Saturday Review*, at the close of an interesting article on Sir Salar Jung (May 27, 1876), "our new guest is the man who, when Delhi had fallen and our power was for the moment tottering in the balance, saved Southern India for England. Sir Salar Jung spared us the expenditure of countless lives and countless millions;" and furnishes in himself, the reviewer might have added, the practical evidence that a Mohammedan may become an effective reformer without abdicating his faith.

In the face of these facts, and with his knowledge of the

---

[16] Ticknor's *History of Spanish Literature*, vol. iii, p. 460.
[17] *Edinburgh Review*, October, 1886, p. 808.

Islam and Race Distinctions.

teachings and spirit of his religion, what must be the feelings of Sir Salar Jung when he reads a work of the temper of *Islam under the Arabs*, in which the author, a British officer of some experience in Mohammedan countries, shows that he not only shares, but is willing to reproduce in elaborate pages, the vulgar estimate held in Christian lands of the Mohammedan religion.

We had marked several other passages in Major Osborn's book for remark, but the want of space compels us to turn to the deeply-interesting and valuable work which, we are happy to say, furnishes a full and complete reply to the principal charges, and gives ample correction to all the erroneous statements and inferences of *Islam under the Arabs*.

Mohammed and Mohammedanism is the second enlarged and revised edition of a course of lectures delivered at the Royal Institution in 1874. The following remarks in the preface to the second edition reveal the lofty aim and eminently catholic spirit of the writer, but can give no adequate clue to the charming style of the composition—the transparent clearness, the vigour, the glowing enthusiasm, with which the subject is handled:—

> To denounce fundamental conditions of Oriental society; to ignore the law of dissolution, to which Eastern no less than Western dynasties are subject; to confuse the decadence of a race with that of a creed; to be blind to the distinction between progressive and unprogressive, between civilised and uncivilised peoples; to judge of a religion mainly or exclusively by the lives of its professors, often of its most unworthy professors; to forget what of good there has been in the past, and to refuse to hope for something better in the future, in despair or indignation for what is—all this may occasionally be excusable, or possibly even necessary; but it cannot be done by me so long as I think it neither excusable nor necessary.

It is a very easy task, and, no doubt, in entire keeping with the feelings of the dominant race, to show the faults committed at different times and in different countries by Mohammedan rulers, in entire obliviousness of the parallel which might, in almost every instance, be adduced from Christian history. But the careful and philosophical historian performs a far more agreeable task to himself, and possibly more profitable to his readers, when he dwells on the acts of philanthropy and heroism, the achievements in literature and science, which, for five hundred years, attended the progress of Islam; and this pleasant task Mr. Bosworth Smith has not only taken upon himself, but has executed in the most admirable manner. If we had any control in the matter we should arrange that an earnest inquirer into the history and principles of Islam should first give to Major Osborn's work, when the series is completed, a careful perusal, and then take up Mr. Smith's book, both as the complement and expounder of the facts collected by Major Osborn.

The influence of race in the matter of religion does not seem to be taken into consideration by the generality of writers on such subjects. To this important element in the development of religious systems Mr. Bosworth Smith frequently calls attention. While it is known that the Christian system has received large modifications as to outward form and expression, and even as to some of its dogmas, from the influence of country and race, it is too generally taken for granted that Islam is a rigidly uniform system; that Mohammedans are all alike, and that the Turk is the type and representative of the whole Muslim world. But nothing could be more erroneous. Says Mr. Smith:—

> The Persians are of a race and genius widely different from the Arabs; but the surroundings and general mode of life are the same in each, and the exception—so far as it is an exception—to the rule I have laid down, tends rather, in its results, to prove its general truth, for the hold of Mohammedanism on them has been much modified by the difference of race. . . . . It cannot be said that the religion proved itself altogether suited to the people. In other countries the scymitar had no sooner been drawn from its scabbard than it was sheathed again. But in Persia the scymitar had not only to clear the way, but for some time afterwards, to maintain the new religion. The Persians corrupted its simplicity with fables and miracles; they actually imported into it something of saint-worship, and something of sacerdotalism; and, consequently, in no nation in the Mohammedan world has the religion less hold on the people as a restraining power. The most stringent principles of the Koran are set at nought.

Mr. Matthew Arnold, following Gobineau, has suggested that the division of the Muslim world into the two great sects of Shiahs and Sunis has its true cause in a division of races rather than in a difference of religious belief.[18] Islam, among the Indo-European

---

[18] *Essays on Criticism*, p. 298.

Islam and Race Distinctions.

races, as in Turkey, Persia and India, is quite different from what it is among the Semitic and semi-Semitic races in Arabia and Africa.

Mr. Gladstone, in his recent pamphlet on the Turkish Question, puts forward the following thoughtful and suggestive paragraph:—

> It is not a question of Mohammedanism simply, but of Mohammedanism compounded with the peculiar character of a race. They are not the mild Mohammedans of India, nor the chivalrous Saladins of Syria, nor the cultured Moors of Spain. They were, upon the whole, from the black day when they first entered Europe, the one great anti-human specimen of humanity. Wherever they went, a broad line of blood marked the tract behind them; and, as far as their dominion reached, civilisation disappeared from view. They represented everywhere government by force, as opposed to government by law.

So far as India is concerned—the country which Major Osborn hopes will be favourably affected by the work he has written—there seems to be very little probability that Christianity, as disseminated by Europeans, will ever secure the ascendency over tribal or national life which either Buddhism or Mohammedanism has attained. The achievements of the Christian religion thus far have been chiefly among the lower classes, who, as in all other countries, having nothing to lose, readily accept revolutionary changes in their politics or religion.

One of the most thoughtful and appreciative observers of the results of Christian Missions in India, in a most elaborate article, which has attracted considerable attention on both sides of the Atlantic, refers to the present status of Christian converts in the following terms:—

> We regard with special interest, but also with special anxiety, the progress which the native Church that has been planted in some districts in India is making towards maturity. It is already distinguished for docility and liberality; but we should wish to see it, on the one hand, freer from inherited faults and failings, and, on the other, more self-reliant, more progressive, more comprehensive, extending with equal zeal and rapidity amongst the higher and the lower classes. At present too large a proportion of the native converts belong to the lower classes and the aboriginal tribes..... When Hindus have become Christians, they have not at the same time become English people, and that means a great deal. It means they have not ceased to be timid, and they have not become self-reliant, highspirited, and manly.[10]

---

[10] *Quarterly Review*, April, 1875.

Christianity, Islam and the Negro Race.

The *rationale* of this state of things is given by Mr. Bosworth Smith as follows:—

In India Mohammedans make converts by hundreds from among the Hindus, while Christians with difficulty make ten; and this, partly at least, because they receive their converts on terms of entire social equality, while Europeans, in spite of all the efforts of missionaries to the contrary, seem either unwilling or unable to treat their converts as other than inferiors. The Hindu who becomes a Christian loses, therefore, his own cherished caste without being admitted into that of his rulers. The Hindu who turns Mohammedan loses his narrow caste, but he becomes a member of the brotherhood of Islam.

If a pariah becomes a Muslim he may rise to the throne. The pariah who turns Christian is a pariah still.

An able and liberal writer in the *Quarterly* endorses this sad view of things. He says:—

A considerable portion of the prejudice with which native Christians are often regarded is owing, we believe, to pride of race. If caste pride prevails largely amongst natives, pride of race prevails quite as largely amongst Europeans. Many of the English in India regard all natives with indiscriminate aversion.

The only Christian effort or quasi-Christian effort which seems to make any way among the higher classes is that inaugurated by Keshub Chunder Sen, but it would seem that his efforts do not find much favour in the eyes of the missionaries, who "feel towards him as Athanasius might have felt towards Ulfilas, the Arian Bishop of the Goths."[20]

Major Osborn no doubt gives a correct account of the results thus far achieved by British rule in India in the following vigorous passage:—

What we have done for India is to convert it into a gigantic model prison. The discipline we have established is admirable, but the people know they are prisoners, and they hate us their jailers. And until a prison is found to be an effective school for the inculcation of virtue, and a jailor a successful evangelist, it is folly to expect the regeneration of India. Reports on her material and moral progress will, of course, continue to be written; but if we estimate the effects of British rule, not by trade statistics, but by its *results on the spirits of men*, we shall find that the races of India have declined in courage and manliness, and all those qualities which produce a vigorous nation, in proportion to the period they have been subjected to the blighting influence of an alien despotism. There is no human power which can avail to arrest the progress of decay in a people bereft of political freedom, except the restitution of that freedom. This

---

[20] Müller's *Chips*, vol. iv, p. 274.

Islam and Race Distinctions.

sentence of doom glares forth from the records of all past history, like the writing of fire on the wall of Belshazzar's palace. It is an hallucination to suppose that British rule in India is a reversal of the inexorable decree.

Strange that one thus capable of appreciating the situation did not strive, by making more adequate preparation for the work he undertook, to do justice to the creed of so large a portion of his fellow-subjects, and thus, as far as in him lay, to diminish by literary tact and fairness the bitterness of grievances, which he admits to be real, but which he alleges can never be removed by the present social and political agencies!

We think we can understand, however, how difficult it must be for a member of the conquering race, especially one of Major Osborn's calling, to entertain any practical sympathy with the feelings and aspirations of the subject race. It would seem that the very qualities which render Anglo-Saxons irresistible as conquerors—that unrelenting sternness and uncompromising hardness—disqualify them for the subtle and delicate task of assimilating subject races and winning their confidence and affection.

Such a work as Major Osborn has proposed to write is no doubt greatly needed; but, until either he himself, or someone else of similar literary aspirations, and at his point of influence, conceives the proper spirit and method which should be brought to the execution of so important a task, we must recommend British officers and intelligent Mohammedans in India to study the valuable work of Mr. Bosworth Smith as a natural and genuine product of the advancing civilisation of the age, supplying at once an interesting illustration of the liberal and tolerant spirit of Christianity, and a most effective agency in the noble work of bringing about that mutual understanding and goodwill, which it would appear is more needed in India than in any other country in the world, between the comparatively small numbers who govern and the millions over whom it is their lot to bear rule.

Africa and the Africans.

THE abolition of slavery in the United States was not an isolated phenomenon. It was an important link in the great chain of events which are leading up to the regeneration of Africa. A Negro writer of the present day on Africa and African questions, therefore, can neither forget American slavery nor the great American Emancipation. He must, ever and anon, like the manumitted Hebrews of old, recall the " house of bondage," not only as the *fons et origo malorum* to a large portion of his race, but as the type and representative of all the oppression which has everywhere afflicted the Negro in the countries of his exile. He must also remember the great deliverance, when the door of his prison-house was forcibly opened, and five millions of his race marched out into the open air of personal freedom, not only as the starting point for a large section of his people on a loftier and nobler career, but as an important step towards the amelioration and reconstruction of his fatherland—as Heaven's intervention in the solution of a great and intricate problem as the pledge and proof of God's providential care and beneficent purposes for Africa and the African.

Before the abolition of slavery in the United States, it was generally taken for granted that, as things had been, so far as the Negro was concerned, so they would continue to be; that there was no other destiny for Africa than to be the hunting-ground for unprincipled men of all other countries, and no other destiny for the Negro than to continue in servitude to the man-hunters and their abettors. And many an intelligent Christian thought he saw in the Bible a clear warrant for this view.

Africa and the Africans.

But hardly had the Negro come out of the house of bondage in America, when traditional views on the subject of his destiny began to fade away among the unwholesome superstitions of the past. Events began to turn attention to his ancestral home. The emancipation of millions of people of a foreign and uncongenial race, in a country governed by republican institutions, could not but awaken serious reflections in the minds of the thoughtful. Here was a new problem for solution, and one which, to the minds of many, presented terrible contingencies. They could not conceive of five millions of blacks living among thirty millions of whites in any other relation than that of servitude, especially when servitude had been the uniform antecedent relation. But that relation had been abruptly severed. The five millions of slaves were now free men.

There were several proposals made for the disposition of this unwelcome and inconvenient element. Many thought that they should be sent to the Great West, and be formed into a "territory" of the United States. Others held that they should be absorbed into the body politic under reconstruction laws. Others proposed their concentration as free men and independent in the Gulf States. Not a few advocated their deportation to the West Indies, or Central America. A small number contended that an endeavour should be made to return them to the land of their fathers. For several years, this last proposition was ridiculed and contemned, but it could not long be suppressed. It was founded upon a principle inherent in humanity. It appealed to the irresistible instincts and sympathy of race, and it has recently gained an immense popularity among the blacks. Organisations for emigration to Africa, called "Exodus Associations," are being formed among them. While we write this, we learn that near two hundred thousand are ready to leave for Africa. Those of the Negroes in the United States who comprehend this movement and aid it, and avail themselves of it, will be elevated, and will save their posterity from perpetual degradation, or, possibly, extinction. Those who ignore it, and fight against it, will be baffled and thwarted in all their attempts at elevation in the land of their former oppressors, if they are not altogether crushed by the odds against them. This is the teaching of all history.

In the meanwhile, events have been co-operating for the opening of Africa. Scarcely had the emancipation proclamation been promulgated, when Livingstone disappeared from the civilised world, and lost himself in the wilds of Africa, just as the intensest interest had been excited in the work of exploration which, as an humble missionary, he had begun. In attempts to ascertain the whereabouts of the lost traveller, more and more of the country was revealed to the outside world; and in the fifteen years which have elapsed since the abolition of slavery in America, more has been learned of Africa by the civilised world than was ever previously known. Explorers from all the leading nations are entering the country from every quarter. One of the Sovereigns of Europe turns aside from the cares of State, and from the great questions now interesting Europe, to give his personal influence to stimulate the work of African exploration and civilisation. The Royal Geographical Society has shown its increased interest and determination in the matter, by instituting an "African Exploration Fund," to be appropriated "to the scientific examination of Africa (especially the central part of the continent), in a systematic and organised manner."[1] A proposition has been laid before the American Congress for a preliminary survey of the countries east of Liberia, with a view to the construction of a railroad from Monrovia to Central Africa. In Africa itself, magnificence and beauty are being disclosed where the most forbidding natural features were expected. More than a dozen lakes have been discovered in regions formerly supposed to contain only "trackless deserts of shifting sand." The continent has been crossed from east to west by youthful and enthusiastic explorers. So that the exiled African, returning to the land of his ancestors, will not be journeying to a country of which he has no knowledge. The general ignorance of this continent, which only a few years ago prevailed, when it used to be said that "our maps of the moon

---

[1] Circular issued by the Royal Geographical Society, 1877.

Africa and the Africans.

were more correct and complete than those of interior Africa," can never again exist.

But, while every effort is made to explore and describe the country, very little attempt is made to study the man of Africa. It is very natural that adventurous travellers should deem it the most important part of their mission to describe the country, to spend their time in telling of what the outside world is consciously and confessedly ignorant, and of which, therefore, there is the greatest anxiety to gather information. The geographical problem presses for solution. As to the Man, there is not this anxiety. The outside world thinks it knows the Man of Africa. Has not the Negro been seen as a labourer in every part of the world? Has he not for centuries been on the plantations in all the Western hemisphere? Have not numerous travellers written about him, and has he not been minutely described by scientific men, from his skull to his heels? But it is beginning to be apprehended now by the more thoughtful, that, after all, the Man of Africa is not understood. There is now more thinking, writing, learning, and talking about Africa than ever before. Still the notions of Europeans are extremely vague about the Man. On two points only they seem to be clear, viz., first, as to the irrepressible or inextinguishable character of the Man—that he will not fade away or become extinct before Europeans, as the American and Australian aborigines have done; and, secondly, that in any calculations looking to the material improvement or aggrandisement of his native home, he cannot be wisely ignored. Further than this, all is dark to the European mind. Only the Negro will be able to explain the Negro to the rest of mankind.

We have travellers in Africa belonging to all the principal nations of the world, and all, in a greater or less degree, indulge in strains of disparagement of the Man. And this not as a rule, and not even generally, from a desire to be unfair, but partly from preconceived notions of the Negro, imbibed from reading or hearsay in the course of their preparation for their journey; partly from the influence of their atmospheric surroundings in the field of their investigations; and partly, also, on the principle that it is easier to pull down than to build up; and that there is a sort of fame attached to the great destroyer. The names of the builders of mighty pyramids may be forgotten with the ages, while the name of the destroyer of a magnificent temple has lingered in the memory of generations.

There is no possibility of entering Africa, either from the east or west, without passing through a belt of malarious country by which the strongest constitutions are affected. A pernicious miasma receives strangers at the threshold of the continent. Their whole nervous system becomes disordered—the action of the liver is deranged. They become the prey of melancholy in its literal, etymological sense, and in this abnormal state of mental impressibility they take the most gloomy views of the people, and reproduce their own preconceived or favourite types of the African. In a letter to the *New York Herald*, Dr. Livingstone says:—

> The irritability produced by disease made me pigheaded. The same cause operates with modern travellers, so that they are unable to say a civil word about the natives. Savages seldom deceive you, if put upon their honour; yet men turn up the whites of their eyes, as if deception showed an anomalous character in the African. Modern travellers affect a tone of moral superiority that is nauseous.

And in his works he frequently warns the reader against accepting, without qualification, the statements of some African travellers about the natives. Dr. Johnson says, "Every man is a rascal as soon as he is sick."

While, therefore, we duly appreciate the geographical or material results of the labours of modern explorers of Africa; while we cannot but admire their gigantic physical and moral courage, the inextinguishable faith in themselves and their destiny which sustained them in their perilous labours, we cannot admit that the philosophical results of their efforts have been satisfactory. When they attempt to transcend the physical or material, there is contradiction and confusion. There is want of clearness in the pictures they draw; and the most skilful and accurate delineator has succeeded in producing but clumsy daguerreotypes or distorted photographs of the superficial life of the people. The European world is, as yet, only in the infancy of its studies in African psychology.

Africa and the Africans.

No European statesman or philanthropist has, as yet, even attempted to grapple with it. Far more difficult of settlement than the sources of the Nile, the intellectual character and susceptibility of the Negro will probably, for ages yet, elude the grasp and comprehension of the most sagacious European. Livingstone was the first of modern Europeans to approach the source of the Nile and indicate its locality; so, likewise, he has come nearer than any other European to understanding the Man of Africa. And, like all true philosophers, he never dogmatises as to the results of his investigations in that direction. He of all travellers made the Man an object of his study, and the benefit of the man the ultimate aim of his labours. "When one travels," he said, "with the specific object in view of ameliorating the condition of the natives, every act becomes ennobled."[2]

In his letter to James Gordon Bennett, under date November, 1871, he says: "If my disclosures regarding the terrible Ujijian slavery should lead to the suppression of the East Coast slave trade, I shall regard that as a greater matter by far than the discovery of all the Nile sources together."

The African is now judged by the specimens in exile and along a coast—more spoilt and debauched than benefited by foreign intercourse—just as the physical character of the interior was inferred, in former times, from the lowlands and swamps seen along the margin of the continent. No Roderick Murchison has arisen yet in the intellectual world to lay down with any definiteness the character of the mental landscape of the Negro. No Professor Hall has yet descried the remote satellite of his genius. Livingstone has come the nearest to fulfilling the office of such a philosopher. He had the first and most important pre-requisite to proficiency in that class of study, viz., sympathy with his subject. He not only loved Africa, but the African. He had an instinctive appreciation of the peculiarities and varieties of African character, and so remarkable a power of blending his observations into a harmonious whole, that he was able, in no little degree, to

---

[2] *Last Journals*, vol. i, p. 18.

emancipate himself, notwithstanding his physical sufferings, from the trammels of his race-prejudices, and with that insight and discrimination which a correct sympathy gives, to select the materials for his delineation of African character—dealing with Africans not only in their abnormal and degraded forms, upon which most travellers love to dwell, but studying the deeper aspects and finer capacities of the people. He has thus become the popular and most trustworthy teacher of the best portion of the Christian world with regard to the African.

Nearly all other modern travellers have regarded the Man of Africa with contempt, in comparison with the natural features—the physical grandeur and material resources—of the country. *Solum melius populo.* Mr. Herbert Spencer, with the aid of his friends, has prepared a basis for a work on African Sociology, in the shape of a classified compilation of materials taken from the works of writers on Africa. But as his facts have been drawn so largely from second-hand sources, and from the writings of travellers whose observations were confined to very small localities, and made under the disturbing influence of disease, we cannot expect that the work, when completed, though it will be one of considerable merit and a monument of industry, will be a trustworthy guide. The author will have relied, to a very large extent, upon isolated cases and *ex parte* statements.

It has been to us a source of surprise and regret to notice that the *Westminster Review*, usually so fair and candid in dealing with the Negro, should have allowed itself—chiefly under the guidance of Sir Samuel Baker—to carry on a discussion on Africa and the African in the spirit and temper manifested in its article on 'Slavery in Africa' (April, 1877). The Reviewer endorses as correct the superficial and contemptuous estimate of Negro character as given by Sir Samuel Baker. With the writings of Livingstone before him, and with numerous admissions in favour of the African from Sir Samuel Baker himself, the Reviewer yet makes every available use of Baker's works, not to accept his liberality, but to emphasise the suggestions of what we cannot but characterise as his inveterate prejudices.

Africa and the Africans.

The intelligent Negro traveller in foreign lands comes across four classes of Europeans. First, the class who are professionally philanthropic. These, at the sight of the Negro, go into ecstasies over this "man and brother," and put themselves to all sorts of inconvenience to prove to this unfortunate member of the human race that they believe God hath made of one blood all nations of men, &c. The second class is composed of those who, at the sight of the Negro, have all their feelings of malice, hatred, and all uncharitableness excited, and who adopt every expedient and avail themselves of every occasion to give exhibitions of their vehement antagonism. The third class regard him with contemptuous indifference, and care to exhibit neither favour nor dislike, whatever his merit or demerit. The fourth class consists of those who treat him as they would a white man of the same degree of culture and behaviour, basing their demeanour altogether upon the intellectual or moral qualities of the man. To the cultivated Negro, of course, the last class is the most interesting to meet, and if he had his choice between classes first and second, he would choose the second. Writers on Africa and the African race may be divided into very much the same classes; and the race has scarcely suffered more from the violent antagonism of its foes than from the false and undue admiration of its friends.

Before pointing out some of the errors of the *Westminster Reviewer*, we will take a brief survey of the past and present history of the African slave trade, and see how far it has introduced waste and disorder into Africa, and prevented the progress of the people. Of course we have no detailed account of the proceedings of the slave-hunters who captured the unfortunate creatures represented on Egyptian monuments; but we have pretty full accounts of the origin and character of the modern slave trade, and we give here a summary from an able and well-informed source:—

> Within two centuries after the suppression of slavery in Europe, the Portuguese, in imitation of those piracies which existed in the uncivilised ages of the world, made their descents on Africa, and committing depredations on the coast, first carried the wretched inhabitants into slavery. This practice, thus inconsiderable at its commencement, became general, and our ancestors, together with Spaniards, French, and most of the maritime powers of Europe,

Christianity, Islam and the Negro Race.

soon followed the piratical example; and thus did the Europeans revive a custom which their own ancestors had so lately exploded from a consciousness of its impiety. The unfortunate Africans fled from the coast, and sought, in the interior parts of the country, a retreat from the persecution of their invaders; but the Europeans still pursued them, entered their rivers, sailed up into the heart of the country, surprised the Africans in their recesses, and carried them into slavery. The next step which the Europeans found it necessary to take was that of settling in the country, of securing themselves by fortified posts, of changing their system of force into that of pretended liberality; and of opening by every species of bribery and corruption a communication with the natives. Accordingly they erected their forts and factories, landed their merchandise, and endeavoured by a peaceful deportment, by presents, and by every appearance of munificence, to allure the attachment and confidence of the Africans. Treaties of peace and commerce were concluded with the chiefs of the country, in which it was agreed that the kings on their part should from this period sentence *prisoners of war* and convicts to European servitude; and that the Europeans should supply them in return with the luxuries of Europe.[8]

Thus began that horrible traffic which for generations has distracted the African continent. The discovery of America stimulated the traffic and intensified its horrors.

Africans were deported to slaughter virgin forests, to test the capability of virgin soils, and to enrich both hemispheres with sugar, tobacco, cotton and wines. And it is due to the terrors of its harbourless coast, the malaria of its mangrove swamps, its burning deserts, its dangerous beasts and reptiles, its impenetrable jungles, its wary tribes prepared either for fight or flight, that Africa was not entirely depopulated to satisfy the greed of Christian nations for slaves, during the last four centuries.

Though, under the pressure of enlightened Christian sentiment, the traffic has been abandoned by Christian nations, still the continent is made to bleed at almost every pore. Notwithstanding all that has been written and said on this subject, those who have seen anything of the horrors of the traffic—which no pen can adequately describe—are solemnly impressed with the necessity of urging continually upon the public mind, with every possible emphasis and reiteration, the importance of its suppression. Livingstone says:—

When endeavouring to give some account of the slave trade of East Africa it was necessary to keep far within the truth, in order not to be thought guilty of exaggeration; but in sober seriousness the subject does not admit of exaggera-

---

[8] *Rees's New Cyclopædia*; art. 'Slavery.'

Africa and the Africans.

tion. To overdraw its evils is a simple impossibility. The sights I have seen, though common incidents of the traffic, are so nauseous, that I always strive to drive them from my memory. In the case of most disagreeable recollections I can succeed, in time, in consigning them to oblivion; but the slaving scenes come back unbidden, and make me start up at dead of night, horrified by their vividness.

Sir Samuel Baker, in his *Albert Nyanza*, describes an attack made upon a village for slaves, as follows:—

Marching through the night, guided by their Negro hosts, they bivouac within an hour's march of the unsuspecting village, doomed to an attack about half an hour before the break of day. Quietly surrounding the sleeping villages, they fire the grass huts in all directions, and pour volleys of musketry through the flaming thatch. Panic-stricken, the unfortunate victims rush from the burning dwellings, the men are shot down like pheasants in a *battue*, while the women and children are kidnapped and secured, the herds of cattle are driven away, and the human victims lashed together, forming a living chain, while a general plunder of the premises ensues.

In his *Ismailia* he say:—

It is impossible to know the actual number of slaves taken from Central Africa annually. . . . . The loss of life attendant upon the capture and subsequent treatment of the slaves is frightful. The result of this forced emigration, combined with the insecurity of life and property, is the withdrawal of the population from the infested districts. The natives have the option of submission to every insult, to the violation of their women and the pillage of their crops, or they must either desert their homes or seek independence in distant districts, or they must ally themselves with their oppressors to assist in the oppression of other tribes. Thus the seeds of anarchy are sown throughout Africa. The result is horrible confusion, distrust on all sides, treachery, devastation and ruin.[4]

Graves and numerous skeletons (says Cameron) testified to the numbers whose lives had been sacrificed on this trying march, whilst slave-clogs and forks still attached to some bleached bones, or lying by their side, gave only too convincing a proof that the demon of the slave trade still exerted his influence in this part of Africa.[5]

Schweinfurth, the German traveller, who travelled for some time in charge of the Nile slavers, and witnessed their diabolical proceedings, says that the "traders of Darfoor and Kordofan are as coarse, unprincipled, and villainous a set as imagination can conceive."

An avenging Nemesis must surely follow in the footsteps of such unparalleled atrocity and wickedness.

---

[4] *Ismailia*, vol. i, pp. 4, 5. [5] *Across Africa*, vol. ii, p. 256.

Christianity, Islam and the Negro Race.

The *Westminster* Reviewer, with all these facts before him, and after quoting from Livingstone a statement which justly attributes the backward condition of Africans to the disturbing influence of the slave trade, chooses to select the very lowest tribes upon which to make his unfavourable comments, and from which to infer the character of the whole race, and seems to suppose that he has clenched and riveted his disparaging work by introducing the following sketch of the Negro as furnished to his hand by Sir Samuel Baker:—

Negroes seldom think of the future; they cultivate the ground at various seasons, but they limit their crops to their natural wants; therefore an unexpected bad season reduces them to famine. They grow a variety of cereals, which, with a minimum of labour, yield upon their fertile soil a large return. Nothing would be easier than to double the production, but this would entail the necessity of extra store-room, which means extra labour. Thus, with happy indifference, the native thinks lightly of to-morrow. He eats and drinks while his food lasts, and when famine arrives he endeavours to steal from his neighbours . . . nothing is so distasteful to the Negro as regular daily labour, thus nothing that he possesses is durable. His dwelling is of straw or wattles, his crops suffice for support from hand to mouth; and as his forefathers worked only for themselves and not for posterity, so also does the Negro of to-day. Thus, without foreign assistance, the Negro a thousand years hence will be no better than the Negro of to-day, as the Negro of to-day is in no superior position to that of his ancestors some thousand years ago.

Such is the indictment against a whole race drawn by an amateur philanthropist, who only saw portions of the people in one corner of the continent, where, by his own account, they are so harassed and persecuted by the slave-traders that progress is impossible. None more eloquently or truthfully than Sir Samuel Baker has described the horrors of the slave trade and its blighting effects upon the country and people. "What curse," he asks, "lies so heavily upon Africa?" He answers:—

It is the internal traffic in slaves. All idea of commerce, improvement, and the advancement of the African race must be discarded until the traffic in slaves shall have ceased to exist.

In a curious paragraph the Reviewer apparently apologises for the slavers by involving the native chiefs who sell slaves in equal, if not greater, guilt; but in the very next sentence he recovers his mental equilibrium and sense of justice, and tells us of—

Crafty slave-dealers, who, under various pretexts, set chief against chief,

Africa and the Africans.

knowing that whichever wins they will be the gainers, obtaining thereby the numerous slaves they covet.

There is nothing surprising in the fact that, under such circumstances, Africans sell each other. Who was it that sold those Angles whom Gregory saw in the slave-market at Rome? Is it not well known that Saxon husbands and parents sold their wives and daughters? Did not slavery prevail in every country in Europe?

Now, suppose that during the days of European ignorance and darkness, when the people sold their own children, the large alien populations of Asia had agreed to make constant incursions into Europe and stimulate the traffic in slaves. Suppose the result of the battle of Marathon had been different and Europe had become the vassal of Asia, and Asiatic hordes had entered its territory for the purposes for which both Europeans and Asiatics have entered Africa, and had continued their depredations to this period, what would be the condition of Europe to-day?

It cannot have escaped the most superficial reader of African history that the ravages introduced by the slave trade have had a distinctly marked effect not only on the personal or tribal character of the inhabitants, but on their social organisation—on the whole industrial and economic life of the country. Their condition for centuries has been one of restless anarchy and insecurity.

Both Livingstone and Baker describe regions free from the slave trade, where the people were superior and had many of the elements of progress; but they enjoy only a sort of insular immunity with all the disadvantages of such a position. Their dwelling-places are like islands in piratical seas, kept, as it were, constantly under martial law, with the means of defence always carried about or accessible at a moment's notice—forever on the alert to hold their own against the traders who menace them from every quarter. These regions the cowardly marauders avoid. Speaking of the warlike Baris, Sir Samuel Baker says:—

> I discovered that these people had never had any communication with the slave-traders, who were afraid to molest so powerful a tribe.

Mr. Stanley, in his address at Cape Town in November last, when fresh from his great achievement of the discovery of the

Christianity, Islam and the Negro Race.

course of the Lualaba-Congo River, described certain inaccessible localities as follows:—

> I can assure you that on this map—and it will probably be the last part of Africa to be explored—there is a part close to Zanzibar which every expedition takes good care to avoid. It lies between Mombassa and Lake Victoria, and there lives there the ferocious tribe of the Wahomba. An expedition of a thousand men could go there and penetrate the country, but with an ordinary travelling expedition it would be impossible. Then there is the Somab country; I should like to see what travellers would make of that. And there is another district which would tax the skill of the best explorer. From the north end of Lake Tanganyika to the south end of Lake Albert Nyanza there is a pretty and very interesting district, but it is a country where you will have to fight if you want to explore it. Here is another little district close to the West Coast, and yet in two hundred years the Portuguese have been unable to explore it. Between St. Paul and a part called Ambriz, a distance of only sixty miles, there is no communication by land, and yet it is Portuguese territory. There are martial as well as pacific tribes.[o]

Still, formidable as are the "martial" tribes, the exigencies of their condition are a perpetual bar to progress.

> We can scarcely enter into the feelings (says Livingstone) of those who are harried by marauders. Like Scotland in the twelfth and thirteenth centuries, harassed by Highland Celts on one side and English Marchmen on the other, and thus kept in the rearward of civilisation, these people have rest neither for many days nor for few.[7]

The Reviewer, after pulling the Negro down to the lowest possible point in the scale of being, to which Sir Samuel Baker in his aggressive dogmatism and satirical humour has reduced him, suggests the uselessness of endeavouring to educate him, in the ordinary sense and by the ordinary methods, we presume, of European education. He says:—

> That the Negro is not incapable of civilisation, has indeed been proved, yet the testimony of Dr. Livingstone would tend to show that education with the Negro does not necessarily fit him for helping to elevate his race. "Educated blacks from a distance" (says Livingstone) "are to be avoided; they are expensive, and are too much of gentlemen for your work."

With regard to the character of the "education" which the Negro has received, and is now, as a general thing, receiving from his European teacher, and to the estimate which the Negro, as he rises in civilisation, intelligence, and culture, will put upon that

---

[o] *Times*, November 30, 1877. [7] *Last Journals*, vol. ii, p. 143.

Africa and the Africans.

"education," we venture to refer the Reviewer to articles dealing with this subject in *Fraser's Magazine* for November, 1875, and May and October, 1876.

Then, as if struck by the injustice of his general line of argument, the Reviewer believes himself to have fallen upon instances which must beyond all cavil substantiate his conclusions. He proceeds :—

> If it should be considered unfair to judge of the Negro in his present condition in his native land, ruined and demoralised as it undoubtedly is by the slave trade, no objection can be raised to an inference drawn from his condition as a free man in our colonies, or in those native free states to which he has been consigned by a freedom-loving people. If we look at the present state of Hayti, Sierra Leone, and Liberia, the attempts of the Negro at self-government are not encouraging; these attempts seem generally to end in anarchy, in a burlesque of everything civilised, and constant revolutions.

Then, as if still conscious of the unfairness of his position, the Reviewer adds :—

> It could, perhaps, hardly be otherwise; we can scarcely expect people downtrodden for ages to develop at once, on recovering their freedom, a love of order and an aptitude for civilisation, which have been with us the slow growth of many centuries. All impartial writers are agreed in considering the *sudden* emancipation of the Negro as a great political blunder.

But the evil in so-called Negro civilised communities lies deeper than anything suggested by the Reviewer—deeper than the downtrodden condition for centuries of the people—deeper, far deeper, than their "sudden emancipation."

Among the evils wrought by the slave trade, none has been more damaging to Africa and the Negro race than the promiscuous manner in which the tribes have been thrown together and confounded in the lands of their exile. And in dealing with the Negro question European writers overlook this fact altogether. There are Negroes and Negroes. The numerous tribes inhabiting the vast continent of Africa can no more be regarded as in every respect equal than the numerous peoples of Asia or Europe can be so regarded. There are the same tribal or family varieties among Africans as among Europeans. And the Reviewer does not seem to be ignorant of this. He says :—

> We must not lose sight of the fact that there are many races in Africa—that the typical Negro with prognathous jaw and woolly hair, who has been so

eagerly sought as a slave in all ages, is quite as distinct from the Kaffir, and from many of the races described by travellers in the interior, as from the diminutive Bushman, the feeble remnant of an older race now extinct.

This is true: there are the Foulahs inhabiting the region of the Upper Niger, the Mandingoes, the Housas, the Bornous of Senegambia, the Nubas of the Nile region, of Darfoor and Kordofan, the Ashantees, Fantees, Dahomians, Yorubas, and that whole class of tribes occupying the eastern and middle and western portions of the continent north of the equator. Then there are the tribes of Lower Guinea and Angola, so much ridiculed by Winwood Reade and Monteiro; all these, differing in original bent and traditional instincts, have been carried as slaves to foreign lands and classed as one. And in speaking of them they are frequently characterised in one or two sentences. Now it should be evident that no short description can include all these people; no single definition, however comprehensive, can embrace them all. Yet writers are fond of selecting the prominent traits of single tribes with which they are best acquainted, and applying them to the whole race. So the Reviewer makes a disparaging inference as to the character and capacity of all Africans from the want of success which has attended the efforts of so-called Negro communities in Christian lands, who, under the government of Europeans, show no marked ability; or who, as in the case of Hayti and Liberia, have set up for themselves, as alleged, ill-contrived, unsuitable, or unstable governments.

In the first place, these Negroes, as far as they are purely African, do not represent even the average intellectual or moral qualities of the African at home. The Africans who were carried into slavery were mostly of the lowest orders—of the criminal and servile classes—the latter of whom had lived for generations at home with "half their worth conveyed away," and who, it was not to be supposed, would improve in manly qualities under the circumstances to which they were introduced in foreign lands. Only here and there a leading mind—a real Man—was carried into captivity. And where these did not succumb under the new conditions, and become "the foul hyena's prey," they invariably took prominent positions among their own people. In the United States and the West Indies there were numbers, whose descendants may be seen to this day wearing the mark of superiority, who were neither criminal nor servile in their antecedents. These inspired the respect, confidence and even admiration of the oppressors of their race; and, for their sakes, the dominant class would have made large concessions to the African; but as no rule could be established to meet exceptional cases, they were obliged to deal with all according to the regulations established for the majority.

And where under the lead of the superior few of the race, as in Hayti, or, under the philanthropic suggestions of the benevolent among their oppressors, they are assisted in the establishment of a separate nationality, as in Liberia, still the specific gravity of the majority has a continual tendency to hamper and thwart the efforts of the minority.

There is a perpetual struggle between the very few who are aiming to forward the interests of the many, and the *profanum vulgus*, largely in the majority.

If any cannot imagine such differences between Negroes and Negroes, perhaps their imagination may be stimulated if we call their attention to differences equally marked which grew up between white men and white men in a highly civilised country. Travellers in the Southern States of America, before the abolition of slavery, described two classes of whites—the rich, aristocratic planters, and the poor, mean whites—"white trash" as they were sometimes called. They were described by all writers, especially Mr. Frederick Law Olmstead, as

Loafers, squatters, dwellers in the woods, hangers-on among the cities, amounting to several millions, and forming, in fact, a numerical majority, and about as ignorant, squalid and brutal as could well be imagined. The dislike which the planters felt to the neighbourhood of the poor whites on account of their thievish habits and contagious idleness induced them to buy out the poor whites as fast almost as they settled near them.

Yet these people enjoyed equal social and political rights with the wealthiest or best educated whites. Now, suppose, by some means, the comparatively wealthy few had been reduced to an equal pecuniary condition with the "white trash," the latter retain-

Y

ing the numerical superiority, and they had been required or had undertaken to form an independent state on democratic principles, without extraneous stimulus or repression, what should we naturally expect to be the result?

The cruel accidents of slavery and the slave trade drove all Africans together, and no discrimination was made in the shambles between the Foulah and the Timneh, the Mandingo and the Mendi, the Ashantee and the Fantee, the Eboe and the Congo—between the descendants of nobles and the offspring of slaves, between kings and their subjects—all were placed on the same level, all of black skin and woolly hair were "niggers," chattels, having no rights that their oppressors were bound to respect. And when, by any course of events, these people attempt to exercise independent government, they start in the eyes of the world as Africans, without the fact being taken into consideration that they belong to tribes and families differing widely in degrees of intelligence and capacity, in original bent and susceptibility.

But the laws affecting other portions of humanity are not supposed by certain writers to affect the Negro. He is an exceptional being, made, if not now by the consent of enlightened men for perpetual servitude, at least for the finger of scorn to point at. Learned reviewers, masters of style, and apparently the ablest minds, do not think it an unworthy amusement to rail at the Negro —to make him the object, if not always of energetic vituperation and invective, of satirical humour and practical jokes. In reading through the African experiences of Sir Samuel Baker, as furnished by himself, especially in his *Ismailia*, one cannot help noticing that however panegyrical the terms in which a benefactor may be introduced on the stage, he is never dismissed without whatever shortcomings he may have had being brought into prominence. He is sure not to be let go without a parting touch of satirical disparagement. In describing the departure from Khartoum (February 8, 1870), he says with a sneer, "I had had to embrace the governor, then a *black* pacha, a *rara avis in terris*." This habit of indulging in caricature for the sake of amusement easily leads to a spirit of misrepresentation and calumny.

Africa and the Africans.

In speaking of the love of music for which Africans are everywhere noted, Sir Samuel Baker says, with a touch of exaggeration:—

The natives are passionately fond of music. I believe the safest way to travel in these wild countries would be to play the cornet without ceasing, which could insure a safe passage. A London organ-grinder would march through Central Africa followed by an admiring and enthusiastic crowd, who, if his tunes were lively, would form a dancing escort of most untiring materials. . . . A man who, in full Highland dress, could at any time collect an audience by playing a lively air with the bagpipe, would be regarded with great veneration by the natives, and would be listened to when an archbishop by his side would be totally disregarded.

After quoting this passage, a grave American divine, in an elaborate article on Africa in an American Review, could see nothing from which to infer any noble qualities in the Negro, and could not let the opportunity pass without indulging in the conventional giggle. Continuing Baker's joke, he still further degrades the impression, in order, apparently, to develop the smile into a "broad grin." He says:—

An African's religion finds vent at his heels. Songs and dances form no inconsiderable part of the worship at a Southern coloured camp-meeting. If we were constructing a ritual for the race we should certainly include this Shaker element.[8]

"An African's religion" is inferred from what takes place at "a Southern coloured camp-meeting." "A ritual for the whole race" must "include the Shaker element." We would assure the reverend doctor that such a "ritual" would be an egregious failure. The "Shaker element" prevails chiefly, if not entirely, among Negroes or "coloured" people, who have been trained under the influence of the denomination of which Dr. Wentworth himself is a distinguished ornament. But only a comparatively small number of Africans are shouting Methodists. The greater portion of the race who are not Pagans are either Mohammedans or Roman Catholics, and *their* "religion" does not "find vent at their heels." The traveller in Africa will find himself in need of far more solid acquirements when passing through Mohammedan districts, than the ability to play the cornet, organ, or bagpipe. It is due,

---

[8] *Methodist Quarterly Review* (New York); January, 1876.

however, to the qualities whose presence is implied by the African's love of music that bilious and irritable travellers pass through their country not only with impunity, but receiving the kindest treatment.

> Wo man singt, da lass dich ruhig nieder,
> Böse Menschen haben keine Lieder.

And here we cannot but call attention to a fact which, in the intelligent negro, undermines his admiration of foreign races, viz., that his race, numerically the weakest, has been through the ages selected for oppression and ridicule by the other branches of the human family. If there are, according to the present estimate, twelve hundred millions of human beings upon the earth, two hundred millions of whom are Africans, we have in the treatment which Africans have received from the rest of mankind one of the remarkable illustrations of the advantage the strong are prone to take of the weak. Ten hundred millions against two hundred millions. Ten persecuting, abusing, ridiculing two. And this has been the case in all the ages, ten against two. And yet, men, apparently thoughtful, affect to wonder that Negroes have appeared in all the historic periods as slaves—have been represented on all the monuments of Egypt as carried in chains in triumphal processions.

But in spite of all, the Negro race has yet its part to play—a distinct part—in the history of humanity, and the continent of Africa will be the principal scene of its activity. The mistake which Europeans often make in considering questions of Negro improvement and the future of Africa, is in supposing that the Négro is the European in embryo—in the undeveloped stage—and that when, bye-and-by, he shall enjoy the advantages of civilisation and culture, he will become like the European; in other words, that the Negro is on the same line of progress, in the same groove, with the European, but infinitely in the rear. The *Saturday Review*, not long since, in a remarkable leading article on American politics, in which some curious inaccuracies occurred, made the following statement:—

> On their own continent, Africans seem to be irreclaimable, but after two or three generations of servitude they begin to resemble inferior Europeans. The

Africa and the Africans.

slave trade may perhaps eventually prove to have been the first cause of Negro civilisation. The mimetic instinct of the Negro race tends, like the similar faculty in children, to accelerate the progress of unconscious education.[9]

This view proceeds upon the assumption that the two races are called to the same work and are alike in potentiality and ultimate development, the Negro only needing the element of time, under certain circumstances, to become European. But to our mind it is not a question between the two races of inferiority or superiority. There is no absolute or essential superiority on the one side, nor absolute or essential inferiority on the other side. It is a question of difference of endowment and difference of destiny. No amount of training or culture will make the Negro a European; on the other hand, no lack of training or deficiency of culture will make the European a Negro. The two races are not moving in the same groove, with an immeasurable distance between them, but on parallel lines. They will never meet in the plane of their activities so as to coincide in capacity or performance. They are not *identical*, as some think, but *unequal;* they are *distinct* but equal; an idea that is in no way incompatible with the Scripture truth that God hath made of one blood all nations of men.

> All are architects of Fate,
> Working in these walls of time;
> Some with massive deeds and great,
> Some with ornaments of rhyme.
>
> Nothing useless is, or low;
> Each thing *in its place* is best;
> And what seems but idle show
> Strengthens and supports the rest.[10]

The African at home needs to be surrounded by influences from abroad, not that he may change his nature, but that he may improve his capacity. Hereditary qualities are fundamental, not to be created or replaced by human agencies, but to be assisted and improved. Nature determines the *kind* of tree, environments determine the *quality* and *quantity* of the fruit. We want the eye and ear of the Negro to be trained by culture that he may see

---

[9] *Saturday Review*, March 24, 1877. [10] Longfellow.

more clearly what he does see, and hear more distinctly what he does hear. We want him to be surrounded by influences from abroad to promote the development of his latent powers, and bring the potentiality of his being into practical or actual operation. He has capacities and aptitudes which the world needs, but which it will never enjoy until he is fairly and normally trained. Each race is endowed with peculiar talents, and watchful to the last degree is the great Creator over the individuality, the freedom and independence of each. In the music of the universe each shall give a different sound, but necessary to the grand symphony. There are several sounds not yet brought out, and the feeblest of all is that hitherto produced by the Negro; but only he can furnish it. And when he does furnish it in its fulness and perfection, it will be welcomed with delight by the world.

When the African shall come forward with his peculiar gifts, he will fill a place never before occupied. But he must have a fair opportunity for his development. Misunderstood and often misrepresented even by his best friends, and persecuted and maligned by his enemies, he is, nevertheless, coming forward, gradually rising under the influences of agencies seen and unseen.

It is the fashion of some friends of the African to deplore his past, or lack of a past, and to infer from this fact an "inferior faculty of self-development" in the race.

But, with the facts before us, we cannot admit the fairness of such an inference as these sympathising critics of the race are disposed to draw. No one who has paid any attention to the subject at all will aver that there is any possibility of development without the interference of a higher type of intelligence or energy, which must either come from without or must be assisted by favourable conditions within, in order to become continuous or general. Mr. Stanley, having become, on a second journey through Africa, better acquainted with the people, takes a far more accurate view of them than he was disposed to do when he passed through the country in his hasty and impatient search for Livingstone.

In his address at Cape Town, he endeavoured to show the kinship in habits, propensity and feeling between the

Africa and the Africans.

black man and the white man, illustrating this by several comparisons between Central Africa at present and the Homeric age.[11] And in his address in London, before the Royal Geographical Society, in February last, he remarked: "It has been said that the African is unimprovable and irredeemable; but that I wholly and utterly deny."

It is a fact that a description of the condition of things in portions of Central Africa truthfully given would read like an account of the earlier ages of Greece and Rome. We have ourselves visited remote and sequestered districts about the head-waters of the Niger, where we have found Negro Mohammedan students devoting themselves to literature with an indifference to the outside world which reminded us of the habits of the monks in the middle ages, who, in retirement and seclusion, pursued literature for its own sake;[12] and if the proceedings of chiefs in council which we have witnessed were written down in plain, unadorned style, the account would read like descriptions in Cæsar's Commentaries of the doings of the Celts in the days of their unsophisticated habitudes. Now, if Greeks, Romans, or Celts had been smothered in the cradle of their civilisation by extraneous violence perpetuated to this time, is it unreasonable to suppose that they would be found at this day in much the same condition that Stanley found some of the African tribes? That these tribes have ever advanced so far is astounding, considering what they have had to contend against.

Through the labours of Mr. Herbert Spencer and other thinkers in that line, it has now come to be regarded as an elementary fact among scientific men that societies are determined in their growth by their environment, whether physical or human. "The self-development of a society is limited by its environment." In primitive and rudimentary societies there may occur exceptional cases of individual power, where mental energy may introduce changes and begin improvements; but if surrounding circumstances are hostile, the influence will die with the introducer, and the

---

[11] *Times*, Nov. 30, 1877.

[12] See Barth's *Travels in Central Africa;* vol. iii, p. 373.

improvements will not be perpetuated. We are told by Mr. Spencer that among the Karens "now and then a little Napoleon arises, who subdues a kingdom to himself and builds up an empire.[18] The dynasties, however, *last only with the controlling mind.*" There have been similar experiences in Africa. Changes of vast importance have taken place in the interior as a result of internal activity—of individual intelligence and energy; but instead of being perpetuated, they have been destroyed by the hostile influences from without. Dr. Barth tells of the ruins of the ancient capital of Bornou, Ghasreggomo, about 13° N. lat., 22° E. long., situated in the finest country in Bornou, with a rich alluvial soil; a country which formerly teemed with hundreds of villages and was laid out in cornfields, but which is now (or was when he saw it) almost deserted, and covered with dense forests and impenetrable jungle, and has become the haunt of the monkey and the hog, the elephant and the lion. Barth noticed also the admirable brick structures of the ruins of former towns in this neighbourhood, so much more durable than the frail buildings of the present day. All this is proof that there was a beginning of social advancement and well-being in the days of security; but Negro slaves were wanted for the Caucasians in North Africa and South-eastern Europe; *razzias* were encouraged, the slave-hunting Tawareks invaded the country, and all progress was checked. And this is only one instance out of thousands which might be recited. Thus the African has gone on from generation to generation furnishing, in remote ages, materials to swell the triumphal processions of Egyptian kings, and, in modern times, strong arms for the plantations of the Western hemisphere, and is taunted by his persecutors (and his friends) with his inability to rise against this pressure.

In no part of Central Africa have any human agencies from without exerted any uplifting power; no planetary influences, according to mediæval theory, have operated to produce any variation from the regular type; and, as we have just seen, there is no internal tendency in any individual or race, as a rule, to vary

---

[18] *Principles of Sociology;* p. 485.

from the ancestral organism. Africa needs wholesome interference from without. There has been interference, but it has been for the most part an interference of violence which, through the centuries, has prevented the survival of any variation from the original type, which would have pushed forward improvements in the country. And now that the effort of the enlightened portion of humanity is to suppress the violent interference and introduce agencies for the improvement of the people, it is of the greatest possible importance that the people be understood. From the want of appreciation of their capacities and susceptibilities, innumerable are the theories proposed for the amelioration of their condition, Sir Samuel Baker advocates military discipline. He says:—

> I believe that if it were possible to convert the greater portion of African savages into disciplined soldiers, it would be a most rapid stride toward their future civilisation. A savage who has lead a wild and uncontrolled life must first learn to obey authority before any great improvement can be effected.[14]

He would apply force everywhere. Civilise Africa by force. They must be "regimented" under captains of industry who will compel them to their task. The scourge and the sword must carry out the views which Sir Samuel thinks good. He concludes a glowing account of one of his military expeditions with the following flourish:—

> The Bari war was now over; on every side the natives had been thoroughly subdued.[15]

Subdued! yes, possibly, but not brought over to respect and affection. It is surprising that Sir Samuel Baker should not have been able to see that his proceedings among the Baris, judging from his own "unvarnished tale," were nothing of which to boast. "It is probable," Livingstone generously says, "that actual experience will correct the fancies which he (Sir Samuel) now puts forth as to the proper mode of dealing with Africans."[10] We cannot help feeling that the erroneous theories held by travellers as to the African seduce them often into serious blunders and grievous wrongs, making the nationality and religion they represent an opprobrium, and exposing themselves or their successors to needless peril.

---

[14] *Ismailia;* vol. i, p. 302.   [15] *Ibid.*, vol. ii, p. 428.   [10] *Last Journals*, vol. ii, p. 155.

Christianity, Islam and the Negro Race.

It is owing, in a great measure, to the inadequate theories held by those who undertake to deal with the African, whether as friend or foe, that while in the colonies along the coast European influence and teaching furnish new elements of commercial and religious life, they are helpless to raise the people above the "mimetic" stage, and endow them with creative or reproductive power. What we want is, that the foreign information introduced should properly *educate* the people—that is, should be so assimilated as to develop, and be fertilised by, native energy. We want to see the foreign leaven so introduced as to spread beyond the coast, transcend the malarious regions of the continent, and, taking possession of the healthier and nobler tribes of the interior, leaven the whole lump. In order to bring about these results, those who from abroad assume to be teachers and guides should study the people so as to be able to deal scientifically and not empirically with them. By this we mean that they should study the laws of growth as they affect or pertain to the Negro race. The present practice of the friends of Africa is to frame laws according to their own notions for the government and improvement of this people, whereas God has already enacted the laws governing in these affairs, which laws should be carefully ascertained, interpreted and applied; for until they are found out and conformed to, all labour will be ineffective and resultless. We may be told that this is a very difficult, if not impossible task, for the European to perform, and that it is very far to look ahead to the time when the Negro shall be able to do this work for himself. This may be so; but what we are aiming to show, is, that in this direction, and this direction only, lies the hope of Africa's future. Her ultimate usefulness and happiness will be secured, so far as human instrumentality can bring them about, on this line; and this is a subject to be carefully studied, especially by the missionary, if Christianity is to take root at all in Africa, or to be to the native anything more than a form of words. A little common sense will do more for this country than a great deal of moral preaching and the loftiest philanthropic purpose without that elementary but rare quality.

We do not expect to see this continent, or any large portions of it, under one government, either foreign or indigenous. But we do expect to see, following the extinction of the slave trade, and the introduction from abroad of facilities for internal communication, the increase of intelligence, the development of wealth, and the growth of free principles. We expect to see the native tribes or communities so evenly balanced among themselves as to bury for ever in oblivion even the tradition of tribal or individual aggression, with a public sentiment so elevated and purified that the general sense against wrong or injustice of any kind will preponderate and render impossible the existence of single malefactors who now have it in their power to distract extensive regions and check the operations of husbandry. And we should expect to see in Africa all the progress we have indicated above as the result of a few years of internal tranquility and order, which the continent has *never* within the memory of man enjoyed. There will be an exhibition of virtues not dreamt of in the Caucasian world, a sudden development of energies latent for ages. "Ethiopia shall *suddenly* stretch forth her hands unto God."

Next, then, to the exploration of the country, the most important preliminary to the general civilisation of the African tribes is the suppression of the slave trade. And it is fit that the nations of Europe should unite for the extinction of the horrible traffic. Shem and Japheth have largely participated in the guilt of the enslavement of Ham. Shem, having lagged behind Japheth in the march of enlightenment, persists in the perpetration of the hideous wrong. But, under pressure, the dilatory brother is being urged on to his duty.

Africa has been spoiled by all the races alien to her, and, under their stimulating example, by her own sons. Other races have passed through the baptism of slavery, as a stepping-stone to civilisation and independence, but none has toiled under the crushing weight of a servitude so protracted and inflicted from so many sources. Milleniums mark the period of the bondage and humiliation of Africa's children. The four quarters of the globe have heard their groans and been sprinkled and stained with their blood. All that passed by have felt at liberty to contemn and plunder. The oppressors of this race have been men with religion, and men without religion—Christians, Mohammedans, and Pagans. Nations with the Bible, and nations with the Koran, and nations without Bible or Koran—all have joined in afflicting this continent. And now the last of her oppressors, tearing from her bosom annually half a million of her children, are nations with the Koran. All travellers tell us that when the Arab traders in East Africa are suppressed the work will be done. This will, no doubt, be accomplished before very long. The Viceroy of Egypt is pledged to England to suppress the traffic, and in a given time to abolish slavery altogether.

It was a long time before the Christian world discovered, or rather admitted, the wrong in the slave trade; and we are persuaded that just as the truth in Christianity produced, though tardily, a Wilberforce and a Clarkson, so the truth in Islam will raise up—is now raising up—Muslim philanthropists and reformers who will give to the Negro the hand of a brother, and perhaps, outstripping their Christian brethren in liberality, accord him an equal share in political and social privileges—a liberality in dealing with weaker races which some Europeans confess themselves unable to exercise.

Dr. Livingstone seems to have thought that there might be some possibility of a Muslim Wilberforce, if we may judge from his immortal prayer, written, according to Mr. Waller, just one year before his death, and recorded on the tablet near his grave in Westminster Abbey, and which, in conclusion, is here most fervently reiterated:—

All I can add in my loneliness is, may Heaven's rich blessing come down on every one—American, English, or TURK, who will help to heal the open sore of the world.[17]—AMEN.

---

[17] *Last Journals*, vol. ii, p. 182.

The Life of Lord Lawrence and its Lessons.

THIS model biography, published in 1883, has already passed through six editions. It has produced remarkable results in the mean time. In the United States it has been received with far more honour than is usually accorded to biographies of illustrious Englishmen. We learn that the United States Government has paid it the unique compliment of ordering a copy to be placed on board every ship in the navy and in every public library in the United States. Such a compliment is by no means undeserved. Mr. Bosworth Smith has performed a patriotic and philanthropic work. He has done a service to England and a kindness to humanity by writing the life of Lord Lawrence as he has written it. That such a work has been so generally and enthusiastically welcomed is a significant and interesting commentary on the intellectual and moral progress of the present generation of Englishmen and Americans, and reassuring as to their future policy in dealing with those whom they still haughtily designate "inferior races."

We purpose in the following pages to gather from this remarkable book some of the practical lessons which we believe it was the aim of the author to inculcate by means of the character and deeds of one of the most interesting and suggestive natures which it has ever been our good fortune to contemplate. There are few books, it seems to us, which could be put with as much advantage into the hands of young men who, entering the civil, military, or naval services of England or the United States, aspire to positions of honour, of responsibility and of trust.

A writer in the *Quarterly Review* (April, 1883), himself, we believe, an old Indian official, tells us that "some months after the funeral at Westminster, when it became known that the widow of Lord Lawrence had committed the task of writing her husband's history to a Harrow Master—to one who had never seen India—there were grievous misgivings and great searchings of heart among the Anglo-Indian legions." It was feared that a civilian who had never visited either India or the Colonies would not have sufficient grasp of the subject—that his ignorance of details and lack of local experience would lead him into serious mistakes.

It was, indeed, a bold undertaking for a comparatively young man with the antecedents of the author, practically a stranger to India and Indian affairs, to come forward as a historian and critic of matters apparently so entirely out of his line; to treat of a period which has not yet passed into the domain of history, seeing that so many who acted amid the scenes described are still living; to deal with facts and principles, with the merits and demerits of various actors, in which not a few survivors still feel a keen interest, and with regard to which they entertain views more or less decided.

It required no little courage to write fully and freely on so important a subject—rather on so many important subjects—with the consciousness that such high authorities as Lord Napier of Magdala, Captain Eastwick, Sir Richard Temple, Sir Bartle Frere, Sir Charles Raikes, Sir Henry Norman, Sir Ashley Eden, Sir Frederic Goldsmid, &c., were waiting to read the record, and to bring to its perusal not only a deep personal interest, but a thorough knowledge of the subject of the biography and of the times and scenes of his activity.

But, after all, considering the large number of works which have been written on India, by men of eminent ability and vast local knowledge, what seemed to be now needed was not so much narrative and description, as critical appreciation of events and personal character; and it is really refreshing to sit down to the perusal of a work not only undefaced by technicalities unintelligible to the ordinary reader, but displaying a practical sagacity capable

The Life of Lord Lawrence.

of forming a distinct view of all the mingled objects with which it has to deal, while it conveys lessons of the highest importance at this particular time, when Indian affairs are becoming more and more a topic of general interest in England.

Mr. Bosworth Smith has not dealt with what may be called the subterraneous elements of the Indian question, which only a few can appreciate or understand, but with what is above ground, and clear to the apprehension of all classes and colours, of all creeds and races. That which gives is real and enduring value to the book is not only that it is eloquent, but that its eloquence is instinct with faith and love; not only that its paragraphs are glowing, but that they glow with passion for goodness, for truth, and for liberty. Whatever else the book lacks, these elements will cause it to live. Two of the Anglo-Indians, whose criticisms we have read, have had an opportunity of correcting what, from their standpoints, seem to be mistakes or omissions in the author. But, upon the whole, they give the work their indorsement. Very few are the real blemishes which their vast experience of the circumstances and details of Lord Lawrence's career could detect or point out.

It is acknowledged on all hands, that, in spite of the enormous difficulties in the way, Mr. Bosworth Smith has been able to give a true picture of a hero and of a stormy period, which even the severest criticism cannot seriously impair—a picture which will, we may believe, influence for good every successive generation of Englishmen. The blows he has dealt, heavy at times, at the cause of war, aggression, cruelty and the pride of race, may be resented in certain quarters now, but they point to a glorious future for England, and for weaker and so-called inferior races over whom she now bears, or may hereafter be called to bear rule. They tend to strengthen, to perpetuate and to diffuse the traditional instincts of his country for the useful and the just. Wherever the book is read in the British colonies, especially among races alien to the Anglo-Saxon, it will inspire confidence and give assurance as to the real aims and motives of the British Government in its colonial administration.

No amount of residence and Government service in India would have given the qualifications for the production of such a work; nor would any amount of mere scholarship have made a biographer of Lord Lawrence such as Mr. Bosworth Smith has proved himself to be. The book might have been written with greater local knowledge; it might have been more at home in technical details; it might even have given a fuller picture of the outward form—the flesh and blood and bones—of Lord Lawrence; but we know of no other living writer who, after having drawn the sketch, prepared the skeleton, constructed the body, could have informed it with the life, the soul, the spirit of the hero. Mere scholarship, or mere geographical or political knowledge of India, would have been helpless to make Lord Lawrence move among us, as he now moves, living, breathing, teaching, inspiring.

> Sudet multum frustraque laboret
> Ausus idem.

Something else was needed, and that Mr. Smith possesses, namely, that thorough sympathy with his subject which arises from similitude of character.

The task was not only within the compass of his mental powers, but entirely congenial to his intellectual and moral tastes. We did not need the assurance of the author that he entered upon his work with a "keen sense of responsibility and with a genuine enthusiasm." This is apparent on every page. Judging from the tone and tendency of the previous works by which Mr. Bosworth Smith became known to the literary world, we cannot imagine that he would have undertaken this, if he had not satisfied himself beforehand that the life and labours of the subject were such as to furnish an opportunity for enforcing those lessons of justice and truth, of tolerance and freedom, which it has been his aim to inculcate. *Mohammed and Mohammedanism*, and *Carthage and the Carthaginians* were composed not for the purpose merely of filling a blank in religious and historical literature, but for high moral ends. No statesman can read his work on Carthage, and no theologian or Christian missionary can read his work on Mohammedanism without getting clear views as to the highest and most effective

The Life of Lord Lawrence.

methods of dealing with questions which frequently confront them in their respective callings.

There is, as we have said, a certain resemblance of mind and spirit between the biographer and his subject. In his delineations, we may readily believe that Mr. Smith is not unfrequently revealing his own life and personal experiences. His vivid descriptions of Lord Lawrence's character give a clue to his own. His representations of that remarkable man are not always pure, dramatic expressions, but they are also self-revelations. He himself has lived inwardly the life he so successfully portrays. He has enjoyed the felicitous domestic surroundings to which, in the experiences of Lord Lawrence, he is so fond of recurring, and with ever-fresh delight.

It cannot be doubted that the wife of John Lawrence exerted a most beneficial influence upon him in softening the hard outline which, in consequence of his peculiar calling, his character was apt to assume. And in this the biographer resembles his subject. It is said that in all his literary labours—a fact which is more than hinted at in his graceful dedication of *Mohammed and Mohammedanism*—Mrs. Bosworth Smith has taken an important part, and, in the work before us—if we mistake not—traces of her influence are everywhere to be seen. It is not our wish to intrude upon the sacredness of domestic privacy, but we are gratified to be able to pay this tribute to one to whose devoted and self-sacrificing labours the world is more largely indebted than it knows, for a great deal that Mr. Bosworth Smith has been enabled to teach it.

In a country like India, the help of such a woman to an English official, who holds a responsible position, or to any thoughtful European, is simply incalculable. Even the letters written from home by such women to their relatives or friends in that distant land have an inspiring effect. Colonel Sleeman, in his *Rambles of an Indian Official*, touchingly refers to this in addressing his sister :—

> Were anyone to ask your countrymen in India (he says to her) what had been their greatest source of pleasure while there, perhaps nine in ten would say, the letters which they receive from their sisters at home. . . . And while thus contributing so much to our happiness, they, no doubt, tend to make us

better citizens of the world and servants of Government than we should otherwise be; for, in our "struggles through life" in India, we have all, more or less, an eye to the approbation of those circles which our kind sisters represent—who may therefore be considered in the exalted light of a valuable species of *unpaid magistracy* to the Government of India.

John Lawrence, throughout the greater part of his career in India, lived under the sweet but effective influence of such a "magistracy," unpaid, indeed, by Government recognition or pecuniary stipend, but reaping a constant reward from the consciousness of duty done or help given to a loved one to rise, in his great work, to higher levels—a reward to her "more precious than gems or stores of gold."

Only a writer of spirit kindred to that of Lord Lawrence, " in reading over thousands of letters" written by his subject for the purpose of preparing a readable biography, would have so borne in mind the cause of the weak and oppressed, as to have noticed that " not a single expression occurred which would wound the pride of the most sensitive of natives," and that " not in one single instance does he use the opprobrious term which is the very first to come to the mouth of too many young officers or casual visitors to India."

The following will be read with admiration and gratitude by thousands in India, in Africa, in America, who are "guilty of a skin not coloured," like the white man's:—

Englishmen there have been, and still are in India, who, priding themselves on their race or their colour, their superior strength of body and strength of will, despise the natives, keep aloof from them, call them by the opprobrious name of "niggers," and strike and maltreat them in a way in which they would not venture to treat a European. But such Englishmen have happily always been in a small minority. They may be found sometimes among the youngest and most empty-headed officers of the army, or among the frivolous and fashionable and scandal-loving society of the great towns. But they are not to be found in the ranks of the civil service, or among those soldier-statesmen who have built up and have preserved our Indian Empire. It is not in the writings, the conversation, or the acts of men like Sir Thomas Munro, or Lord Metcalfe, like Outram or Havelock, like Henry or John Lawrence, and of the hundreds of good men and true, of whom these are, after all, but the most brilliant representatives, that we can find a word or deed indicative of other than the deepest and most affectionate interest in the helpless and voiceless millions over whom they rule. . . . These are the men who know the natives, who sympathise with them and have learned to love them; who, in the spirit of a truly imperial race, look

The Life of Lord Lawrence.

upon themselves as the servants of those whom they rule, and rule by serving them; who do everything that in them lies to bridge over the yawning gulf, which, by our fate or by our fault, still separates colour from colour, race from race and creed from creed.[1]

Throughout his life, even in the early Delhi and Punjab days, John Lawrence had set his face strongly against practices which it is easier to understand than to describe, and which were then all too common among our countrymen in India. No one whose character was not above suspicion in these respects could hope to stand well with him, even in the early times. . . . No one ever dropped an impure word or made an impure allusion in his presence. No one ever scoffed at religion, whether his own or that of the natives. No one ever spoke contemptuously or harshly of the natives themselves without receiving from him a stern and sometimes a sledge-hammer rebuke. On one occasion, a lady who was sitting at the Vice-regal table allowed herself to sneer at the Bible. Sir John Lawrence looked sternly on her and said, with all his dignity, but with more of sorrow than of anger in his words, " How can you speak like that of God and of God's book, in the presence of these young men ? " The next minute he was talking with her of other subjects as if nothing had happened. But the rebuke had done its work on her and on the assembled company. On another occasion, a young officer in the army, who was talking, after the manner of his kind, contemptuously of the natives, happened, in Sir John's hearing, to speak of them as "those niggers." " I beg your pardon," said Sir John, " of what people were you speaking ? " And here again the rebuke did its work right well. Thus the Vice-regal Court was in his time what, happily, it has been in the case of most of our Viceroys, and what the English Court has been throughout the reign of Queen Victoria—the centre, as far as its chief occupant could make it so, of everything that was pure, everything that was lovely, everything that was of good report and from it, as from a fresh fountain, flowed forth lessons of purity, of simplicity, of reverence, of manliness, of hard work, of all the domestic charities which were felt more or less through all ranks of English society in India. Would that it had always been so in India before and since ! Would that it may always be so hereafter ! Would that intelligent and inquiring natives may never find one of their most forcible arguments against Christianity in the language, in the actions, in the policy, in the surroundings of its so-called Christian rulers ![2]

This is the first time, so far as we know, that this subject—one of great importance to the coloured races of the globe, and which is generally considered too delicate to be handled or too insignificant to deserve attention—has been treated with such dignity and seriousness and in a work destined to wield so wide an influence. The intelligent English-speaking African, even more

---

[1] *Life of Lord Lawrence*; by R. Bosworth Smith, M.A. (vol. i, pp. 157, 158).
[2] *Ibid*; vol. ii, pp. 511, 512.

than the Indian, has frequently, in his reading and in his travels, to encounter gratuitous insults, and from quarters where he would naturally not look for them. A few months ago, an English Dissenting clergyman, whom we will call Mr. A., was a passenger from New York to Liverpool on one of the White Star steamers. He had lived in the Southern States of America, and though now living in London and in charge of a respectable congregation there he could not conceal the prejudices which had grown upon him in America. There sat opposite to him at the Captain's table—assigned seats there by the consideration and courtesy of the Captain himself—two passengers of African descent—one, a lady of education and culture, wife of a diplomatic officer of the United States, on the way to join her husband; the other, the presiding officer of a literary institution in Africa. Mr. A. did not feel at home in the company of his coloured fellow-passengers, and not unfrequently went out of his way, in speech and manner, to exhibit and emphasise his uncomfortable state. There sat on his right hand another English Dissenting clergyman who had been spending a few weeks in America, but who possessed all the qualities of a Christian gentleman and scholar. This gentleman was often shocked by the utterances of his brother minister in defence of Negro slavery, and always rebuked him for them. On one occasion, at the dinner-table, while the passengers sitting near them were proposing and answering conundrums, in which the African passengers participated, he suddenly said: "Now, tell me, where is the Negro mentioned in the Bible?" Several answers were given, which he would not accept as correct. At last, when it was "given up," he blurted out, with rude and vulgar emphasis, the wretched pun, "Nigger demus," to the general disgust of the company.

Mr. James Parton, in a remarkable article, published, not very long ago, in the *North American Review*, on 'Antipathy to the Negro,' says:—

> This colour repugnance is usually observed to be strongest in the meanest. Among the educated people of the Southern States it was never half so strong as in the "white trash" and in the adventurers from other regions who had an

The Life of Lord Lawrence.

interest in flattering the poor "white trash." The man who made the disturbance about the coloured person in the omnibus was generally a snob more or less disguised. He might be a gorgeous gambler, a sham D.D., a pushing store keeper, a small politician; but, commonly, the soul of a scamp was in him. In the North it was never the really educated man or women who felt aggrieved at the presence of a decent coloured man.

Would that these sentences conveyed "the truth, the whole truth and nothing but the truth." But, if we are to judge from outward appearances, they do not do so. We cannot see the soul. But there are, we regret to say, some outwardly respectable persons in England, as well as in America, who speak and write in a manner which indicates the kind of soul referred to by Mr. Parton. One of the most flagrant cases is that of Dr. Edward A. Freeman in his last work on America. During a visit which we paid, in 1882, to the United States, we found a feeling of wide-spread indignation among the intelligent coloured classes in view of the insult offered them by Dr. Freeman, in his articles on the United States. These articles appeared in the *Fortnightly Review* and *Longman's Magazine*. They are now republished in a volume.[3]

The following are some of his more offensive utterances:—

The bestowal of citizenship on the Negro[4] is one of those cases which show what law can do, and what it cannot. The law may declare the Negro to be the equal of the white man; it cannot make him his equal. To the old question, "Am I not a man and a brother?" I venture to answer: No. The Negro may be a man and a brother in some secondary sense; he is not a man and a brother in the same full sense in which every *Western Aryan* is a man and a brother.

The eternal laws of Nature, the eternal distinction of colour, forbid the assimilation of the Negro.

We are told that education has done, and is doing, much for the younger members of the once-enslaved race. But education cannot wipe out the eternal distinction that has been drawn by the hand of Nature.

I cannot help thinking that those in either hemisphere who were most zealous for the emancipation of the Negro must, in their heart of hearts, feel a secret shudder at the thought that, though morally impossible, it is constitutionally possible that, two years hence, a black man may be chosen to sit in the seat of Washington and Garfield.[5]

---

[3] *Some Impressions of the United States;* by Edward A. Freeman, D.C.L., LL.D.—London, 1883.

[4] Dr. Freeman writes the word with a small "n."

[5] Dr. Freeman is an ardent and untiring opponent of the Mohammedan religion, which teaches that it is morally possible and religiously right that, if

Christianity, Islam and the Negro Race.

To me at least the Negro is repulsive. Of the two, one is more inclined to hail a man and a brother in the Indian than in the Negro. Such Indians as I saw were certainly less ugly than the Negroes. But then they lacked the grotesque air which often makes the Negro's ugliness less repulsive. Not repulsive, like the Negro, from the more lines of the face, they were repulsive from the utter lack of intellectual expression.

Very many approved when I suggested that the best remedy for whatever was amiss would be if every Irishman should kill a Nergo and be hanged for it. Those who dissented, dissented most commonly on the ground that, if there were no Irish and no Negroes, they would not be able to get any domestic servants."

Dr. Freeman knows that there are many Negroes, men and women, in America, who can read, and will read, his book, and he thoughtlessly flings these insults into their faces. He knows, also, that these people are manfully struggling to rise against a heavy burden of prejudice and contempt, and he wantonly piles up arguments against them for the use of their oppressors. Is Dr. Freeman a Christian, or has he, for the nonce, thrown off his incrustation of modern culture to give full play to the pure latent Briton ? Or is it the old Norman pride ?

The jargon of describing the Negro as " unfit for freedom " being now, to a great extent, obsolete, his personal peculiarities, as he is seen chiefly in the countries of his exile, must be brought forward for ridicule, in order to intensify the prejudice against him and perpetuate the social hostility by which he is oppressed. Prejudice is, partly, an instinct, and, partly, a result of surrounding circumstances. Sometimes it has a mercenary quality, or, rather, originates in mercenary motives. The prejudice against the Negro, in America, is both instinctive and circumstantial; in Englishmen, it may be only instinctive, the result of race-pride or exclusiveness; but it has, at times, in Englishmen in America, partaken of a mercenary nature. It used to be said, in the days of slavery, that Englishmen who had accepted Southern hospitality always had Southern sympathies. Possibly the inability of the historian of the *Norman*

---

a black man has the necessary qualifications, he should rise to the head of the Government, and sit in the seat of the Sultan—a doctrine which, in the history of Islam, has often been practically carried out. Ought the Negro to follow Dr. Freeman's teaching on this subject, or Mohammed's ?

^c *Some Impressions of the United States* ; chap. x.

The Life of Lord Lawrence.

Conquest on this subject may be accounted for by the fact that he has a son who has become a Virginia planter. Shortly after the civil war, it was, and it probably still is, the fashion, with some leading spirits of Virginia, to denounce Negro education and enfranchisement as necessarily hostile to the industrial interests of the country; and Dr. Freeman could not escape the contagion, while on a visit to his son, in 1881-82. Indeed, he says himself, referring to this very subject, " What I venture to say on the housetops has been whispered in my ear in closets by not a few in America, who fully understand the state and needs of their country."

Dr. Freeman is, probably, not aware that the " whisperers " in " closets " are numbered by loyal Americans among the " unreconstructed," who feel regret for the absence of those laws and regulations by which the Negro was doomed to be a perpetual chattel, and which fostered that race hostility, which, by the excess of its violence, served not indeed to prevent the amalgamation of the races—for that was going on continually—but as the pillar and buttress of slavery. The agitation against the Negro by Americans in some parts of America is intelligible and, perhaps, natural, though it is, in a great measure, unjust and unreasonable. But it is strange indeed that an Englishman should go out of his way to add fuel to the fire, and, it can only be accounted for, by the fact, that, in the Southern States, foreigners have thought it prudent, at times, not only to profess to share, but even to excite, the popular antipathy against the Negro, that they might utilise it for their own ends. Dr. Freeman, indeed, warns the reader in his preface that " the impressions are those of one who looks at things for *his own purposes*, and from his own point of view." Mr. Herbert Spencer, who visited the United States not long after Dr. Freeman, did not, in recording his impressions of the country, say a single word which might increase the load of odium under which the Negro labours, and he was probably as keen in his appreciation of the " state and needs of America " as his distinguished countryman. But, true to his English instincts, that eminent philosopher did not think it creditable to " hit a man when he is down." The absence

Christianity, Islam and the Negro Race.

of any "axe to grind," and freedom from obligations incurred in any particular section of the country, left his nobler nature its full play.

But Dr. Freeman parades his antipathy not only to the Negro, but to the Irish, the Indian, the Chinese. He selects for his persecution the weaker races. There are blows to give, he thinks, but none to take. We do not object to his criticisms, coarse as we deem them, of the looks of the different races; for good looks or bad looks in individuals or classes depend upon the standpoint from which the objects are viewed. Stanley tells us that when he came out of the interior of Africa, where, for two years, he had been accustomed to the black or bronze colour of the natives, the white complexion of the foreigners he met on the coast at first repelled him. He says:—

<small>The sight of the pale faces of the Embomma merchants gave me the slightest suspicion of a shiver. The pale colour, after so long gazing on rich black and richer bronze, had something of an unaccountable ghastliness.

I could not divest myself of the feeling that they must be sick; yet, as I compare their complexions with what I now view, I should say they were olive, sunburnt, dark.[7]</small>

Winwood Reade, in his *African Sketch-Book*, gives an amusing and suggestive account of the impressions of an intelligent African youth in the interior of Africa, on his first seeing a white man. We would commend to Dr. Freeman a perusal of that account, if, with all his research, he has not yet learned that what may be "ugly" in Europe is not necessarily "ugly" in China, India, or Africa. If Dr. Freeman were bound to travel in Africa, we venture to predict that the natives would never make any disparaging comments—whatever their opinions—upon his personal appearance, where he would be likely to hear them; and this, from an innate good breeding, which, though they lack mental culture, is ever visible, in spite of what may be called their unpolished exterior.

But does it not occur to such writers as Dr. Freeman that the world is tired of hearing stereotyped phrases of contempt for the African? For three hundred years this has been going on. The

---

[7] *Through the Dark Continent*, vol. ii, p. 462.

world is tired, and is now changing its tone. The enquiry among the most earnest men is, What can be done to lift up this race? How shall that vast continent, from which millions have been torn to engage in unrequited toil for strangers, be delivered from the disadvantages of ages? These are the problems to which some of the best and most vigorous minds of the age are directing their attention. The Rip Van Winkles have lost their influence. The rising generation of English scholars has very little sympathy with the narrow, racial prejudices of their fathers. And, with such teachers to guide them, as Mr. Bosworth Smith, the youth now in the schools of England, when they come upon the stage of action, will eliminate from their literary and scientific discussions those relics of barbarism—the opprobrious terms now applied to foreign and weaker races—and they will wonder how, with all the refinement and culture of their predecessors, there could have been exhibited that odious selfishness, that want of magnanimity and consideration for others, which often disfigure their literary productions.

It is a significant sign of the times and of the progress of liberal sentiments in England that the great reputation of Mr. Carlyle, who believed that "God had put a whip in the hand of every white man to flog the Negro," is undergoing the shock and revision which were sure to come when that large population, which he characterised as "mostly fools," recovered from the fascination of one who, as time goes on, will seem to them, more and more, a stupendous charlatan. We were amused, not long since, at the excitement and bitterness created in certain quarters by Mr. Froud's straightforward honesty in publishing the picture which, with severe but repulsive truthfulness, Mr. Carlyle had drawn of himself. The worshippers of a generation have revolted at the hideousness of their fetish; and the enlightened Negro feels a sense of relief that the real character of one who sneered at the philanthropies of Christianity and the humanities of the age, and ridiculed what he called "Nigger emancipation," has been disclosed, and *by his own hands*. The agencies for good are mightier than the agencies for evil. A righteous Nemesis may be slow, but it is sure. The ploughman of Ayrshire has proved a deeper thinker and truer prophet than "the philosopher of Chelsea." The song of the rustic poet will ring down the ages when the sensationalisms and affectations of his cynical countryman are all buried in their merited oblivion.[8]

> For a' that and a' that,
> It's coming yet for a' that,
> That man to man the world o'er
> Shall brothers be for a' that.

As it has happened to Mr. Carlyle, so will it happen to all who use the gifts bestowed upon them by the common Father of all to ridicule or oppress any portion of His creatures. They will be classed, in the ultimate judgment, even of men, with poltroons and cowards, who think it necessary to pull down others in order to assure a standing and opportunity for themselves; and in the great hereafter they will rank with Dante's contemptible herd—

> le genti dolorose,
> C'hanno perduto il ben dell' intelletto,
> * * * * * * *
> Fama di loro il mondo esser non lassa;
> Misericordia e Giustezia gli sdegna.[9]

We are glad to notice that, in the midst of an interesting and absorbing narrative of the siege and capture of Delhi, Mr. Bosworth Smith pauses to record his indignation at baseness and brutality, and to brand with just condemnation the deeds of Captain Hodson. We do not care to reproduce here the horrible charges which, on substantial evidence, direct and collateral, are preferred against the man; but this we may say, that in our opinion Hodson was, morally speaking, one of the worst specimens of all of whom we have ever heard or read as claiming relationship with Englishmen.

Α'ἴσχιστος δὲ ἀνὴρ ὑπὸ Ἴλιον ἤηλθεν.[10]

It is consolatory to believe that there were only two other Englishmen like Hodson in India, and we are glad that their names

---

[8] How much there is (says Professor Max Müller) in Carlyle's histories that might safely be consigned to oblivion.—*India*, p. 16.

[9] *Inferno*, iii.

[10] *Iliad*, ii.

The Life of Lord Lawrence.

are not given by the biographer. Mr. Bosworth Smith's reference to a life of this man by his brother, "extolling him as a model of Christian chivalry and honour," reminds us of a passage in Macaulay's terrible indictment of Barere. And as it fell to the lot of Barere, under the caustic pen of that brilliant essayist, so has it fallen to the lot of Hodson, under the indignant and incisive pen of Mr. Bosworth Smith. We imagine that from the eminence of infamy on which Mr. Smith has placed his character, no attempt to prove him a "model Christian" will ever take it down.

The animadversions on the proceedings of Frederick Cooper seem to us even more necessary than the impaling of Hodson. Hodson was an exceptional character, rough-hewn and of a base nature. Cooper represented the ordinary English official of whom hundreds go to India and the colonies. He was of finer nature and higher culture than Hodson, and his example, if not reprobated and condemned, as it has been in this book, might be followed by the large number who, in the English service, are likely to secure positions similar to that which he held.

We do not see, however, that full justice has been meted out to John Nicholson. There is about this man, we must admit, a great deal that is attractive; and, perhaps, in the fearful crisis through which British India was then passing, such a character—"turbulent and imperious"—was necessary. He was evidently courageous, deserving to the full, no doubt, the enconiums bestowed upon him by Lord Lawrence in an after-dinner speech at the "Great Durbar of Lahore;" but we confess that our admiration is marred when we read the curt and apparently unfeeling note in which he announced to the Chief Commissioner the death of a man who had fallen by his nervous and fatal shot—

> Sir,—I have the honour to report that a man came into my compound to-day intending to kill me, and that I shot him dead.
>
> Your obedient servant,
> JOHN NICHOLSON.

His cool and apparently indifferent remark after hacking to death a brave enemy who had stood manfully prepared to die at his post, has a touch of the unmanly in it. The Reviewer in the

Quarterly, thinks that Nicholson is aptly described by the lines which Horace applies to Achilles—

> Impiger, iracundus, inexorabilis, acer,
> Jura sibi negat, nihil non arrogat armis.

Whatever else he possessed, he seems to us to have been devoid of many of the elements of the real hero. Whether we contemplate him from a military or ethical point of view, we cannot but regard his character as seriously incomplete and defective. "In the English," says Mr. Bosworth Smith, "as in all imperial races, there is an element of the wild beast." Nicholson exemplifies this remark. Perhaps in all conquering races this indomitable element is a necessity—this overbearing and insolent spirit, which alone knows how to conquer. But *we* shudder in the presence of a nature so relentless and implacable.

No one can fail to read with interest and admiration the following passing tribute paid to the weak—the natives who bore their part in the capture of Delhi:—

> The coolness and the courage of the old Sikh Artillerymen, who had been picked out by Sir John Lawrence in person, and of the despised Musbi Sikhs, whom he had also sent down to Delhi, were as conspicuous as that of the Europeans themselves. And the passive endurance of the water-carriers and native servants, who, amidst the hatreds of colour and race which the fierce conflict had engendered, had not always received the best of treatment at their masters' hands, and were now expected to wait on those same masters amidst storms of shot and shell, was, perhaps, more wonderful than either.[11]

Mr. Bosworth Smith is not a philanthropic agitator, but he is intensely patriotic. He is intensely English, swayed by the noblest feelings of his people. He is anxious for the honour of England. He wishes that England should be everywhere feared and loved, especially in her colonies. He believes that England, upon the whole, possesses more of the elements and possibilities of beneficent and conservative rule than any other European nation; and he never loses an opportunity to point out that it is the aim of the Imperial Government that righteousness should at all times enter as a dominant, predominant factor in English policy toward weaker races. But he is also, at the same time,

---

[11] *Life of Lord Lawrence;* vol. ii, p. 184.

The Life of Lord Lawrence.

aware that, under colonial rule, such a policy is not always carried out. He is anxious that it should be. He is anxious that full scope should be given for the just ambition of native races, and that their abilities should be utilised in every way compatible with the rights and welfare of all; and he believes that such a course comes " within the range of practical politics." He looks upon the possibilities of the British Empire precisely as Dean Stanley looked upon the possibilities of the Church of England, as able to make room, not for one race only, nor for one element of human nature only, but for all the races and all the various elements of the whole world. Not that he would bring them all to a dead uniformity. He would respect the religious and social institutions of alien and non-Christian races, and he would not interfere with their harmless customs.

Those acquainted with the character and temper of the men who, happily for humanity, come to the head of the Government at home from both the great parties, know that Mr. Bosworth Smith by no means exaggerates when he represents Henry and John Lawrence as the embodiment of the spirit and intention of the Imperial Government. "Taking them both together," he says, " the chivalry, the generosity, the sympthy of the one ; the strength, the judgment, the magnanimity of the other; the name of Lawrence may, now and forever, present to the people of India the noblest impersonation of English rule—a rule unselfish and unaggressive, benevolent and energetic, wise and just." [12]

Considering the peculiarities of human nature, the excellencies and defects which are almost always found in some of the ablest rulers, it is not to be wondered at that the beneficent conceptions of the Imperial Government should find realisation in the administrative acts of but comparatively few of its representatives abroad ; and this, because the majority of men lack that imaginative sympathy which enables us to put ourselves in the place of others.

Of one of the most distinguished of the British rulers of India Mr. Bosworth Smith says :—

---

[12] *Ibid.*, vol. ii, p. 160.

Christianity, Islam and the Negro Race.

Lord Dalhousie seems, from his letters, hundreds of which lie before me, to have been unable to clothe himself sufficiently with the feelings, the prejudices, the aspirations, the ideas of those over whom he ruled; and he was unable, therefore, to understand how the natives of India, recognising, as many of them did the general benevolence of our intentions and the undoubted beneficence of our rule, were yet disposed to look back with yearning and regret on the days when, if they were oppressed, plundered, murdered, they were so by men of their own race, their own language, or their own creed. . . . Nor is there in the whole of his letters, brilliant and incisive and racy, as they all are, a single sentence which inclines the reader to pause and say, as he does again and again, when he is reading the much less brilliant and incisive letters of Metcalf, or Outram, of Henry or John Lawrence, "Here is a man whose chief claim to rule India was that he so thoroughly understood her people. If, therefore, there has been no abler, or more commanding, or more conscientious, or more successful Governor-General of India than Lord Dalhousie, there have been, in my opinion, Governors-General who were more sympathetic with the natives and more beloved.[18]

The West African settlements, the only ones of the British colonies with which we are acquainted, notwithstanding all the drawbacks of climate, have numbered among their rulers, especially within the last twenty years, some of the best representatives of the English spirit. The names of Sir Arthur E. Kennedy, Sir John Pope Hennessy, Sir Samuel Rowe, Governor A. E. Havelock, will long be remembered on these shores as reflecting one of the best traditions of Downing Street.

One of the chief faults of the Indian administration, to which Mr. Bosworth Smith often incidentally alludes, is that it leaves so few outlets for native talent, has so little real insight into the native character, and is too anxious to engraft Western progress wholesale on Eastern conservatism and stagnation. It is gratifying to know that in the colonies in West Africa—thanks to the enlightened efforts of some of the rulers to whom we have referred—matters, in these respects, are improving. The fault which administrators find with the natives is a want of regular and continuous development. Their later career does not seem to fulfil the promise of their earlier years. But this happens, more or less, in all countries and among all races. Everywhere the talents and conduct of boys or young men develop them-

---

[18] *Ibid.*, vol. i, pp. 484, 485.

selves very differently. Some are precocious, expand with a show of rapidity, and then, all at once, stand still or deteriorate. But, in the West African settlements, this is perhaps more noticeable, and so it will be in all colonies where Englishmen rule over an alien and weaker race. The remedy is, " more outlets for native talent," greater " insight into native character," and less anxiety to engraft European progress wholesale on African conservatism and stagnation. A more comprehensive system of education and better teachers would, in a short time, give the natives all the accomplishments in which they are now so deficient; and they would soon prove that Nature has not denied them the talents and the perseverance necessary to adopt the manners and the habits suited to positions of responsibility and trust under an enlightened government.

The following is worthy of reproduction, preservation, and wide circulation: After the fall of Delhi, some of John Lawrence's friends wrote to him expressing their earnest hope that he would " plough up Delhi;" others, that he would at least destroy the Great Mosque. In reply to the latter proposal, he writes to Pelham Burn, who had consulted him in the matter, "I will on no account consent to it. We should carefully abstain from the destruction of religious edifices, either to favour friends or to annoy foes." And, when some of the chief authorities in his province—and many of them his intimate friends—came in solemn deputation to him to urge the same step, and pointed out, as a convincing argument, that to destroy the finest place of Muslim worship in the world would be felt as a blow to their religion by Muslims everywhere, he first reasoned out the matter calmly with them, but finding that he could produce no effect, he jumped up from his seat, and, slapping the foremost of them on his back, said, " I'll tell you what it is: there are many things you could persuade me to do, but you shall never persuade me to do this; so you may as well spare your pains." [14]

Thus the mosques of Delhi were not desecrated; that the inhabitants were not left to shift for themselves as homeless outcasts; that the whole city, with its glorious buildings and its historic memories, was not levelled with the

---

[14] *Ibid.*, vol. ii, p. 222.

Christianity, Islam and the Negro Race.

ground and the plough driven over its site; in one word, that the lasting shame emblazoned in letters of blood and fire in the annals of Imperial Rome, by her ruthless destruction of Carthage and Corinth, is not written in equally indelible characters in the annals of English rule in India, was due, in great part at least, to the justice and the humanity, the statesmanship and the Christian spirit of John Lawrence.[15]

Lord Lawrence did not parade his religion, says his biographer:

> No more sincere Christian ever lived. He walked as in the sight of God. He read the Bible every morning of his life with prayer, and regarded it as the only, and as the sufficient, guide to heaven. But he rarely talked on religious questions, and still more rarely did he make use of the phraseology which was current in religious circles of the strictly Evangelical type. The religious expressions made use of in his letters are of the simplest and most childlike kind.[16]

The following testimony is borne by Captain Eastwick, an intimate friend, who himself partakes largely of the Lawrence spirit. The hospitalities of his pleasant home in London are always accessible to the deserving stranger of whatever race or colour. He says:

> No man understood better than Lord Lawrence that living for others is the first step towards living for God. The extent to which he laboured in this sphere of Christian charity is known only to the cherished partner of his earthly pilgrimage, the partaker of his joys and sorrows, and the sole sharer of every secret of his inner life. . . . From the earliest period of my acquaintance with him he was a decided Christian; a simple, God-fearing man, who, to the best of his ability, translated into daily practice the precepts of the Bible.[17]

The celebrated letter of Lord Lawrence, in reply to Colonel Herbert Edwards, wherein he lays down the course which a Christian Government should pursue in dealing with non-Christian subjects, has been generally studied in Asia, Europe, Africa and America, and furnishes very important hints to Christian missionaries and missionary committees. It shows the "insight, grasp, calmness and toleration of a Christian statesman." The letter was written, under his instructions, by his Secretary, now Sir Richard Temple, who has borne, since that time, a part in the government of nearly every province in India, and is distinguished as an enlightened friend of Christian missions. We quote one or two striking passages:—

---

[15] *Ibid.*, p. 226.   [16] *Ibid.*, vol. ii, p. 270   [17] *Ibid.*, vol. ii, p. 325.

The Life of Lord Lawrence.

Sir John Lawrence, I am pleased to state, says the Secretary, entertains the earnest belief that all those measures which are really and truly Christian can be carried out in India, not only without danger to British rule, but, on the contrary, with every advantage to its stability. Christian things done in a Christian way will never, the Chief Commissioner is convinced, alienate the Heathen. About such things there are qualities which do not provoke or excite distrust, nor harden to resistance. It is when unchristian things are done in the name of Christianity, or when Christian things are done in an unchristian way, that mischief and danger are occasioned.

The greatness of Lord Lawrence was English greatness. He cannot be regarded as an isolated phenomenon in the modern history of England. He embodied in himself the characteristics of the English people. He was the result of the soundness of the central character of England. The beginning of his career in India witnessed the beginning, in England, of that series of reforms which, in the last fifty years, have changed the whole of the economic and political character of Great Britain. No other period in the modern parliamentary history of that great country has been so fruitful of beneficent measures; in none has there been such a variety of philanthropic legislation. During the first decade of John Lawrence's residence in India, the Reform Bill, the Bill for the Abolition of Slavery, the Bill for the Removal of the Disabilities of the Jews, the Poor Law Amendment, the Tithe Commutation Acts, were fully discussed and passed by Parliament.

In the subsequent decade, under the guidance of Sir Robert Peel, the same spirit of improvement was displayed in financial and commercial changes, ending with the abolition of the Corn Laws and of the Navigation Laws. The speeches delivered in Parliament and elsewhere in England during the discussion of these measures, were all, no doubt, eagerly read and studied by John Lawrence in his remote sphere of labour, and they were in themselves a liberal education. Living in a strange country, among a strange people and unfamiliar surroundings, and anxious to keep abreast of events as they happened at home, it is probable that he enjoyed greater opportunity and had greater inducements for studying and mastering the questions which came before him in letters and newspapers, than he would have had in England. While in the districts of Delhi and Paniput, he was accumulating those treasures of experience, he was, at the same time, getting instruction from the noble utterances of such able teachers as Brougham, Macaulay, Thomas Fowell Buxton, and acquiring those habits of which the results are seen all through his subsequent labours, whether in the Indian Council, the Palace at Calcutta, or the House of Lords. His mind was getting direction from the great orations of Bright, Cobden, Peel, Gladstone, Disraeli. He grew up and his first official deeds were performed during the time that the greatest orators of the present century were swaying the minds of the English people, creating an enthusiasm for the masses, and finding co-operation in the Muse of the greatest contemporary poet, who taught in stirring song that

> Kind hearts are more than coronets,
> And simple faith than Norman blood.

Under such influences was the character of John Lawrence formed—a character which, it cannot be doubted, was the result of the constitutional history and national character of England. It was an evolution—a blossom which took shape from the rising sap, and was tinted by the light of English history.

It is matter for gratulation that the *Life of Lord Lawrence* has been added to the literature of Great Britain—a literature upon which the sun never sets, and which may be compared to a beautiful and variegated landscape. The traveller over it is surprised and delighted at each turn of the road. There are stretches which, beautiful with fragrant flowers, minister to the æsthetic intuitions and necessities of his nature; along these he loves to linger; but the only feeling that remains, after he has passed them, is one of exhilaration. There are others where luscious fruits abound, which, besides delighting the eye, regale the appetite and satisfy a craving deeper than mere artificial taste. Here he finds not only delight, but profit. There are beautiful and charming works in English literature which are only beautiful; they do not nourish. There are others which feed the hungry, while they send the rich empty away; others, still, minister to the taste of the rich, while they leave the poor to starve; while others once more afford sustenance to the needy and guidance and help to the rich. The *Life of Lord Lawrence* belongs to the last class. Mr. Bosworth Smith has

The Life of Lord Lawrence.

fulfilled the conditions laid down by the poet for complete success in literary art :—

> Omne tulit punctum, qui miscuit utile dulce
> Lectorem delectando pariterque monendo.[18]

The atmosphere of the book is refreshing and uplifting. It will bear protracted reading aloud in any thoughtful circle. Its moral and intellectual tone throws a brightness over virtue and benevolence, and makes vice and brutality seem darker. It brings to mind the experience one has in a tropical tornado when it is just approaching. The quarter of the heavens whence it proceeds looks blacker from the clearness of the sky in the opposite direction. The storm clouds deepen in their density and gloom, while the sun appears to shine with increased intensity in the opposite quarter. So the unsparing vindictiveness, savage brutality and insatiable avarice of Hodson, the stern and calculating cruelty of Cooper, the fierce and distorted temperament of Nicholson, seem more repulsive in the light of the exalted heroism, the generosity and love of the Lawrences, and other noble characters, who have been made to pass before us. The light gives a greater depth to the shadow.

Taking into consideration the moral influence of this work, it is, we venture to think, far more important to humanity than any of the productions of the fine arts—of sculpture, painting, or music. So far as their effect upon human progress is concerned, what are the frescoes of the Vatican, the exquisite grace of Raphael, or the sublimity and energy of Michael Angelo, compared to the practical and philanthropic influence of such a book? Viewing its effect upon the welfare of humanity, we would not exchange it for all the awful and beautiful things in the Sistine Chapel. Its triumphs are not æsthetic, but humanitarian. The high problems of political and social economy and ethics, of race, education, religion and diplomacy, are all dealt with in a truly Christian spirit. Not taste but righteousness is consulted, and the great law is enforced, by precept and living examples, of doing unto others as we would that they should do unto us.

---

[18] *Horace*, ' Epistola ad Pisones.'

We sincerely hope that this work may not remain an isolated phenomenon in the biographical literature of England. We trust that the successors of Lord Lawrence may find biographers who may be not only disciples but successors in spirit, of Mr. Bosworth Smith. In one sense, Lord Lawrence will have no successor. There are some qualities which are individual and belong to a particular time—and only to that time—neither communicable nor transmissible. Lord Lawrence could not form a Lawrence school any more than Shakespeare could train a Shakespeare. A doctrine, a principle, a method, a discovery, may be communicated or transmitted. But how shall a spirit be embodied? Who shall give to others that "heroic simplicity," that rapid penetration into the obscurities of a question, that prompt intuition into peculiar cases, which cannot be judged by general rules, and which distinguished Lord Lawrence? These gifts are personal and peculiar.

But *non omnis moriar*.

The essential principles underlying all that Lord Lawrence wrote and thought and did will be as true a hundred years hence as they are to-day; and from these principles, as from a mine of wealth, many generations of Indian statesmen may gather treasures new and old, bearing alike what is the practical ideal at which Indian rulers ought to aim, and what are the dangers which it most behoves them to avoid.[10]

It has been a joy and a profit to us to study these volumes, and we lay them down with regret that we could not deal with more of the important questions they suggest. We should be puzzled to say which has given us the greater pleasure, the beauty and the skill with which the story has been told, or the sentiments of justice and love which permeate the record. The two chapters on 'John Lawrence as Conqueror' and 'John Lawrence as Pacificator' ought to be published separately in tract form, and scattered over not only the British Empire, but the world. We have been able to deal with but one side of the work—that side which makes it so encouraging to non-European races, and so instructive to Englishmen who have to deal with them, either as rulers, missionaries or traders, and that side, probably, which will give to the work its most permanent influence and value.

---

[10] *Life of Lord Lawrence;* vol i, p. 809.

The Life of Lord Lawrence.

We congratulate Mr. Bosworth Smith on his great achievement. He has erected a *monumentum ære perennius*, which will ever be an honour to his country.

It will be a delight to remember both the hero and his biographer. The country which is proud to have produced John Lawrence must be proud to have produced Bosworth Smith. The land of Achilles is also the land of Homer. We look for immediate and direct results from the influence of this book; and we look for remote and far-reaching results. It will make itself felt in existing society, and in the thinking and actions of generations yet unborn.

The Mohammedans of Nigritia.

IN the present discussion, by Nigritia must be understood all the region of West Central Africa embraced between Lake Tchad on the east, and Sierra Leone and Liberia on the west, and between Timbuktu on the north, and the Bight of Benin on the south, including the Niger from its source to its mouth. The European travellers who have described various portions of this country are Mungo Park, Denham and Clapperton, the Landers, Laing, Caillie, and more recently, Richardson, Barth, Overweg, Vogel, and Winwood Reade; the Liberian travellers are Benjamin Anderson James L. Sims, and George L. Seymour.

The country east of Lake Tchad to the Red Sea is occupied largely by Mohammedans; but we will now deal only with the countries west of Lake Tchad, in which are situated the well known cities of Kano, Sokoto, Illorin, Timbuktu, Sego, Kankan, Timbo, Musardu.

This part of Africa, although so near to Europe, seems to have been shut out from the knowledge of Europeans, until the publication of the travels of Mungo Park, about one hundred years ago. His descriptions are characterised by a marvellous fidelity and accuracy. It is a remarkable fact that the accounts of the earlier African travellers are, as a rule, more trustworthy than the statements of more recent adventurers. In all delineations which depend for their intelligibility upon the reflective power, and not merely upon the perceptive organs, the older travellers are far

superior to their successors. There are some transactions—
or, rather, there is a condition of things—which can be made
intelligible only by an imaginative delineation of their accompaniments. Alike in the statement of facts which need only to be
narrated, in order to be understood, and in the delineation of
conditions, which need the help of the imagination in order to their
thorough appreciation, the older African travellers are far safer
guides than those who, in countless numbers, are following them.
The earlier travellers came out unfurnished with any previous ideas
of the objects they were to explore. Their minds seem to have been
a complete *tabula rasa* in relation to the country and people. The
result was that the facts were given as they appeared to them,
not coloured or modified with a view to support or disprove any
theory. The greatest masters in any art are those who have first
trodden the way. Others must necessarily be imitators. It has
been so with sculpture, painting and music; and it is so with travels
in Africa. In an old Atlas, published at Amsterdam, in 1665, the
position of the Victoria Nyanza, there called "Zaflan lacus," is laid
down with wonderful accuracy, whereas Central Africa appears
almost as a pure blank in the maps of forty years ago. For the
Nigritian country, therefore, we would recommend Mungo Park's
Travels; and, after his, those of Denham and Clapperton, Caillie
and the Landers. The modern traveller is hampered by a commercial
exigency. He is under the necessity of making a book that will sell;
and he is more anxious to conform to, and perpetuate popular
notions, than to give a faithful portraiture of what he sees, for he
would then have to walk in the old goove. He must bring forth
something new, something original, something sensational. Sir
Richard F. Burton, an experienced African traveller, has recently
made the following just observation :—

> In Africa, strangers had two things to learn; in the first place, what there
> was, and in the second place what there was not; and generally, what there was
> not was more circumstantially reported than what there was.[1]

In the days of Park, Denham and Clapperton, the countries
which they visited were chiefly Pagan. They are now, through

---

[1] Remarks at Meeting of Royal Geographical Society, June 29th, 1885.

the energy and zeal of Negro converts to Mohammedanism, all under the rule of Islam. They enjoy a settled constitution, a written code of laws, and a regular government.

Mohammedanism was not quite half a century old when it was introduced into North-western Africa. Its conquests swept like a whirlwind over the northern portion of the continent, from Egypt to the Atlantic. An incident illustrative of the passionate faith, the vigour and fervour of its first propagators, is given by Gibbon:—

> The title of "Conqueror of Africa" is justly due to Akbah. He marched from Damascus at the head of ten thousand of the bravest Arabs. . . . It would be difficult, nor is it necessary, to trace the accurate line of progress of Akbah. . . . He plunged into the heart of the country, traversed the wilderness in which his successors erected the splendid capitals of Fez and Morocco, and at length penetrated to the verge of the Atlantic and the Great Desert. . . . The career, though not the zeal, of Akbah, was checked by the prospect of a boundless ocean. He spurred his horse into the waves, and raising his eyes to Heaven, exclaimed, with the tone of a fanatic, "Great God! if my course were not stopped by this sea, I would still go on to the unknown kingdoms of the West, preaching the unity of Thy holy name, and putting to the sword the rebellious nations who worship any other gods than Thee."[2]

Through the irrepressible energy of these indomitable Arabs, the Mohammedan religion superseded a higher creed, which seemed powerless to penetrate the continent. Various reasons have been assigned for the failure of the North African Church to maintain its position, and extend its influence. These reasons refer mainly to defects in the Church itself, to its internal differences and dissensions;[3] but it did not yield to the attacks of the Eastern propagandism without determined and protracted resistance.

> It must not be believed (says Cardinal Lavigerie) that the African church disappeared at a single thrust from the Arab's sword. This is a mistake too widely spread, and against which our filial piety feels bound to protest.

Leo XIII has just proclaimed it loudly, with an authority that dispenses with the necessity of any further proof. In the Bull 'Materna Ecclesiae caritas,' he says:—

> Even as the Church of Africa had grown and increased with honours, even so it accepted its destruction with dignity. The Faith of those unhappy popula-

---

[2] *Decline and Fall of the Roman Empire*, chap. li.
[3] Lloyd's *North African Church*, p. 18.

The Mohammedans of Nigritia.

tions did then struggle long and desperately with its persecutors. Fourteen times, according to the account of Ebn-Khaldoun, it was driven back by the sword into apostacy, and, fourteen times, it returned to its ancient Faith. In spite of the banishment to the deserts of Arabia of multitudes of men of all ranks—senators, wealthy lords, women, children, simple plebeians ; in spite of solicitations, seductions, caresses, the Catholic Church remained steadfast at its post at Carthage and in Tunis proper, for more than six centuries after the Mussulmans' conquest. We have proof of this in the letters of Popes Saint Leo IX and Saint Gregory the Great, during the 11th century and during the 13th, in the testimony of the historian of the Crusades, who mention in the time of St. Louis, regiments belonging to the Sultan of Tunis composed of Christian natives.[4]

But, notwithstanding so much faith, so many catastrophes, and such heroism, the Crescent superseded the Cross. We are disposed to regard it as a question at least open to entertainment, whether, upon the whole, the continuance and growth of the Christians in the North of the continent would have promoted the welfare or contributed as much to the future civilisation of the people, as the triumph of the Saracens. When we consider what has happened to the native races of other continents where Christianity is said to have established itself, we are inclined to the conclusion that the North African Church failed because it was not competent to deal with the indigenous races of the country. The Gospel, pure and simple, would have been an unspeakable blessing. But it would not have come pure and simple. A writer in the *Church Missionary Intelligencer* (July, 1885) candidly says :—

It is cheering to observe that as the veil is gradually being withdrawn from unknown Africa, some attempt, however incommensurate with the resources of a Christian nation, is being made to send to the population the only blessing which can *possibly compensate them for the privilege of being made known*, namely, the glorious Gospel of Christ.

There is no evidence that Christianity, or, rather, professing Christians (in all we say we refer to the *professors*, not the system) would have been less unscrupulous in their dealings with natives of Africa, than they have been with the natives of America, of Australia, of New Zealand. We can hardly doubt that, in the wake of Christianity, would have followed such transactions as would have inspired the eloquent and indignant pen of some

---

[4] *Annals of the Propagation of the Faith;* March, 1885.

Prescott or Robertson. There would have been the counterparts of Cortez and Pizarro, and probably no Las Casas to check, if he could not altogether prevent, the extermination of the aborigines. The greater divergence of race would have intensified the antagonism. The successful invaders would have assumed a right to the persons and labour of the natives, slavery would have been the normal condition of the aborigines, and the cruelty and rapacity of their European masters would have exceeded anything witnessed in the New World—a whole continent would have lain prostrate at the feet of unprincipled greed and irresponsible tyranny.

Mohammedanism, in Africa, has left the native master of himself and of his home; but wherever Christianity has been able to establish itself, with the exception of Liberia, foreigners have taken possession of the country, and, in some places, rule the natives with oppressive rigour.[5]

Mr. Anthony Trollope, in his work on South Africa, says the white people of Natal told him there were no workmen to be found,

---

[5] In a pamphlet issued in 1884, by the Committee of the Wesleyan Foreign Missionary Society, they make pathetic and forcible appeal, in behalf of the "Natives in Bechuanaland, and the Transvaal, against European oppression." The Committee says—

1st. *It is a fundamental law of the constitution of Boer Government that no Native can purchase or hold land in his own name.* The natives, therefore, simply occupy land under the Boer, its owner. No amount of genius or skill, no measure of industry or enterprise on the part of the native, can ever raise him to the position of a joint-ownership.

2nd. They are further oppressed by "The Location System" which may be thus described: A Municipality, however large or small, formed by the Boers of any town, enacts that the natives shall not be allowed to reside within the area of said town, but shall have a portion of land assigned to them somewhere in the neighbourhood, on which they must locate. A tax is exacted from the occupant of every shanty in the "location."

3rd. The "Curfew Bell," *with its most invidious associations*, afflicts them.

4th. There is the absence of all marital laws and rights of the native people within the area of the Transvaal. They have no standing within the "fundamental law" of the Boer as to marriage.

5th. The natives are plundered with impunity by the Boers under the title of "Commands."—*The English Government and the Natives in Bechuanaland and Transvaal.* Published at the Wesleyan Mission House, London, 1884.

The Mohammedans of Nigritia.

though the streets were full of Zulus, who will do anything for a shilling, and half anything for a sixpence. In Bloemfontein, no coloured person is allowed to walk about after eight o'clock in the evening. And, with the unfeeling hardness of the cold Northern intellect, the eminent novelist makes the following comment:—

> There are cases in which justice—abstract justice—cannot be executed. Had justice only been done, there would have been no United States, no British India, no Australia, no New Zealand, no South Africa. Humanity, forbearance and Christianity must put themselves as closely as possible into alliance with physical supremacy, and, together, make the best they can of the bargain.[o]

This is not the way the Founder of Christianity taught it to the world. He said, "All things whatsoever ye would that men should do unto you, do ye even so to them."

Christianity, then, failed in North Africa, and a people was brought from a distance, of a race cognate with the African, whose social sympathies, and foreseeing, and discriminating laws as to food and drink, and other matters—supported, as they believed, by Divine sanction—supplied elements for the preservation of the natives. The Atlantic interposed its threatening billows to the progress of Islam; the Sahara interposed its perilous sands to the progress of Christianity. The propagators of Christianity constructed for themselves the conveyances in which they crossed the Atlantic. The bearers of Islam had the "ships of the desert" created for them. The ocean was a highway for Christianity; the desert a highway for Islam. Europe could not penetrate Africa; Arabia could. A slave and an African was the mother of Ishmael, the progenitor of the founder and first followers of Islam. Shem and Ham unite in Mohammed. Instances of the union of Shem and Ham are frequent in Holy writ. We have Joseph and the Priestess of On; Moses and the Ethiopian woman; Solomon and Pharaoh's daughter. They have been together in ruling and in serving, on the throne and in the dungeon. So, when the descendants of the union of these two great families appeared in the north and north-east of Africa with their religion, Central Africa

---

[o] Trollope's *South Africa*, p. 108.

readily opened to them. The desert gave forth water, and the fever tempered its intensity. Japheth and Ham have never yet come together in large numbers, except in the capacity of master and slave. And, if the present attempt of Europeans to take possession of the vast regions of the Congo could succeed—but happily it cannot—they could not make their acquisition of any value without introducing a system of enforced labour, which is slavery.

After the first conquests of the Muslims in North Africa, their religion advanced southward into the continent, not by arms, but by schools, and books, and mosques, by trade and intermarriage. They could not have brought a force sufficient to subjugate the people, for they had to deal with large, powerful and energetic tribes. The Nigritian and Soudanic tribes have never been subdued by a foreign foe, but they have, over and over again, driven back both Arabs and Europeans. We learn from a distinguished African geographer, that when the Portuguese discovered and took possession of the western coast, they found a Negro king who had not only extended his conquests from the centre of Housa to the border of the Atlantic, and from the Pagan countries of Mosé, in 12° north latitude, as far as Morocco, but governed his subjects with justice, and adopted such of the customs of Mohammedanism as he thought conducive to civilisation.[7]

Major Denham gives a graphic account of the disastrous issue of two expeditions made by Arabs against natives, armed only with spears and arrows, in one of which he himself nearly lost his life. In both cases the rout was complete—the Arabs fled in dismay. When Major Denham was flying, in a naked and miserable state, from the victorious enemy, he experienced something of the hospitality of the African, of which Mungo Park gives so many interesting instances. A young African prince pulled off his own trousers and gave them to him."[8]

---

[7] See Cooley's *Negroland of the Arabs*.

[8] *Narrative of Travels and Discoveries in Northern and Central Africa in the Years 1822, 1823 and 1824;* by Major Dixon Denham, of His Majesty's 17th Regiment of Foot; and Captain Hugh Clapperton, of the Royal Navy.—London, 1826.

The Mohammedans of Nigritia.

Neither by the wars of the ancients, nor by the improved methods of modern warfare—neither for political nor religious ends—have foreigners been able to penetrate and occupy the Soudan. It was after the great tribes had been peaceably converted to Islam that we hear of Jihads—military expeditions to reduce Pagans to the faith. This religious propagandism, conducted by native warriors, has been carried on with wonderful activity and success during the last fifty years. Thirty years ago, a religious devotee and military genius—a native of Futah Toro, Al-Hajj Omaru—reduced large districts on the Upper Niger to the faith of Islam. He received the title, "Al-Hajj," "The Pilgrim," after he had performed the pilgrimage to Mecca. He was well versed in the Arabic language and literature, and wrote a number of books on his travels, and on religious subjects, which are in circulation throughout Nigritia.º

He has had several successors in the work of disseminating the Mohammedan creed; and they are rapidly bringing the whole of Africa north of the equator under the influence of the Crescent. The most important kingdoms in this portion of the continent which are still subject to Paganism are, Dahomey and Ashantee, and their conversion is a question of a short time only. There is, at this moment, an energetic promoter of the Jihad, having under his command scores of thousands of zealous Mohammedans anxious for the spoils of time and the rewards of eternity. By means of these, he is reducing to the faith the most warlike and powerful tribes. His name is Samudu, born about forty years ago, in the Mandingo country, east of Liberia. His fame has gone far beyond Nigritia, all through the Soudan. It has crossed the Mediterranean to Europe, and the Atlantic to America. A narrative of his proceedings now lying before us, written in Arabic, by a native chronicler, contains an interesting account of his method and achievements. The introductory paragraph we translate as follows:—

This is an account of the Jihad of the Imam Ahmadu Samudu, a Mandingo, an inhabitant of the town of Sanankodu, in the extreme part of the Koniah

---

º A sketch of Al-Hajj Omaru's life is given by Lieutenant Mage, in his *Voyage d'Exploration dans le Soudan Occidental.*

country. God conferred upon him His help continually after he began the work of visiting the idolatrous Pagans, who dwell between the sea and the country of Wasulu, with a view of inviting them to follow the religion of God, which is Islam.

Know all ye who read this—that the first effort of the Imam Samudu was at a town named Fulindiyah. Following the Book and the Law, and the Traditions, he sent messengers to the King at that town, Sindidu by name, inviting him to submit to his government, abandon the worship of idols, and worship one God, the Exalted, the True, whose service is profitable to His people in this world and in the next; but they refused to submit. Then he imposed a tribute upon them, as the Koran commands on this subject; but they persisted in their blindness and deafness. The Imam then collected a small force of about five hundred men, brave and valiant, for the Jihad, and he fought against the town, and the Lord helped him against them, and gave him the victory over them, and he pursued them with his horses until they submitted. Nor will they return to their idolatry, for now all their children are in schools, being taught the Koran, and a knowledge of religion and civilisation. Praise be to God for this.

Alimami Samudu then went to another idolatrous town called Wurukud, surrounded by a strong wall, and skilfully defended, &c.

The same course was adopted as with the former town, and this is the method pursued in all his operations. Large and powerful states which, two years ago, were practising all the irrational and debasing superstitions of a hoary Paganism, are now under the influence of schools and teachers, and the regular administration of law. In 1872, the present writer visited Falaba, the capital of the Soolima country, two hundred and fifty miles east of Sierra Leone, as Special Commissioner to the King from the British Government. He found the King and his people intelligent, warlike, brave, and energetic, but determined Pagans. For fifty years, the Foulah Mohammedans, by annual military expeditions, had striven to bring them over to the faith of Islam, but they had always successfully resisted every attack. To-day, however, Falaba is Mohammedan, having fallen two years ago, before the troops of Samudu, under the melancholy circumstances detailed in the following letter, addressed to us by the Government Interpreter of Sierra Leone:—

Freetown, Sierra Leone,
October 30, 1884.

Dear Sir,—I am sure you will be sorry to hear that Falaba is taken. As you have visited that region of country on two occasions, I know that you must take a deep interest in it. The King, Royal Family, and principal men, were killed;

The Mohammedans of Nigritia.

and the rest of the inhabitants hurried into slavery, in countries above and below Falaba, by the captors, under the command of Alfa Samudu and Mahmudi Daranii. The latter is reported to have since died. It is reported that when Sewah, King of Falaba (well known to you), found that he could do no more to save his capital, together with its inhabitants, and numerous villages, from being taken by the armed Mohammedans, he invited the whole Royal Family, and many of the principal persons, into a large house, where he had a large quantity of gunpowder, and addressed them in the following words:—

"Falaba is an ancient country, and never has been conquered by any tribe; it has always been ruling, and never has been ruled. I will never submit to Mohammedanism. If any of you choose to become Mohammedans, you are at liberty to do so." All unanimously replied "They would rather die than become Mohammedans."

The King then threw a lighted torch into the powder, which immediately caught fire, and the whole place and people were burnt to death. Thus was Falaba taken by the great Mohammedan war, now coming to the coast. It is reported that Suluku, the chief of Big Boumba, in the Limba country, has surrendered and taken a new name, Ahmadu Sofala. Should I learn anything further, I will inform you. With kind regards,

I remain, dear Sir,
Your obedient Servant,
THOMAS G. LAWSON,
Dr. E. W. Blyden. *Govt. Interpreter.*

This letter was published in the *West African Reporter* (Nov. 22, 1884), upon which the Editor remarked as follows:—

The capture of Falaba, the capital of the Soolima country, by the troops of Alfa Samudu, will form an important epoch in the history of the Western Soudan. The brief but graphic description of the circumstances of the capture of this important city, as given by Mr. Lawson in this issue, will be read with painful interest. . . . For more than three months, Falaba successfully resisted the forces of Samudu, commanded by three distinguished generals—Fode Darami, Infalli and Bilal. These men believed themselves to be fighting for the establishment of the true religion, and for the freedom and security of trade. Falaba felt itself fighting for national life. The strife was exacerbated by fanaticism on the one hand, and the phrensy of personal peril and menaced independence on the other. At length, Samudu gave orders to cease active operations, and having a large number of men and vast resources at his command, established a siege, which he maintained with relentless vigour, for several months, until the fatal surrender. Starvation did what his troops could not do.

The troops of this energetic commander are now moving westward toward the Atlantic. He has no quarrel with Christians, whom he treats with consideration and respect, and he would be an important auxiliary in the interior operations of Christian Governments on the coast, if only they knew how to utilise him. He displays in all his dealings a soldierly, as well as fatherly, heroism; so that he has the art, as a rule, without carnage, of making his iconoclastic message acceptable to the sympathies of the Pagans whom he summons to the faith. In every town taken, either by force of arms or by its own voluntary submission, he plants a mosque and schools, and stations a teacher and preacher. He lays great stress upon education. He trusts to the Koran and to the schools far more than to the sword, as instruments for the determination of the great moral and political controversy between him and the Pagans, and for the general amelioration. Indeed, throughout Mohammedan Africa, education is compulsory. A man might now travel across the continent, from Sierra Leone to Cairo, or in another direction, from Lagos to Tripoli, sleeping in a village every night, except in the Sahara, and in every village he would find a school. There is regular epistolary communication throughout this region in the Arabic language—sometimes in the vernacular, written in Arabic characters. Bishop Crowther informed us that he received a letter at Lagos, which had come across the continent from Tripoli.

The book chiefly taught in the schools, and with a view to the educidation of which all other books are studied, is the Koran. It is called *Alkitab*, "The Book," *par excellence*, just as the Bible is by us. It is composed in the purest Arabic, and offers many difficulties to those not acquainted with the idom of the Desert Arabs, who alone speak the language in its perfection. The books which, beside the Koran, are taught in all the schools, are various theological treatises and the *Moallakat*—the six poems, which, in a literary contest of all Arabia, before the days of Islam, carried off the prize for grammatical excellence, purity and style. One of these poems was written by a Negro, and won the special admiration of Mohammed. Another work which is much studied is the *Makamat, or Assemblies of Hariri*, which are said, in fifty books or parts, to contain the whole Arabic language. This work is the result of the literary system of a period in which not only the sciences, but the useful arts of life, were sacrificed by the ingenious and studious of a great nation to a profound grammatical research into the structure and resources of their own most copious language. The theological student, anxious to master Hebrew, and the Hebrew Scriptures, should know enough Arabic to read the *Makamat*. Gesenius, in his lexicon, frequently explains a Hebrew root by reference to this treasury of Semitic philology.

The African Mohammedans are still in that period in which devotion to the one divine book, and to whatever serves to illustrate it, supersedes every other feeling. Great attention is paid to grammatical analysis; indeed, the language is said to have been first reduced to system by Abu'l Aswad, Father of the Black of African extraction.[10] Nearly every Mandingo, or Foulah trader, or itinerant teacher, carries among his manuscripts the *Alfiyeh* of Ibn Malik, the most complete and celebrated of the Arabic grammatical poems. The regular subjects of study are grammatical inflexion and syntax, rhetoric, versification, theology, the exposition of the Koran, the traditions of the Prophet, and arithmetic. But, besides treatises on serious subjects, they have an abundance of light reading, story books, &c. Richardson says:—

> Yusuf has been reading an Arabic book, which I at first thought was some commentary on the Koran; but to-day I was undeceived. He related what he read. It reminded me of *Gulliver's Travels*. A tall man walks through the sea, cooks fish in the sun, and destroys a whole town, whose inhabitants had insulted him, by the same means that our comparative giant saved the palace of Liliput from conflagration.[11]

There are numerous native authors who have written in the Arabic, Foulah, Mandingo, and Jalof languages; but great reverence is paid to Arabic; it is the language of devotion, of civil and ecclesiastical law, of inspiration. It is the opinion of the Nigritian Mohammedans that Abraham spoke Arabic. They say it was carried—by the Father of the Faithful, the Friend of God, and his son Ishmael—into Arabia, where it was kept, and was not allowed to be diffused until it was enshrined by the message of the Prophet. After it was embodied in the Koran, where it would be certain of preservation, it was allowed to go forth and to come into contact

---

[10] *Biographies of Ibn Khallikan;* vol. i, p. 662.
[11] *Narratives of a Mission to Central Africa;* vol. i, p. 57.

with other rites and customs; and they affirm that the Africans were the first people to whom it was sent.

There is, no doubt, some ground for the opinion of the African Mohammedans as to the antiquity of the Arabic language. Hebrew is regarded by Semitic scholars as really a dialect. Arabic comprises many peculiar and original formations, pointing to a remoter time and much earlier stage. And it is remarkable that a language confined to the Arabian peninsula until the seventh century after Christ should have attained such copiousness. And when it came into contact with new conditions, and strange races and customs, such is its wonderful elasticity that it adapted itself, not only by adaptations of existing roots, but by words already formed and in use, to the intelligible expression of the innumerable new notions, and even to the new ideas of modern thought and life. It is adapted to the solitudes of the desert, and to the multifarious and complex activities of the city; to the simple nomadic life of the Bedouin, and to the artificial civilisation of Alexandria, Beyrut and Bagdad. "In Arabia, as in Greece," says Gibbon, "the perfection of language outstripped the refinement of manners, and her speech could diversify the fourscore names of honey, the two hundred of a serpent, the five hundred of a lion, the thousand of a sword, at a time when this copious dictionary was entrusted to the memory of an illiterate people."

But it is interesting to meet, and to be able to converse with, one of the learned men from the heart of Nigritia, who knows nothing of the scientific discussions and discoveries of the day. It is our privilege, as we write this—one we rarely enjoy—to have the company, almost daily, of such a character. He is a man, not much over thirty, of the Mandingo tribe, now visiting the coast for the first time. He is learned in all the theological, controversial and political literature of Arabia and of his native country; is himself the author of several small treatises, speaks Arabic fluently and several native languages, and is now taking English lessons. He has in his possession two copies of the Arabic Bible (Beirut translation), and is familiar with its contents. We asked him to give, in writing, his opinion on several points on which we had conversed. We send you his views in his own handwriting (Arabic) on the Bible, on Slavery, on Pictorial and Plastic Representations, marked respectively No. 1, No. 2, No. 3. It might, perhaps, interest your readers if you could give a *fac-simile* of each, or a portion of each, in the pages of the *Review*. We give below translations :—

THE BIBLE AND THE KORAN.

Manifest differences between the Holy Bible and the illustrious Koran are presented to the careful observer. *We mention* five.

In the book of Genesis (chap. i and v. 27) it is said, " God created man in His own image, in the image of God created He him." This is contrary to his word, the Exalted, in the chapter on ' Counsel ' (*Koran*, xlii, 9). " Creator of the heavens and the earth ! He hath made for you pairs from among your own selves, and pairs from cattle—by this means he multiplies you. *There is naught like Him.*"

Again ! in Genesis, chap. ii, ver. 2, 3, it is said : " He *rested* on the seventh day." This is also contrary to the word of the Exalted, in the chapter on ' The Cow ' (*Koran*, ii, 111). " Maker of the Heavens and the Earth ! and when He decreeth a thing, He only saith to it, ' Be,' and it is." This is the truth accepted by us, that God (may He be exalted) does not work by means of tools—only by His word. " Be," and it is. This is truth without contradiction. Glory be to Him. Weariness be far from Him. Rest is sought only after weariness or fatigue, and fatigue comes from effort through labouring with the hand or with implements, and this is not applicable to the method of our Lord. (May he be honoured and glorified !)

Again : in the book of Exodus, xxxii, v, 2-4, it is said, " And Aaron said unto them, break off the golden earrings which are in the ears of your wives, of your sons and your daughters, and he received them and fashioned it with a graven tool after he had made it a golden calf." This is contrary to the words of the Exalted in the chapter, ' Ta Ha ' (*Koran*, xx, 90-92), "And so did Samiri cast, and he brought forth to them in bodily shape a lowing calf, &c., &c. And Aaron had before said to them—O my people ! by this calf are ye only proved, and verily your Lord is the Merciful : follow me, therefore, and obey my bidding.[12]

Again : in the Gospel of John (chap. xix, 16-18), it is said, " And they took Jesus, and led Him away ; and He, bearing His cross, went forth into a place called ' The Place of a Skull,' which is called in the Hebrew, ' Golgotha,' where they crucified Him and two others with Him, on either side one and Jesus in the midst." This is contrary to the words of the Exalted in the chapter on ' Women ' (*Koran* iv, p. 156). Their saying, " Verily, we have slain the Messiah, Jesus the son of Mary, the Apostle of God. . . ."

---

[12] See note on this passage in Rodwell's translation of the *Koran*. Mohammedans affirm that Aaron was opposed to the making of the calf.

Yet they slew him not, but they had only His likeness,[18] and verily, they who differed about Him were in doubt concerning Him. No sure knowledge had they about Him, but followed only an opinion; and they did not really slay Him, but God took Him up to Himself.

Again: In the prayer, "Our Father, who art in heaven." This is contrary to His word (May He be exalted). "Praise be to God, the *Lord of all creatures*." The import of the words, "Our Father," is an affirmation of Fatherhood on the part of God, the Truth, and disowns his Lordship (May He be glorified), and rejects the servitude (*servanthood expresses* the idea of the original letter) of the creature affirming sonship on their part.

This is not a doctrine acceptable to the people who hold to the unity[14] of God. The words, "Lord of all creatures," affirm dominion, sovereignty, on the part of God, the Truth, for this is His prerogative, and submission and obedience on the part of the creature, which is their proper position. It is finished.

No. 2.—SLAVERY.

Saith God, the Exalted (and He is the most righteous of speakers): Verily, the most honourable of you in the sight of God is the most pious of you (*Koran*, xlix, 13).

From this the intelligent may understand that no creature can be a slave to a creature. God suffereth one to come into the possession of another as a test of the compassionate or merciful disposition of the possessor, and the nature of his gratitude to Him, the Exalted; and for the possessed (the slave), a test of the measure of his submission to the decree and power of God. And that it may be made manifest to thee that God is the controller of His creatures, verily the Exalted may make His enemy ruler over His friend, as He tried His servant Joseph—the righteous, the honourable, son of the honourable, *who* was son of the honourable, who was son of the Friend of God. He made him the slave of Potiphar, a ruler in Egypt, and he submitted to the decree of his Lord and to His power; and God changed his servitude to the most excellent rank, and made him chief and King over the people of his time. Very often a man purchases a slave with his money, and he serves him till he dies; and notwithstanding this, he is nearer to God than his master, as was the case with the Children of Israel who, in their time, on account of the revelation granted to them, were superior to all other people; yet God gave them in servitude to Pharaoh, with all his arrogance and Heathenism, until the period of the departure of Israel by the hand of his patient and prudent servant Moses, the son of Amram (Peace be upon them both). This was a trial to them, and a humiliation for their sins. Therefore, O man of understanding, be not arrogant over your slave or make yourself superior to him. Seek from him with kindness what God has decreed to you of profit

---

[13] Literally, "*One was made to appear to them like Jesus.*"—Rodwell. The Mohammedans believe it was an *eidolon*, and not Jesus Himself, who was crucified.—Palmer's translation of the *Koran, in loco*.

[14] Not only the oneness, but the unapproachable singularity of the Divine Being.

from him, and know that God, who made you ruler over him, is able to make him ruler over you. Thank God for His gift, and be not ungrateful. Gratitude secures favour, ingratitude dismisses it. Saith God (May He be honoured and glorified) in his Book—chapter on the 'Prophets' (*Koran*, xxi, 36)—"For trial, we will prove you with evil and with good, and unto us shall ye return." Oh God, I entreat Thee grant me firmness in the faith and preservation in this world, and in the next. Oh God! bless our Lord, Mohammed, and keep him safe, and all the Prophets and the Apostles, brethren of Mohammed. May the blessing of God be upon them all. Praise be to God, Lord of all creatures.

No. 3.—PICTURES.

Moses and Jesus (Blessing and peace upon them), were prophets indeed, and in truth. Their excellence and superiority are not hidden, but they have no followers. I have not seen their followers, nor have I heard of them from the mouth of men. I have not seen among them, *i.e.*, those to whom has been given the Bible, any opposition to the making of images and figures in their houses and churches, and on walls. I have even seen in the markets loaves of bread made into figures—some to resemble men, and some other things. Now, among things well understood by those to whom there is the slightest perception in this: that in the Holy Bible, God, through the prophets and their followers, forbade the making of images and the worship of them. He has explained that He is a jealous God, and said, "Thou shalt not make unto thyself any graven image, &c." Is this abrogated? Why, then, is not the verse shown by which it is abrogated? And if you ask them concerning this, what is their answer? Do they not say that this is an old prohibition? Or they say, "When we make images and pictures it shows our intelligence;" or, "God has forbidden the *worship* of images, not the *making* of them. Verily this is the delusion of Satan to them. The house has neither foundation nor support. Know that the *making* of images, as well as the *worshipping* of them, after receiving the Divine revelation against it, is a work of the devil; who, through his envy of the believing followers of the prophets, whispers this wickedness into the hearts of the servants of God—from among those who have the books of Moses and Jesus and our Prophets, and deceives many, except those who believe and do the things that are right of the people of Mohammed. Some of those of whom we have heard, of the followers of Moses and Jesus, who bow down before images, say falsely that they are the images of those whom they love and honour, of the prophets, and great men who followed them—that they worship God (May He be glorified) by means of these images. But they do not perceive that such work is contrary to the command of God, and cannot be pleasing to Him. They are carried away by this mockery of Satan, who rejoiceth in their degradation through these deeds of theirs. May the curse of God rest upon the devil and his associates; and may God separate between the people of Mohammed and the accursed, as He separates between them and His Forgiveness and His Paradise. He is over all things mighty!

It must be interesting to every intelligent and earnest Christian, to get the glimpse which these papers which we have laid before them, give of the views and feelings of the Negro Mohammedans of Africa, on the questions discussed. It will be seen in No. 1, that one of the most precious doctrines of Christianity has no place in the Koran—the doctrine of the atonement of the vicarious sufferings and death of Christ.

It will, no doubt, strike the reader with astonishment, also, to learn from the same paper, that the Fatherhood of God, as understood by Christians, is not accepted by Mohammedans. With them the Lord is King of Kings and Lord of Lords, the Sovereign of the universe, Lord of all creatures. The description of God, in the Koran, is as follows:—

> God! there is no god but He; the living, the subsisting; neither slumber seizeth Him, nor sleep; His, whatsoever is in the Heavens, and whatsoever is in the Earth! Who is he that can intercede with Him but by His own permission? He knoweth what is present with his creatures, and what is yet to befall them; yet naught of His knowledge do they comprehend, save what He willeth. His throne reacheth over the Heavens and the Earth, and the upholding of both burdeneth Him not, and He is the High, the Great!" [15]

The Muslim's idea of God is that of a Being too exalted to have any relations with his creatures, even remotely resembling earthly relationship. Their system admits neither anthropomorphism nor circumlocutions of any kind. They would accept the unrivalled definition of God as given by the Westminster Assembly's *Shorter Catechism*. But, notwithstanding this distance to which the God of the Mohammedan is removed, yet they act far more fully than some who would condemn them upon the other idea, which is a result of the belief in the Fatherhood of God, viz., the Brotherhood of men. "Write me down," said Abou ben Adhem, "as one who loves his fellow-men." Many Christians who say "Our Father," reject the truth in practice. Recent American papers are full of illustrations of the extreme difficulty experienced in that eminently Christian country on the question of dealing with the Negro on the broad platform of Christian brotherhood. The Annual Council of the Diocese of Virginia has just adopted a Canon (May, 1886)

---

[15] Sura ii, p. 256.

which provides a separate organisation for the coloured Episcopalians, to be known as the "Coloured Missionary Jurisdiction" of the Diocese of Virginia. There were cast for the measure 114 votes out of 164. No doubt, these 114 voters said "Our Father" every morning and evening. The Bishops of the Methodist Episcopal Church, South, in their quadrennial address (May, 1886), held the following language:—

> The attitude of the Negro toward all the institutions of the country is a problem, civil and spiritual, which becomes hourly more difficult of solution. Nor must we, on the other hand, be hurried forward by sentimental extravagance in the direction of the discoloured current of social equality, through the agency of the schoolroom, the congregation, or the conference; for there is no *conceivable result* that would compensate for the *crime against Nature* which this theory deliberately contemplates.[10] But this is a reproduction of the doctrine of the late Bishop Pierce, formally announced on the occasion of his golden wedding, February 3, 1884. He said:—The Negroes are entitled to elementary education, the same as the whites, from the hands of the State. It is the duty of the Church to improve the coloured ministry, but rather by theological training than by literary education. In my judgment, *higher education, so called, would be a positive calamity to the Negroes.* It would increase the friction between the races, produce endless strifes, elevate Negro aspirations far above the station he was created to fill, and resolve the whole race into a political faction, full of strife, mischief, and turbulence. Negroes ought to be taught that the respect of the white race can only be attained by good character and conduct. Their well-doing and well-being, all right-minded citizens desire, and would rejoice in. Agriculture and all the mechanical pursuits are open to them, and in them they might find lucrative employment. In these directions they may support their families, get property, and become valuable citizens. If Negroes were educated, intermarriages in time would breed trouble; but of this I see no tendency now. *My conviction is, that Negroes have no right on juries, in legislatures, or in public office.* . . . The whites can never tamely, and without protest, submit to the intrusion of coloured men into places of trust and profit, and responsibility.[17]

The views which Southern bishops are enforcing by elaborate

---

[10] We copy these paragraphs from the correspondence of the New York *Independent* (May 13, 1886). The correspondence describes the address as "an able and comprehensive document, in plain and vigorous English." The Editor makes no remark.

[17] *Methodist Review;* May, 1886, p. 339.

argument, Southern professors are putting in telling epigrams. "Poor Sambo!" exclaims Professor Noah K. Davis, " he asks for bread, and you build him a college; he asks for a fish, and you send him a professor." Dr. Curry calls this epigrammatic wit.[18]

But, with all this, the Negro is hopeful for the future. We wish we could share this hope; but we do not believe that what race-prejudice begrudges to the fathers will be conceded to the children. In spite of the barriers which argument and ridicule and outrage strive to put into the way of the education of the proscribed class, many will, no doubt, rise to heights of scholarship and become adepts in science, while the oppressors may grow in liberality; but the involuntary limits of their mental and social sympathies will always prevent them from according to their former chattels, of a distinct race, equal, or rather identical, privileges, with themselves. John F. Morgan, in the *North American Review*, July, 1884, says, in view of the future, "The same party which claims to have emancipated the Negro, will become the most active in his disfranchisement."

In the same *Review* (November, 1884), Prof. E. W. Gillian, speaking of the efforts to elevate the freedmen, says:—

> The final result must be race-antagonism, growing in intensity, and menacing malignant evils. One race must be above, the other below, with a struggle for position. Equality is impossible. *The African must return or be returned to Africa.*

The *Christian Recorder* (June 24, 1886) says that, "A few weeks ago, a distinguished man in the Methodist Episcopal Church, deferred the consideration of the question of social equality to the year 1986." Let us hope that, in 1986, hundreds of thousands of Christian Negroes from the United States will be, in this hemisphere, successfully vying with their Mohammedan brethren in reclaiming the continent from Paganism, and introducing the reign of the Prince of Peace. Long before that time the "colour line" will have been washed out by the broad Atlantic, and the white man, rejoicing in the homogeneousness of his great country, will wave in triumph across the briny deep, to the "brother in

---

[18] *Ibid.*; July, 1886, p. 626.

black," the handkerchief of social recognition, and wonder at the former aberration of opinion on this subject. In the meanwhile, it seems to be expected that the Negro in America will "order himself lowly and reverently to all his betters."

But the Christian Negro meets with trouble from his brethren of a different race in other quarters than the United States. The British Wesleyans of the West Indies, on account of the preponderance of the coloured population, find it impossible, after one hundred years of labour in those islands, to organise a West Indian Conference.[10] The leading official organ of English Wesleyans, in an elaborate article on 'Wesleyan Foreign Missions,' which caused some stir at the time of its publication, thus describes the situation:—

Taking the Islands as a whole, the Colonial element is not strong. The coloured population greatly predominates. This is true of the West Indian Churches generally. It is barely fifty years ago since slavery was abolished in the West Indies. As a rule, every man who is over fifty years of age was once a slave, redeemed by British justice, with British gold. With rare exceptions, every man who is over thirty years of age is the child of parents who were born in slavery—a slavery which was the tradition of generations. The evils which that slavery had so cruelly inwrought into the enslaved race cannot all be remedied in the course of the first generation. Where freedom does not flourish, conscience must needs be exotic. Duplicity breeds distrust. The knowledge that notions of truth and honesty are commonly lax, will necessarily hinder one from confiding in another. That the coloured men of the islands are, in many cases, able to assert their rights, and to hold themselves equal, in conscious integrity and business power, to the best among their whiter comrades, need not be denied. The truth remains that, in more islands than one, it is difficult to persuade one darkskinned man to trust another. Lay officers are few and hard to find. These things have been too often affirmed to be regarded as strange. They were known to the Missionary Committee three years ago as fully as they are known to-day; and it is an open secret that, because they were known, the Committee was in no haste for the constitution of the Conference.[20]

No wonder, after such a statement, we should find that at the Wesleyan May Meeting, in July, 1886, there was not a little discouragement. The English correspondent of the Sierra Leone *Methodist Herald* says, under date June 15, 1886:—

---

[10] We learn that since this was written the West Indian Conference has been organised.

[20] *London Quarterly Review*; July, 1885.

Christianity, Islam and the Negro Race.

Sincere heart-searchings and close self-examination, have been occasioned in many quarters by the falling-off in missionary contributions, as reported at the present Anniversary of the Wesleyan Missionary Society, as well as by the diminished attendance at the Exeter Hall and some other meetings, and the decrease of membership. Hence we have had much correspondence in our religious papers, especially in the *Christian World*, on the question, 'Is Methodism declining?'

By an interesting coincidence the writer of the letter from which we take this extract is no other than the veteran Wesleyan missionary—now retired—the Rev. William Moister, who has been in labours so abundant, both in Africa and in the West Indies. When he read the startling sentences in the *London Quarterly*, he must have recalled his own statements, made twenty years ago, as to missionary success in the West Indies. In his *History of Wesleyan Missions* (p. 92), he says:—

In the West Indies, we can point to Christian ministers, physicians, lawyers, magistrates, legislators, philosophers, of African descent, who perform their duties with as much efficiency and dignity as persons of any other country, although some of them have had but slender means of raising themselves to their present honourable position.

If the statement of the *London Quarterly* is not the invention of prejudice, what a falling-off there must have been in the last two decades.

In the United States there are the Methodist Episcopal Church and the African Methodist Episcopal Church, having the same creed, polity and language. The separation is caused by the elemental differences of race and colour; evidently no fault of the Negro Church; for it displays on its banner, with almost pathetic distinctness and reiteration, the sentiment of which Mohammedans do not admit the first part, but practise the second, "God our Father; Man our brother." The formal and continuous holding forth of this truth would be superfluous, if it were universally recognised. But its presentation by the weaker—by the so-called inferior and despised party—wears to us the aspect of a humiliating appeal for recognition and sympathy—the *argumentum ad misericordiam*. It is the "Am I not a Man and a Brother?" of the days of Slavery. The excellent device of the *Christian Recorder* would have weight, it seems to us—we mean, not inherent, but relative weight—if it were displayed by the stronger and superior, with a view of attracting the weaker. But coming from the weaker, it appears to us that the desired effect is destroyed. All force is withdrawn from the strongest phrases in the language when employed by those who cannot command, but only beg. The offer of liberality is effective only when made by those who have the means to be liberal. The offer of beneficence on the part of those who have no benefits to confer, is meaningless. We do not say that those who have adopted the motto have no justification for it. They have not only strong foot-hold in reason and common sense, but they have good ground in the Gospel of Christ. We do not believe that such a brotherhood is beyond the possibilities of Christianity. We believe that the purpose and tendency of the system is to make hearts divided by the distinctions of race, or rank, or intellect, clasp one another in the close embrace of a common faith. Was not this its effect in the primitive Church? Our Mohammedan friends are charmed by that beautiful picture drawn by Luke of the simple and loving life of the Apostolic Church—"And all that believed were together, and had all things common; and sold their possessions and goods; and parted them to all men, as every man had need. . . . . And the multitude of them that believed were of one heart and of one soul; neither said any of them that ought of the things which he possessed was his own; but they had all things common." The theory of the Church of Christ, as taught by the Divine Founder and his immediate successors, is a spiritual Kingdom whose citizens are all sons of God, and therefore brothers and sisters one of another. "For this cause" says St. Paul, "I bow my knees unto the Father of our Lord Jesus Christ of whom the whole family in earth and heaven is named." But, alas, in a materialistic age, the noble device held forth by the *Christian Recorder* is simply "the voice of one crying in the wilderness." *Vox clamantis in deserto.*

The views of our author on 'Slavery' (No. 2) are very different from those attributed to Muslims by the popular opinion of Christian countries. But they are the views held throughout the Mohammedan world. "Slavery, from the first to the last," says Mr. Palgrave, "after the manner in which it is practised here (in Arabia) from time immemorial, has little but the name in common with the system, hell-branded by those atrocities of the Western hemisphere."[21] Mohammed, at the beginning of his mission, caused such excitement among the slaves by the liberality of his teaching, that some of the large slaveholders found it necessary to remove their slaves from the vicinity of his labours, lest they should all turn converts. His system was a social, as well as a religious and political, revolution. Says an able reviewer:—

Under Mohammed there sprang up, *ex necessitate rei*, a form of democratic equality, more absolute than the world has elsewhere seen. Claims of birth and wealth could be of no value, or the presence of a master whose favour implied the favour of the Deity. The proudest Arab could not murmur if God chose a slave like Zeid to be the leader of armies, and visibly confirmed his choice with the seal of victory. It is a principle, also, of the new sect, that Islam extinguished all relations. The slave, once a Muslim, was free; the foe, once a Muslim, was dearer than any kinsman; the Pagan, once a Muslim, might preach, if the Prophet bade, to attentive listeners. Mohammed was enabled, therefore, at all times to command the absolute aid of every man of capacity within his ranks. No officers of *his* throw up their commissions because they were superseded. If he selected a child, what then? Could not God give victory to a child? Moreover, all the latent forces which social order restrains were instantly at his disposal. Every strong man, kept down by circumstances, had an instinctive desire to believe in the faith which removed at a stroke every obstacle to his career. To this hour, this principle is still of vital importance in all Mohammedan countries. A dozen times has a Sultan, utterly ruined, stooped among his people, found—in a water-carrier, a tobacconist, a slave, or a renegade—the required man; raised him in a day to power, and supported him to save the empire. If the snuff-dealer can rule Egypt, why should he not rule Egypt? He is as near to God as any other Mussulman, save only the heir of the Kalifate; and accordingly, Mohammed Ali finds birth, trade and want of education, no obstacles in his path. The pariah who, in Madras, turns Christian, is a pariah still; but if he turns Mohammedan, the proudest Muslim noble will, if he rises, give him his daughter, or serve him as a sovereign, without a thought of his descent.[22]

Mohammed appointed a Negro slave, Bilal, to call the faithful to prayer at the stated times. And from those Negro lips the beautiful sentiment first found utterance—"Prayer is better than sleep: Prayer is better than sleep." It is repeated every day throughout the Mohammedan world; and the most distinguished

---

[21] *Eastern and Central Arabia;* vol. ii, p. 271.
[22] *National Review,* October, 1861.

The Mohammedans of Nigritia.

European of which history can boast is, in Asia and Africa, an unknown personage by the side of the slave, Bilal. Mohammed gave this man precedence to himself in Paradise. On one occasion the Prophet said to Bilal, at the time of the morning prayer, "O Bilal, tell me an act of yours from which you had the greatest hopes; because, I heard the noise of your shoes in front of me in Paradise, in the night of my ascension."[23]

It is said that the intellectual part of Christendom is in revolt against the received forms of Christianity; that there is a growing alienation from the recognised standard of belief; but among African Mohammedans, the Church of the people is identical with the intellect of the people. The possibilities of every individual in the nation, whatever his race or previous condition, give social stability and spiritual power to the system. Frederick Douglass, as a Mohammedan, would have been a *waleess*—a saint of the religion, an athlete of the faith; as a Christian, his orthodoxy is suspected, and his very presence is deprecated in a church in the capital of the nation; and further south, his domestic relations would probably earn him a home in the penitentiary.

In No. 3, on 'Pictures,' &c., our author says, "Jesus and Moses have no followers." The intelligent Mohammedan from the interior who visits the Christian settlements on the sea-board, is struck with the discrepancy between what he has read in the Bible and what he sees in the customs of the people. He knows nothing of the argument, from necessity or expediency, by which, in Christian countries, much of the letter and spirit of the Word is set aside and neutralised.[24] In a conversation with our learned friend, he expressed his surprise at what he regarded as the sinful taste for pictures displayed in the houses of Christians whom he had visited, and quoted the Second Commandment to support his view. We said, "They have them simply as a part of house furniture, as ornaments, and not as objects of worship." He replied, "Why

---

[23] *Mischat-ul-Masabih;* vol. i, p. 285.

[24] Some things there may be in the structure of society to-day, as in the days of Moses—as in all the days since Moses—which must be tolerated temporarily, because of the hardness of men's hearts.—*Methodist Review;* July, 1886, p. 598.

are they not satisfied with the ornaments which Nature has furnished in such lavish profusion around them—the blue sky, the white clouds, the beautiful flowers, the living birds, the real horses, sheep, and goats, the prolific cow?" &c. We then asked him to put his opinion on the subject in writing, when he wrote at once No. 3.

Besides the passage in the Koran which forbids the making of images, Mohammed, in private instructions, constantly impressed upon his followers the evil of such practices. The Prophet said, "Those will be punished the most severely, at the day of resurrection, who draw likenesses of God's creation." "If you must make pictures, make them of trees, and things without life."[25]

This prohibition has not been without its advantages to the Negro convert to Islam. His Arab teacher having no pictures by which to aid his instruction, was obliged to confine him to the book. In this way, his thinking and reasoning powers were developed rather by what he read and heard than by what he saw. He saw neither busts nor pictures, but men. He did not study books, but character. And among the first lessons he learned was, that a man of his own race, a Negro, assisted at the birth of the religion he was invited to accept; and, in his subsequent training, his imagination never for one moment endowed the great men of whom he heard or read with physical attributes essentially different from his own. When—in 1873, at the court of the Mohammedan King of Futah Jallo, three hundred miles north-east of Sierra Leone, we saw him, surrounded by his venerable chiefs and sheikhs, all men of fine forms, who looked to us more like the old prophets and kings than any other group we ever saw—we asked him what was his conception of the personal appearance of Mohammed and the first Khalifs, he replied: "They looked just like the men you see here." This man had never seen a picture, and his imagination reproduced the great men of Islam in the forms with which he was familiar. So, the boys who are being educated in the Nigritian schools are not subject, like their Negro brethren in Christian lands, to those intermittent exertions of the faculty of insight which,

---

[25] *Mischat-ul-Masabih;* vol. ii, p. 869.

sometimes make them look upon themselves as full men, with all the possibilities of men; but at other times, forced by the only pictorial examples they see of greatness, to doubt their capacity to attain to the excellence they admire. The white boy who looks at the glories of the canvas, or the exquisite forms brought out in the marble, feels an elevation of sentiment, a rush of inspiration and aspiration. He grasps some fragment of the beauty of the marble, or gathers some flying whisper from the magnificence of the canvas, and echoes it back in the language of his own consciousness, and feels, "I, too, am a white man!" The Negro youth sees only the surface—it is all obscure allegory to him, and his feeling is frozen into language subtler than the marble he looks upon, as he asks himself, "What part or lot have I in this?" While, therefore, he stands in art galleries amid admiring crowds, there never was a man to whom a yellow primrose is, in so true a sense, nothing more than a primrose.

Bishop Turner complains that, in the United States, even in the estimate of the generality of Negroes, "White is God, and black is the Devil." What wonder that it is so? The Negro imbibes this lesson through every avenue of his soul. For him, then, there would have been no loss if the Second Commandment had been rigidly enforced: "Thou shall not make unto thyself any graven image, or any likeness of anything that is in heaven above, or that is in the earth beneath, or that is in the water under the earth."[20] This verse is omitted in the shorter catechism, both of the Lutherans and of the Roman Catholics. One can hardly see why since it is given, in full, in Luther's Bible and in the Vulgate. Dogmatic motives, probably, caused the omission by the Roman Catholics, as one of the chief methods of instructing the masses in the Middle Ages was supplied by art. "The only teaching of the people," says Dean Milman, "was the ritual." Artists were employed to execute on the walls of churches, picture histories. Church, chapel, corridor, were completely transformed into one great and harmonious picture. Such paintings were the books of

---

[21] Exodus, xx, 4.

Christianity, Islam and the Negro Race.

the unlettered people. "*Illiterati, quod per Scripturam non possunt intueri, hoc per quaedam picturae lineamenta contemplantur*"—was the Declaration of the Synod of Arras, in 1205. One of the popular artists of that day is made to say, "We painters give attention to naught, but to make male or female saints on the walls and on our panels, thereby, to the great despite of the demons, to render men more devout and better."

Happily for the development of the Negro in Africa, a different method has been adopted in his training. No art can represent him. The "rich black and richer bronze" of his complexion has never yet been reproduced in marble or on canvas; and neither brush nor chisel can give his peculiar expression. Any representation made of him must be untrue to Nature. He can, therefore, dispense with plastic or pictorial art as a means of perpetuating his memory, and we see that, as a means of his education, it is worse than useless.[27]

Let Negro readers of this paper ponder the views of one of their learned brethren from the heart of Nigritia, innocent of race-oppression and race-prejudices, and know that there are millions like him, on this continent, who hold these views.[28] In their eyes, Michael Angelo, Raphael, Leonardo, Georgione, Titian, were all sinners of the deepest dye, working, in their sublimest performances, under an afflatus, not from above, but from below. The Moses of Michael Angelo, rising before us in all its commanding sternness, as the figure before which Pharaoh trembled, would be

---

[27] We have discussed this subject more fully elsewhere.—See *Fraser's Magazine*, Nov., 1875; and *Edinburgh Review*, January, 1878.

[28] Cardinal Lavigerie, of Algiers, who is said to be the best living authority in regard to the extent and influence of Mohammedanism in Africa, says that, "There are at present, from the Soudan to the Niger and Senegal, more than sixty millions of Mussulmans." We are glad to see it announced (*Christian Recorder*, June 17, 1886) that a Negro—Rev J. C Aylor—who has just graduated in a full course of Theology at the Reformed Theological Seminary, New Brunswick, N.J., has finished a special two-years course in Arabic. This is the first case, as far as we know, of any Negro in the United States devoting himself to the study of this language; and yet, for effective missionary work, in the most important part of Africa, a knowledge of Arabic, is indispensable. More Negroes read and write this language than any other.

The Mohammedans of Nigritia.

pronounced a falsehood, as the artist never saw Moses—*amal Shaitan*—the work of Satan.

The question of the future of Islam in Africa is one which is claiming the attention of the thinkers in Europe. The opinion seems to prevail that it has lost its power to influence the nations of Europe and Asia, and this is owing to decadence of the race among which it had its rise. A vigorous German writer in *Die Nation* (May 29, 1886), in a review of a recent work on Zanzibar, thus speaks of the Arab :—

> The Arab of to-day, gifted as he is, if he learns, it is little more than to read, to write, and the Koran; all other knowledge is gone to sleep. Even its medical science, which gave to Europe its first physicians, has dwindled into domestic medicines and magical art; and industry, in the general absence of needs, has declined from the construction of the Alhambra to the manufacture of the most primitive implements. The spirit has lost its impulse to an all-embracing activity; the body does not need it. The nobles buy European products. Our own science shows itself incapable of making any impression on their peculiar mental organisation.

But, whatever may be the case in Arabia, there is an irrepressible activity—intellectual, commercial, political and religious—among the adherents of the creed in Nigritia. They pursue an extensive agriculture; they spin, weave, sow, work in the metals, engage in the craft of the potter and of the tanner. Dr. Barth (1849-1855) travelled through a large portion of this country. He describes certain districts as abounding in rich pastures, in valleys of very fertile land, and in mountains clothed to their summits with noble trees. The towns and cities were walled, and respectably built; the markets were numerously attended, and a considerable trade carried on. He found commerce radiating in every direction from Kano, the great emporium of Central Africa, and spreading the manufactures and the productions of an industrious region over the whole of Western Africa. The fixed population of this city he estimated at 30,000; but, on the occasion of the great fairs, at 60,000.

The principal commerce of Kano consists in native produce; namely, the cotton cloth woven and dyed here, or in neighbouring towns, in the form of tobes; turkedi, or the oblong piece of dress of dark-blue colour worn by the women; the zenne, or plaid of various colours. There is also a large trade in sandals and tanned hides, and in the cloth fabrics manufactured at Nupe. Throughout these districts a large variety of European goods may be seen. Arabic books, printed at Morocco and Fez, in red morocco binding, form an important article of traffic. The *Koran*, the *Traditions of Bochari*, the *Commentaries*, &c., are exchanged by Moorish traders for the fine cloth manufactured by the Nigritians, and for gold dust and gold trinkets.

There is in this country an activity not suspected by the outside world. Boys, who go from remote districts to the great centres of trade, wonder at the crowds and the different wares, as country youth in England and America wonder when they visit such centres as London or Liverpool, Boston or New York. And they have not the remotest idea that in any other portion of the globe—if, indeed, the knowledge of the existence of any other portion of the globe has dawned upon them—there exists so populous, so industrious, so wealthy a community.

And all this industry and activity is controlled by the Mohammedan tribes. In Central Africa, Islam is an aggressive, conquering force; and it is, of course, infinitely superior to the Paganism which is has abolished. It has established in the minds of its adherents the sense of responsibility beyond this life, and the fear of God; and this sentiment—which is the condition of all other progress—it is not only diffusing, but transmitting to posterity. This is the element which has given stability and upward impulse to the social and political forces of advanced countries, and it will have the same effect in the dark corners of this continent. And what is an interesting fact is, that in this vast region—as large as the whole of Europe—no such question can arise as Bishop Foster solemnly put the other day: " What shall be done with Rum?" This problem has never yet arisen, and will never arise. There is no necessity for Dr. Talmage's proclamation of a " universal strike against strong drink." We can count upon at least, sixty millions of water drinkers.

It is said that General Gordon had an idea of utilising the

The Mohammedans of Nigritia.

Muslim power, with Khartoum as a centre, for carrying on the work of civilising the millions of equatorial Africa. He believed that Mohammedanism possessed enough truth for this regenerating work. In his Journal, under date September 12, 1884, he says:—

> I am sure it is unknown to the generality of our missionaries in Muslim countries, that, in the Koran, no imputation of sin is made to our Lord; neither is it hinted that He had need of pardon; and further, no Muslim can deny that the Father of our Lord was God (*vide* chap. iii of Koran), and that He was incarnated by a miracle. Our bishops content themselves with its being a false religion; but it is a false religion possessed by millions on millions of our fellow creatures. The Muslims do not say Mohammed was without sin; the Koran often acknowledges that he erred; but no Muslim will say "*Jesus sinned.*" As far as self-sacrifice of the body, they are far above the Roman Catholics, and consequently above Protestants. . . . . The God of the Muslims is *our* God.[20]

We do not envy the man who deems himself sufficiently enlightened to be able to smile at the beliefs and proceedings of this people; and dissenting, as we very decidedly do, from many of their doctrines, we dissent still more emphatically from the bigotry which refuses to recognise in their teachings and methods, many of the elements of goodness, of truth and righteousness. Now, what prospect is there of the spread of the Gospel among these people? We have purposely reserved for the close of our discussion the question which must chiefly excite the interest of the Christian world, viz.: What is the disposition of the African Mohammedan in relation to the religion of Jesus, and how far are they accessible to its influence? Let the following fact answer.

Sometime ago, through the benevolence of an English lady, we were able to send a large number of Arabic Bibles and Testaments to different countries which lie behind Liberia and Sierra Leone. Among acknowledgments which have come to us of their receipt and circulation from parties to whom we sent them, is the enclosed Arabic letter, marked No. 4, of which the following is a translation:—

> Praise and glory to the Creator of the earth and the heaven. This letter comes from the youth, native of the Futah country, to the possessor of honour and knowledge, namely, the learned Abd-ul-Karim, called among the Christians Mr. Blyden. Peace to you, and to your family. How are you? I am in good

---

[20] *The Journal of Major-General Gordon at Khartoum.*

health. I have received the books which you sent me. I distributed them among the people, and I distributed them as you directed me—I sent one copy to Mohammed Akibu, in the town of Dinkerawi. I gave two copies to Almanie Sanusi; one to Murri Ishmael; one to Almanie Amara Silla; one to Baraka, a stranger from Sego. I sent six copies to our country, Futah Jallo. I gave several to the little boys at Fulah town. When the news spread, the people asked me, "Where have you procured books like these?" I told them that a Christian man, who loves the Muslims, gave them to me, that I might give them to you to read, that we might all be one. They wondered. I then took a passage from the Koran (sura ii, verses 2nd and 3rd), which is as follows:—

"The God-fearing are those who believe in the unseen, and observe prayer, and out of what we have bestowed upon them, expend for God; *and who believe in* [the Koran] *what hath been sent down to thee;* and *what hath been sent down before thee* [the Bible]." It was their opinion that the Koran superseded the Tourat (Old Testament) and Injil (New Testament): that God revoked the Tourat and Injil when he revealed the Koran. I told them, "No! this book is the Tourat and Injil." They then rejoiced very much and said, "A deed like this is better than sending liquor." Many believe that there is no other book, and no other religion leading to Heaven, except that of Mohammed. He is their intercessor and guide to Heaven. When I first saw the Holy Bible in the Arabic tongue, a learned man informed me that the original tongues were Hebrew and Greek. I wondered, and I entered upon the reading of it, and I saw things different to what I had seen in the Koran, the great (John xiv, 6, and x—). "Jesus said unto him, I am the way, the truth, and the life: no man cometh unto the Father but by me." "I am the door; by me, if any man enter in, he shall be saved, and shall go in and out and find pasture." I took these two verses and wrote them on the back of each one of the books and gave it to them, and they promised me to read it. And after some days there came to me a man named Alfa, and sojourned with me fifteen days, that I might explain to him some of the verses in the Gospel. The words were Matt. xx, 30. He said, "How does the Koran promise us *houris* in Heaven?" I said to him, "Be patient; only read on and your burden will be lightened." He wondered. The sending of religious books to the people is a beautiful work. Therefore, I send this letter to you to inform you of what has taken place among us. One of them to whom I gave the books, said, "The words which I read in this book, do the Christians have words like these?" I said, "Yes," and he contradicted me twice. He said, "Those who have books like this, never get drunk." There are left with me now ten copies of the Psalms, and three of the whole Bible. I never give a copy to any except to those who know the Arabic language. When the time for the caravans comes, I will send the remainder as you have directed me. May the Lord your God bless you and keep you. Peace from your friend, MOMODO WAKA.

Written on the sixth day of the month of Ramadhan, in the year of the Hijra, 1201 (June 18, 1885).

It will appear that the Mohammedans do not object to reading the Christian Scriptures, and that they pay close attention to their contents. Many of those who visit Sierra Leone for trade, purchase Arabic Bibles at the bookstore there. It is a great thing to know that they read the Bible. Now, where is the living evangelical teacher to propound to them, and follow up with Gospel teaching, the question of Philip to the Eunuch, "Understandest thou what thou readest?"

The Christian world seems slow to understand who the instruments in this work must be. Just as Africa has been, and is being, conquered for Islam, not by Arabs, but by Negro converts to the system, so will she be conquered for Christianity by the Negro converts to the religion. No others can do it. The American war furnished the symbol of the method of Africa's regeneration. The war, in the Divine purpose (whatever man's plans and intentions may have been), was evidently for the freedom of the Negro;[80] and no success could crown its arms until the Negro himself was called to the front. "We thought, first," says Frederick Douglass, "we could carry on the war politely. It was to be done by gentlemen—by white men. We fought with our soft, white hands, while we kept our hard, black hand chained behind us. But, after a while, we learned wisdom; and we put an eagle on the Negro's button, a musket on his shoulder, and a knapsack on his back, and told him to help, and he did help. He responded full two hundred thousand strong.[81]

So, for the spiritual war which is being carried into Africa, the Church must utilise the African. No cheering news will come from the front until some of those millions who assisted in procuring the temporal emancipation of the race are allowed and assisted to take part in the great work of the spiritual redemption of their Fatherland. Providence has already prepared the political and ecclesiastical organisations. Liberia is the pioneer in the political movement, founded by far-seeing Christians, philanthropists and statesmen, in America. Let her be generously assisted and sup-

---

[80] Colonel McClure, of the Philadelphia *Times*, in his great lecture on 'The Lessons of the War,' delivered at Lexington, Va., June 16, ignores this issue.

[81] *Lectures on John Brown.*

ported in her advance into the continent. The African Methodist Episcopal Church in the United States (soon to be joined by the African Methodist Episcopal Zion Church, and similar organisations), in machinery and appliances, and in physical adaptation, leads the way. The Negro Baptists of the South are already in the field. There are Negro Presbyterians and Negro Episcopalians. These will all be utilised when a few more years, and a little more experience, have satisfactorily demonstrated to the American Church the utter impracticability of the present methods. "Arm the Negroes! Arm the Negroes!" will again ring through the American nation. Arm the Negroes, in the name of Christ, if Africa is to be conquered for Christ. "The solution of Africa in America," said the late Bishop Haven, with true Christian insight, after visiting this vast country, "is America in Africa;" and there can be no other solution. Bishop Taylor is calling for Negro recruits from America, for his great inward march from Liberia. May the response be large, generous, multitudinous!

African Colonisation.

THE series of brilliant explorations of Africa witnessed by the present generation has filled up the larger part of the blank spaces on maps of the "Dark Continent," and a country has been revealed such as the outside world, fifty years ago, never suspected. Previous to that time, the little that, from the coast settlements, could be discerned of the interior, encouraged the belief that not only was it inaccessible, but unworthy of the pains and sacrifices required to attempt access. But, within the last five-and-twenty years a whole library has been written, giving minute particulars of the country and people in the heart of the continent; unfolding regions that seem fresh from the hands of God; only waiting the energies of man to bring to perfection the numerous products of the soil—great rivers, extensive pasturage and tillage, cities of respectable size, a large inland commerce, countless millions of people; in some parts with the rudiments, at least, of history, and with a capacity for receiving and contributing to an advanced civilisation.

These discoveries have turned the attention of Europe to Africa with renewed curiosity and interest. And, very recently, this interest has so much increased that the competition among the leading European powers for the possession of territory on the coast has been described by the London *Times*, with no touch of exaggeration, as "The Scramble for Africa."

An European writer, delighting in epigrammatic rhetoric, has recently said, "The eighteenth century stole the black man from his country; the nineteenth century steals his country from the black man." And, just as the stealing of the man in the eighteenth century originated in philanthropic ideas, so the motive for stealing his country in the nineteenth century is put into philanthropic language. The nations engaged in the " scramble " are all models of the highest civilisation, and their aims and purposes are all in the interest of enlightenment and progress. The Congo Conference laid down admirable rules for occupation and protectorates, whatever the native may have to say against them. But they will not countenance any acts against right and justice. They are at once the invaders of his country and the protectors of his rights. The spirit of the international alliance is the spirit of liberty and equity for Africa.

But it does not seem probable to us that what foreigners have failed to accomplish in all the past ages will be achieved by their descendants of this generation. Modern Europe, with all its vast machinery of intellectual and material progress, and with all its humanitarian intentions—with all its appliances for civilising, instructing and elevating—stands paralysed before difficulties not a whit less appalling than those which, for centuries, have confronted European efforts in this country. To any thinking man, of whatever race, who, living in West Africa, surveys the current of events, the reflection must bring a feeling of discouragement that the very extension and multiplication of means of foreign communication with the country, which give material facilities for the task of her regeneration, throw moral obstacles in the way of its accomplishment, by allowing or encouraging counteracting social forces to have equal access to the field.

It is in view of the physical obstacles which beset the efforts of foreigners, and of the moral difficulties raised by the introduction of European civilisation that we purpose, in the following pages, to attempt to show how closely all prospect of regenerating the African continent is connected with human elements in the United States, which seem to be superfluous there, and with the principle represented by the American Colonisation Society.

The Negro, in exile, is the only man, born out of Africa, who can live and work and reproduce himself in this country. His residence in America has conferred upon him numerous advantages. It has quickened him in the direction of progress. It has pre-

African Colonisation.

disposed him in favour of civilisation, and given him a knowledge of revealed truth in its highest and purest form. We believe that the deportation of the Negro to the New World was as much decreed by an all-wise Providence, as the expatriation of the Pilgrims from Europe to America. When we say that Providence decreed the means of Africa's enlightenment, we do not say that He decreed the wickedness of the instruments. When the deportation first began, it was looked upon as simply the transportation of Africans to America for purposes of labour; but with a view, also, as Sir John Hawkins made Queen Elizabeth believe,[1] to their spiritual improvement. But, in course of time, human passions became mixed up with, and wicked hands prosecuted, what it had been before determined should be carried out; and the enterprise, having, at first, a beneficent aim and a humane form, became the slave trade, with all its unspeakable enormities. It was not the first time that wicked hands were suffered to execute a Divine purpose. No special guilt on the part of the African, no special merit on the part of the European, made one the slave and the other the master. Many a wicked man became master, and flourished the rod of the oppressor over the head of his moral and intellectual superior. The good are often in distress; the wicked in prosperity. "They are not in trouble as other men; neither are they plagued like other men."

Says Cotta, in Cicero's treatise on the Nature of the Gods, arguing against a moral government of the world—

> Why did the Carthaginian overbear, in Spain, the two Scipios, the bravest and the best of men? Why did Maximus bury his son, who had already been consul? Why did Hannibal slay Marcellus? Why did the field of Cannæ snatch away Paulus? Why was the body of Regulus given up to the cruelty of the Pœni? Why did not his own roof cover our Africanus? . . . The day would fail me, were I to tell of the evils that have befallen the righteous; no less so, were I to recount the successes of the wicked. For why did Marius die so happily in his home in a ripe old age, and consul for a seventh time? Or, why did Cinna, the cruellest of all men, rule so long?[2]

But the Christian has been taught, that whatever is done,

---

[1] Walker's *History of the Slave Trade*, p. 37.
[2] *De Natura Deorum*; lib. iii, c. 32.

is done, not from the caprice of the gods, but because it seems good in the sight of a merciful Father, infinite in wisdom, power, justice, holiness, goodness and truth. No grief, therefore, at the recollection of the ravages in Africa; no memory of the evils of the "middle passage"; no abhorrence of successful and damnable crime; no indignation at the iniquities of unparalled oppression in the house of bondage, can prevent us from recognising the hand of an over-ruling Providence in the deportation of Africans to the Western world, or interfere with our sense of the incalculable profit —the measureless gains—which, in spite of man's perversity, cruelty and greed, must accrue to Africa and the Negro race from the long and weary exile.

Africans were carried away by millions. There is no means of estimating the number. Had they been taken to the foreign school as individuals, and been brought back after their training, the desirable results would not have been attained. Individuals might have lost their knowledge of their own people, and their interest in them; or, receiving foreign training, under circumstances of personal isolation, might have received it under a sort of mental protest as having no relation to the interest or happiness of their people at home; or, returning to their country as the prophets of a new era, they would have shared the proverbial fate of the solitary reformer among his own people. They were, therefore, carried away in such numbers, that, while under the control of a civilised people of a different race, and undergoing the process of enforced improvement, they might be sufficiently numerous to find among themselves encouragement, sympathy and support, amid the rigours of their schooling; and, on returning might exert the influence of organised communities, able to introduce and establish wholesome reforms.

Careful observers have noticed that the Negroes have retained their manliness, self-reliance and self-respect, to a far greater degree in those sections of the United States, and in the West Indies, where they could exist in large numbers, and where the climate more nearly resembled their own, than in countries where the paucity of their numbers and an uncongenial climate made

African Colonisation.

them always feel like strangers. And in tropical, or semi-tropical countries, they were, though slaves in some respects, masters of the situation; for they had often to instruct their European overseers in the art of tropical agriculture, and in the value and use of tropical productions. They had the advantage, at times, of being able to dictate, and to see their suggestions adopted. But, in temperate climes, where for six months of the year, they had to deal with frost, ice and snow—with a flora and fauna entirely unknown to them—they were obliged to ignore all their past experience. Their knowledge previously gained amounted to nothing. They had to be told everything, and to render, even in the merest trifle, mechanical obedience; hence, they hung in helpless dependence upon their masters. For them the *modus vivendi* was absolute submission. Whenever they moved they must move in the track of their guides. Reason and judgment were abdicated, and the mimetic faculty took their place. No such combination against their oppressors as occurred in Hayti or Jamaica, was possible to them. Nature, instead of affording them the sympathy and shelter of her recesses, repelled them. The wintry stars, in their courses, fought against them; and trusting to the white man became as complete an instinct as keeping their balance. Though the condition of the Negroes of the Northern States was theoretically better than that of their brethren in the South, they have not held their own either in numerical or intellectual importance. They have steadily decreased in numerical and social status.

In the meanwhile, the Fatherland has been left a prey to European greed, and to its own untutored devices, enjoying only here and there, isolated efforts of a timid and cautious philanthropy.

The chief obstacle to the wholesome influence of Europeans in Africa is the climate. From the earliest antiquity this has been the insuperable barrier. Barth says that the relics of Roman dominion in North-central Africa are chiefly sepulchral monuments.[3] Such monuments, alas, are still the melancholy reminders,

---

[3] *Travels, &c., in North and Central Africa, in the Years* 1849–1855; vol. i, p. 156.

all along the West coast, of European efforts. And notwithstanding the increase of foreign conveniences, and the vast progress accomplished in climatology, the climate of Africa produces on European constitutions the same fatal effects. Recent advices state that the mission of the London Missionary Society, on Lake Tanganyika, is nearly abandoned, on account of the repeated deaths of the missionaries. The Rev. Bowen Rees, one of the missionaries, in tendering his resignation to the Committee, pathetically says:—

> Having been unwell since I have settled in this country, and there being at present no signs of my getting well; also, that I see my fellow missionaries falling one after the other, I am convinced that Europeans are not qualified, physically, for the climate of this part of Africa. Consequently, I feel that I am compelled to return home as soon as possible.

Given a healthy climate, or even a less pernicious climate, for Europeans, and all other difficulties would be overcome. But it is a melancholy fact, that wherever, and as far as they can penetrate and live, the concomitants of their successful residence have largely hindered the improvement which their presence is supposed to stimulate.

Bishop Foster, of the Methodist Episcopal Church, by his address before the General Missionary Committee of his Church, in November last, has furnished serious matter for thought and reflection. The Bishop has travelled, and knows whereof he affirms. We do not know whether he has visited West Africa, but this we know, that, whatever may be the fact in other parts of the world, every word of his address, so far as it applies to this country, should be emphasised by capitals. We will give the testimony on this subject of the earliest of modern explorers of this portion of Africa, and the result of the observations of the very latest.

Mungo Park recorded his impressions as follows:—

> Although the Negroes, in general, have a great idea of the wealth and power of Europeans, I am afraid that the Mohammedan converts among them think but very little of our superior attainments in religious knowledge. The white traders in the maritime districts take no pains to counteract this unhappy prejudice. . . . . The poor Africans, whom we affect to consider as barbarians, look upon us, I fear, as little better than a race of formidable but ignorant Heathen.[4]

---

[4] *Travels in* 1795, 1796, 1797; p. 161.

African Colonisation.

The Landers observed, that the natives, in proportion as their aspect and attire showed symptoms of intercourse with Europeans, became always more barbarous and lawless.[5]

A century has made no change for the better. Mr. Joseph Thomson, the well-known traveller, visited the Nigritian countries last year, and in a recent article detailing his experiences, he says:—

My voyage along the coast of Africa, and visits to all the principal places, have astonished me profoundly. I looked forward with pleasure to a study of the influence which a century of contact with civilisation has effected in the barbarous tribes of the seaboard. The result has been unspeakably disappointing. Leaving out of consideration the towns of Sierra Leone and Lagos, where the conditions have been abnormal, the tendency has been everywhere in the line of deterioration. There is absolutely not a single place where the natives are left to their own free will, in which there is the slightest evidence of a desire for better things. The worst vices and diseases of Europe have found a congenial soil, and the taste for spirits has risen out of all proportion to their desire for clothes. . . . . In these villages, men, women, and children, with scarcely a rag upon their persons, follow you about beseeching you for a little gin or tobacco. Eternally gin, tobacco, or gunpowder. These are the sole wants aroused by a century of trade and contact with Europeans.[6]

When Mr. Thomson speaks of places "where the natives are left to their own free will, he means, places where the unbridled propensities of godless Europeans are unchecked by law or public sentiment. In these places the morality with which the natives come into contact is of the lowest character. The generality of the trading agents act upon the theory that European trade with Africa is a species of one-sided contract, in which all the benefit must be on the side of the European, and all the disadvantages on the side of the African. They are men, as one of their own countrymen has recently described them, "who left their country for their country's good." They bring with them the arts and the strength of civilisation, but, personally, they are at large from the influence of its higher principles. They resemble the men who resorted to David in the cave of Adullam: "Every

---

[5] *Journal of an Expedition to Explore the Course and Termination of the Niger;* by Richard and John Lander, 1832.

[6] *Good Words;* January, 1886.

one that was in distress, and every one that was in debt, and every one that was discontented." Such reckless spirits are utterly indifferent to the character of the method, or to the moral results of their intercourse with the natives.

But those sad results occur, not only "where the natives are left to their own free will," but even where civilised governments are supposed to control, and where the "conditions are described by Mr. Thomson as "abnormal." The strict application of Free-trade principles to the sale of spirits, within, and in localities adjoining, British colonies, is attended with deplorable consequences; and often, by the disturbances created, the philanthropic objects of Free-trade are largely defeated. Sir Arthur Conynghame, in his work, *My Command in South Africa*, gives the following melancholy account:—

> The facility with which these untamed savages (Kaflrs) can obtain any amount of villainous drink, is one of the most fruitful sources of danger. Some of the chiefs, being aware of the evil, forbid canteens in their localities, and have repeatedly requested that the same prohibition should be extended among the adjoining (British) districts. The answer of authority has always been, " that the natives should place a moral restraint on themselves, and not imbibe more than is beneficial; and that trade cannot be impeded, simply because it may engender evil consequences among the natives.

What a "simply." During the visit of Cetewayo, King of the Zulus, to England, a few years ago, a deputation from the British National Temperance League called upon him, to urge their views as to the evils produced in native races by the use of spirituous liquors. After they had spoken, the King replied as follows:—

> I can only say that, as a nation, my people are, so to speak, abstainers; or, at all events, they are not accustomed, nor do they, as a people, partake of spirituous liquors. The beer which they use, which is actually a food, is like gruel—our beer is really a food; but the others—your spirits and your intoxicants—are death. It may be interesting to the gentlemen of the deputation, to know that there was an order issued, or a proclamation by me, that spirits were not to be introduced, or allowed to enter my country. But I think that the right place to shut the door is the side from which the spirits come. It is no good my shutting the door on my side, for I have no distilleries. But I think the proper way would be for the Natal Government to assist, by placing restrictions upon the introduction of spirituous liquors into my country.

The Zulus are celebrated as logicians. The above is a specimen

African Colonisation.

of the unanswerable answers which, in verbal fence, they are accustomed to give to Europeans.

Rev. R. H. Nassau, M.D., of the Presbyterian Mission on the Ogowe, writes (Dec. 31, 1884):—

> The inroad of intoxicating liquor into the mission premises, and used by Church members and inquirers, distressed us exceedingly, and burdened our hearts as the carking care of station work alone would not have done.

Rev. David A. Day, of the Lutheran Mission in West Africa, with pathetic indignation, says:—

> The vilest liquors imaginable are being poured into Africa in shiploads from almost every quarter of the civilised world. On one small vessel, in which myself and wife were the only passengers, there were, in the hold, over 100,000 gallons of *New England rum*, which sold on the coast for one dollar a gallon in exchange for African produce.

The religious press in West Africa is loud in its denunciations of the infamous traffic. *The Methodist Herald* (December 9, 1885), published at Sierra Leone by natives, making grateful record of the proceedings of the Missionary Conference held at Bremen, October 27, to protest against the trade in spirits, says:—

> In considering the advance of European civilisation into Africa, one of the chief sources of anxiety for the future in the minds of intelligent Africans is the introduction of ardent spirits, which seem to be, along the coast, the chief article of European traffic with the natives. It is gratifying, therefore, to see that the attention of one of the most powerful of the European Governments whose citizens are enlarging their trade with the country, is being earnestly and seriously directed to this evil. We do not believe that the article is indispensable to the African trade. The spirits introduced are confined to the coast, the interior natives knowing little or nothing of them. If European traders would agree to eliminate the articles from their African trade, they could do a far more flourishing business without them. Money the natives now spend for the poison would be devoted to far more useful things. The revenue of civilised Governments would not be diminished. We have hope that, owing to the energetic protests being made in various Christian countries against the manufacture and sale of the poison, Africans will be saved the melancholy fate which has befallen some other races, through their contact with foreigners who are indiscriminate in their trade.

Mr. Stanley, who has been, for many years, a close and sympathetic observer of missionaries and their work in this country, says:—

> Pious missionaries have set forth devotedly to instil into the dull, mindless

tribes the sacred germs of religion; but their material difficulties are so great, that the progress they have made bears no proportion to the courage and zeal they have exhibited.[7]

The indefatigable traveller turns, with more hopeful prospects and for wider beneficial results, to "the missionaries of commerce." But we have seen how, as a rule, their work has affected the African.

The next agency proposed for Africa's regeneration is COLONISATION. From the preceding discussion it may be inferred that no great hopes can be placed on the achievements of European colonists. There is, first, the physical difficulty which unfavourably affects the colonists; and next, the moral difficulties which injuriously affect the natives. European colonists have been able to settle in no large numbers in equatorial Africa.

The equatorial regions of Africa (says Mr. Stanley) have for ages defied Islamism, Christianity, science and trade. Like the waves beating on a rocky shore, so Islamism has dashed itself repeatedly from the North in its frantic effort to reach the line of the equator. Christianity has also made ineffectual attempts, for the last three centuries, to obtain a footing in the same region, but ignorance of the climate caused its retirement. Science has directed strategic assaults upon the closely-besieged area, and has succeeded in retiring with brilliant results; its success, however, has been only temporary, as Trade, which ought to have followed, stood dazed with the difficulties which the pioneers encountered. . . . . Civilisation, so often baffled, stands railing at the barbarism and savagery that presents such an impenetrable front to its efforts. . . . . Had a few of those waves of races, flowing and eddying over Northern Africa, succeeded in leaping the barrier of the equator, we should have found the black aboriginal races of Southern Africa very different from the savages we meet to day.[8]

The fact is, we should not have found them at all; and this is the reason why the races who drink the waters of the Niger and the Congo, and dwell on the borders of the great lakes, have been severed from the interests of Europe by insurmountable barriers of sand, and by inhospitable shores.

In South Africa, where European settlements have been possible, the results for the aborigines have been far from encouraging. During the three-quarters of a century that England has held that

---

[7] *The Congo, and the Founding of its Free State;* vol. ii, p. 377.

[8] *Congo Free State;* vol. ii, pp. 372, 373.

African Colonisation.

portion of the continent, her administration has been attended by ceaseless troubles, and the clash of arms has rarely been silent, for many years at a time. Nothing but the extraordinary vitality of the Kafirs has kept them from extermination. An able writer in the *Edinburgh Review*,[p] said sometime ago:—

There is one most striking and all-important peculiarity, in which the Kafirs differ from almost all aboriginal tribes with which our colonists have come in contact. To the Red Indians, and New Zealanders, the Australians, and even their own Hottentot neighbours, Christian (European) civilisation has been as an Upas tree, destroying them by its diseases, or still more fatally poisoning them by the infectious contamination of its drunkards and debauchees; but the Kafirs have shown that they can live on the borders of a civilised community, and unless killed off by war, or by famine caused by war, they keep up their numbers.

The history of European civilisation has, indeed, but too plainly proved how hard it is for a strong race to do more for a weak race than to bestow upon it its vices; and too quickly deducing from the sad facts of this history the conclusion that that which is hard must be impossible; there are many persons who advocate severe measures against the Kafirs, as against all savages, on the principle that it is more humane to kill them quickly with powder and shot than slowly by drink or disease. The Boers, we are told, are great readers of the Old Testament; and comparing themselves to the Israelites, as did the Puritans of New England, they shoot a native on the strength of a text out of Joshua.

But events, every day occurring, are forcing the world to accept the truth, that Europeans cannot occupy equatorial Africa, either for their own advantage, or that of the natives.

They cannot occupy it by *force*. One of the officers of Samudu, the celebrated Mohammedan military chieftain of Nigritia, said to the present writer a few weeks ago: "As long as it is not possible for the white man to send armies composed of iron men, who need no food or drink, who are impenetrable by sun or rain, so long will it be impossible for them to take our country by war, or to achieve and maintain ascendancy away from the coast." In the interior, European artillery and ironclads, nitro-glycerine and panclastite are of no avail. With all the appliances of modern warfare, the troops of the most wealthy of European nations found the Nort-eastern Soudan inaccessible. The Marquess of Salisbury,

---

[p] July, 1854.

in announcing the policy of the new Conservative Government, in the House of Lords (July 6, 1885), referred to the British invasion of the Soudan as follows :—

> One of the most complicated and entangled problems ever submitted to a Government to solve, is the problem of the present position of Egypt. . . . Now, the first of all the difficulties with which we have to contend, is, that we have a triumphant enemy on the frontier. On the frontier at Khartoum, and on the frontier at Suakim, we have an enemy who, at all events, according to his own ideas, has been triumphant in the recent struggle. He has prevented us from attaining the objects we had in view, and he has seen us retire from the ground which we occupied.

In the entry made in his Journal under date September 17, 1884, General Gordon said :—

> From a *professional military* point of view, and *speaking materially,* I wish I was the Mahdi, and I would laugh at all Europe.

Under date September 12th, he wrote :—

> The people are all against us, and what a power they have ; they need not fight, but have merely to refuse to sell us their grain. The stomach governs the world, and it was the stomach (a despised organ) which caused our misery from the beginning.[10]

It is impracticable to occupy the interior of Africa by *European colonies.* It is being found out that, even if the insuperable climatic difficulty could be overcome, the resources of Africa are not so conveniently accessible as the imagination of enthusiasts had pictured.

On the 15th of November, 1884, the Plenipotentiaries of all the Powers of Europe, and of the United States, met in conference at Berlin. One of the objects of this illustrious gathering was to decide the formalities to be observed for the valid annexation of territory in future on the African Continent. No assembly of such importance in connection with Africa had ever met in Europe before, if we except the Congress of 1815, at Vienna, which made the celebrated declaration against the slave trade. In keeping with the understanding arrived at in Berlin, Germany, France, England, Italy and Portugal, have been appropriating African territory. But the most elaborate bit of recent machinery for the occupation and civilisation of Africa is that at the head of which stands

---

[10] *The Journals of Major-General Gordon, at Khartoum.*

African Colonisation.

that Royal philanthropist, Leopold II, King of the Belgians. He has already, with more than regal munificence, lavished a vast fortune in the Congo country with a view to the extinction of Slavery and the introduction of a select civilisation among the aborigines. It is a noble purpose, a magnificent aim, to build up a civilisation in Africa by free labour. But Europeans have never achieved such a result in the tropics. No Europeans will ever go to the Congo and work as farmers or labourers. Serious drawbacks are presenting themselves. Dr. Fischer, the recent German traveller, in his work entitled *More Light on the Dark Continent*, scouts the idea that Europeans will never be able to colonise Africa. The natives, he says, will not work without being compelled; and therefore, slavery, or life service, as he puts it, is inevitable.

Mr. William P. Tisdel, United States Agent to the Congo Free State, in his Report to the Department of State, dated June 29th, 1885, gives a startling account of the condition of things in the Congo Free State.[11] According to his statement it was an exception to find a white man anywhere in good health. Out of six hundred whites who had contracted with the Association to serve for three years, only five have been able to remain the full time. Only two Americans have ever been employed by the Association, and of these, one returned to the United States, ill with African fever, and committed suicide while under its effects; and the other was left by Mr. Tisdel, dangerously sick, in the Congo country. It is said that the Belgian Government have appointed an independent Commission for the investigation of the circumstances of the new State.

It appears that the Germans did not hit upon an El Dorado when they annexed Angra Pequena. Several Saxon miners who went out when the acquisition was first made, and hopes were brilliant, have returned home. They report unfavourably on the scarcity of water.

Another recent observer, Mr. W. Montague Kerr, in a paper read before the Royal Geographical Society (November 30, 1885),

---

[11] *United States' Consular Reports;* No. 55 (August, 1885), pp. 551, 552.

describing 'A Journey Overland from Cape Town, across the Zambesi, to Lake Nyassa,' said—

> It had not been his good fortune to fall upon any extraordinarily fertile spots which would offer inducements to the inhabitants of overcrowded Europe. In every instance, the discouragements had been greater than the inducements, to foster the colonisation of Africa by European subjects.[12]

Mr. Kerr took the opportunity to bear the following testimony to the character of the natives—

> From the time he left the Cape of Good Hope till he arrived at the shores of Lake Nyassa, he was never robbed of a single bead or a yard of cloth, though, for months, the goods were completely at the mercy of the natives.

From what we have seen, it will appear that Europe must give up the idea of regenerating Africa through colonies of her own subjects. Hearty, thrifty, energetic colonisation for whites, must be in climates where the winter or cold weather brings its healthy and recuperative influences to body and mind. Nature will not allow herself to be tied down to the theories of even the wisest and most benevolent of men, however high their aims or exalted their motives. Those who, instead of humbly searching for a knowledge of Nature's laws, arrogate to themselves the right of making laws for Nature, must always fail. Expelled with a pitchfork, she will ever return.

After this survey of the nature of the difficulties which confront and attend European effort in Africa, we are forced to the conclusion—which any careful reader will have seen was with us, from our protracted experience and observation on the spot, a foregone conclusion—that the instruments for the regeneration of this continent are the millions of Africans in the Western hemisphere, where, after nigh three hundred years of residence, they are still considered as strangers. It seems to us that European and American workers for Africa should recognise this fact; and those nations who actively co-operated in the work of their deportation should as earnestly co-operate in the work of their restoration. This is the redress which Nature is waiting for before she will lend a finger to European effort. Justice must precede mercy. Be

---

[12] London *Times*, December 1, 1885.

African Colonisation.

just before you are generous. Under some Assiento Contract[13] the work of restoration should begin. We are sometimes told that the descendants of Africa are in America *to stay* there. A similar view was taken of slavery, by the generality of masters, in the days when it was surrounded by all the safeguards that intelligence and wealth, and even piety, could contrive. It was thought that by Divine arrangement, the institution was to be perpetual, and not simply disciplinary and preparatory. Different views on that subject now prevail. The Negro never accepted the abnormal relation as permanent, and was ceaseless in his prayers for deliverance, and *looked* for deliverance. So now, not a few seem to think that all the preparation of the days of bondage, and all the instruction now imparted, are simply to produce a population of domestic servants, to be kept in a subordinate place by the dominant race. This Samson for African achievements is to grind at the mill of the Philistines. The great Artist and Architect is to fail of the ideal foreshadowed :

Amphora cœpit
Institui ; currente rota cur urceus exit? [14]

But, as in the days of slavery, so now, the Freedman feels something in his soul—" God put it there," he says—which tells him that, if not for himself, at least for his children, there are scenes of wider freedom, higher duties and larger proprietorships, in the land whence his ancestors were torn.

And in Africa there is sympathetic response. The elder natives tell of the bitterly-tragic scenes which took place on the coast, as children in the grasp of the murderous trader were being wrenched from the embrace of their parents—the wail of sorrow and unutterable grief which went up to heaven, and the prayers— *prophetic* prayers—the passionate and fervent appeals to the Judge of all the earth, not for vengeance on the robbers, but for the return

---

[13] For forty years, during the last century, England, under the Assiento Contract, had the monopoly of carrying Negroes to the Western world.

[14] *Horace*: 'Ars Pœtica,' 21 :—

A vase was meant; how comes it, then, about,
As the wheel turns, a common jug comes out?
Sir Theodore Martin's Translation.

of the stolen ones. Those sublime and awe-striking prayers are still before the throne of Supreme Justice, waiting to be answered; and they will not cease to be heard until, by the return of the exiles, they are merged in such music of exultation and triumph, as has never been heard since the morning stars sang together, and all the sons of God shouted for joy.

To the present generation of whites and blacks in America, it may seem that the Negro "is there to stay," but the next generation will take a different view. Descendants of Africa have never been permitted to feel at home in those countries, even where they are most numerous, and where the geographical and climatic conditions are congenial. Freedmen from Brazil and other parts of South America, are continually making their way back to the Fatherland, anxious to breathe again the ancestral air, and to lie down at last, and be buried with their fathers.[15]

In the United States, notwithstanding the great progress made in the direction of liberal ideas, the Negro is still a stranger. The rights and privileges accorded by constitutional law, offer him no security against the decrees of private or social intolerance. He is surrounded by a prosperity—industrial, commercial and political—in which he is not permitted to share, and is tantalised by social respectabilities from which he is debarred. The future offers no encouragement to him. In the career of courage and virtue, of honour, emolument and fame, which lies open to his white neighbours, and to their children, neither he himself, nor his sons or daughters, can have any part. From that high and improving fellowship, which binds together the elements from Europe, however incongruous, the Negro child is excommunicated before he is born.

One fatal drawback to the Negro in America is the incubus of imitation. He must be an imitator; and imitators see only results —they never learn processes. They come in contact with accom-

---

[15] It is stated that the new Governor of Lagos, Captain Alfred Moloney, C.M.G., looks with favour upon the return, to the part of the coast under his jurisdiction, of the exiles from South America; and with a sagacious and judicious statesmanship, is disposed to do all in his power to facilitate it.

African Colonisation.

plished facts, without knowing how they were accomplished. They never get within, so as to see how a thing originates or develops. Therefore, when they attempt anything, they are apt to begin at the end, without the insight, patience or experience which teaches that they begin at the beginning. They are impatient theorists—in the literal sense—who can neither understand, nor wait for the slow results and precarious combinations of arduous and prolonged effort. Hence they are ready to criticise processes, to find fault with details. The destructive faculty is largely developed; but to originate, and point out methods of effective action, is impossible to them. John Jasper is a respectable Negro preacher of Virginia, who has constructed his own theory of the solar-system; and the fact that he has constructed something, and has the temerity to explain and defend his theory against the theories of the learned, causes a large following, and he has lately been invited to lecture in Europe as a curiosity. His earnestness and acuteness, in spite of his defiance of grammar, and his ignorance of scholastic methods, command the respect of the intelligent listener. It is easier to smile at his scientific perversity, than to give the reasoning by which the mighty results of astronomy have been obtained.

Whatever may be said of the advantages of education and civilisation, and a great deal is being said just now, and, perhaps, so far as the Negro is concerned, a great deal ought to be said—it seems certain that such advantages are not without serious dangers. It is our earnest belief that a real independent moral growth, productive of strength of character and self-reliance, is impossible to natures in contact with beings greatly superior to themselves. This is one reason, we suppose, why our spiritual training was not entrusted to angelic beings, why "we have this treasure in earthen vessels." Everybody knows that a powerful, massive character—though it be nearly perfect—may positively injure those within the circle of its influence by giving them a bent in a direction opposite to their own natural tendencies, so as to make it extremely difficult, if not impossible, for them to shake themselves free.

This is one of the great drawbacks to the introduction of

civilisation by foreigners into Africa. In the European settlements on the coast there are visible the melancholy effects of the fatal contagion of a mimic or spurious Europeanism. Some who have been to Europe, bring back and diffuse among their people a reverence for some of the customs of that country, of which the more cultivated are trying to get rid. But, happily, the inhospitable and inexorable climate prevents this pseudo-civilisation, called "progress," from spreading to the interior. The tribes still retain their simplicity and remain unaffected. And may they remain so until they pass by normal and regular progress and natural steps to a higher plane on the line of their own race-development, when European habits and customs will be aimed at as accessories, rather than a principle of life.

But, besides the drawbacks in the learning of the schools, the educated Negro, in the United States, in the enjoyment of the advantages of culture, has come in contact, throughout the period of his training, with influences which warp him in the direction of self-depreciation, even more powerfully than the books which he reads, or the teachers to whom he listens. The instruction of the schools does, to a certain extent—perhaps to a great extent—improve, but it can neither reverse or supersede the far more efficient education which comes from the experiences of daily life, which—

<blockquote>Week in, week out, from morn till night,</blockquote>

control and give direction to the mind.

Living as the wards of a people, who, out of their own *habitat*, instinctively dread deterioration—the loss of vitality and vigour—and who believe that their existence and growth depend upon constant self-assertion, as against all alien comers; and who, therefore, can neither give place nor opportunity to their former slaves, the Africans must be subjected to experiences which, in spite of the training received in the schools, must warp them out of the moral and intellectual perpendicular, and incline them to the attitude and practices of the creature who either climbs or crawls. Bishop H. M. Turner, of the African Methodist Episcopal Church, is constantly calling attention, in his outspoken

African Colonisation.

A writer in *Macmillan's Magazine* (April, 1885) says: "It is our bad luck at present that there are only two independent English nations." The writer has probably not heard of Liberia. By recent negotiations, the territory of Liberia has become conterminous with that of the British Colony of Sierra Leone. On the occasion of the settlement of this long-pending question, the British Commissioner, Sir Samuel Rowe, remarked:—

> The happy duty, now devolved upon me, of signing, on behalf of Her Majesty, the Queen of Great Britain and Ireland, that Convention, which, having been signed also by the accredited Commissioners of the Government of Liberia, will, I trust, set at rest those differences, which, from time to time, have impeded the progress of civilisation, and lessened, perhaps, the harmony which it always is desirable should exist between States whose territorial limits are conterminous. . . . . . Sister States, side by side on this Eastern shore of the broad Atlantic, peopled by members of the African race, who have adopted the habits of Western civilisation, cannot be other than united by the ties of one common duty; and that duty is, the furtherance of civilisation in this African land, amongst those native tribes, their immediate neighbours, who have not enjoyed the opportunities afforded to the inhabitants of Sierra Leone, and to the emigrants from the United States to Liberia, of becoming acquainted with that higher life and purer thought, which we of the Northern clime maintain pervades the people of Europe and America.

It is now expected that the relations of Liberia and Sierra Leone will become more intimate, and that there will be, in course of time, uniform tariff regulations, by which the trade of the two countries may be carried on under the same rules. And this would seem not unreasonable, when it is considered that the Mannah River, fixed by England as the south-east boundary of Sierra Leone, and the north-west boundary of Liberia, is not an ethnological frontier, but cuts off and takes into Sierra Leone, a portion of the Vey tribe, the majority of whom are in the recognised limits of Liberia; so that British subjects and Liberian citizens speak across the boundary to each other in the same aboriginal tongue, and obey foreign laws couched in the same European language, and based on the same system of jurisprudence. Gallinas and Sulymah belong, geographically and ethnographically, to Liberia; they belong, politically and territorially, to Sierra Leone, through the accidents of diplomatic management. The idea of joint-legislation, then, it may be seen, is by no means alien to the purposes and aims of the two communities, nor is it repugnant to the spirit of the age. The impression has been produced in West Africa, by articles in American newspapers, and private letters from the United States, that the American Government is likely, in future, to take greater practical interest in Liberia than has been hitherto customary. Whether this notion is well founded or not, it is evident that, in view of the vast energies, pecuniary, intellectual and moral, being expended by Europe upon the solution of the African problem, the United States cannot sit much longer as an indifferent spectator, possessing, as she does, to a far greater extent than any other nation, the facilities for effective work on this continent.

It is not for nothing, that to the United States has been committed the trust of millions of Africa's descendants, the natural and appointed agents in the regeneration of the continent; and it is not without meaning, that they should have been set at liberty at the precise period when the vast field of their future energies was being opened to the gaze of an astonished world. It cannot be unwise for the United States Government to employ some of its surplus capital—not too much—in opening the way to a career for millions of people, who can have none in a country to whose material progress they have so largely contributed. We looked in vain in the last Message of President Cleveland, for a single reference to the continent of Africa, the original home of millions of his hapless fellow-citizens, who are anxious to return. But we do not imagine that this was the silence of indifference. It was rather, we suspect, the reticence which often comes from earnest practical interest—the silence which scans the distance before taking the leap.

It seems to us, that the United States Government is now standing, so far as Africa is concerned, at the parting of the ways. And if the lingering at the bifurcation be not too long, or long enough to cause insuperable doubts and fears, the hesitation will do good, and Africa may hope for great things from the new *régime*.

But some of the best friends of colonisation have entertained

African Colonisation.

doubts as to whether such an enterprise ought to be, or can be, legally assisted by the United States Government. Daniel Webster, the great expounder and defender of the Constitution, had no doubt on this score. He said, shortly before his death :—

> It appears to me that this emigration is not impracticable. What is it to the great resources of this country to send out a hundred thousand persons a-year to Africa? In my opinion, without any violation of the analogies which we have followed in other cases, in pursuance of our commercial regulations, it is within our Constitution—it is within the powers and provisions of that Constitution, as a part of our commercial arrangements—just as we enter into treaties and pass laws for the suppression of the slave trade. If we look, now, to other instances, we shall see how great may be the emigration of individuals, with slight means from Government.[80]

Mr. Webster then referred to the vast emigration from Ireland to the United States, under the stimulus of "very slight Governmental support."

On the several grounds of justice, humanity and expediency, it seems to us that the Government should give its aid. In contemplating the possibility of such assistance, the only drawback that occurs to us is that the immigration might be so excessive as to imperil the vital interests of the colony. But this would depend, greatly, upon the class of people sent. A few ambitious and turbulent spirits, who, in America, supposed themselves to be ascending in the scale of political life, and determined, on their arrival in Africa, to make way for themselves by the methods of American demagogism, would soon upset the nascent institutions of the young Republic. But thousands of industrious, hard-working farmers and mechanics, would be no source of danger or anxiety. They would go to work, and the aborigines would gladly welcome them as returning brethren, similar to themselves in aspect, in origin, and in destiny. With such immigrants, however numerous, we can imagine no serious difficulty. As long as Liberia includes vast tracts of fertile land unoccupied and uncultivated, there will be space and opportunities to afford safe outlets for any inconvenient accumulations of working energy. Where abundance of land is so easily accessible, there is no danger of local congestions of population. They will be allured

---

[80] Address before the American Colonisation Society, January, 1852.

to the rich forests and the fruitful plains, and will very soon find out that Africa is the best country in the world for an absolutely poor man. Meat, fire, and clothing, may also be regarded as luxuries in a climate so genial, and to them, so *congenial*.

There are in the various counties of Liberia—Montserrado, Bassa, Sinou, Maryland—in the rich countries drained by the St. Paul's, the St. John's, the Sinou, the Cavalla and the San Pedro Rivers—eligible sites for profitable farms, for villages and towns, commanding a lucrative trade in the valuable products of the wealthy interior. And there is an active, intelligent native population ready for co-operation, for an interchange of ideas, of produce, of transactions, and of capital, which must unite their country with Liberia by the closest civil and social, as well as political, ties. Their Government, as a rule, has very few of the features of what is understood by royalty, or monarchy. The *people* govern, and they furnish everywhere most interesting specimens of Republicanism.

The Christian Church in the United States should recognise the instruments at their door for the African work.

It would seem to have been designed that Christianity should not come into Africa from Europe, where it had been taken from its Semitic mould, and either Latinised or Teutonised; but that it should cross the ocean, and acquire larger freedom and greater elasticity, under new conditions, and be imparted to millions of Africans, who should be the bearers of it to their Fatherland. American Christianity, though having its roots in Europe, differs from European Christianity in many important respects—in the wide tolerance which pervades it, in the form which it has assumed, and the impression which it leaves on the mind. It is the religion of a democratic people.

Liberia is blamed because she has made no greater progress. But where, in Western Africa, has there been greater progress in proportion to the means used or effort put forth? At Senegal, the authorities are perplexed by the obstructive operations of hostile Mohammedans. At the Gambia, the adjacent tribes, when they please, disorganise the trade by wars. Sierra Leone is one

African Colonisation.

hundred years old, and the aborigines around it are ready, at any time, to defy its authority, and menace its existence. At the Gold Coast, the Ashantees periodically put the Settlements in jeopardy. Lagos is under the influence of the interior tribes. Foreigners are confined to the coast, or admitted to the wealthy and populous inland districts by the edicts at Abbeokuta. At Gaboon, Dr. Lenz tells us, that the whole native population is being rapidly driven to the interior by the Fans. In the Congo country, serious difficulties environ the situation. Liberia, and her influences, compare favourably with all these.

APPENDIX.

THE REPUBLIC OF LIBERIA.

NO agency has yet been tried for Africa's regeneration which promises so much and is capable of so much for the permanent welfare of the people as the method of the American Colonisation Society in the establishment of Liberia. All other efforts from abroad may be classified under two heads—the disorganising and the corrective. The work of one set of foreigners is to introduce the agencies of helpfulness; of the other, the instruments of mental and moral degradation. The missionary represents the one; the trader the other. In districts subject only to Pagan rule, the traders really govern the country. Everything is made to subserve the interest of their trade. They appeal to the cupidity of ignorant chiefs, and fix the standard of morality. The missionary is helpless.

European colonies, though existing for a higher purpose, and though under their protection and stimulus the missionary can do an unmolested and even apparently aggressive work, yet, in such colonies, the measure of progress allowed to the natives must be limited, seeing that the power and prestige of the Europeans and the promotion of European interests must be made the first consideration.

The United States, then, have furnished Africa with the most effective instrument of unlimited progress and development in the Republic of Liberia. The basis of the Liberian political life is the

2 F

Appendix.

American Constitution and Laws. But the earlier legislators of the new State very soon discovered that American precedents, in not a few important respects, would have to be set aside; and it is creditable to their statesmanship that they were able to introduce with prudence such modifications into the American system as made it applicable to their new circumstances and practicable for their purposes. Their successors are finding more and more that as they advance into the continent and develop national life new modifications will be necessary. These must take place if there is normal growth—if the nation is to be the true expression of the race. The friends of Liberians abroad cannot help them to national or racial expression. They must fight their own battles and achieve their own victories, if they are not to be overawed, depressed and overcome, not so much by the merits and virtues as by the vices and failings of foreigners, whose literature they read and whose commodities they purchase.

The theory upon which Liberia was founded has thus far stood the test. It is a theory with definite practical consequences, which every one who is earnest in the desire for African regeneration and acquainted with the facts must accept, and which no one in these days, however antagonistic to the Negro in exile, will strenuously oppose.

In the European colonies along the coast there may be the evidences of material prosperity, but it proceeds with the heavy and crushing indifference of the car of Juggernaut, and, like the conductors of that ponderous vehicle, it looks upon the possible destruction of individuals as no serious evil; as possibly for their own good and for the advancement of the cause. There is no recognition, therefore, of the fact that there are hearts that feel, no notice taken of sensibilities that may be rudely lacerated, no effort to nurse the well-spring of a nobler life within. The native is, as a rule, simply the victim of an unsympathetic apparatus of political and commercial machinery.

The Republic of Liberia.

In Liberia matters are entirely different. The people, with all the drawbacks incident to their necessarily isolated life, have the legislative control of at least five hundred miles of coast, and of an indefinite interior. They recognise the necessity—the prime necessity—of the moral and religious emotions. Their minds are strengthened and expanded by the wide and glorious prospects which their independent nationality and the vast continent on which they live with its teeming millions of their blood relations open before them; and they stretch out their hands to the United States for the return of their exiled brethren, to increase their civilised and Christian force. They ask for greater educational and religious facilities. They could have greater material prosperity; but they look upon the life as more than meat, and the body as more than raiment. For more than half a century they have resisted the appeals of Europeans for an indiscriminate trade in the country, and have thus kept an extensive region both on the coast and in the interior in a virgin state waiting for their brethren from abroad, who will know how to protect themselves against the influence of a vicious foreign trade, and who will be able to introduce in a regular and healthful form the blessings of freedom and civilisation. As an example of the work in promotion of a genuine Christian civilisation which Liberia, as an independent nation, whose laws are final, has the power of performing, see the recent law enacted against Sabbath-breaking, which applies only to the seaboard and to the proceedings of foreign vessels (*African Repository*, July, 1887). You would understand the import of this fact and its bearing upon Christianity in this country if you could see how all along the coast out of Liberia the Sabbath is disregarded by foreign traders, while the missionaries look helplessly on. In course of time, Liberia will banish the traffic in spirits from the whole of her domain; and in this effort she will be sustained by the great Mohammedan trading community on the east and north.

Now, here is an instrument—indigenous, sympathetic and

Appendix.

permanent—for the aggressive work of the American Church. If American Christians will deal with this question earnestly and wisely, they can in a few years revolutionise the Nigritian countries. America possesses the elements—the human instruments—now needed for the work in Africa, and they are anxious to come. This desire of the Negroes for emigration to the fatherland is sometimes said to be exaggerated by colonisationists; but I find in *The Church at Home and Abroad* the following from Rev. H. N. Payne, Field Secretary of the Freedmen's Board:—

"Much as the coloured people are attached to the places where they grew up, thousands of them would gladly go to Arkansas, to Texas, or *to any other place* where they would better their condition; but they cannot raise the money to emigrate, and must stay and suffer where they are."

Now here is disinterested testimony, put not half as strongly as the facts warrant. The *any other place* is Africa; and if these hapless creatures do not name Africa in the utterance of their tearful longings, it is because thousands do not dream that there is any possibility of ever getting to this distant country. I found, during my travels in the South, in 1882, that hundreds were turning their faces to Arkansas and Texas, who had never heard of Liberia or of the American Colonisation Society.

Now, ought not the Church, in contemplating the magnitude of the work in Africa, to consider whether this superfluous energy might not be utilised? Here, at least, is the physical basis of a great moral and physical superstructure. Do not go about lamenting your incapacity to help Africa when you have with you the elements of effective assistance, but which, on account of its apparent insignificance, you despise. Remember Longfellow's baffled and disheartened artist:—

> Then a voice cried, "Rise, O Master;
> From the *burning brand of oak*
> Shape the thought that stirs within thee!"
> And the startled artist woke—

The Republic of Liberia.

> Woke, and from the smoking embers
>   Seized and quenched the glowing wood;
> And therefrom he carved an image,
>   And he saw that it was good.
> O thou sculptor, painter, poet!
>   Take this lesson to thy heart:
> *That is best which lieth nearest;*
>   Shape from that thy work of art.

Do not wait until you have trained the Negroes up to your ideal—in your peculiar modes of thinking. You cannot make them Anglo-Saxons. You never will make them so in spirit and possibilities, if I interpret the providence of God aright. The Hebrews in Egypt remained illiterate and ignorant, though surrounded for four hundred years by the splendours of a brilliant civilisation. That civilisation was not for them, though they had, by providential direction, been brought into contact with it. It was not suited to the peculiar work for which they were destined. So the children of Africa among you have in them the possibilities of a great work in the Fatherland. Remove them from the pressure in your country to the freedom and congeniality of their ancestral home, and so open a wider sphere, for the play and development of their social, moral, and spiritual nature. It is not the best plan to rely upon college training to fit them for work in Africa.

The fugitive Hebrew slaves, without the learning of the schools, received the law for their guidance—found the truth for their race—in the solitudes of the desert. In Africa, the merest rudiments of Western learning will have more power upon the Negro than the highest culture in America. There is something in the atmosphere, in the sunshine, the clouds, the rain, the flowers, the music of the birds, that makes the *a b c* of your culture more valuable to him than all the metaphysics and philosophy you can possibly give him in America.

In contrasting the results of the methods of his Mohammedan teachers upon the Negro with those produced upon him by the efforts of his Christian guides and instructors, one is reminded of

Appendix.

the old story of Falconnet, a vain French artist, who was once lecturing a class of students on the horse of Marcus Aurelius. For a time he was critical and captious, pointing out little faults of detail and contrasting them with a more perfect anatomical model of his own. But at last the spirit of the artist overcame professional jealousy, and he exclaimed, "After all, gentlemen, that ugly horse lives, and mine is dead." Something of the same feeling comes over the thoughtful observer as he studies the results of the two religious systems upon the African. The Christian Negro, equipped with all the apparatus of the schools, appears at a disadvantage by the side of his Mohammedan brother. The training of the latter is admitted to be faulty and imperfect, but he is at home in Africa and dominant in the land of his fathers. After all, the ugly horse is *alive.*

If Christians in America will trust to the healing and restorative power of Nature, and will help the thousands to migrate to Africa, and then, under the influence of the earth and sky and sea of the ancestral home, will further assist them with elementary schools and plain Gospel preaching, and with tools for mechanical and agricultural work, Africa will soon lift up her head.

The methods generally pursued, apart from the principle of the Liberian enterprise, will never cause Christianity to penetrate the interior with any hope of bringing the tribes under its sway. Of another thing I am not much less assured, that Mohammedanism —unless Liberia is strengthened and stimulated by an increase of civilised population and schools—will extend its influence to the sea along the whole of Upper Guinea, and will control the indigenous tribes. This it will do with the countenance and support of European governments, dependent for their revenues upon a trade largely under the control of the sober and energetic Moslems.

The religion of Arabia has the advantage of numbers in its work in Africa. The religion of America may also have this advantage, if the Church there will get near enough to the unsophisticated

The Republic of Liberia.

Negro to understand his broken utterances about Africa. Dr. Ellinwood told the General Assembly at Omaha that "the Mohammedan College in the little African state of Tripoli, with one thousand students, sends to the interior not less than three hundred missionaries every year; and the great Azar in Cairo, with ten thousand students, sends to the Moslem mission fields not less than two thousand a-year."

The Nigritian Mohammedans are wonderful propagandists. Half scholars, half merchants, they are devoted to trade, literature and religion; they are also pilgrims and adventurers. You will find them in every important city on the coast; and in the interior they haunt the busy centres of trade and lead in all the places of popular devotion. They have in their favour certain elements of truth—enough to make them grow and thrive. The Koran appears to the cursory and superficial reader self-contradictory, dull—"a tissue of incoherent rhapsodies;" but it is impregnated with a few grand ideas, which stand out strongly from the whole. On the St. Paul's River one frequently sees huge trees standing on high banks overhanging the stream, with just enough root in the soil to hold them, but growing in all the luxuriance of the trees in the fertile valley or on the rich mountain side. These river-side trees are a picture of Islam. It is a mighty tree standing on apparently very little soil, but soil enough to hold it. Every rising tide seems to threaten its downfall, but the water recedes; freshets come and go, and leave it more firmly rooted in the earth than before. It is a power to be reckoned with, then, in all attempts to evangelise Africa; and no isolated missionary effort can resist the organised force it brings.

Bishop Taylor has recognised this important fact, and he is endeavouring to demonstrate the feasibility and necessity of *colonies* for the greater and ultimate success of mission work in Africa. He has recently wisely adopted Liberia as a base and strategic point for his operations, where, protected in his rear by a regular govern-

Appendix.

ment in sympathy with his work, he will not be subject to the intrusion of the many conflicting influences to which he is exposed in the Congo country.

Shall Liberia, for the want of a generous and far-sighted sympathy, be compelled to linger in the unhealthy regions of the coast, circumscribed in the field of her operations, and paralysed by physical and moral malaria, while thousands of possible agents of an effective work, within and beyond her borders, wander uselessly about your country, asking, "Who will show us any good?"

In the great speech of Dr. Ellinwood before the Assembly, so full of the philosophy and the results and the hopes of foreign missions, not one word is said of the work in Africa, or of the future of this continent. Perhaps she is so near America, in the millions of her representatives there, that she is regarded as a part of the home mission field. Then deal with her as a part of your household, and remember the apostolic estimate of the man who fails to provide for his own household.

ED. W. BLYDEN.

African Colonisation.

and energetic style, to the disadvantages of the Negro in America; but nowhere has he given a more vivid presentation of the dreary and discouraging subject, than in a recent short article in the *Quarterly Review*, of his Church.[16] To some, his picture will, perhaps, appear as a repulsive photograph. Still, he writes with a kindly indignation—with a deep and fervid earnestness, and a surprising humour and fun, that compel attention. He says:—

> I need not repeat my well-known convictions as to the future of the race. I think our stay in this country is but temporary, at most. Nothing will remedy the evils of the Negro, but a great Christian nation upon the continent of Africa. White is God in this country, and black is the Devil. White is perfection, greatness, wisdom, industry, and all that is high and holy. Black is ignorance, degradation, indolence, and all that is low and vile; and three-fourths of the coloured people of the land do nothing day and night but cry: "Glory, honour, dominion and greatness to White." Many of our so-called leading men are contaminated with the accursed disease or folly, as well as the thoughtless masses; and, as long as such a sentiment pervades the coloured race, the powers of Heaven cannot elevate him. No race of people can rise and manufacture better conditions while they hate and condemn themselves. A man must believe he is somebody, before he is acknowledged to be somebody Hundreds of our most educated young men will put on as many airs over a position that requires them to dust the clothes of white men, as a superior man would over an appointment to the President's Cabinet. I deny that God himself could make a great man out of such a character, without a miracle—
> "Mit dummheit Kämpfen Götter selbst vergebens."[17]

The imagination of the Negro has been taken captive by his surroundings. His consciousness is not sufficiently disengaged to enable him to respect his own peculiarities. He can conceive of nothing different from his surroundings; and he does not wish to conceive of anything different, believing as he does that the Ultima Thule of progress has been reached by the Anglo-Saxon. The Negro of the most powerful intellect must work by the pattern before him, and reproduce only what he has seen with his bodily eyes. The ideal faculty has not fair play, or any play at all. He is bound to endless imitation. If any original image is formed in his mind, it must be banished, or it is crowded out by the pressure of the actual. There is neither time nor opportunity to

---

[16] *The African Methodist Episcopal Church Review*, January, 1885.
[17] "With stupidity the gods themselves struggle in vain."

work it out. He must spend his days longing for the crumbs of social and political existence which fall from the white man's table :—

> Simile ad uom che va di porta in porta
> Mendicando la vita.

There must be Africans in America who feel all this, who feel that they have a life of their own—a life destined to last; who protest against many things they see around them, even while they are bound to respect them. We are told that when Michael Angelo looked at the lofty dome of the cathedral at Florence, he exclaimed, "I will not make one like you; I cannot make one better than you." There must be, among the seven millions, some, if not many, who share the proud humility of the great artist. To such, at times, there must come the tears of another artist: not, however, because they have exhausted their ideals, but from the conviction that there is no opportunity to work them out; and that, even if there were such opportunity, the result would mean nothing amid incompatible and unsympathetic surroundings; that, like the monolith in Central Park, though fitted to beautify and adorn other scenes for thousands of years, the result of their conceptions, if not still-born, would rapidly crumble to decay under the action of an inhospitable and uncongenial climate. To such, there must be a longing for other scenes, where, forgetting the things that are behind, they may reach forward to things which promise vitality, usefulness and prosperity to their race. But there are many, alas, who may never gain the fructifying atmosphere—who must always resemble those figures one sees in museums in Europe, which would be magnificent if they were complete; as they now stand, they are only splendid torsos—melancholy suggestions of unattainable possibilities.

It is a curious and suggestive fact, however, that the Negroes of country districts in the Southern States, who have had the slenderest educational opportunities, enjoy a comparative freedom from the deleterious effects of the general oppression. They are largely unsophisticated. They have neither been elevated nor vitiated by the conventionalities of society. Their condition is not the deplorable one of their educated brother, who feels, with greater keenness, the disabilities to which he is subject; and whose case, in many instances, is that of a despised man—as Bishop Turner points out—who despises himself and his race. The Southern Negro denizens of rural districts make, therefore, as a rule, better colonists in the Fatherland than those who are able to declaim, in the language of the schools, about the wrongs and rights of the race, but whose sympathies and admiration go to the dominant class— who step out of the ranks of their own people, without elevating themselves above them—continually wandering away from the crowd in sullen and contemptuous isolation, but compelled always to keep the same social and political plane. These make unsatisfied and unsatisfactory colonists. The pioneer and self-sacrificing spirit is altogether absent from their mental, moral and physical constitution.

It should not be surprising that a people, living under such conditions, should find it difficult to recognise any leader among themselves; or that those, whom circumstances have thrust to the front, should suffer from the jealous and irritable susceptibilities of those forced to follow. Everything tends to disintegration and dissolution —to the separation of chief friends and the making a man's foes those of his own household, or race. A man like Frederick Douglass who is, by common consent, acknowledged to be *primus*—hardly *primus inter pares*—standing among his people, like the Bartholdi statue among the steeples of New York—is often selected for ill-mannered criticisms, by some to whom his labours assisted in bringing, not only freedom, and ability to write and speak, but the freedom to walk and move without feeling the friction and hearing the clanking of the ancestral chains. These things tend to increase and perpetuate the difficulties of the coloured man's position. The prejudices against him, now slowly dying out—alas, too slowly!—are thus unfortunately perpetually confirmed and fanned.

But the Negro's residence in America, in spite of all drawbacks, has been of incalculable advantage to him; nor has it been without peculiar benefits to the dominant race. The discussions which have arisen in consequence of his presence there have taught numerous wholesome lessons to the ruling class. One book on the subject of the Negro's wrongs unsealed the fountain of tears in all countries and among all races. Human rights have been better understood, and have been placed upon a firmer footing than ever before. The assumption of the right to hold slaves was deeply rooted in the minds of men, derived from antiquity, transmitted in the writings of philosophers, and accepted by all legislators, Asiatic, European, African and American. This right was unqestioned until Negro emancipation first established the principle that no circumstances justify the making or holding of slaves. And it may be, as Dr. Reeve contends,[18] that the presence of the Negro in the Western world is still necessary to teach other lessons equally important in the direction of Christ-likeness, to the hard and conquering Anglo-Saxon; to impress upon him the truth of the essential sociability and solidarity of humanity. We can quite believe that if the day should ever come when this man of love, and suffering, and song, shall leave the United States, after his 260 years of residence, there will be left an insatiable void. Taking this view of the work of the Negro in America, we can earnestly say of those who choose to remain, "Peace be within their walls, and plenteousness within their palaces;" for our brethren and companions' sake, we wish them prosperity.

But still we believe that there is a wider sphere, and there are loftier achievements, for those who come to take part, on the spot, in the work of the regeneration of Africa.

An Eglishman who visited the United States in the Autumn of 1884, has made the following remarks on the condition of the Negro in the country :—[19]

> The Negro is eager to learn, and is steadily improving his position. But the old antagonism of the races is as strong as ever; if, indeed, not stronger than ever. . . . . The black man is despised as of old, and no one hails him as a

---

[18] Dr. J. B. Reeve, a Negro clergyman, of Philadelphia, in the *African Methodist Episcopal Church Review*, July, 1885.

[19] *Macmillan's Magazine*, November, 1885.

African Colonisation.

brother. His children must go to separate schools—he must travel by separate cars on the railway.[20] Will it be so always with these six millions of free citizens of the American Republic. It is a grave and difficult question. . . . . In an alien land, at least, he has not the independent vitality which gains respect for its originality and strength; at best, he is but a weak imitator of his old enslavers. What may be the future of the dark continent and its inhabitants, is one of the great problems of the world. But it is my own conviction, that the tribes and peoples which have been sold from it into slavery, will never reach the height of perfect manhood in the countries of their exile, until the race from which they spring develops a new endemic civilisation in Africa. . . . The new experiment with the African must be made in his own magnificent home.

After this survey of the European in Africa, and the African in America, it is difficult to escape the conclusion forced upon Bishop Haven, after visiting Liberia, that the solution of Africa in America, is America in Africa; and further, that the solution of Africa in Africa, is Africa in America. This brings us to a consideration of the work and its results, of the only agency which is labouring to bring about the solution by the means just suggested, namely, the *American Colonisation Society.*

This Society had its origin in a sympathy with the noblest aspirations of the bondman in exile. Its object was to secure for him not only personal liberty, but effective political organisation, in the land of his fathers. It is the only agency capable of effectively obliterating painful recollections, by providing, for him, in the ancestral home, a future worthy of his ambition. But the objects of the Society were not simply to affect the political status of the comparatively few descendants of Africa in America. The most eminent among its founders looked to the higher results to be produced upon Africa, recognising, as they did, even at that time, the impossibility of effective white agency in this land. Just as they believed that the black man could not be prosperous and comfortable in America, so they read in the dispensations of Providence, that Africa had been absolutely interdicted to the white man. Daniel Webster, in almost the last public address he made, said solemnly, as from the verge of the eternal world :—

---

[20] The Jubilee Singers, at one time the guests of the Prime Minister of England, are refused accommodation in the hotels of their native country.

Christianity, Islam and the Negro Race.

Gentlemen,—There is a Power above us which sees the end of all things from the beginning, though we see it not. Almighty God is His own interpreter of the ways of His own Providence; and I sometimes contemplate with amazement—and, I may say, with adoration—events which have taken place through the instrumentality of the cupidity and criminality of men, designed, nevertheless, to work out great ends of beneficence and goodness, by our Creator. . . . . African slaves were brought hither, to the shores of this Continent, almost simultaneously with the first tread of a white man's foot upon this, our North America. We see in that—our shortsightedness only sees—the effect of a desire of the white man to appropriate to himself the results of the labour of the black man, as an inferior and a slave. Now let us look at it.

These Negroes, and all who have succeeded them, brought hither as captives, taken in the wars of their own petty provinces, ignorant and barbarous, without the knowledge of God, and with no reasonable knowledge of their own character and condition, have come here; and here, although in a subordinate—in an inferior, in an enslaved—condition, have learned more, and come to know more, of themselves and of their Creator, than all whom they have left behind them in their own barbarous kingdoms. It would seem that this is the mode—as far as we can judge—this is the destiny, the rule of things, established by Providence; by which knowledge, letters, and Christianity shall be returned by the descendants of those poor ignorant barbarians, who were brought here as slaves to the country from which they came.[21]

The Hon. Edward Everett, in one of his inimitable orations, said :—

Mark the providence of God, educing out of these natural disadvantages (disadvantages to man's apprehension), and this colossal moral wrong—the African slave trade; out of these seemingly hopeless elements of physical and moral evil—out of long cycles of suffering and crime, of violence and retribution, such as history can nowhere parallel—educing, I say, from these elements, by the blessed alchemy of Christian benevolence, the means of the ultimate regeneration of Africa. . . . . All other means have been tried in vain. Private adventure has miscarried; strength, and courage, and endurance, almost superhuman, have languished and broken down; well-appointed expeditions, fitted out under the auspices of powerful associations and powerful Governments, have ended in calamitous failure; and it is proved, at last, that the Caucasian race cannot achieve this long-deferred work.

When that last noble expedition, which was sent out from England—I think in the year 1841—under the highest auspices, to found an agricultural settlement in the interior of Africa, ascended the Niger, every white man out of one hundred and fifty sickened; all but two or three—if my memory serves me—died; while, of their dark-skinned associates—also one hundred and fifty in number—with all the added labour and anxiety that devolved upon them, a few only were sick; and they, individuals who had passed years in a temperate

---

[21] Address before the American Colonisation Society, January, 1852.

African Colonisation.

climate, and not one died. I say, again, Sir, you Caucasian, you proud Anglo-Saxon; you self-sufficient, all-attempting white man, then, you cannot civilise Africa. You have subdued and appropriated Europe; the native races are melting before you in America, as the untimely snows of April before a vernal sun; you have possessed yourself of India; you menace China and Japan; the remotest isles of the Pacific are not distant enough to escape your grasp, nor insignificant enough to elude your notice—but *Central Africa confronts you, and bids you defiance.* Your squadrons may range or blockade her coast; but neither on the errands of peace, nor on the errands of war, can you penetrate the interior. The God of Nature, no doubt for wise purposes, however inscrutable, has drawn across the chief inlets a cordon you cannot break through. You may hover on the coast, but you dare not set foot on the shore. Death sits portress at the undefended gateways of her mud-built villages. Yellow fevers, and blue plagues, and intermittent poisons, that you can see as well as feel, await your approach as you ascend the rivers. Pestilence shoots from the mangroves that fringe their noble banks; and the glorious sun, which kindles all inferior nature into teeming, bursting life, darts disease into your languid system. No, *you* are not elected for this momentous work. The Great Disposer, in another branch of His family, has chosen out a race, descendants of this torrid region, children of this vertical sun, and fitted them by ages of stern discipline, for the gracious achievement.

> From foreign realms and lands remote,
> Supported by His care,
> They pass unharmed through burning climes,
> And breathe the tainted air.

Sir, I believe the auspicious work is begun; that Africa will be civilised—civilised by her offspring and descendants. I believe it, because I will not think that this mighty and fertile region is to remain for ever in its present state; because, I can see no other agency adequate to the accomplishment of the work, and I do behold in this agency a most mysterious fitness.[22]

The objects and aims of the Colonisation Society, at the time of its organisation, seventy years ago, met the sympathy of leading statesmen and divines in all parts of the United States, as offering a solution of the difficulties at once legitimate and eminently humanitarian. But there were two classes who could not tolerate its pretensions, namely, those who looked upon the institution of slavery as having Divine sanction, and, therefore, permanent, and those who thought it the "sum of all villanies," and insisted upon its immediate abolition. It was a significant fact, often remarked in the days of the struggle, that the Colonisation Society was

---

[22] Delivered before the American Colonisation Society, January, 1868.

charged by the one with having "abolition affinities and tendencies," and by the other with being "the twin sister of slavery." The most elaborate and ingenious argument against Colonisation we have ever seen was from the pen of a Southerner, Professor Thomas R. Dew, of William and Mary College, Virginia. In an exhaustive article, written in 1832, in defence of Slavery, the Professor uttered the following prediction of the result of Colonisation:—

> We look confidently to the day, if this wild scheme should be persevered in for a few years, when the poor African slave, on bended knee, might implore a remission of that fatal sentence which would send him to the land of his forefathers..... We do not see how the whole scheme can be pronounced anything less than a *stupendous piece of folly*.[28]

"This wild scheme" has been persevered in for more than fifty years since the prophet spoke, and thousands of African *ex*-slaves (a class not contemplated in his prophecy) are to-day imploring aid to reach the land of their "forefathers;" and the promoters of the "wild scheme," not yet defunct, are unable to supply facilities for the transportation of earnest applicants for passage. Fifty years hence (*we* now prophecy), the current of African humanity setting eastward will be absolutely irresistible.

From the Northern, or Abolition standpoint, the reasoning which has most forcibly impressed us is summed up in an eloquent paragraph in a letter denouncing Slavery, addressed, in 1839, to Jonathan Phillips, Esq., by Dr. W. E. Channing.

No man can say, positively, what ought to be done in a matter of such serious importance as the destiny of a race. But men are prone to dogmatise on questions entirely beyond them. They often prefer to be guided by what, from the circumstances of their training, they think God ought to do, rather than to study, with unbiased temper, His providence, and find out what He has done and is doing. The fact, however, is, that the Anti-Slavery and the Colonisation Society were both born of the liberal and emancipative tendencies of the age. In the early days of the abolition move-

---

[28] *The Pro-Slavery Argument*, p. 899.—Charleston: Walker, Richards and Co., 1852.

African Colonisation.

ment, some of its promoters favoured a scheme of colonisation of the blacks. Benjamin Lundy, editor of *The Genius of Universal Emancipation*, obtained, about the year 1835, a grant of land from the Mexican Government on which to settle coloured people.[24] Mr. Garrison was a Colonisationist before he became an Abolitionist. It was the misapprehension of the policy of the Colonisation Society, in its full scope and meaning, that furnished the theme and motive of the satire of Garrison, the invective of Douglass, and the rhetorical pyrotechnics of Phillips.

Nearly all the founders of the American Anti-Slavery Society have passed away. Of the founders of the American Colonisation Society and the pioneers of Liberia, among the few living are Hon. John H. B. Latrobe, President of the Society; Dr. James Hall, the founder of the County of Maryland, in Liberia; and H. M. Schieffelin, Esq., New York, the founder of a promising settlement in Liberia—all full of years and honour. The active life of Mr. Latrobe has been coeval with the life of Liberia. It was he who suggested, or rather formed, the name of LIBERIA, from the Latin word *liber;* and the name of its capital *Monrovia*, from that of President Monroe. He has had only four predecessors in the office of President of the Society; Justice Bushrod Washington, elected in 1817; Charles Carroll, of Carrollton, elected in 1830; Ex-President James Madison, elected in 1833; Hon. Henry Clay, elected in 1836. Mr. Latrobe was elected in 1853. The records of the Society for the sixty years of its existence are full of the most remarkable specimens of eloquence, delivered from time to time with inexhaustible fervour and freshness by this veteran colonisationist. We have read them nearly all, and all are so impressive that we find a difficulty in selecting any for especial tribute or recognition. Even the platitudes of the African cause are made luminous and instructive by the ardour of his zeal and the glow of his intelligence. These early friends of colonisation have seen Liberia in her darkest hours; they have all exceeded

---

[21] *Life of Samuel J. May;* Boston, 1876: p. 140.

Christianity, Islam and the Negro Race.

the allotted years of man, but they are still strong in the hopes for the Negro nationality, which inspired their early efforts; and they are realising that they did not exaggerate their prognostications of the future of the colony.

> Those only (exclaimed Mr. Latrobe, with thoughtful enthusiasm) accomplish great ends among men, who are prophets with a conviction of the truthfulness of their visions, and who have the patience to wait without despondency. No doubter ever won a battle or realised a fortune. Our success, up to this time, in the prosperity and order of our colonies; in the contentment, healthfulness and numbers of their people; in the commerce that has sprung up around and with Liberia; far surpasses the like experience of all preceding colonisation. We have had, in truth, nothing to discourage us.[25]

But, in view of the great work to be done, the narrowness of its resources, and the vast ignorance prevailing among multitudes of Negroes on the subject of their Fatherland, the Society is still the "voice of one crying in the wilderness." They persist, however, with the same intense and profound belief in the rightness and righteousness of their cause; and stand, with regard, both to the past and the future, like the Chevalier Bayard, *sans peur et sans reproche*.

No one can read the accounts—their own reminiscences—put before the world from time to time, by these veteran friends of Liberia, of the early days of the colony, without feeling that it was a daring enterprise on the part of the Colonisationists to plant peaceful settlements on the coast of Africa, which, at the time they began operations, was the scene of war, plunder and piracy. In 1822, the year after the settlement was founded, the British Minister at Paris wrote:—

> There seems to be scarcely a spot on that coast (from Sierra Leone to Cape Mount) which does not show the traces of the slave trade, with all its attendant horrors; for, the arrival of a ship in any of the rivers on the windward coast, being the signal for war between the natives, the hamlets of the weaker party are burnt, and the miserable survivors carried off and sold to the slave-traders.[26]

---

[25] Address delivered at the Anniversary of the American Colonisation Society January 17, 1854.

[26] Sir T. Fowell Buxton on the 'Slave-trade, and its Remedy.'

African Colonisation.

In 1825, Mr. Ashmun, the first Governor of the Colony, wrote to the Society:—

> From eight to ten, and even fifteen, vessels were engaged at the same time in this odious traffic, almost under the guns of the settlement. In the month of July contracts were existing for eight hundred slaves to be furnished in the short space of four months, within eight miles of the Cape (Monrovia). Four hundred of these were to be purchased for two American traders.[27]

Several times, through the diabolical intrigues of the miscreant traders, the settlements were on the verge of extinction. But the courage and energy of the resolute colonists thwarted the plots of the demons.

With all their alleged contempt of the Negro, colonisationists had faith enough in him to believe that he could hold his own away from the leading-strings of his master. Mr. Ashmun, the white Governor, and the only white man in the colony, at the time when the slave-traders were concentrating their forces in the neighbourhood of Monrovia for its destruction, expressed entire confidence in the ability of the colonists to maintain their position. "The colony only wants the right," he writes to the Society; "it has the power to expel this traffic to a distance, and force it, at least, to conceal some of its worst enormities."

In the United States, many influential slaveholders supported the Society, gave liberty to their slaves, and sent them to Liberia, because they believed in their manhood, or rather, in their possibilities of manhood. Ex-President Monroe assured Elliott Cresson, that eminent philanthropist and colonisationist, "that if adequate funds were possessed by the Colonisation Society, he could procure ten thousand slaves, by voluntary emancipation, in his native state alone."[28]

The struggles of the early Liberian colonists against the ignorant opposition of their own untutored people, stimulated by slave-traders, have a species of pathos and romance to which the struggles of the first colonists in America offer nothing similar. The battles of the African pilgrims were not for empire over an alien race; not for power or dazzling wealth; but for room in the

---

[27] Gurley's *Life of Ashmun*, p. 261.   [28] *African Repository*; 1839, p. 298.

land to which they had a hereditary right, *De vita et sanguine certant*.[29] The pathetic aspect of their position was, that they had to confront a ferocity, not natural, but generated under the dark influence of incarnate fiends—to fight against a people allied to them by blood, and probably, identical in their antecedents, who would gladly have welcomed them but for the malevolent interference of those supreme criminals of humanity—*hostes generis humani*—who had ruthlessly robbed their fathers of their homes.

We could here recite—if this were the place for it—the thrilling experiences of these courageous pioneers. We could tell of their hardships and heroism, of their hunger and thirst and nakedness, of their chills and fever; of their confronting, with axe in one hand and gun in the other, the illimitable forests and the malarious swamps; of the devotion and bravery of their women, by whose unswerving fidelity and magical inspiration one was made to chase a thousand, and two were able to put ten thousand to flight. But it is enough to say that they were triumphant over all obstacles, and succeeded in laying in suffering and sorrow, and in indomitable faith, the foundation of a State. The colony, in the twenty-seventh year of its existence, became an independent Republic, and as such now enjoys the confidence and respect of all foreign nations.

The late Bishop Haven, after seeing Liberia, in 1877, wrote:—

The St. Paul's River is the heart of Liberia, the key to its future, the hope of the African in Africa. In no other colony is there such developed country life. Sierra Leone is city; South Africa is white; the rest is savage. This is country, and country always; and country only makes country. Let Liberia fill up her land with farms, and she will conquer Africa. . . . .

It only remains to be seen whether America will help her firstborn—her representative, her child still, in every pulse—to win this honour for herself and for us. Such an enterprise will give our trade and manufactures a new impulse. Let the North Pole remain in its icy isolation; while this vaster, nobler, and more useful undertaking is furthered by our Government.

The heroic William Taylor, "Bishop of Africa," after holding his first Conference at Monrovia, in January, 1885,[30] wrote of Liberia as follows:—

---

[29] *Æneid;* xii, 786.

[30] Bishop Taylor is now (January 30, 1883) holding his second Conference at Grand Bassa, Liberia.

African Colonisation.

Liberia is the garden spot of West Africa; splendid soil, well watered, good spring water for use, salubrious climate, and more exempt from flies and mosquitoes than any tropical country in which I have laboured. I am very sorry that the Liberian Government has, by bad management, got into debt. I hope our Government will feel maternal interest in it, and help it out of its embarrassment. . . . . If our Government won't help the Liberians, our coloured people should give them one dollar each—about a million of them—for the sake of their race. There is a grand future yet for Liberia, if they will learn by what they have seen and suffered, in the past fifty years.

We might cite here the concurrent favourable testimony of several naval officers, American and English, who have, from time to time, visited Liberia; but space allows us to give only one. It is the testimony of that most distinguished and useful officer, Commodore Perry. After spending some time on the Liberian coast, he wrote:—

In truth, I cannot but believe that the colony of Liberia is firmly and permanently established; and that it possesses, at this early period of its existence, the germ of a powerful empire, to be populated by a class of people hitherto unknown, at least to modern times—*a community of blacks, destined to enjoy all the advantages of civilisation, and to exercise its full share of political influence in the family of nations.*

Liberia is a Republican State, modelled after the United States. She is superior in self-reliance and self-control to Sierra Leone, now on the eve of her centennial anniversary. In that British colony, the foreign soldier—and, until very recently, the Bishop of the Church of England—took part with the civil officer in the work of government. And, to this day, when the Governor is absent, his place is supplied by the "Officer commanding the Troops." In Liberia, there is no standing army; and if any difference is observable in the public security of the two places, the difference is not to the disadvantage of the Republic.

With astonishing success has Liberia been able to impress the aboriginal tribes in favour of her Government and laws. While the neighbouring colony of Sierra Leone is, not unfrequently, troubled by raids of marauders into British territory, the aborigines, throughout Liberia, are getting to understand the political creed of the Republic, and to sympathise with the national aims. They are beginning to look upon Liberia as their own—a social, political and industrial commonwealth, which includes them, and contemplates their highest interest; so that, with no large material resources for offensive or defensive purposes, the Republic is able to keep in check the predatory tendencies of the wayward elements.

> Celsa sedet Æolus arce,
> Sceptra tenens; mollitque animos, et temperat iras.[81]
> Æolus, throned on high, the sceptre sways,
> Controls their mood, their wrath allays.
> *Conington's Translation.*

The theory of the American Colonisation Society is verified, as their *protegés* take their place in Liberia, and come under the influences of the Fatherland. As they advance to maturity in the ancestral home, the propensity to imitation grows weaker and weaker, and their improving faculties gradually divert them from the models they left in the house of bondage, to ideal standards, more in accordance with their tastes and instincts. *White* is dethroned, and *black* takes its proper position. The habit of thinking, of observation, of reflection—without the disturbing action of any alien influence—adds, as it were, a new eye to the mind; slumbering faculties are aroused; and they learn many things, which, with less freedom to be themselves, less responsibility, and less necessity for intellectual concentration, it would have been impossible for them to acquire.

The men, who, as a rule, succeed in Liberia, are of two classes: Firstly, those who were born, or have grown up, and were educated in the country; and, secondly, adult emigrants of humble educational attainments, who have been taught to use their muscles, and to rely upon themselves; and who, on their arrival, feel that they have entered a new school, where they have much to learn. Excellent fruits of their former schooling are not lacking. They make good farmers, good carpenters, good brickmakers, good shoemakers, good blacksmiths—in short, they prove to be capable in most of the ordinary branches of useful industry. Large numbers of them are members of the various Christian Churches, and are, as a rule, orderly in their walk, and firm in their

---

[81] *Æneid* i, 56, 57.

African Colonisation.

belief. Their views of morals are often criticised as defective, yet, they display in their new homes, sterling moral qualities; not only habits of industry, but of obedient subordination; of reverence for authority, human and Divine. They come from that set of men who won the admiration of the world, for their fidelity and self-control, during the crisis which came upon their masters five-and-twenty years ago, and, of whom, the following testimony is born by an ex-slaveholder of learning and culture:—

> When the South was largely overrun by a hostile soldiery; when every able-bodied white man of that section had been hurried to the front; when none were left for the protection of our women and children but mere boys and infirm old men, our slaves cultivated our fields, protected our property, and stood by our families in their helpless condition, thus becoming an element of strength instead of weakness, of security rather than danger.[82]

History shows no parallel to this. Europe, from all precedent, looked on at the commencement of the Civil War with an indescribable intensity of interest and anxiety. The *Times* despatched its able and graphic correspondent, Mr. W. H. Russell, to the scene. Writing from the spot, he said, reflecting the feeling of the Old World:—

> If the Negroes occasion any trouble, there is no saying how far the difficulties of the Slave States may not go; but, at present, they are possessed with a confidence, *which may be blind or farseeing,* that their slaves will remain quiet, if not faithful; and the absence of any white element from the population o whole districts is very remarkable. The spectacle of an uprising of 4,000,000 of Negroes in the plantations, burning, plundering, and destroying the whites, is one which, I confess, I am not humanitarian or Abolitionist enough to be prepared to desire or to enjoy.

The slaveholders trusted to the loyalty of their slaves—to those whom the world believed to be in the utmost degradation, and in the depths of savagery—and were not disappointed. It might have been otherwise if they had been alone, or altogether, responsible, for slavery; but it was an inheritance, which they could not have got rid of by any safe or normal means. They were, as we believe, providentially, the guardians of Africa's future re-

---

[82] *The Education of the Negro;* an Address by Gustavus J. Orr, LL.D., State School Commissioner of Georgia.—1880.

Christianity, Islam and the Negro Race.

generators; and while, as individuals, they may have been at times punished for abuse of their trust, yet, when it was possible, and probable, in the view of strangers—when the instinctive reasoning of the human conscience concluded that the time had come for retaliation and retribution by human hands — this awful calamity was not permitted. They were not allowed to suffer, *as a class*, through the unbridled passions of their slaves, for a relationship and its concomitants which they did not originate, and could not abruptly terminate. They suffered only so far as they failed to recognise the handwriting on the wall, stating that the time had come, and pointing out the methods for safe emancipation. Pharaoh was punished, not for having held the Hebrews in bondage, but for refusing to let them go when commanded to do so.

Yet, when everything else connected with the Negro's residence in America is forgotten, this wonderful story of his loyalty and self-control, will be recited to generations yet unborn, as a brilliant page—perhaps the only brilliant page—in the record of Africa in America. Surely, if all the years of toil and suffering are not sufficient to strengthen the appeal for help now made by thousands of these people, who are anxious to return to the land of their fathers; surely, this last act of theirs, this incomparable, this more than loyal devotion, ought to bring abundant assistance and relief to the "cry of the exile towards the graves of the beloved over the sea, that weeps and is not weary."

The refusal to listen to these pathetic appeals, constantly made through the Colonisation Society—this melancholy chorus that comes from the south and south-west, on every wind that blows—may bring the punishment, at least, of remorse. We are "verily guilty, in that we *saw* the anguish of his soul when he besought us, and we would not hear." Yes; when he *besought* us. We look in vain in the wills of dying millionaires for one cent given to aid the return of these faithful servants. But we are sure, if these wealthy stewards of God's gifts could have heard the bitter cries on board those "floating tombs of gasping humanity, on the mighty deep," as they bore away their suffering freights to the Western world, they would be anxious to make some compensation,

African Colonisation.

if only in sending back one who may be anxious to return. Let the facilities to return to their ancestral land be given to this people; let a generous God-speed be extended to them; let them be urged to take possession of the hills and plains awaiting their advent:

> Ply all the sinews of industrious toil,
> Glean up the refuse of a generous soil;
> Rebuild the towns that smoked upon the plain,
> And hope the sun will gild their roofs again.

This merciful dealing with the needy will be twice blessed—blessing him that gives, and him that takes.

Next to the Christian religion, the most important element of strength and prosperity in Liberia, is her possession of the English language. This gives her an advantage with the outside world, for it connects her with the life of the most vigorous and progressive of modern nations. "The English Language," says President Eliot, "is the native tongue of nations which are pre-eminent in the world by force of character, enterprise and wealth; and whose political and social institutions have a higher moral interest, and greater promise, than any which mankind has hitherto invented." It is the language in which knowledge, secular and religious, is most abundantly diffused; two great nations being engaged in printing and circulating in it, in the cheapest possible form, the best thoughts of past and contemporary humanity. It partakes of the character of the people who speak it, and is, therefore, a wonderful stimulus. The native African, like all Oriental or tropical people, can see no reason or propriety in extra work, as long as he has enough to supply his wants. But he is imitative. And as the English language is diffused in his country, vivified by its domiciliation on the American continent,[30] with its constantly-increasing vocabulary, its numerous words and phrases—some of which, produced by a restless and invincible activity, suggest and inspire activity—the native will be raised unconsciously; and, in spite of hereditary tendencies and surroundings, will work, not, then, in order to enjoy repose—the *dolce far niente*—but to be able

---

[30] 'The American Language,' is the subject of an interesting chapter by Mark Twain. The language spoken by the Liberians, is known throughout the adjacent interior countries as "'Merican."

Christianity, Islam and the Negro Race.

to do more work, and to carry out higher objects, Climate, after all, is not an insuperable barrier to progress. Every variety of climate has produced an indigenous civilisation, by outward stimulus.

One of the most important counteracting influences to Mohammedanism in Africa, will be the pressure of the English language. Dr. Nassau Lees, says, that the Koran was written for conquerors; so the English language, with its multitudinous books and newspapers, is the language of conquest—not of physical, but of moral and intellectual conquest.[84] The schoolmaster against the soldier; the primer against the sword. It has everywhere, on the coast, driven out other European languages. The French are struggling against its irrepressible aggressiveness in their own colony at Gaboon. Dr. Lenz found the language at Cameroons, the new German acquisition, to be universally English. Official notices are drawn up in English and German. Dr. Fischer, says, that in Zanzibar the natives say, "All good things come from England." Mr. Joseph Thomson has been recently making treaties on behalf of the English African Trading Company, with the most powerful tribes on the Niger. They refused to entertain the proposals for similar arrangements of a German trading agent.[85] And where the English language once takes root, it is a permanent occupant. In the West Indies, we find the Danish, Dutch and Swedish flags floating over an English-speaking population. The only rival in Africa that will offer anything like stubborn resistance to the pretensions of English, is Arabic. But the increasing desire of the interior tribes for material advancement, and the effort to hold communication with the outside world, which, for them, as Liberia and Sierra Leone extend eastward, will be more and more the English-speaking world, will diminish the practical importance of Arabic, and be a powerful stimulus to their civilisation and Christianisation. The force of material interests will divert the Pagan element from Mohammedan influence.

---

[84] In the steamship, in the railway, in the thoughts that shake mankind.
[85] London *Times*, Oct. 27, 1885.

www.ingramcontent.com/pod-product-compliance
Lightning Source LLC
Chambersburg PA
CBHW072129220426
43664CB00013B/2187